Key Geography for GCSE

David Waugh

Former Head of Geography
Trinity School
Carlisle

Tony Bushell

Head of Geography
West Gate Community College
Newcastle upon Tyne

D1806302

Book 2

Stanley Thornes (Publishers) Ltd

► Contents ◄

Weather, climate, vegetation and soil

World studies

Geographical skills

Index

How is weather measured and recorded?

A

Weather is the day-to-day condition of the atmosphere. It includes temperature, precipitation, pressure, wind speed and wind direction. These climatic elements are measured, usually once a day, by reading a group of scientific instruments – the maximum and minimum thermometer (diagram **A**), rain gauge (diagram **B**), barograph (diagram **C**), anemometer (diagram **E**) and wind vane (diagram **F**).

Temperature is measured, in °C (degrees Celsius) by a **maximum and minimum (six's) thermometer**. During the day the alcohol it contains heats up and expands, pushing the mercury higher on the maximum scale. At night the alcohol cools down and contracts, so the mercury reads lower on the minimum scale. In each case the position of the extreme temperature is recorded by a pin. The pins have to be drawn back (reset) to the mercury each day using a magnet. On the thermometer shown, the maximum was 28°C and the minimum 8°C.

B

Rainfall is measured using a **rain gauge**. This is a metal cylinder which contains a collecting bottle and a funnel. It is partly sunk into the ground for stability in the wind and away from trees and buildings which would shelter it. The rim is 30 cm above ground level to avoid splashing. The rainwater is transferred to a measuring glass and recorded in millimetres (mm).

Pressure is recorded on a **barograph**. The metal cylinder contains a vacuum. Attached to it is a lever and a pen. The pen records onto graph paper attached to a rotating drum. As air pressure increases (or decreases), the cylinder is pressed downwards (or rises) raising (or lowering) the lever and pen. Air pressure is recorded in millibars (mb).

C

The **Stevenson screen** stores several of these meteorological instruments. It is painted white to reflect sunlight, and has slatted (louvred) sides to allow the free circulation of the air and to keep out direct sunlight. It is located away from buildings which could give too much protection. It is placed on grass.

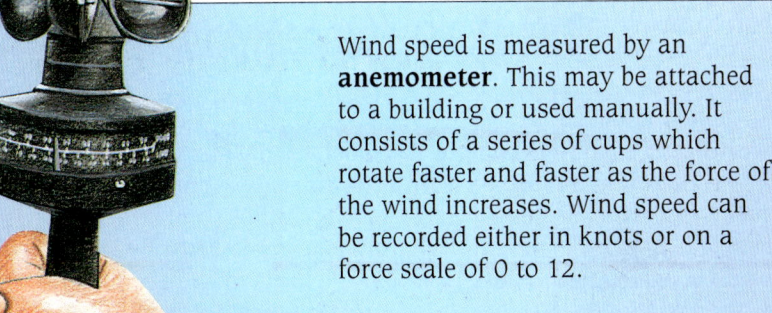

Wind speed is measured by an **anemometer**. This may be attached to a building or used manually. It consists of a series of cups which rotate faster and faster as the force of the wind increases. Wind speed can be recorded either in knots or on a force scale of 0 to 12.

Wind direction is measured by a **wind vane**. The arrow points to the direction from which the wind blows. In the example the wind is from the north-east.

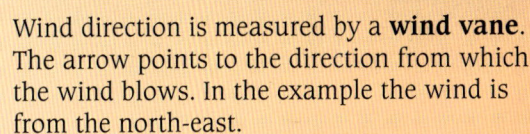

If weather measurements are recorded over a period of time, usually 30 years, we get the average conditions for a place. These average conditions give the expected **climate**. In Britain, for example, we expect to get cool summers, mild winters and rain throughout the year. What we actually get is often different from what we expect!

Activities

1 What is the difference between weather and climate?

2 **a)** Name the scientific instrument used to measure each of the following:
   • temperature
   • precipitation
   • air pressure
   • wind speed
   • wind direction.
   b) Describe the method of recording each one.

3 **a)** Using the scientific instruments named in Activity 2, measure and record accurately the weather for a period of one week.
   b) Record your results by either drawing graphs or producing them on a computer.

Summary

By measuring and recording daily weather conditions over a long period of time it is possible to give a generalised description of the long-term climate of a place.

What are the seasonal differences in climate in Britain?

Britain has a variable climate. This means that the weather changes from day to day, which makes it difficult to forecast accurately. Britain's average climate, as described on page 5, is cool summers, mild winters and rain spread evenly throughout the year. However, it should be pointed out that not **every**

- year will have a cool summer, a mild winter, or an even distribution of rainfall
- place will be cool, or mild, or wet at the same time.

In other words, the British Isles has annual, seasonal and regional variations in climate.

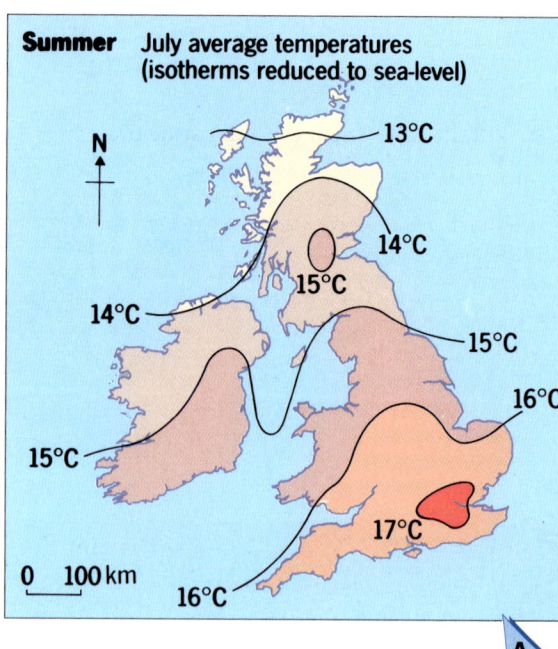

Summer July average temperatures (isotherms reduced to sea-level)

A

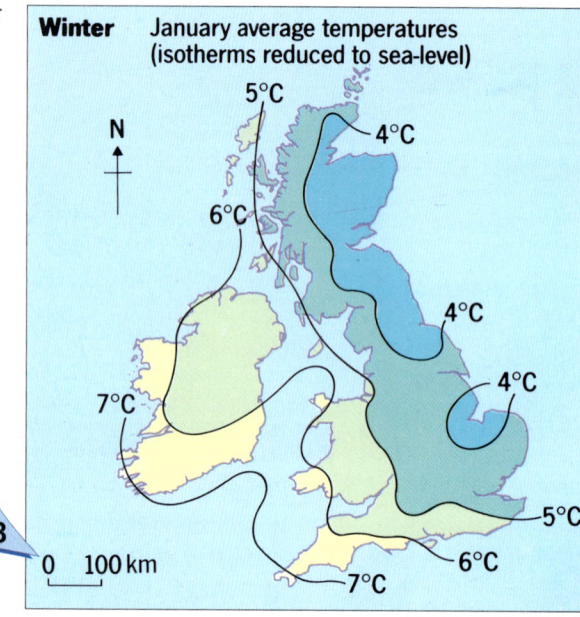

Winter January average temperatures (isotherms reduced to sea-level)

B

The seasonal distribution of temperature

Maps **A** and **B** show **isotherms** for July (summer) and January (winter). An isotherm is a line drawn on a map joining all places with the same temperature. Isotherms usually ignore the actual height of places and are reduced to sea-level. This makes it easier to both recognise patterns on a map and to make comparisons between places.

Summer The isotherms on map **A** show that temperatures:
- are highest in the south-east of England
- decrease from south to north
- are higher over land than over the sea.

Winter The isotherms on map **B** show that temperatures:
- are highest in the south-west of England
- decrease from west to east
- are higher over the sea than over land.

The reasons for the seasonal and regional differences in temperature in the British Isles are explained on pages 8 and 9.

The annual and seasonal distribution of rainfall

Map **C** shows the expected amounts of rainfall over the British Isles in an average year. It is accompanied by six graphs. Three are for places

C

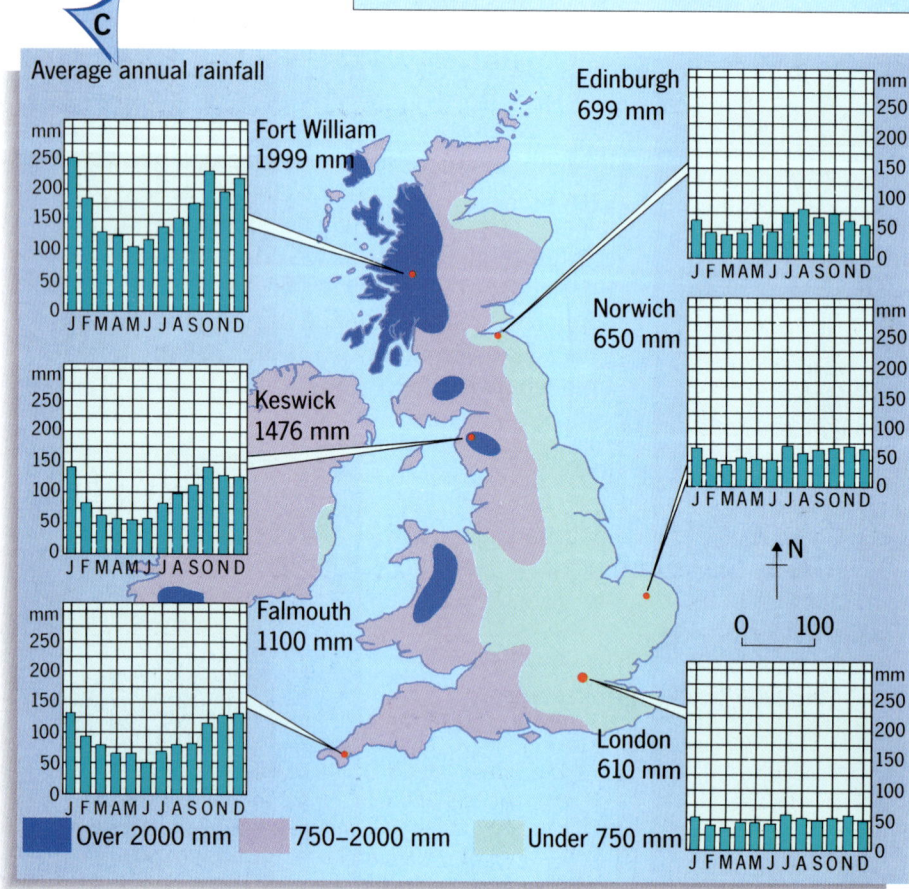

Average annual rainfall

Fort William 1999 mm

Edinburgh 699 mm

Keswick 1476 mm

Norwich 650 mm

Falmouth 1100 mm

London 610 mm

Over 2000 mm   750–2000 mm   Under 750 mm

in the west of Britain and three for places in the east. The map and graphs show that annual rainfall totals:

- are highest in the north-west of Scotland
- decrease rapidly from the north-west of Scotland to the south-east of England.

The graphs also show a contrast in the seasonal distribution of rainfall. Whereas places in the west receive most rain during winter (October to February), places in the east tend to get most rain in July (summer). The reasons for the annual and seasonal differences in rainfall in the British Isles are explained on pages 10 and 11.

Map **D** shows the British Isles divided into four quarters. The quarters were obtained by taking two isotherms:

- the 5°C January isotherm, which divides the milder west and the colder east in winter
- the 15°C July isotherm, which divides the warmer south from the cooler north in the summer.

The resultant map shows, in a simplified form, the seasonal and regional differences in climate in the British Isles.

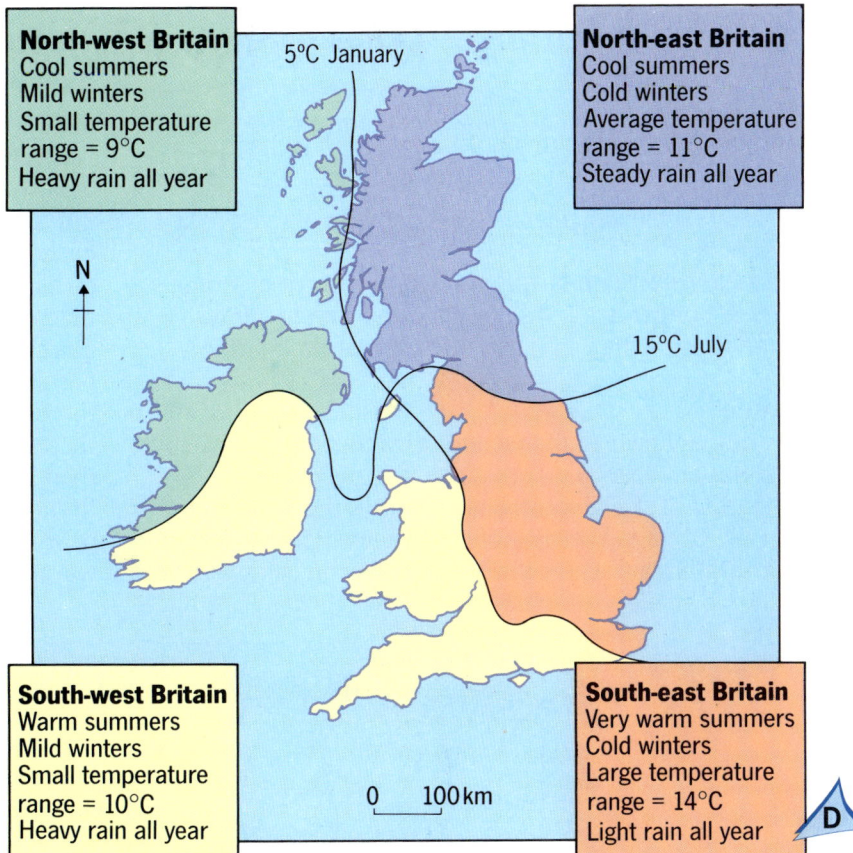

North-west Britain
Cool summers
Mild winters
Small temperature
range = 9°C
Heavy rain all year

5°C January

North-east Britain
Cool summers
Cold winters
Average temperature
range = 11°C
Steady rain all year

15°C July

N

South-west Britain
Warm summers
Mild winters
Small temperature
range = 10°C
Heavy rain all year

0   100 km

South-east Britain
Very warm summers
Cold winters
Large temperature
range = 14°C
Light rain all year

D

E

	Jan	Feb	Mar	Apr	May	June	July	Aug	Sep	Oct	Nov	Dec
Temperature (°C)	4	5	7	9	12	15	18	17	15	12	8	5
Rainfall (mm)	48	42	36	44	48	38	60	56	48	54	56	46

Activities

1 **a)** Copy and complete graph **G** by adding the information from table **E**.

2 **a)** Which two of the four quarters in diagram **D** do you think graph **F** and graph **G** fit?
   b) Give five reasons for your answer, referring to:
   - January temperatures
   - July temperatures
   - annual temperature range
   - total rainfall
   - season with most rainfall.

3 Copy and complete table **H** by ranking the four quarters named on diagram **D**.

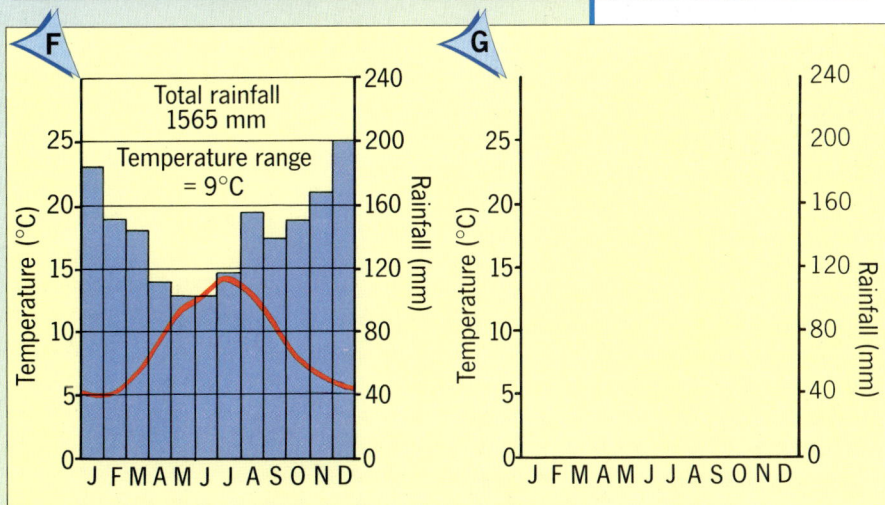

F

Total rainfall
1565 mm

Temperature range
= 9°C

G

H

Britain	North-west	North-east	South-west	South-east
Warmest in summer				
Mildest in winter				
Highest range in temperature				
Most rainfall				

Summary

The British Isles is said to have cool summers, mild winters and rain spread throughout the year. However, these seasonal patterns of climate vary from year to year and from region to region.

▶ *What factors affect temperature?* ◀

The maps on pages 6 and 7 showed significant seasonal differences in temperature between places in the British Isles. On a larger world scale, these differences in temperature are even greater. There are several reasons why, for example:

- the south of Britain is warmer than the north in summer
- the west of Britain is warmer than the east in winter
- some parts of the world are much warmer than others.

Latitude

Places that are near to the Equator are much warmer than places that are near to the poles. This is due to a combination of the curvature of the Earth, the angle of the sun in the sky, and the layer of atmosphere which surrounds the Earth (diagram **A**). At the Equator the sun is always at a high angle in the sky. When it is overhead it shines vertically downwards. Its heat is concentrated upon a small area which, as a result, warms up rapidly and becomes very hot. Going towards the poles, the sun's angle in the sky decreases. As the rays now have a greater area to heat, it takes the land longer to warm up and temperatures remain much lower than those at the Equator. The atmosphere surrounding the Earth contains dust, smoke and other solid particles. These particles absorb heat. As the sun's rays pass through the atmosphere at a more direct angle, and therefore more quickly, at the Equator than nearer the poles, then less heat is lost. These are the main reasons why places in the south of Britain are warmer than places further north in summer (map **A** page 6), and why equatorial areas are warmer throughout the year than the British Isles.

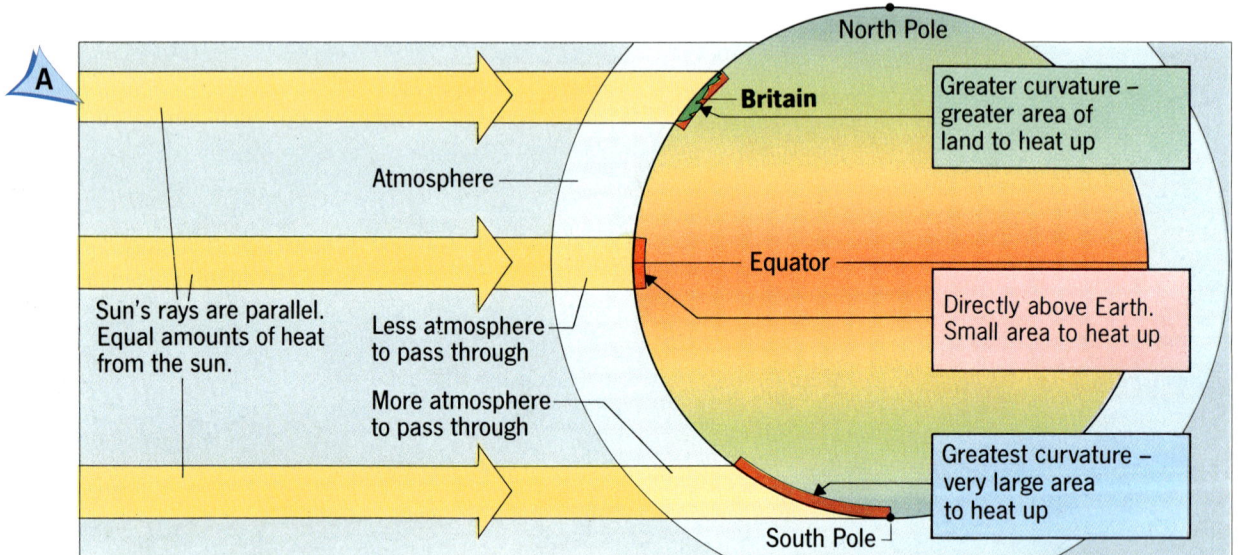

A

Sun's rays are parallel. Equal amounts of heat from the sun.

Atmosphere

Less atmosphere to pass through

More atmosphere to pass through

North Pole

Britain

Greater curvature – greater area of land to heat up

Equator

Directly above Earth. Small area to heat up

Greatest curvature – very large area to heat up

South Pole

Distance from the sea

Liquids are less dense than solids. Consequently the sea is less dense than the land, and so heat from the sun can penetrate through the water to a greater depth. As the sea moves, it allows heat to be transferred downwards. In comparison only the extreme surface of the land heats up. This means that the sea takes much longer to heat up than the land in summer but, once warmed, it retains its heat for much longer in winter. This is why places that are near to the coast are much cooler than places inland in summer but are warmer than places inland in winter. It also explains the shape of the 15°C July isotherm for Britain (map **A** page 6), and why the west of Britain is warmer than the east in winter (map **B**, page 6). It also explains why Britain has a smaller annual range in temperature (map **B**).

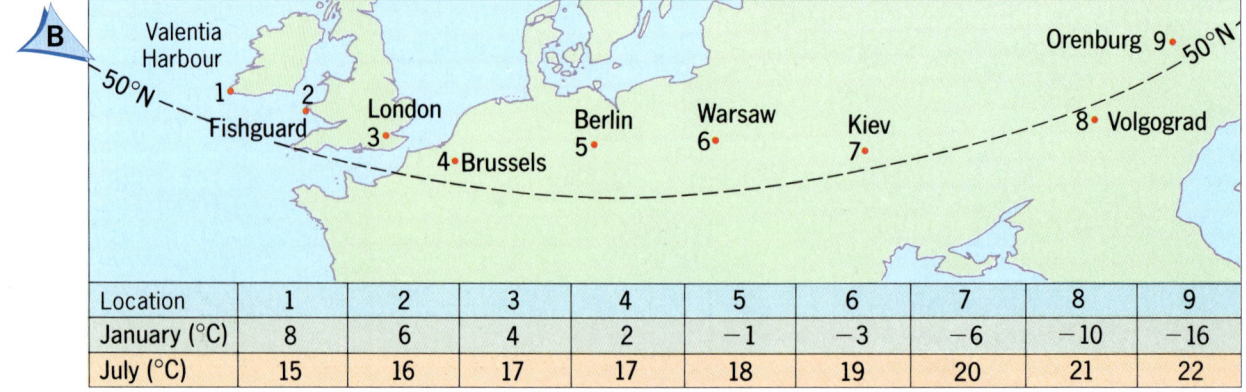

B

Valentia Harbour

Fishguard

London

Brussels

Berlin

Warsaw

Kiev

Orenburg

Volgograd

50°N

1
2
3
4
5
6
7
8
9

Location	1	2	3	4	5	6	7	8	9
January (°C)	8	6	4	2	−1	−3	−6	−10	−16
July (°C)	15	16	17	17	18	19	20	21	22

Prevailing winds

The temperature of the wind depends upon the type of surface over which it passes. If the prevailing wind blows from the land, it will be warm in summer but cold in winter. If, as in Britain, the prevailing wind comes from the sea, it will lower temperatures in summer but raise them in winter (diagram **C**). This also helps to explain why places in the west of Britain have cooler summers, milder winters and a smaller annual range of temperature than places further east.

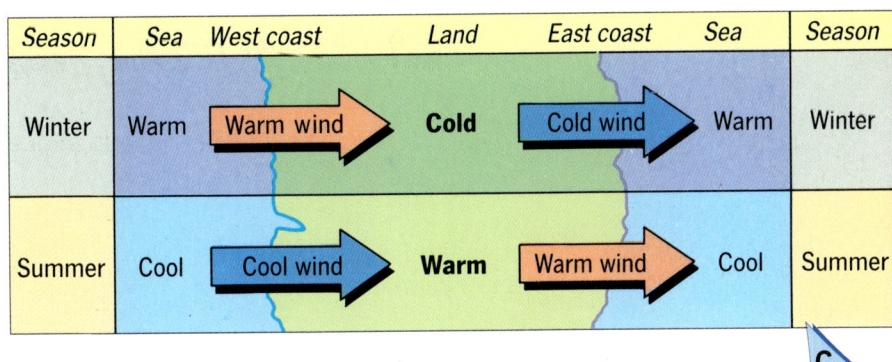

Season	Sea	West coast	Land	East coast	Sea	Season
Winter	Warm	Warm wind →	Cold	Cold wind →	Warm	Winter
Summer	Cool	Cool wind →	Warm	Warm wind →	Cool	Summer

C

Relief of the land (altitude)

Mountains have much lower temperatures than the lowlands that surround them. Temperatures decrease, on average, by 10°C for every 1000 metres of height. This is because there are fewer solid particles in the upper air to retain the heat, and so the heat is rapidly lost into space. This explains why snow lies for several months each winter in the Scottish Highlands, and throughout the year on several high mountains on the Equator (e.g. Mount Kenya and Kilimanjaro in Africa, and Chimborazo and Cotopaxi in South America).

Aspect

Aspect is the direction in which the land, a slope or a building faces. For example, places in Britain facing south are warmer throughout the year than places facing north, and places facing west are warmer in winter than those facing east. Aspect, which often has an important effect on local climates, is an example of a **microclimate** (diagram **D**).

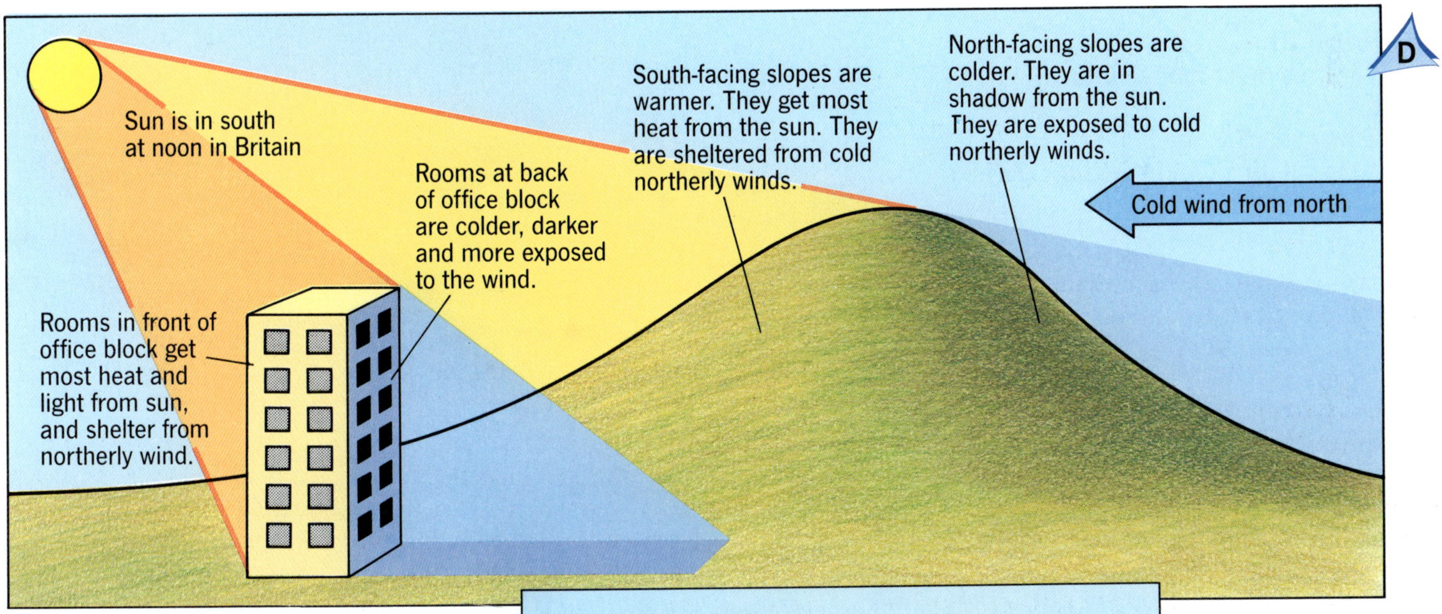

D

Sun is in south at noon in Britain

Rooms at back of office block are colder, darker and more exposed to the wind.

Rooms in front of office block get most heat and light from sun, and shelter from northerly wind.

South-facing slopes are warmer. They get most heat from the sun. They are sheltered from cold northerly winds.

North-facing slopes are colder. They are in shadow from the sun. They are exposed to cold northerly winds.

Cold wind from north ←

Activity

Referring to diagram **E**, explain, with the aid of diagrams, why:
a) **A** is warmer than **B** in summer
b) **C** is warmer than **D** in winter
c) **C** has a lower annual range of temperature than **D**
d) **B** is warmer than **E**
e) **E** is warmer than **F**.

E

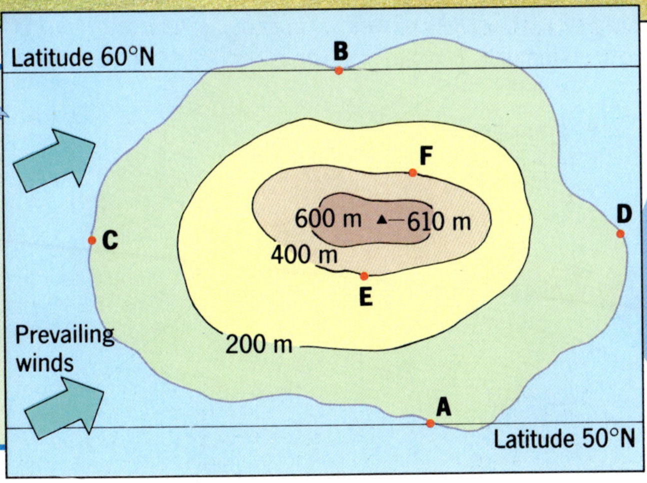

Latitude 60°N

Prevailing winds

600 m ▲—610 m
400 m
200 m

Latitude 50°N

Summary

The temperature of a place depends upon its latitude, its distance from the sea, the direction of the prevailing wind, its altitude and its aspect.

▷ What are the main types of rainfall? ◁

Map **C** on page 6 described the uneven distribution of rainfall over the British Isles, but it did not attempt to give reasons for this. It did not ask why, for example:

- Britain receives rainfall throughout the year
- the west of Britain receives more rainfall than the east
- places in the west receive most rainfall during winter (October to January)
- places in the east often have July as their wettest month.

Diagram **A** shows the several stages in the rainmaking process. Britain receives three types of rainfall – **relief** (diagram **B**), **frontal** (diagram **C**) and **convectional** (diagram **D**). In each case warm, moist air is forced to rise and cool. Condensation causes rain to form, or snow if the temperature is below freezing point. The main difference between the three types of rainfall is what causes, or forces, the warm air to rise.

Relief rainfall

Britain receives relief rainfall throughout the year due to the:

- prevailing south-westerly winds which bring warm, moist air from the Atlantic Ocean
- presence of coastal mountains which force the air to rise and cool.

West coasts receive more rain than east coasts due to the prevailing winds coming from the south-west.

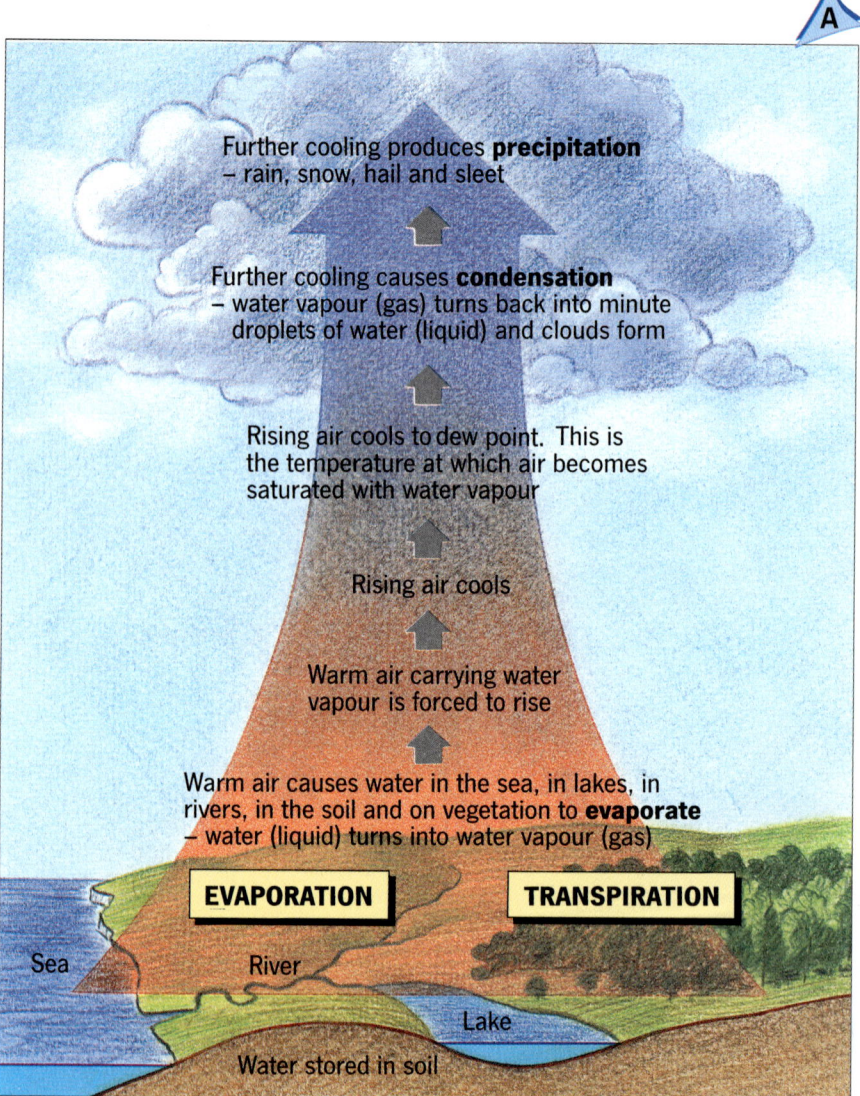

A

Further cooling produces **precipitation** – rain, snow, hail and sleet

Further cooling causes **condensation** – water vapour (gas) turns back into minute droplets of water (liquid) and clouds form

Rising air cools to dew point. This is the temperature at which air becomes saturated with water vapour

Rising air cools

Warm air carrying water vapour is forced to rise

Warm air causes water in the sea, in lakes, in rivers, in the soil and on vegetation to **evaporate** – water (liquid) turns into water vapour (gas)

EVAPORATION   **TRANSPIRATION**

Sea   River   Lake

Water stored in soil

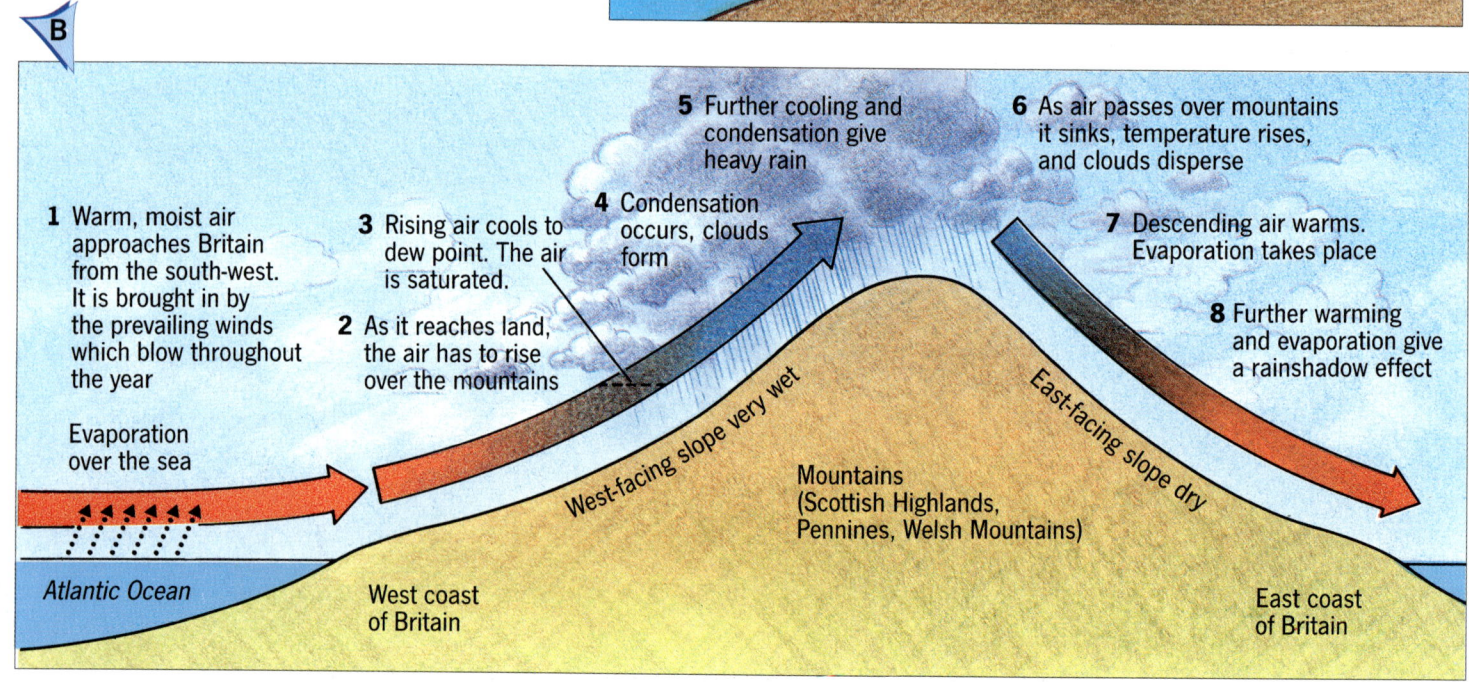

B

1 Warm, moist air approaches Britain from the south-west. It is brought in by the prevailing winds which blow throughout the year

Evaporation over the sea

2 As it reaches land, the air has to rise over the mountains

3 Rising air cools to dew point. The air is saturated.

4 Condensation occurs, clouds form

5 Further cooling and condensation give heavy rain

6 As air passes over mountains it sinks, temperature rises, and clouds disperse

7 Descending air warms. Evaporation takes place

8 Further warming and evaporation give a rainshadow effect

West-facing slope very wet

East-facing slope dry

Mountains (Scottish Highlands, Pennines, Welsh Mountains)

Atlantic Ocean

West coast of Britain

East coast of Britain

Frontal rainfall

Frontal rain results from the meeting of a warm mass of air and a cold mass of air. As the two air masses have different temperatures, they will have different densities and so do not mix easily. The boundary between warm and cold air is called a **front**. As warm air is lighter than cold air, it is forced to rise over the cold air. Frontal rain occurs in depressions which form to the west of the country, over the Atlantic Ocean (page 12). In a depression warm, moist air from the tropics is forced to rise over colder, drier air from polar regions. Depressions:

• usually approach the British Isles from the south-west and so give more rain to western parts of Britain

• are more frequent in winter which explains why western parts of Britain receive most of their rainfall during that season.

Convectional rainfall

Convectional rainfall is caused by the sun heating the ground. The heated ground will, in turn, warm the air which is in contact with it. As the air warms, it gets lighter and is forced to rise in strong upward convection currents. Water on the ground's surface will evaporate and will also rise. As the warm, moist air rises in convection currents, it cools and often gives thunderstorms. Convectional rainfall, which occurs most afternoons on the Equator (page 18), is most likely when the sun is at a high angle in the sky. Britain is usually too cool for this type of rainfall apart from places in the east and south-east which have the highest summer temperatures (map **A**, page 6). This explains why July is often the wettest month in the east of Britain.

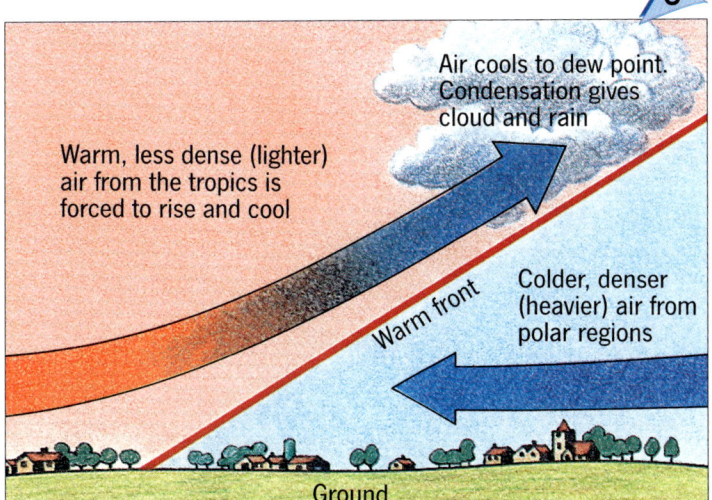

C

Air cools to dew point. Condensation gives cloud and rain

Warm, less dense (lighter) air from the tropics is forced to rise and cool

Warm front

Colder, denser (heavier) air from polar regions

Ground

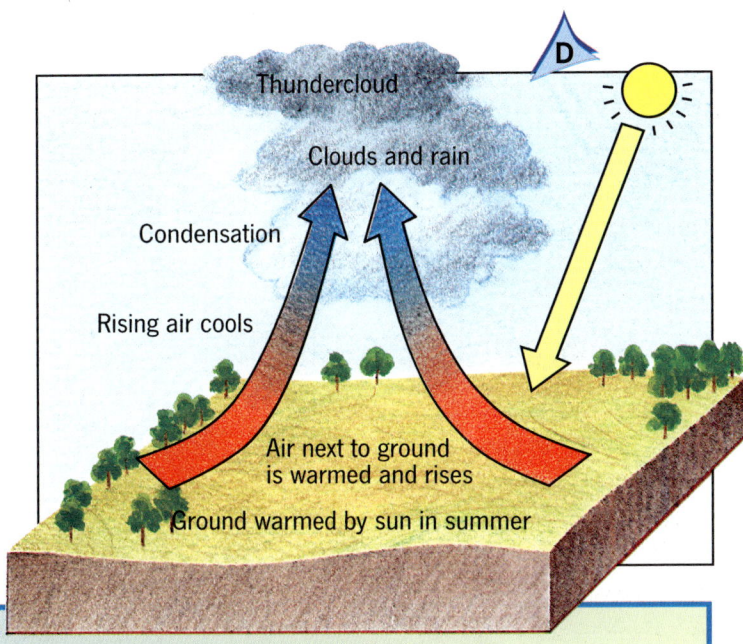

D

Thundercloud

Clouds and rain

Condensation

Rising air cools

Air next to ground is warmed and rises

Ground warmed by sun in summer

Activities

1 a) Put the following phrases in their correct order to answer the question, 'Why does it rain?'

rising air cools • further cooling gives condensation • warm air and water are forced to rise • warm air causes water in the sea and lakes to evaporate • further cooling causes precipitation • air is cooled to dew point.

b) Give three ways by which warm, moist air is forced to rise.

2 Along the top of table **E** are several factors which affect the distribution of rainfall in the British Isles. Copy the table and tick the appropriate boxes to show which of these factors affect the three distributions listed in the left-hand column.

E

	Prevailing south-west wind	Mountains on western side of Britain	Depressions come from the Atlantic Ocean	Depressions are most frequent in winter	Convectional thunderstorms
West of Britain gets more rain than the east					
Places in the west get most of their rain in winter					
Places in the east often have July as their wettest month					

Summary

Rain is caused by warm, moist air being forced to rise and cool. The three main types of rainfall in the British Isles are relief, frontal and convectional.

What is the weather like in a depression?

Britain's weather, for much of the year, is dominated by the passing of **depressions**. Depressions are areas of low pressure which usually bring rain, cloud and wind to the British Isles.

Most depressions develop to the west of the British Isles over the Atlantic Ocean. This is where a mass of warm, moist tropical air from the south meets a mass of colder, drier polar air from the north. The two air masses, because they have different temperatures, have different densities (weight). This prevents them from easily mixing (page 11). Instead, the warmer air, which is less dense (lighter) is forced to rise over the more dense (heavier) colder air. As the warm air rises it creates an area of low pressure at ground level. The boundary between two air masses is called a **front**. There are two fronts in a typical depression:

1 The warm front, which passes first, is where the advancing warm air is forced to rise over the cold air.
2 The cold front, which follows, is where the advancing cold air undercuts the warm air in front of it.

In both cases the warm, moist air is forced to rise. If it cools to dew point it condenses to form cloud and to give frontal rain (page 11). Although each depression is unique, the usual weather which they bring on their eastward journey across the British Isles has an easily identifiable pattern (diagram **A**).

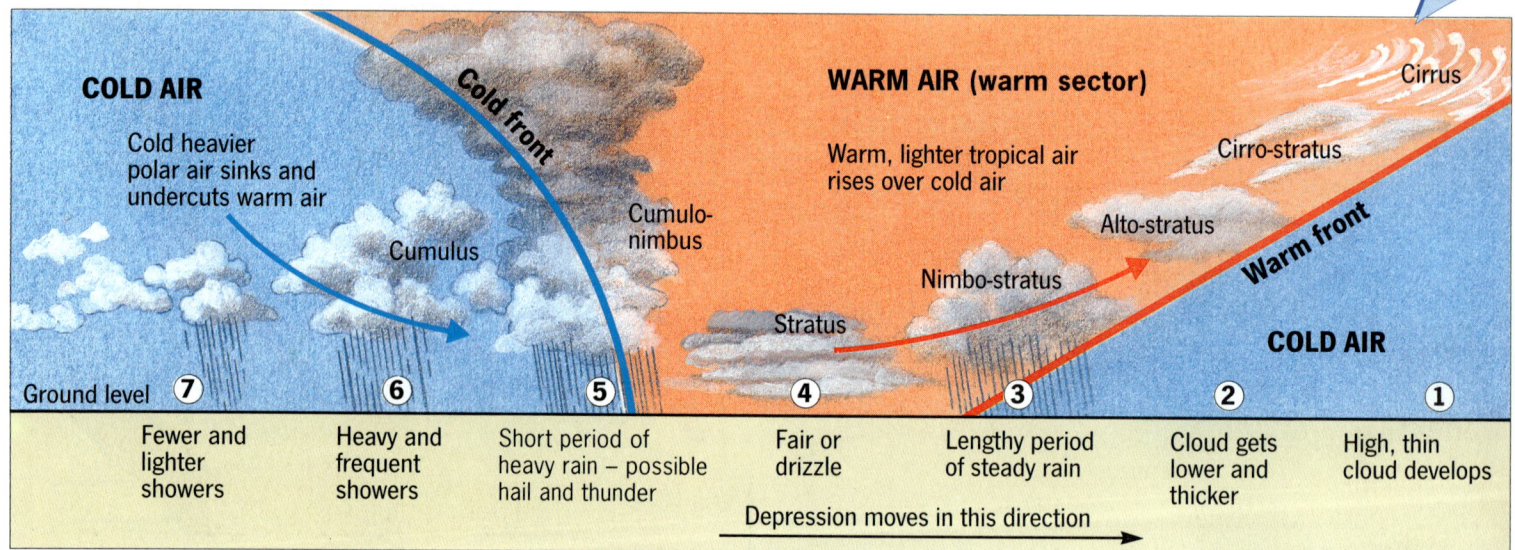

The first sign of an approaching warm front of a depression is the formation of high, thin clouds (cirrus). In time the clouds get lower and thicker (stratus). Winds slowly begin to increase in strength and blow in an anti-clockwise direction from the south-east. As warm air rises there is a rapid fall in atmospheric pressure. As the warm front passes, temperatures rise and winds become stronger, blowing from a south-westerly direction. Steady rain falls for a lengthy period from the low, thick clouds (nimbo-stratus).

The weather within the warm sector is a little less predictable. Light rain or drizzle may continue, or the clouds may break to give weak sunshine. Winds usually decrease in strength.

The most extreme conditions occur as the cold front passes. Winds often reach gale force and swing round to the north-west. Rainfall is very heavy, and can at times be accompanied by hail and even thunder (cumulo-nimbus clouds). The rain, however, is of shorter duration than that at the warm front. As the cold air replaces the warm air, temperatures fall and atmospheric pressure rises. In time the heavy rain gives way to frequent and heavy showers and winds slowly begin to decrease in strength. Temperatures remain low due to the winds which continue to come from the north-west. Eventually the showers die out and the clouds disperse to give increasingly longer sunny intervals. Usually, however, this is just a short lull before the approach of the next depression and the repetition of a similar weather sequence. An average depression can take between one and three days to pass over the British Isles.

Diagram **A** is a section, viewed from ground level, through a typical depression. Diagram **B** shows three weather maps, viewed from the air, drawn at different times during the passing of a depression. Weather maps have their own weather symbols (page 15). In diagram **B** the warm front is shown by the red line and the cold front by the blue line. The black 'circular' lines are **isobars**. Isobars are lines that join up places of equal pressure. The closer together the isobars are on a weather map, the stronger the wind will be.

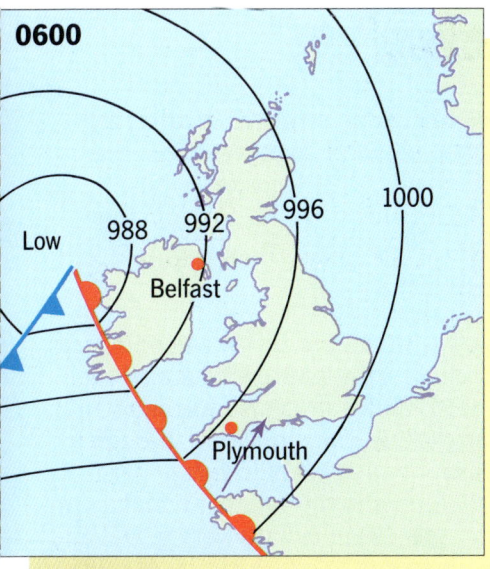

0600

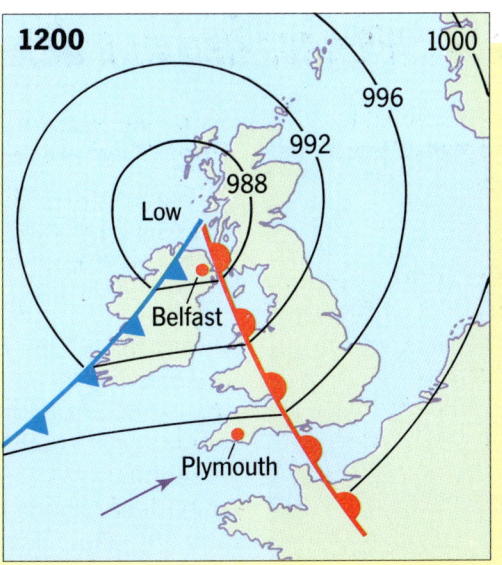

1200

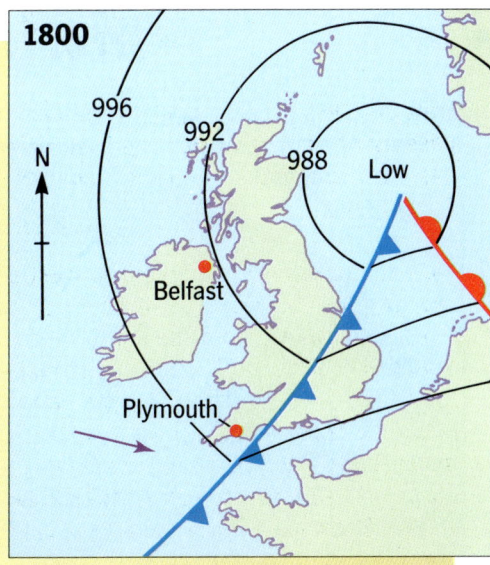

1800

Plymouth
Dry and sunny. Light clouds and rain approaching from west. Winds gentle but increasing from the south-east. Temperatures expected to rise.

Plymouth
Rain clearing to give patchy cloud and clear spells.
Strong winds from the south-west.
Warm.

Plymouth
Stormy weather.
Gale force winds from the north-west.
Heavy rain giving way to showers.
Colder, becoming brighter later.

B

Activities

1 **a)** Make a copy of diagram **C**.
  b) Mark and label the following:
    • warm front
    • cold front
    • warm sector (warm air)
    • area of low pressure
    • lengthy period of steady rain
    • short period of heavy rain.

2 Use diagrams **A** and **B**, together with the written information on these two pages, to complete table **D** to describe the weather associated with the passing of a typical depression.

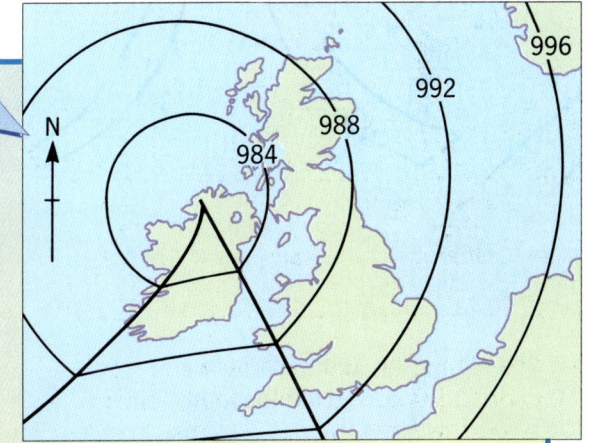

C

⑤ After the cold front passes	④ As cold front passes	③ During the warm sector	② As warm front passes	① As the warm front approaches	Weather conditions	
					Temperature	**D**
					Pressure	
					Cloud amount and type	
					Precipitation	
					Wind direction	
					Wind speed	

3 Use diagram **B** to:
  a) Describe the weather conditions at Belfast for 0600 hours, 1200 hours (noon) and 1800 hours.
  b) Explain why the weather at Belfast changed during this period of time.
  c) Give a short forecast for the expected weather at Belfast 0000 hours (midnight).

Summary

Britain's weather is dominated by the passing of depressions. These form when warm, moist air meets colder, drier air. They are areas of low pressure which bring cloud, rain and wind to the British Isles.

▷ What is the weather like in an anticyclone? ◁

A Satellite photo of an anticyclone

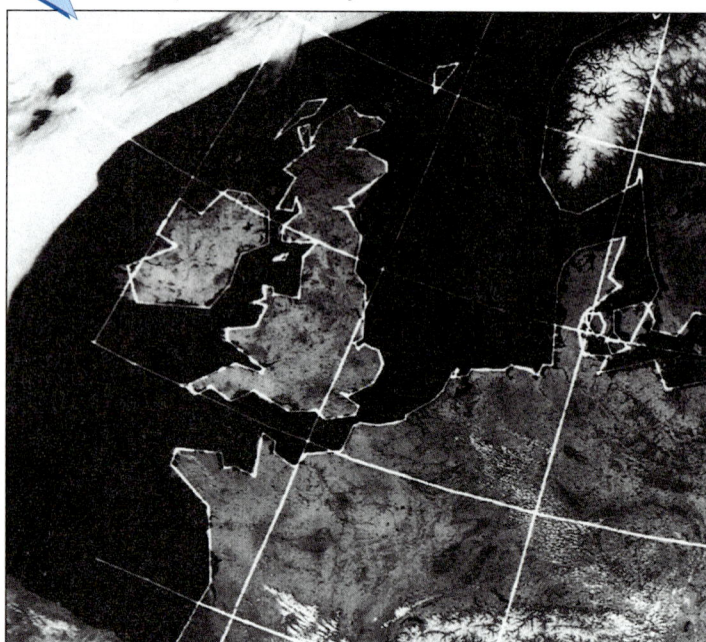

Anticyclones are areas of high pressure. They affect the British Isles far less frequently than do depressions. The weather associated with them is the opposite to that brought by depressions. Once anticyclones develop, they tend to remain stationary for several days, giving very dry, bright and settled conditions.

Anticyclones form in places where the air is descending. As more and more air descends, the 'higher' will become the atmospheric pressure. Descending air is also warming air which means that it can pick up more moisture through evaporation. As condensation is unlikely in these conditions, clouds rarely form and the weather remains fine and dry (photo **A**). Wind speeds are usually very gentle and at times may die away altogether to give a period of calm. Winds blow in a clockwise direction.

There are, however, important seasonal differences in the typical weather associated with anticyclones. In summer, when the sun is higher in the sky, temperatures rise quickly and daytimes are hot and sunny (photo **B**). At night the clear sky allows the heat to escape and temperatures can fall rapidly. As it is the ground surface that loses heat, some condensation can occur to give dew and mist. The dew and mist soon disperse when the sun rises the next day. During winter, when the sun is at a low angle in the sky, daytime temperatures remain low but the weather will be dry and bright. At night, the clear skies again allow a rapid loss of heat. Condensation at ground level at this time of year leads to the formation of frost and fog (photo **C**). These may persist for all, or most of, the next day due to the sun's lack of heat.

B Weather in a summer anticyclone

Synoptic charts

Synoptic charts are maps which can show several weather conditions at one particular time, e.g. midday. The weather conditions can include temperatures, pressure, cloud cover, types of precipitation, wind speeds and wind direction. The daily weather map as shown on television or in a newspaper (map **D**) aims to give a clear, visual and simplified forecast. Synoptic maps issued by the Meteorological Office use official symbols which give weather conditions at specific weather stations (diagram **E**). Each station (diagram **F**) shows five weather conditions while a sixth, atmospheric pressure, can be obtained by interpreting the isobars.

C

Weather in a winter anticyclone

	Highest temperature in degrees celsius		Rain showers and sunny intervals
⑫	Highest temperature in degrees celsius		Rain showers and sunny intervals
☀	Sunny		Thunderstorms
☁	Cloudy and bright		Snow
☁	Cloudy and dull		
☁	Cloudy with sunny spells	⑤→	Wind direction and speed
☁	Rain		

Britain today: The south-west of England will be cloudy, wet and windy. Western Britain will be mainly cloudy and bright. Eastern Britain will be sunny and warm.

F

Official weather symbols

Present weather

- ═ Mist
- ≡ Fog
- , Drizzle
- ; Rain and drizzle
- • Rain
- ✳ Snow
- ▽ Rain shower
- ⛛ Snow shower
- ⎔ Hail shower
- ☇ Thunderstorm

Wind speed (knots)

- ◎ Calm
- ⌐ 1–2
- ⌐ 3–7
- ⌐ 8–12
- ⌐ 13–17

For each additional half-feather add 5 knots

- ⌐ 48–52

Wind direction

Arrow showing direction wind is blowing from i.e. ⟶ west

Temperature

Shown in degrees Celsius i.e. 15°

Cloud

- ○ Clear sky
- ◐ 1/8 covered
- ◕ 2/8 covered
- ◑ 3/8 covered
- ◑ 4/8 covered
- ⊕ 5/8 covered
- ◕ 6/8 covered
- ◑ 7/8 covered
- ● 8/8 covered
- ⊗ Sky obscured

Fronts

- ▬ Warm
- ▲ Cold
- ▲▬ Occluded

E

Weather station

Temperature (degrees Celsius) — **15**

Cloud cover

Present weather

Wind direction

Wind speed (force)

Activities

G

1 Photo **A** was taken during the middle of a day in June. Give an accurate and detailed weather forecast for England and Wales for the afternoon of that same day.

2 The weather conditions in a depression and an anticyclone are very different. Make an enlarged copy of table **G** and complete it to show the main differences.

3 a) Describe five weather conditions at the two weather stations shown in diagram **H**.

b) Draw two weather stations and add the following weather information:

i) Place **X**: temperature – 26 °C; present weather – mist; wind direction – NE; wind speed – force 1; cloud cover – 1/8 covered.

ii) Place **Y**: temperature – 12 °C; present weather – rain; wind direction – SW; wind speed – force 8; cloud cover – 8/8 covered.

	Depression	Anticyclone	
Pressure			
Wind direction			
Wind speed			
Cloud cover			
Precipitation		*Summer*	*Winter*
Temperature			

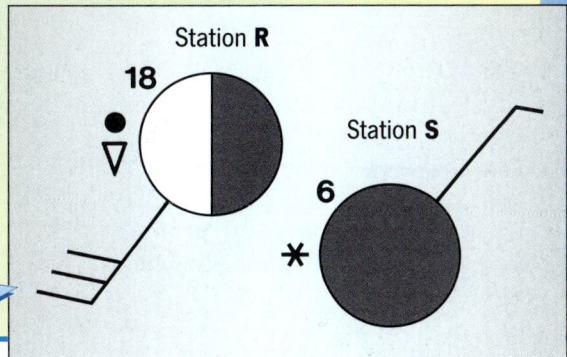

Station **R**

18

Station **S**

6

H

Summary

Anticyclones are areas of high pressure which usually give lengthy periods of fine, dry and settled weather. Synoptic charts are used to show the weather conditions for a particular place at a given moment of time.

Interpreting cloud patterns and synoptic charts from weather satellites

Synoptic charts are often issued along with **satellite images** (photos **A** and **C**; maps **B** and **D**). Satellite images are photos taken from space and sent back to Earth. They are essential when trying to produce a weather forecast or for making short-term predictions about likely changes in the weather. Satellite photos, which usually have lines of latitude and longitude superimposed upon them, show images of cloud patterns (photo **A**).

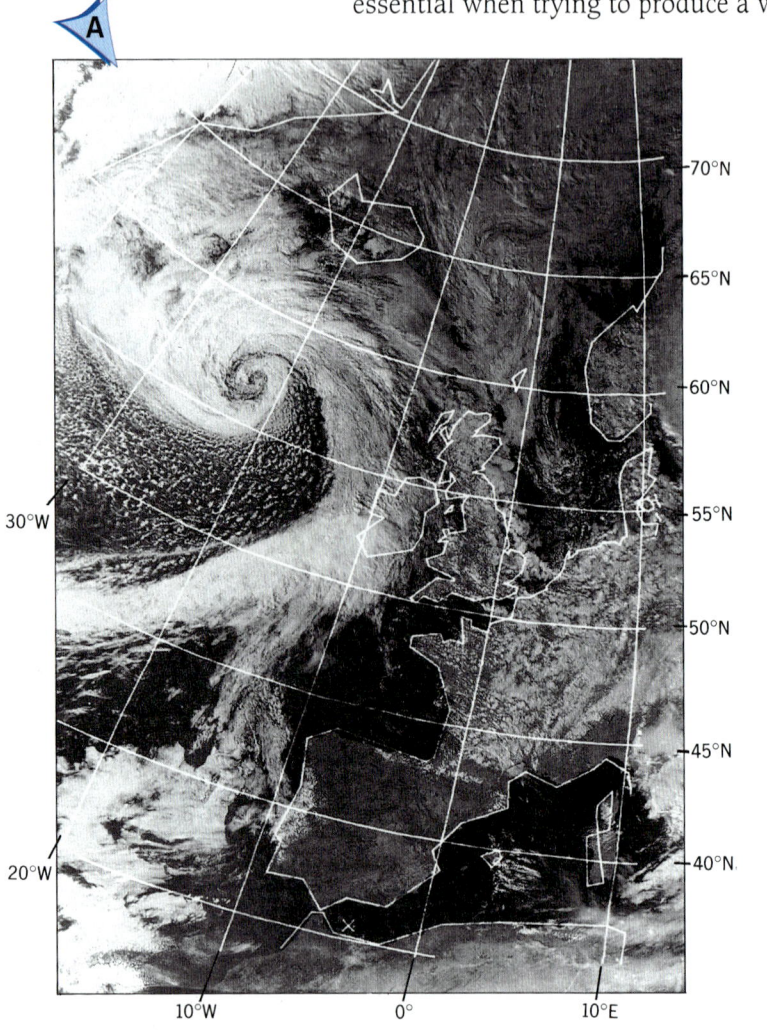

A

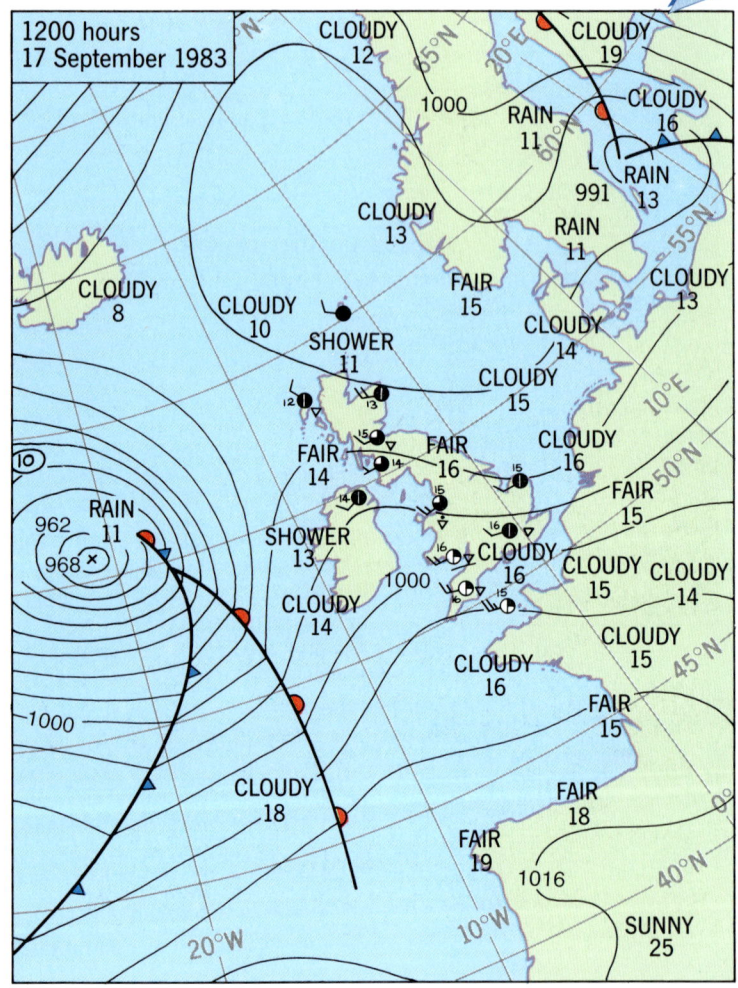

B

Photo **A** shows a typical depression approaching the British Isles. It was taken two and a half hours before synoptic chart **B**. The cloud pattern, in white on the photo, shows the points listed below.

- The centre of the depression is a mass of swirling cloud (latitude 57°N, longitude 22°W).
- The warm front is a thickening band of cloud which is beginning to obscure the coastline of Ireland. The warm front, marking the advance of the depression, lies to the east of the cold front.
- The cold front is a long tail of cloud extending south-westwards back into the Atlantic Ocean.

- The occluded front is a very thick band of cloud resulting from the cold front having caught up with the warm front. As there is no warm sector in an occlusion, there is no chance of any clearing skies as is possible between the fronts of some depressions.
- A band of heavy showers, shown as patches of cloud, follow behind the cold front (between latitude 50° to 55°N and longitude 15° to 30°W).

Photo **A** also shows an area of clear skies over Spain and the western Mediterranean which indicate the existence of an anticyclone.

Photo **C** is part of a sequence of satellite images which were taken to show the passage of the depression seen in photo **A**. It was taken 24 hours after photo **A**. The full sequence of images indicated the direction and the speed at which the cloud, and therefore the depression, moved. Forecasters use information from satellite images together with data collected from weather stations on land and weather ships at sea, to draw synoptic charts (maps **B** and **D**). By relating satellite images to synoptic charts forecasters are able to describe and interpret changes in the weather.

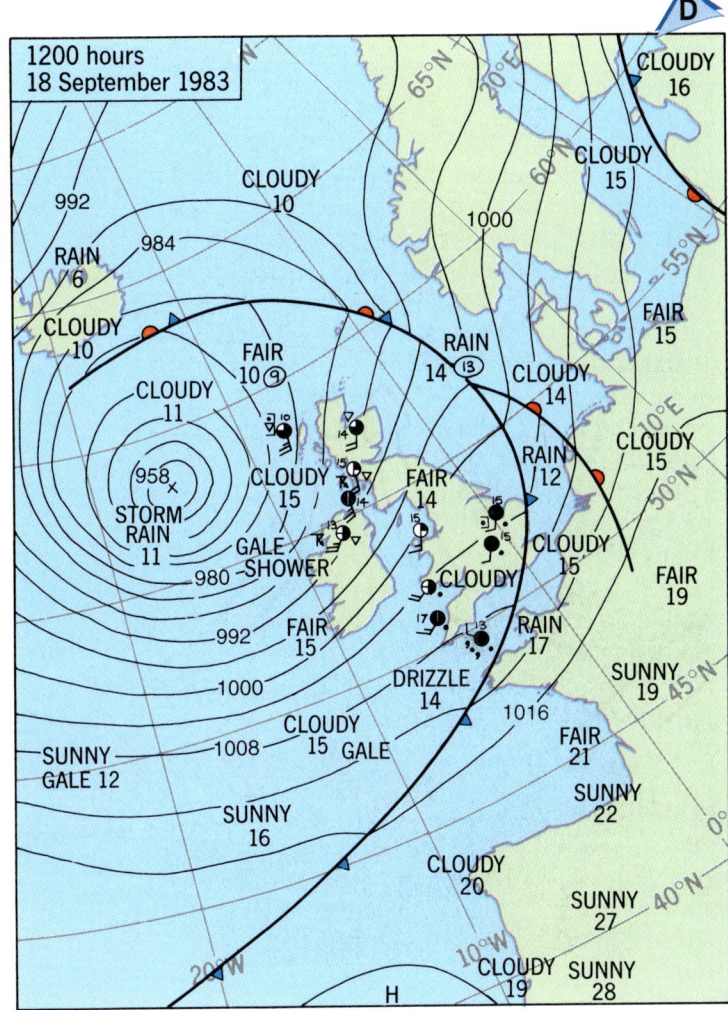

Activities

1 What is the difference between a satellite image and a synoptic chart?

2 Match up the cloud patterns shown in photo **A** and in the description on page 16 with synoptic chart **B**.

3 Describe and give reasons for the changes in:
   a) cloud pattern
   b) weather conditions
   over the British Isles between 1200 hours on 17 September 1983 and 1200 hours on 18 September 1983.

4 How did the weather over Spain differ from that over England and Wales during the period of the forecast?

Summary

Satellite images are photos taken from space and relayed back to Earth. They show cloud patterns which, together with synoptic charts, help forecasters to describe and to predict the weather.

The equatorial climate

Places with an equatorial climate lie in a narrow zone which extends roughly 5° either side of the Equator (map **A**). The zone is not, however, continuous. It is broken by the Andes Mountains in South America and the East African Plateau in Africa.

Graph **B** is a climate graph for Manaus. Manaus is located 3° south of the Equator in the centre of the Amazon Basin in Brazil. It is typical of an equatorial climate in that it is hot, wet and humid throughout the year. The climate is unique in that it has no seasons, and a daily weather pattern that is repeated virtually every day of the year.

Temperatures

Temperatures are high and constant throughout the year and the annual range of temperature is very small (2°C). The major influence on temperature is the position of the sun. Even when it is not directly overhead, it always shines from a very high angle in the sky (page 8). Evening temperatures rarely fall below 22°C while daytime temperatures, due to afternoon cloud and rain, rarely rise above 32°C. Places on the Equator receive 12 hours of daylight and 12 hours of darkness every day of the year.

Rainfall

Annual rainfall totals of places located directly on the Equator exceed 2000 mm a year. The rain falls most afternoons in heavy convectional thunderstorms (page 11). These storms result from the high morning temperatures evaporating large amounts of water from the many rivers and swamps, and from the rainforest vegetation. Manaus, because it is 3° from the Equator, has a short, drier (but not dry) season when the overhead sun has 'moved' to a position north of the Equator. Heavy dew forms during most nights.

Although equatorial areas experience strong vertical air movements, surface winds are light and variable. There are no prevailing winds.

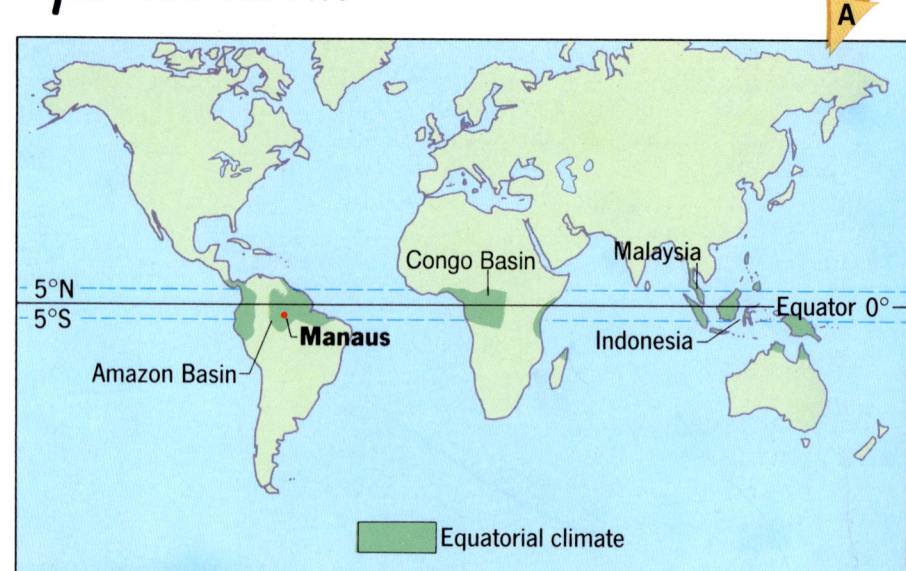

A

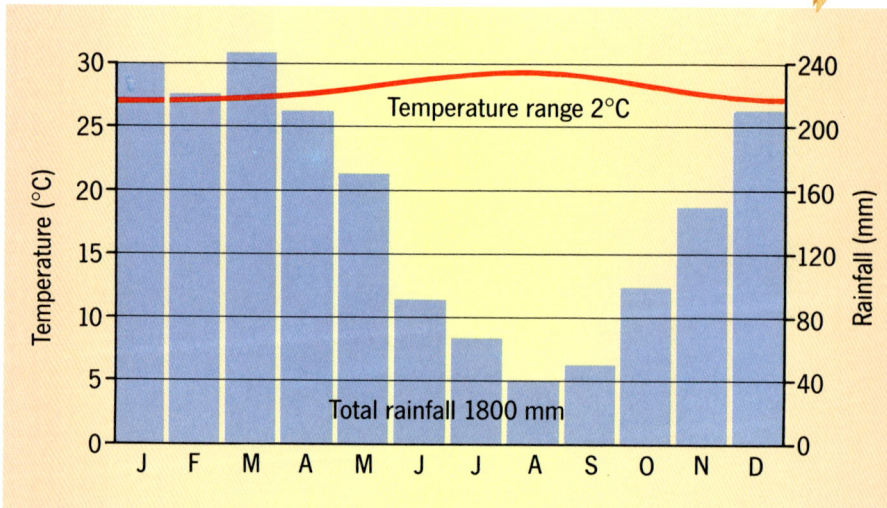

B

Activities

1 **a)** Describe the location of those places with an equatorial climate.
   b) With the help of an atlas, name four countries with an equatorial climate.
   c) Give four differences between the climate graph for Manaus and a climate graph for a place in your home region.

2 Why do equatorial climates have:
   a) high temperatures throughout the year and a low annual temperature range
   b) heavy convectional thunderstorms during most afternoons?

Summary

Equatorial climates, which are hot, wet and humid throughout the year, are usually located within 5° north or south of the Equator and where there is low relief.

Hot desert climates

With the exception of the Sahara which extends across Africa, hot deserts are located mainly on west coasts of continents between latitudes 15° and 30° north and south of the Equator (map **C**). Graphs **D** and **E** are climate graphs for two places in the Sahara. Graph **D** is for Cape Juby (28°N) on the Atlantic coast in southern Morocco. Graph **E** is for Khartoum (15°N) in Sudan. Although both places have limited rainfall, there is a considerable difference in their temperatures.

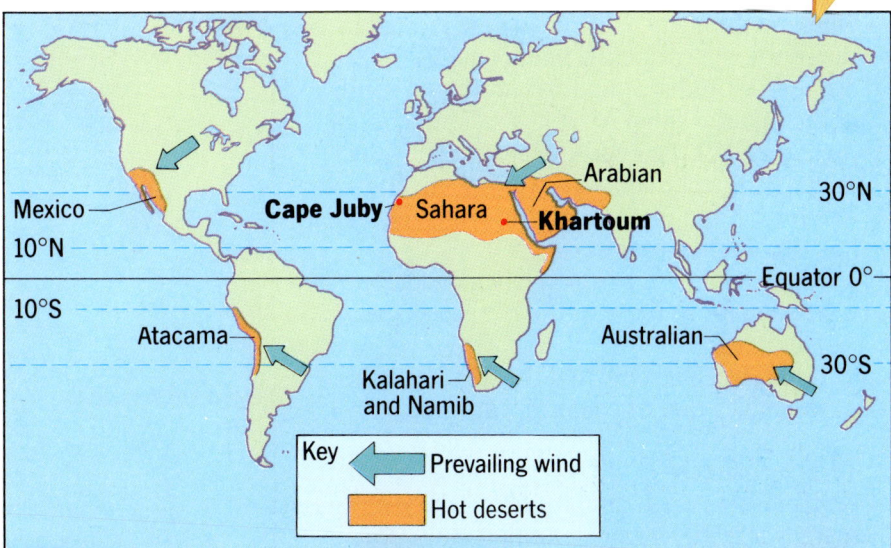

Temperatures

Temperatures are highest when the sun is directly overhead at the Tropic of Cancer, and lower when it is in the opposite hemisphere. Khartoum is warmer than Cape Juby throughout the year because it is nearer to the Equator. Cape Juby is almost as warm as Khartoum in January but is much cooler in summer due to the moderating influence of the sea. Coastal temperatures are also lowered in summer by a cold offshore ocean current (page 24). Away from the sea the cloudless skies of the central Sahara allow daytime temperatures to reach 50°C, and night temperatures to drop to near freezing.

Rainfall

Although deserts, by definition, are dry, none is completely rainless. The lack of rain is due to several factors.

* Prevailing trade winds blow from the east and therefore across dry land.
* Prevailing winds have to cross mountain ranges so that most deserts lie in a rainshadow.
* Descending air at the Tropics warms (page 22), picks up moisture and creates areas of high pressure (page 14).
* When winds do blow from the sea they have to cross a cool surface and so cannot pick up much moisture.

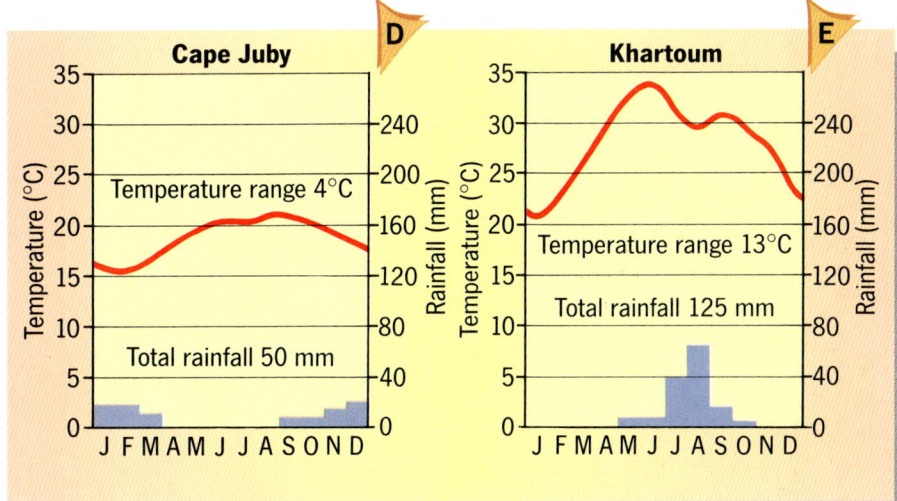

Khartoum gets most of its rain in summer when the overhead sun can trigger occasional convectional downpours. Cape Juby gets a little rain in winter when the prevailing winds blow, for a short time, from the Atlantic Ocean and give some relief rainfall. Coastal areas also get fog when warm air from the land drifts out to sea to meet colder air.

Summary

Hot desert climates are usually located on west coasts of continents between 15° and 30° north and south of the Equator. They are hot and dry throughout the year although coastal areas are much cooler than places that are inland.

Activities

1 **a)** Describe the location of those places with a hot desert climate.
  b) With the help of an atlas, name six countries that have a hot desert climate.
  c) Give four differences between the climate graph for Khartoum and a climate graph for a place in your home region.

2 **a)** Why do hot deserts have:
    i) high temperatures throughout the year
    ii) very little rainfall?
  b) In hot deserts why do coastal areas have lower summer temperatures and a larger annual temperature range than places that are inland?

Tropical continental (savanna) climates

Places with this type of climate are located in the centre of continents, approximately between latitudes 5° and 15° north and south of the Equator (map **A**). It is also found on the higher land of the East African Plateau which straddles the Equator. Graph **B** is a climate graph for Kano in northern Nigeria. The climate has two distinct seasons.

1 A very warm, dry season when conditions are similar to those of the hot desert (page 19).

2 A hot, wet season when the weather more resembles that of equatorial areas (page 18).

Temperatures

Temperatures are high throughout the year and there is a relatively small annual range. The cooler (though not by British standards) season occurs when the sun is overhead in the opposite hemisphere. Temperatures rise as the angle of the sun in the sky increases (page 8), only to fall slightly at the time when there is most cloud and rainfall. Most areas are too far inland to be influenced by any moderating effect of the sea. Several places with this climate are in upland areas where temperatures are slightly reduced due to the increase in relief (altitude, page 9).

Rainfall

During the dry season the prevailing trade winds blow from the east. Any moisture that they carried will have been shed long before they reach the central parts of continents. The dry season is shorter towards the Equator and longer away from the Equator. The rainy season coincides with the time when the sun is overhead and the dry prevailing winds die away. The higher temperatures result in warm air being forced to rise to give frequent afternoon convectional thunderstorms (page 11). Unfortunately the length of the rainy season and the total amounts of rain are unreliable (page 23), while the heavy nature of the rain can do more damage than good (page 26).

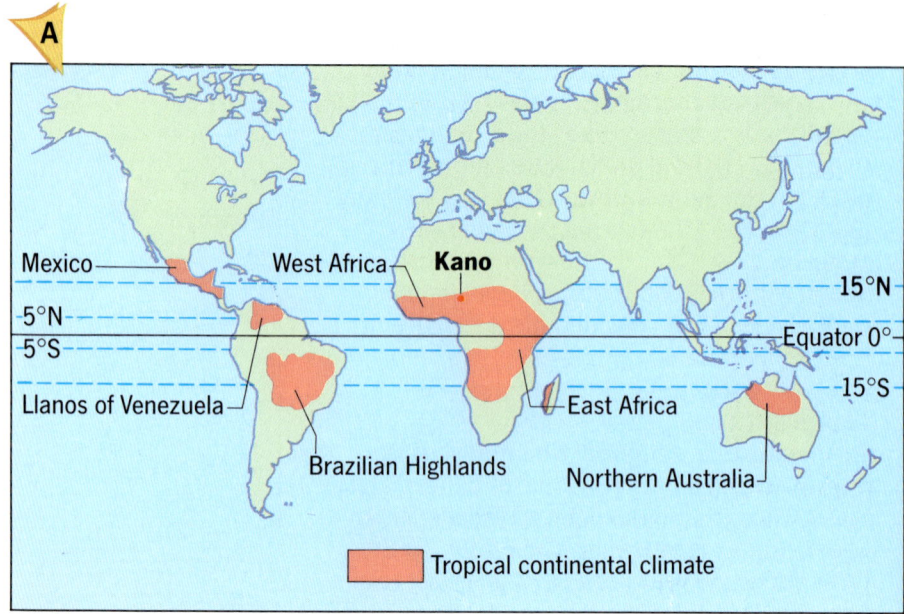

A

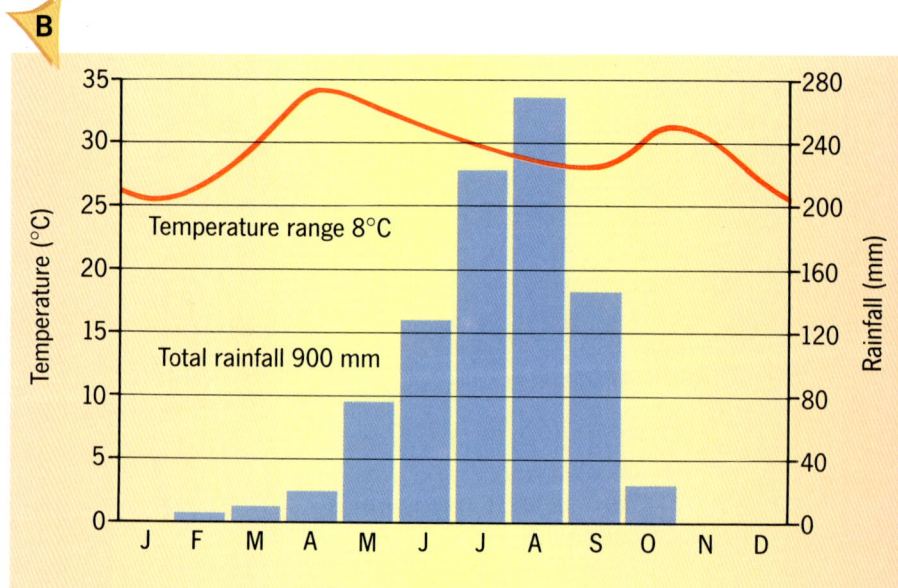

B

Temperature range 8°C

Total rainfall 900 mm

Activities

1 **a)** Describe the location of those places with a tropical continental climate.

b) With the help of an atlas, name four countries that have a tropical continental climate.

c) Give four differences between the climate graph for Kano and a climate graph for a place in your home region.

2 Why do tropical continental climates have:
a) high temperatures throughout the year
b) a dry season and a wet season?

Summary

Tropical continental climates are usually located in the centre of continents between 5° and 15° north and south of the Equator. They have a very warm, dry season and a hot, wet season.

The Mediterranean climate

Places with a Mediterranean type of climate are located on west coasts of continents between latitudes 30° and 40° north and south of the Equator (map **C**). The exception is the area surrounding the 'inland' Mediterranean Sea. Graph **D** is a climate graph for Athens in Greece. The Mediterranean climate has two distinct seasons.

1 Hot, dry summers when the weather has similarities with that of the hot deserts (page 19).
2 Warm, wet winters when the weather more resembles that of the British Isles (page 6).

Temperatures

Temperatures can be very high in summer. This is partly due to the sun being at a high, though never directly overhead, angle in the sky and partly because the prevailing trade winds blow from the warm land. Places on the extreme west coast are, however, cooler due to the moderating influence of the sea and the presence of a cold ocean current (page 24). Winters are warm partly due to the moderating influence of the sea and partly because of the prevailing winds which blow from the sea at this time of year. Many Mediterranean areas have high coastal mountains which lower temperatures considerably.

Rainfall

Summers often experience drought conditions due to the prevailing winds blowing from the dry land. Rain, when it does fall, often comes in short but heavy convectional thunderstorms. Winters can be very wet. This is due to the prevailing winds blowing from the sea and depressions moving eastwards which, together, give relief and frontal rain. Snow falls at higher altitudes.

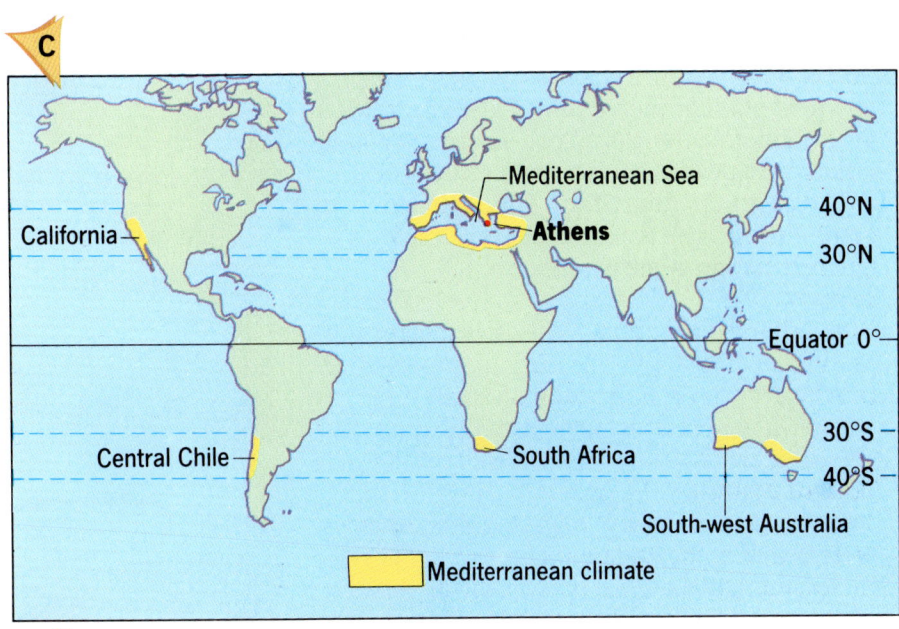

C

Mediterranean Sea
California
Athens
40°N
30°N
Equator 0°
Central Chile
South Africa
30°S
40°S
South-west Australia
Mediterranean climate

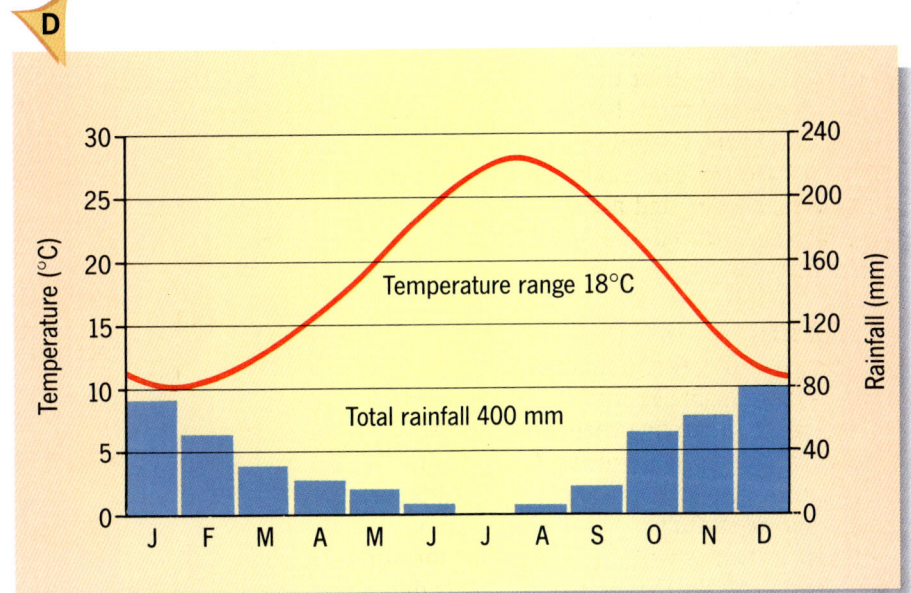

D

Temperature range 18°C

Total rainfall 400 mm

Activities

1 **a)** Describe the location of those places with a Mediterranean type of climate.
   b) With the help of an atlas, name six countries that have a Mediterranean climate.
   c) Give four differences between the climate graph for Athens and a climate graph for a place in your home region.

2 Why do Mediterranean climates have:
   a) hot, dry summers
   b) warm, wet winters?

Summary

Mediterranean climates are usually located on west coasts of continents between 30° and 40° north and south of the Equator. Most places have hot, dry summers and warm, wet winters.

How does atmospheric circulation affect the pattern of world climates?

When describing the location of four of the world's climate types (pages 18–21), it was pointed out that each type had a recognisable distribution pattern. This pattern results mainly from the circulation of air within the atmosphere. To understand **atmospheric circulation** you should be aware of three processes, which are described in table **A**.

The general circulation of the atmosphere is shown in diagram **B**. The diagram shows three circular movements, or **cells**, in each hemisphere. The most important cell, on a global scale, is the Hadley Cell. The cell consists of four segments.

1 With the sun always high in the sky, the ground on the Equator becomes very hot and water on the surface is evaporated. The hot air and water vapour rise in convection currents and an area of low pressure develops. As the rising air cools, it condenses to give the heavy rainfall associated with the equatorial climate.

2 The cooled air spreads out towards the poles and continues to cool.

3 The colder air begins to sink. As the air descends it warms, picks up moisture and forms an area of high pressure. High pressure areas, where condensation rarely occurs, are associated with the cloudless skies of the desert climate.

4 On reaching the ground some of the air returns to the Equator. As it does so it continues to warm and to pick up moisture. It is this surface movement of air that forms the trade winds.

Not all of the descending air in the Hadley Cell returns to the Equator. Some of this warm, moist tropical air (in the northern hemisphere) travels northwards. This surface movement of air in the Ferrel Cell is the cause of Britain's prevailing south-westerly winds. Depressions form where the warm, moist tropical air meets the colder, drier air from the polar cell. The warm air is forced to rise over cold air to give the frontal rain and the frequent low pressure systems (depressions) that are characteristic of the British type of climate (page 11).

The location of the world's major types of climate does not, however, depend solely upon atmospheric circulation. Due to the tilt of the Earth, the position of the overhead sun appears

A

1	When air next to the ground is heated, it expands, gets lighter and rises. As the amount of air next to the ground decreases, an area of **low pressure** is formed.
2	When air in the atmosphere is cooled, it becomes denser and heavier and so descends. As the amount of air next to the ground increases, an area of **high pressure** is formed.
3	Air moves, as wind, from areas of high pressure to areas of low pressure. However, air does not move directly from areas of high pressure to areas of low pressure. If it did then the direction of the prevailing winds in Britain would be from the south. Instead, due to factors such as the rotation of the Earth, most winds come from the south-west.

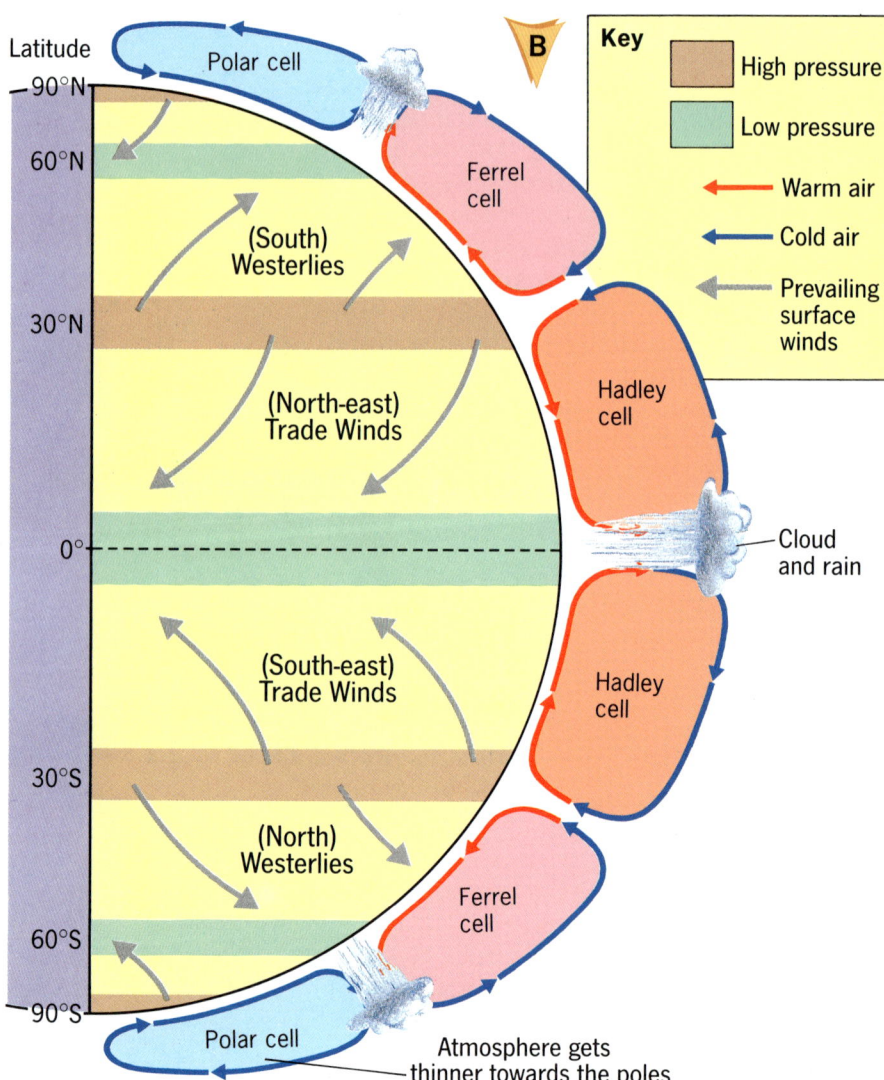

to change between seasons. On 21 June the sun is overhead at the Tropic of Cancer. As the sun 'appears' to move northwards, the equatorial low pressure belt moves several degrees north of the Equator. The result is that the prevailing wind belts, as shown on diagram **B** and map **D**, also move northwards. The reverse occurs on 21 December. At this time of

the year the overhead sun, the equatorial low pressure, and the prevailing winds all move southwards. It is this seasonal change in pressure, and the resultant prevailing winds, that are responsible for the seasonal changes in the Mediterranean and tropical continental types of climate (diagram **C**).

The location of the four types of world climate described in this unit, together with that of the British type, are shown on map **D**. However, this map, like others that show the distribution of world climates, has to be interpreted with care!

- The map has been simplified, due to its scale, and so it cannot show local variations.
- The boundary between two climatic types is shown as a thin line. In reality this change between two adjacent climates is gradual and takes place over a wide area.

C

Climate type	Pressure	Prevailing winds	Rainfall
1 British type	Low all year	South-westerly all year	Frontal and relief all year
2 Mediterranean (transition between British type and hot desert)	Low in winter	South-westerly in winter	Frontal and relief in winter
	High in summer	North-east trades in summer	Very little
3 Hot deserts	High all year	North-east trades all year	Very little
4 Tropical continental (transitional between hot desert and equatorial)	High in 'winter'	North-east trades in 'winter'	Very little
	Low in 'summer'	None in 'summer'	Convectional rain
5 Equatorial	Low all year	None	Convectional all year

Key

- 🟩 Low pressure
- 🟫 High pressure
- → Prevailing winds

Climate types

- 🟩 Equatorial
- 🟧 Hot desert
- 🟥 Tropical continental (savanna)
- 🟨 Mediterranean
- ⬛ British

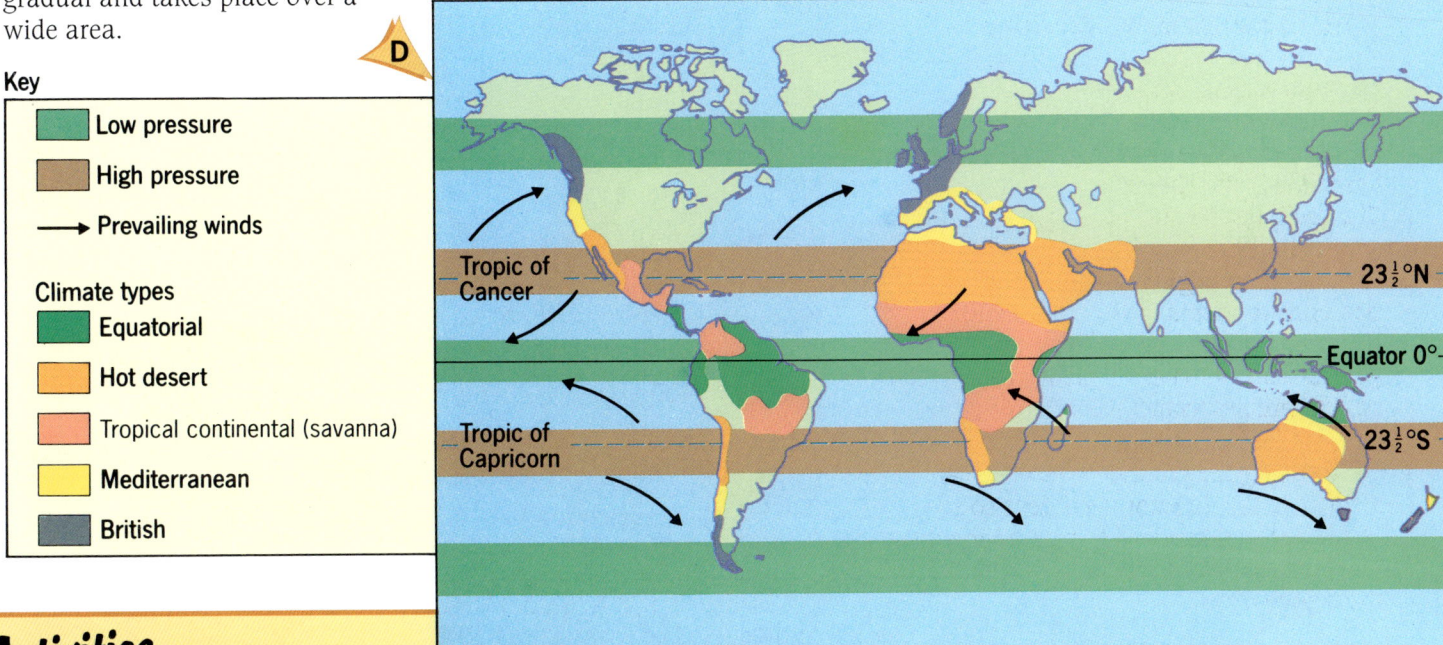

D

Tropic of Cancer — 23½°N — Equator 0° — Tropic of Capricorn — 23½°S

Activities

1 Explain how areas of low pressure and areas of high pressure are formed.

2 Diagram **E** shows the two Hadley Cells, one either side of the Equator.
  a) Copy the diagram and add eight arrowheads to show the direction of air movement.
  b) Label the three boxes either 'high pressure' or 'low pressure'.
  c) Briefly describe the differences in climate between an area with low pressure all the year and an area with high pressure all the year.

E

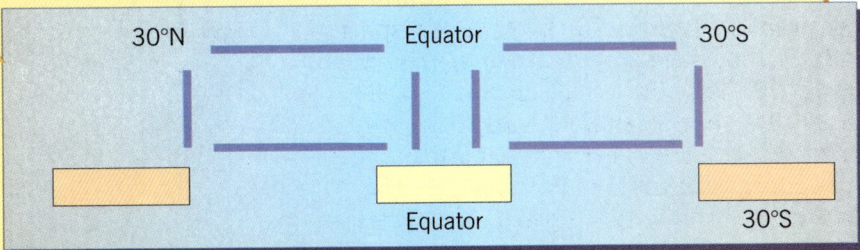

30°N   Equator   30°S

Equator   30°S

3 Explain how atmospheric circulation influences the climate of the British Isles.

Summary The general circulation of the atmosphere is the main factor affecting the world pattern of climatic types.

How do ocean currents affect the climate of coastal areas?

Ocean currents are surface movements of water. They are caused by prevailing winds, which result from the circulation of the atmosphere, blowing over the surface of the ocean (diagram **A**). The main ocean currents follow circular routes – clockwise in the northern hemisphere and anticlockwise in the southern hemisphere (map **B**).

Ocean currents often flow parallel to the coastlines of continents. Where they do, they usually have a considerable influence upon the climate of those coasts. Exactly how ocean currents influence the climate depends largely upon whether the current is classified as being warm or cold. Warm currents take water from tropical areas towards polar areas, e.g. the North Atlantic Drift. They are described as

warm because they raise the temperatures of coastal areas, making them warmer than would be expected for their latitude. In contrast, cold currents take water from colder latitudes back towards the Equator, e.g. the Californian Current. Consequently they lower the temperatures of coastal areas.

Newfoundland and the British Isles lie at approximately the same latitude (map **B**). However, while the seas off Newfoundland are frozen for several months each winter, the North Atlantic Drift keeps Britain ice-free. Even so, anybody falling into the sea off the west coast of Britain in winter is unlikely to survive if left in the water for more than a few minutes!

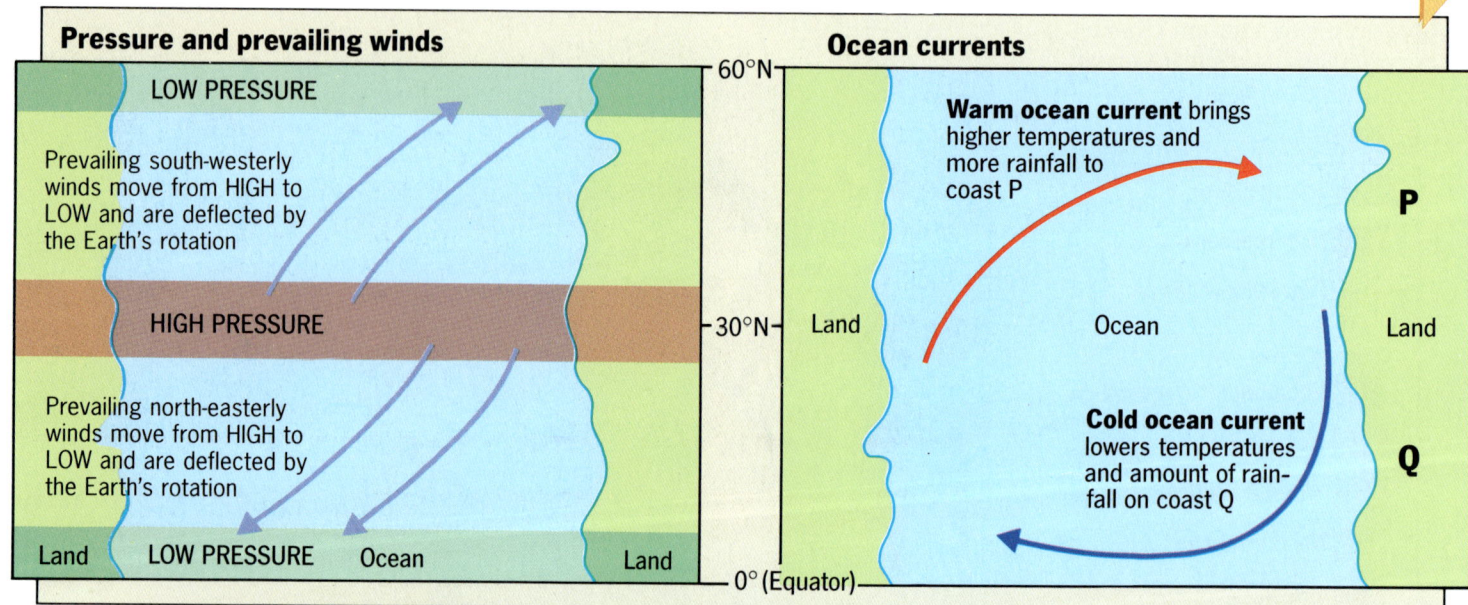

A

Pressure and prevailing winds

LOW PRESSURE

Prevailing south-westerly winds move from HIGH to LOW and are deflected by the Earth's rotation

HIGH PRESSURE

Prevailing north-easterly winds move from HIGH to LOW and are deflected by the Earth's rotation

Land LOW PRESSURE Ocean Land

Ocean currents

60°N

Warm ocean current brings higher temperatures and more rainfall to coast P

P

Land Ocean Land

30°N

Cold ocean current lowers temperatures and amount of rainfall on coast Q

Q

0° (Equator)

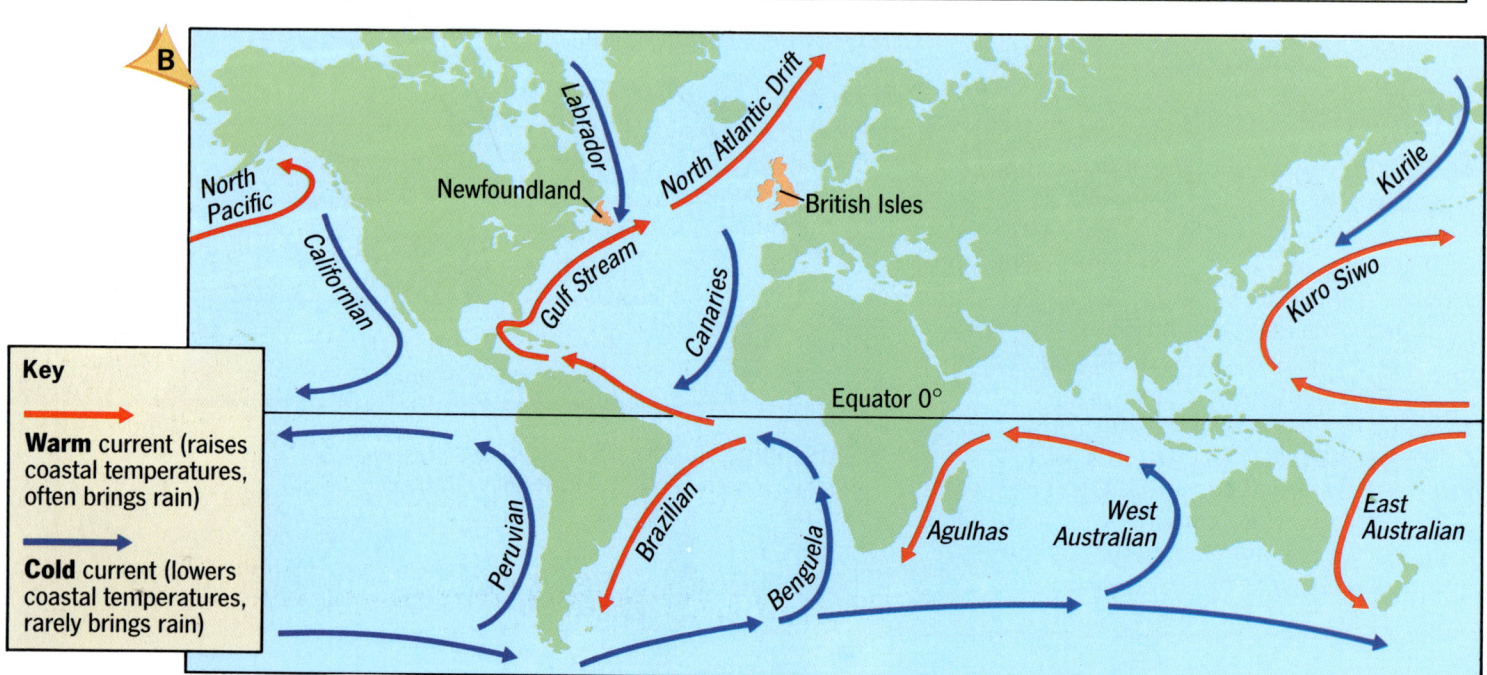

B

North Pacific

Californian

Labrador

Newfoundland

Gulf Stream

North Atlantic Drift

British Isles

Canaries

Kurile

Kuro Siwo

Equator 0°

Key

Warm current (raises coastal temperatures, often brings rain)

Cold current (lowers coastal temperatures, rarely brings rain)

Peruvian

Brazilian

Benguela

Agulhas

West Australian

East Australian

Table **C** describes and explains how two contrasting ocean currents, the warm North Atlantic Drift and the cold Californian Current, have very different influences upon the coastal climates of areas which they affect.

C

Type of current	Location	Source and direction of current	Effects on temperature	Effects on precipitation	Other climatic effects
Warm	Influence of North Atlantic Drift on the climate of the British Isles	Begins in Caribbean Sea and Gulf of Mexico. Flows up east coast of USA as the Gulf Stream, then north-east across the Atlantic Ocean.	Raises temperatures in winter by several degrees – mild. Lowers them in summer – cool.	Allows much moisture to be picked up. This gives heavy and reliable rainfall throughout the year.	Warm air meets cold air to form depressions and gives strong winds (gales).
Cold	Influence of the Californian Current on the climate of California	Begins off west coast of Canada and flows southwards.	Lowers temperatures in summer by several degrees – relatively cool. Raises them a little in winter – warm.	Prevents moisture from being picked up. Gives little rainfall and adds to desert conditions to south.	Warm air drifts out to sea over cold air to give fogs.

Activities

1 **a)** What are ocean currents?
   b) With the help of an annotated diagram, explain how the pattern of ocean currents in the Atlantic Ocean is related to prevailing winds.

2 Diagram **D** shows part of an ocean which lies north of the Equator.
   a) Are the currents flowing clockwise or anticlockwise?
   b) Is current **A** a warm or a cold current? Give a reason for your answer.
   c) Is current **B** a warm or a cold current? Give a reason for your answer.
   d) Make an enlarged copy of table **E**. Complete it to show likely differences in the climate between places **X** and **Y** which are located on the same coast of a large continent.

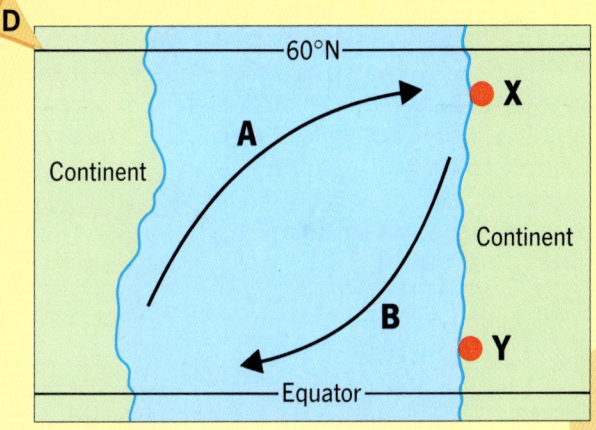

D

60°N · A · X · Continent · Continent · B · Y · Equator

E

	Temperatures		Precipitation	
Place	Summer	Winter	Amounts	Type
X				
Y				

Summary

The global pattern of ocean currents is related to prevailing winds and the general circulation of the atmosphere. Ocean currents have a major influence upon the climates of adjacent coastal areas.

3 Climatic problems

► Why is rainfall unreliable in some parts of the world? ◄

Rainfall in the British Isles is reliable. We know that in a usual year it will rain every few days, rainfall will be spread evenly throughout the twelve months, and that the total amount for each place can be fairly accurately predicted. Occasionally some seasons are wetter and others drier than is expected, but annual totals are nearly always within 10 per cent of the expected average total (map **A**). The driest summer ever recorded in England and Wales was in 1976. It caused a serious drought. Yet it was followed by the second wettest winter ever recorded and so, over a twelve-month period, rainfall virtually averaged itself out.

Not only is rainfall reliable in Britain, but so too is water supply. When it does rain it usually falls steadily for a period of several hours. This allows time for the water to infiltrate into the ground where it can be stored for use in drier periods. The British Isles rarely gets the severe storms that cause rapid surface run-off and flash floods. Britain also has the money and technology to build dams so that surplus water can be stored in reservoirs and then piped where and when it is needed. On a global scale, many countries still do not have a guaranteed supply 'at the turn of a tap'.

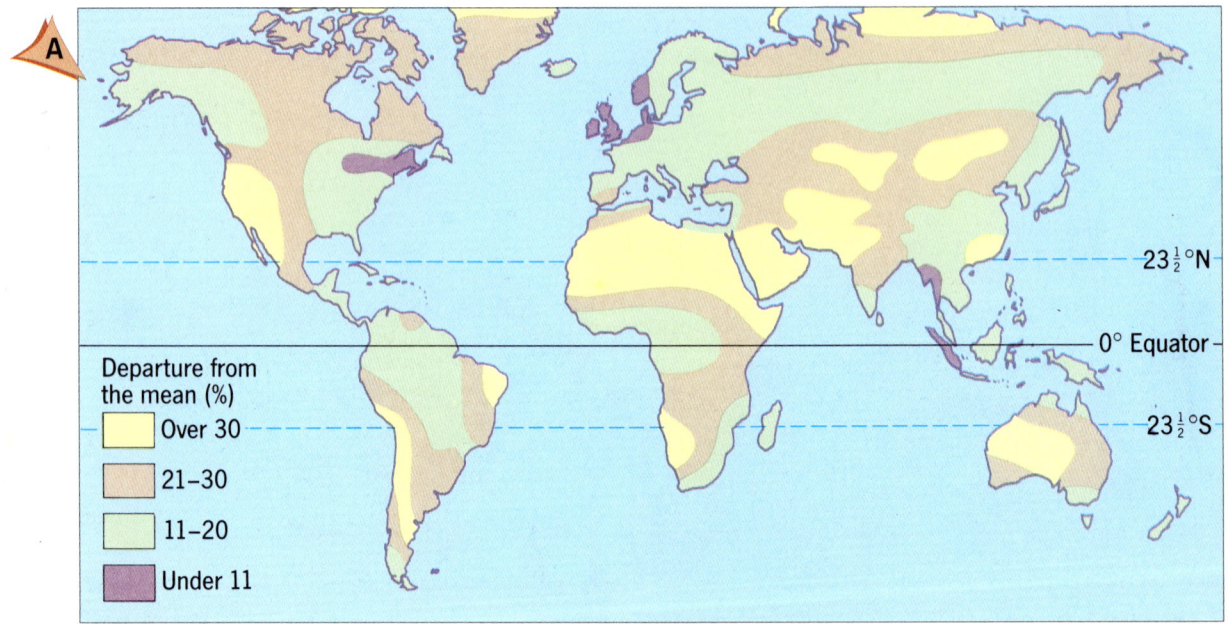

Departure from the mean (%)
- Over 30
- 21–30
- 11–20
- Under 11

23½°N
0° Equator
23½°S

There is a relationship between reliability of rainfall (map **A**), the pattern of world climatic types (page 23) and the circulation of the atmosphere (page 22). This relationship is summarised in table **B**. Rainfall is usually reliable in places where there is less than a 20 per cent departure from the mean (average). Rainfall is least reliable in areas with over a 30 per cent departure from the mean, areas which are are

also usually either too dry or too cold for permanent human settlement. It is those climates with a pronounced wet and dry season, especially in tropical continental areas (page 20), where rainfall is most unreliable in relation to human activity. Here, in some years, the rains may fail to arrive. In other years, when it does rain, total amounts can come from just a few heavy storms. The rain will then be too heavy to

Departure from the mean (%)	Atmospheric pressure	Vertical air movement	Surface prevailing winds	Rainfall distribution	Effectiveness of rain
Under 20	Low	Rising air cools, (i) Equatorial (ii) British type	Equatorial – none condenses and gives rain the sea	Throughout the year British type – south-west from	Equatorial – heavy but intercepted by vegetation Britain – steady
20–30	Seasonal – tropical continental	Rising air giving rain for part of the year. Descending air giving no rain for rest of year	Either too far inland or dry trade winds	Wet season and a dry season	Heavy storms; little interception; less effective and much surface run-off
Over 30	High (i) Hot desert (ii) Polar	Descending air warms, so no condensation	Trade winds from dry land	Very little	Ineffective – short, intense storms

allow infiltration and so the precious water is lost through surface run-off and flash floods. As the rainy season coincides with the time of highest temperatures then evaporation rates, and therefore water loss, will also be at their greatest. Drought frequently occurs in countries along the southern fringes of the Sahara Desert when annual rainfall totals fall below average for several successive years. Unreliable rainfall is one of several important reasons why so many countries with a tropical continental climate, especially in Africa, have remained economically less developed. This creates a vicious circle since, because they are economically less developed, they have less capital and technology to improve their water supply.

Diagram **C** gives some of the consequences of unreliable rainfall upon human activity in Kenya. In a normal year it is estimated that Kenya receives enough rainfall, if it was spread out evenly, to sustain a population several times greater than it has at present. Unfortunately the distribution of rainfall and population does not always match, and rainfall is not always reliable.

C

Maasai herder
We depend upon our cattle, sheep and goats. When the rains fail, there is overgrazing and eventually our animals will die.

Industrialist
We need energy to manufacture goods. We have to rely upon hydro-electricity. If the rains fail, reservoirs dry up and the power stations have to close down. We had big power cuts in Nairobi in 1992.

Wildlife worker
Drought also kills wildlife. In the 1970s thousands of elephants died.

Villager
We have no piped water. If the rains fail, rivers and waterholes dry up and we may have to walk many miles to get water.

Farmer
We need water for our crops. We need more crops since our population is growing so rapidly. If the rains do not come at the right time, and in sufficient quantity, our crops will fail and we will be short of food.

Government official
Kenya is an economically developing country. We do not have enough money to build dams to store water for times of drought. We have several dams but not enough. One big dam was built for us using French money but that accounts for two-thirds of our national debt.

Activities

1 Give three reasons why rainfall in the British Isles is reliable.

2 **a)** Write out the paragraph below using the correct word from each pair in brackets.

Rainfall is most unreliable in areas with (high/low) pressure, when air is (descending/rising) and (cooling/warming), where winds blow from the (land/sea), and when it falls in (long/short) (storms/periods).

  b) Which two of the following four climates have the least reliable rainfall:
  • equatorial   • tropical continental
  • hot deserts   • British type?

3 **a)** How does an unreliable water supply affect a country such as Kenya?

  b) Do you agree or disagree with the statement made in diagram **D**? Give reasons for your answer.

D

The most serious single climatic hazard in an economically less developed country is the variability and uncertainty of rainfall.

Summary

The distribution of areas with a markedly unreliable rainfall can be related to the general pattern of atmospheric circulation and to specific climatic types.

What are the causes and effects of global warming?

Heat from the sun passes through the atmosphere. During the day this heat warms up the surface of the Earth. On clear nights, much of this heat is lost (radiated) back into space and temperatures fall rapidly. On cloudy nights temperatures do not fall as low because the clouds act as a blanket retaining some of the heat. The atmosphere consists of various gases, of which oxygen and nitrogen make up 99 per cent. The remaining 1 per cent includes variable amounts of the two natural gases of carbon dioxide and ozone, and pollutants such methane, sulphur dioxide and nitrogen oxide. It is changes in the amounts of these variable gases and pollutants which are a cause of concern to scientists.

Carbon dioxide is important because it helps to trap heat. The ability of this, and other, gases to insulate the Earth is referred to as the **greenhouse effect**. The natural greenhouse effect is essential as without it the Earth's average temperature would be 33°C lower than it is. (During the last Ice Age temperatures were only 4°C lower than they are today.) Recent human activity has led to an increase in the greenhouse gases. This is causing world temperatures to rise, a process known as **global warming** (diagram **A**).

Causes

Graph **B** shows the major causes of global warming. The most important single factor has been the burning of fossil fuels in power stations, factories, homes and by road transport. As it is the economically more developed and industrialised countries that use up most of the world's energy, they are the ones largely to blame for global warming (graph **C**). A second cause is deforestation (pages 38–43), especially the burning of the tropical rainforests in economically developing countries.

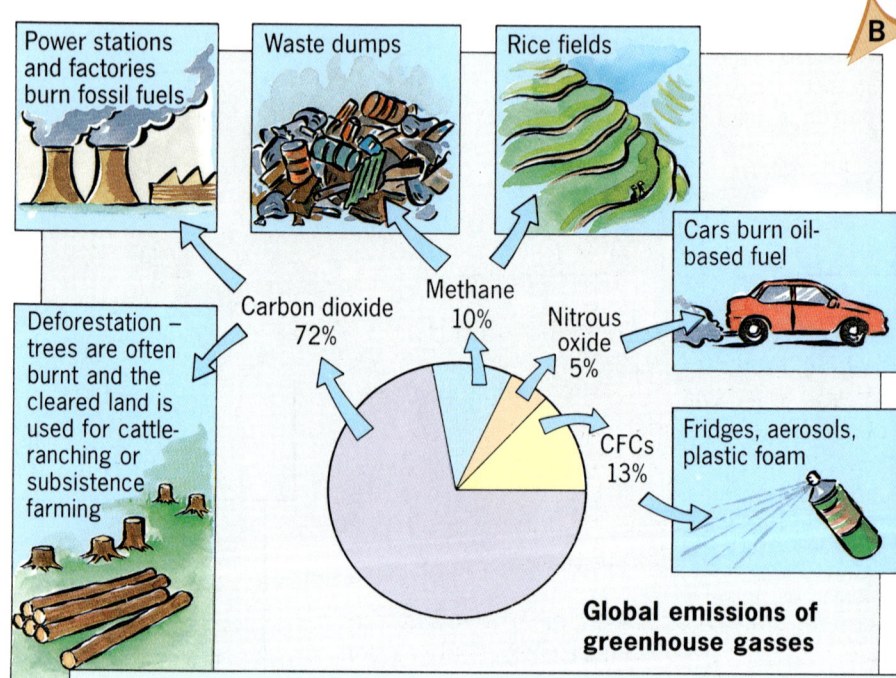

A

The greenhouse effect

Carbon dioxide level is increased by burning fossil fuels and cutting down forests

Sun's heat

Some heat escapes

Less heat escapes

Carbon dioxide in atmosphere

Carbon dioxide traps heat being reflected by the Earth

Warming increases water vapour in air

B

Power stations and factories burn fossil fuels

Waste dumps

Rice fields

Cars burn oil-based fuel

Deforestation – trees are often burnt and the cleared land is used for cattle-ranching or subsistence farming

Carbon dioxide 72%

Methane 10%

Nitrous oxide 5%

CFCs 13%

Fridges, aerosols, plastic foam

Global emissions of greenhouse gasses

Consequences

Although global warming results mainly from activities within a relatively few countries, its consequences affect all parts of the world. Indeed, it is likely that its effects will be greatest in many countries which, at present, are not major contributors to greenhouses gas emissions. This is because gases released into the air, and the resultant rise in temperature, do not stop at national boundaries. Global temperatures have risen by 0.5°C in the last 100 years. Estimates suggest that, without controls on greenhouse gas

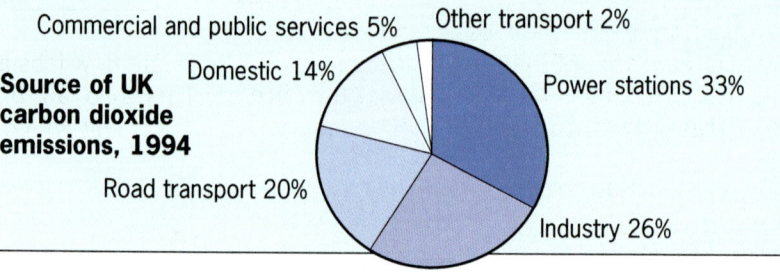

Commercial and public services 5%

Other transport 2%

Source of UK carbon dioxide emissions, 1994

Domestic 14%

Power stations 33%

Road transport 20%

Industry 26%

emissions, temperatures could rise by up to 0.5°C each decade over the next 100 years (graph **D**). The major global effect is the predicted rise in sea-level. Scientists are suggesting that as air temperatures rise:

- sea temperatures will also rise; as the sea expands, due to the extra heat, its level could rise by between 0.25 and 1.5 metres
- ice caps and glaciers, especially in polar areas, will melt; this could result in an overall rise in sea-level by up to another 5 metres.

Even a half-metre rise in sea-level could flood 15 per cent of densely populated Bangladesh, 25 per cent of Egypt's arable land, and submerge several low-lying islands in the Indian and Pacific Oceans (map **E**).

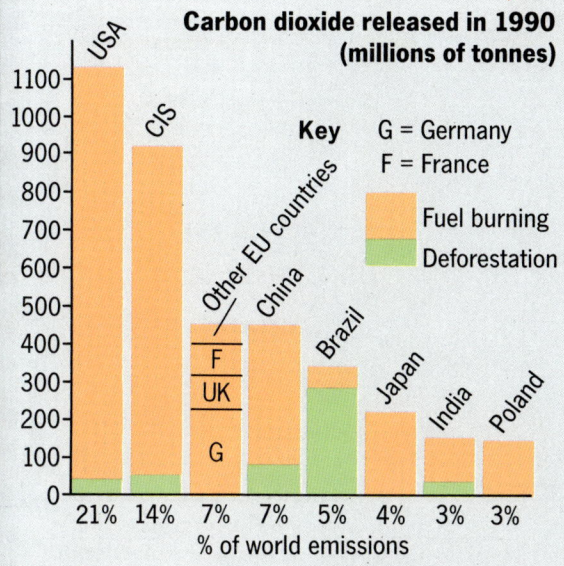

C

Carbon dioxide released in 1990
(millions of tonnes)

Key   G = Germany
       F = France

Fuel burning
Deforestation

% of world emissions

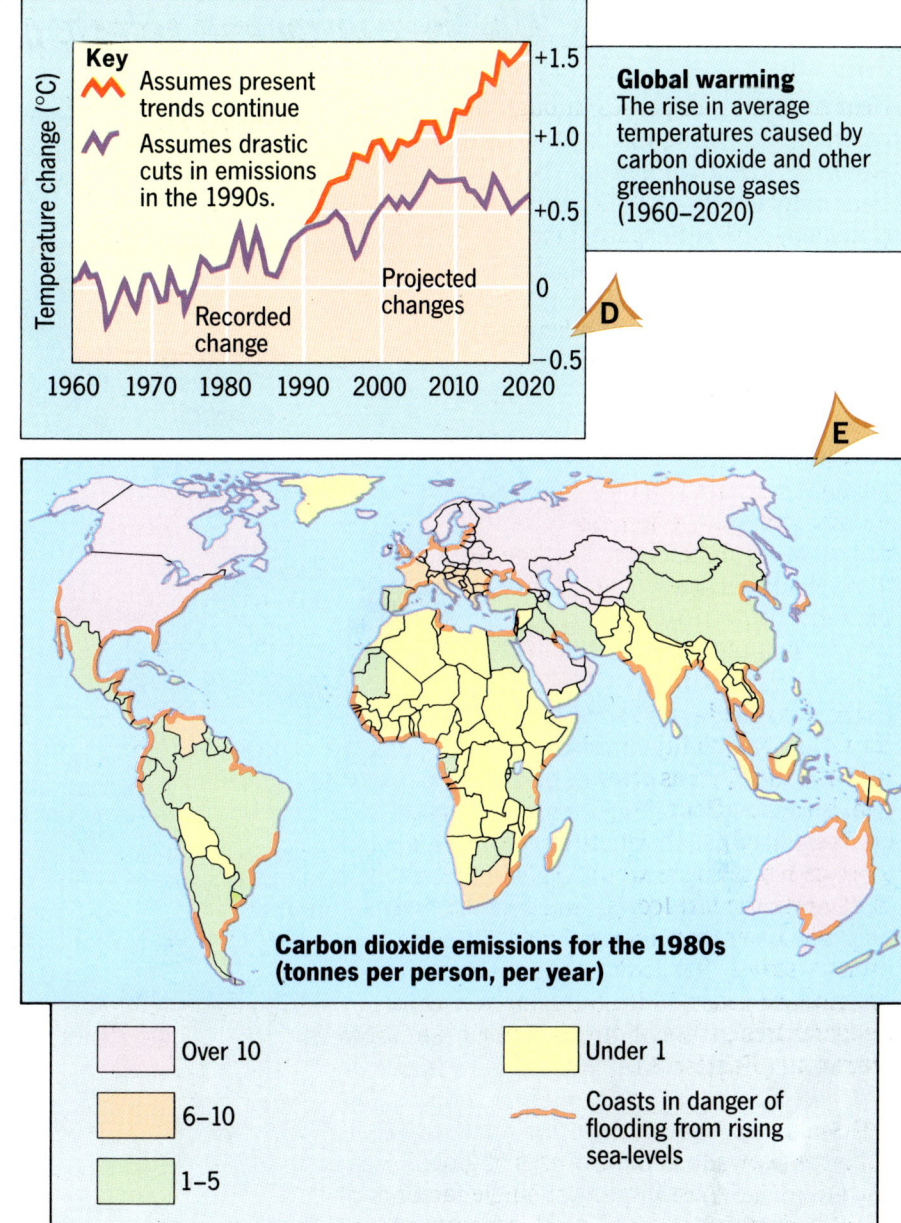

D

Key

Assumes present trends continue

Assumes drastic cuts in emissions in the 1990s.

Temperature change (°C)

Recorded change

Projected changes

Global warming
The rise in average temperatures caused by carbon dioxide and other greenhouse gases (1960–2020)

E

Carbon dioxide emissions for the 1980s
(tonnes per person, per year)

Over 10

6–10

1–5

Under 1

Coasts in danger of flooding from rising sea-levels

Other predicted effects of global warming include an increase in storms and hurricanes in tropical areas and a decrease in rainfall in most of the world's major cereal growing areas. The latter would result from air being able to hold more moisture as it gets warmer. As a result there will be a decrease in rainfall totals and an increase in its unreliability (page 26).

Gaining international agreement to reduce the releases of greenhouse gases, especially carbon dioxide, is difficult. Industrialised countries are reluctant, claiming that the high economic costs involved could cause job losses and a lowering of their standards of living. Developing countries are reluctant, believing that they need to increase energy consumption if they are to create new jobs and raise their living standards. They also fail to see why they should help solve a problem which they did not create.

Activities

1 **a)** Draw a labelled diagram to explain the greenhouse effect.
  b) i) What are the four main greenhouse gases?
    ii) What is the source of each of these four greenhouse gases?
  c) Which countries contribute most to the greenhouse effect?

2 **a)** How is global warming predicted to affect the world's
    i) temperatures
    ii) sea-level
    iii) cereal production?
  b) i) Why is international agreement on the reduction of greenhouse gases necessary?
    ii) Why is it difficult to get this international agreement?

Summary

Global warming is caused by an increase in the emission of greenhouse gases, especially carbon dioxide, by a relatively few industrialised countries. As the consequences will affect the whole world, there is a need for international co-operation and agreement.

Why is acid rain an international problem?

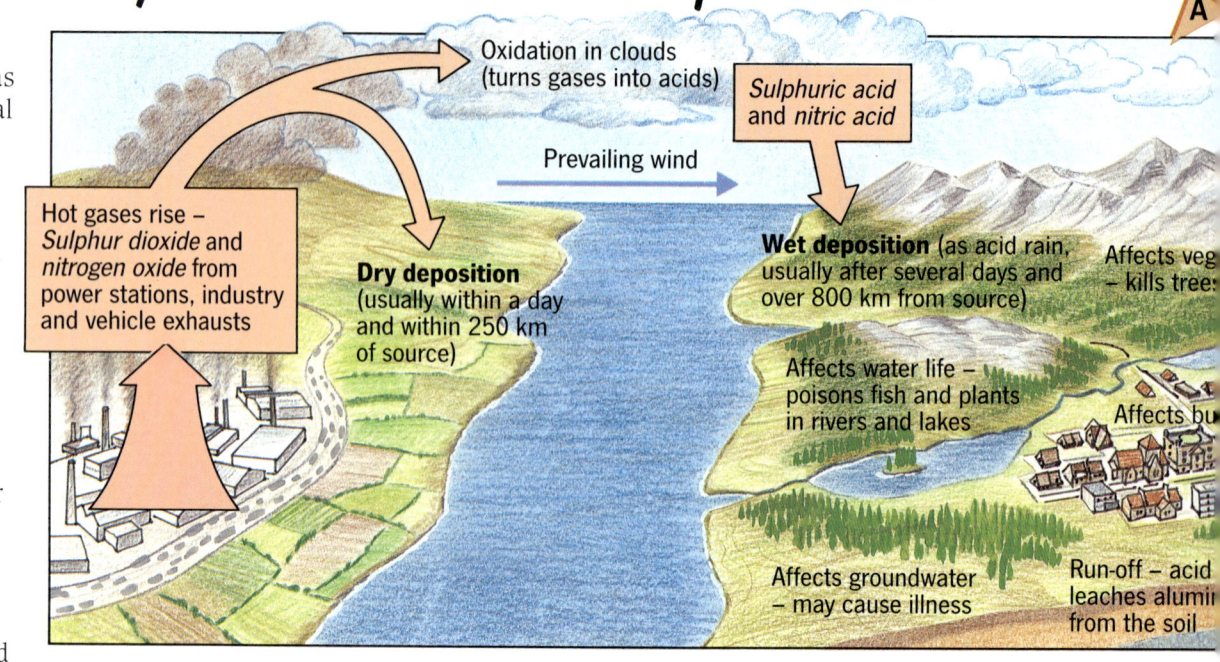

Acid rain, resulting from air pollution, has become a major global environmental problem. The main pollutants are:

*   sulphur dioxide which comes from thermal power stations and industry
*   nitrogen oxide which comes from thermal power stations and motor vehicle exhausts.

These pollutants are carried by prevailing winds across seas and international boundaries (diagram **A**). Some are deposited directly onto the Earth's surface. The majority are converted into acids which fall to the ground as acid rain. Unpolluted rainwater, which is slightly acidic, has a pH value of between 5 and 6 (graph **B**). Acid rain has pH readings of under 5. Parts of north-east North America and north-west Europe have readings of under 4.0 (map **C**).

The effects of acid rain (diagram **A**) include:

*   The destruction of forests as acid rain destroys tree roots (photo **D**). The trees are then more likely to suffer from drought and disease.
*   Making freshwater lakes so acidic that fish and plant life is poisoned. Over 4000 lakes in Sweden are 'dead'. British and Canadian lakes are also becoming increasingly affected.
*   Contaminating freshwater supplies which might, in time, become harmful to health.
*   Increasing the acidity of soil which, unless lime is added, reduces the quality of crops.
*   The chemical weathering of buildings and statues (photo **E**).

Acid rain is an international problem because it is blown across oceans and continents ignoring political boundaries. Many countries produce acid rain (map **C**). Some, like Britain, Germany and the USA, 'export' it while others, such as Norway, Sweden and Canada, 'import' it. Any solution to the problem requires international co-operation. This is not easy as the countries most affected by acid rain are often not the same ones that are responsible for causing it.

Diagram A labels:
Oxidation in clouds (turns gases into acids)
Sulphuric acid and nitric acid
Prevailing wind
Hot gases rise – *Sulphur dioxide* and *nitrogen oxide* from power stations, industry and vehicle exhausts
Dry deposition (usually within a day and within 250 km of source)
Wet deposition (as acid rain, usually after several days and over 800 km from source)
Affects veg – kills trees
Affects water life – poisons fish and plants in rivers and lakes
Affects bu
Affects groundwater – may cause illness
Run-off – acid leaches alumin from the soil

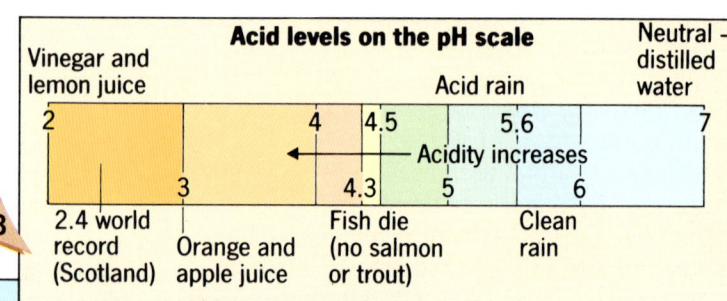

B

Acid levels on the pH scale		Neutral – distilled water
Vinegar and lemon juice	Acid rain	

2 · · 4 4.5 5.6 · 7
3 4.3 5 6
Acidity increases

2.4 world record (Scotland) · Orange and apple juice · Fish die (no salmon or trout) · Clean rain

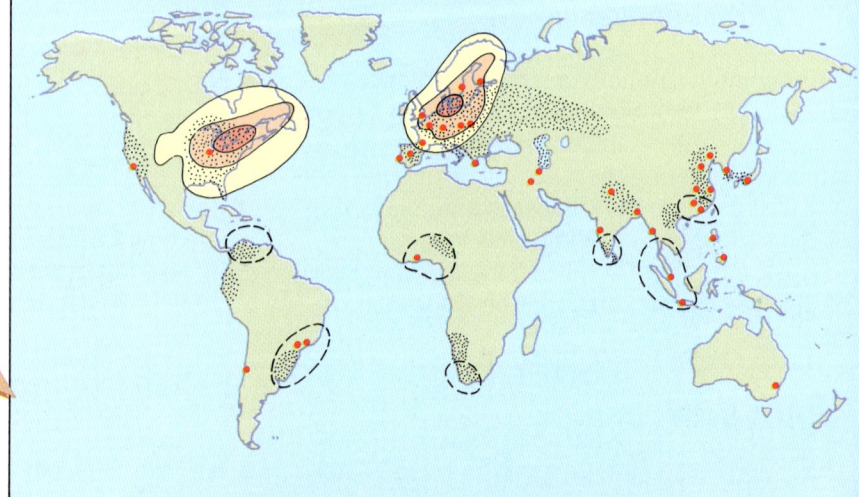

C

Regions where sulphur and nitrogen oxides are released in high concentrations, mainly from burning fossil fuels

Areas where acid rain is a potential danger

• Major cities with high levels of air pollution (including nitrogen and sulphur emissions)

Areas of heavy acid deposition

pH less than 4 (most acidic) | pH 4 to 4.5 | pH 4.6 to 5

How might the effects of acid rain be reduced?

There are several ways by which sulphur dioxide emissions from power stations may be reduced. These include burning coal which contains less sulphur, removing sulphur from coal before it is used, using a new type of boiler which allows the sulphur dioxide to remain in the ash, and removing sulphur from waste gases after it is used. The latter method involves spraying sulphur dioxide with water. This converts the gas into sulphuric acid which can then be neutralised by adding lime. Unfortunately all of these methods are expensive and increase the cost of electricity to the user. Britain is committed to reducing sulphur dioxide emissions by 60 per cent of their 1980 levels by the year 2000 and 71 per cent by 2005. So far they have been reduced by 30 per cent. Some European countries say this is too little and is taking too long, but it has been achieved by phasing out coal-burning power stations in favour of cheaper gas-fired stations. This phasing out has accelerated the decline of Britain's coalmining industry as the demand for coal falls.

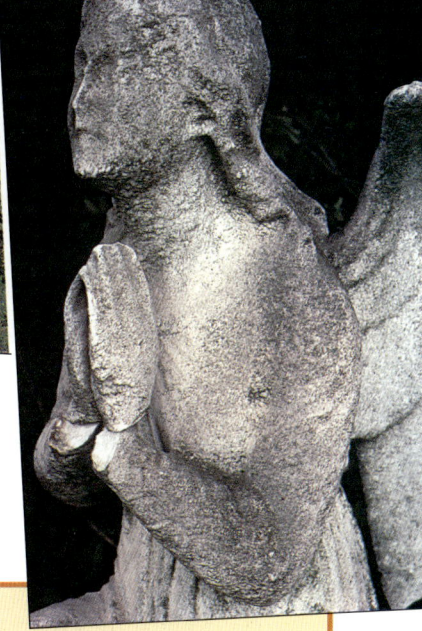

D Damage to trees caused by acid rain – Poland

E Acid rain damage to a stone statue in New York City, USA

Emissions from cars have been reduced by using unleaded petrol and fuel injection. Further attempts, such as recirculating exhaust gases, are likely to add to the cost of a new car.

Activities

1 **a)** What is acid rain?
   b) What, according to graph **F**, are the two major producers of
     i) sulphur dioxide
     ii) nitrogen oxide?
   c) Describe five problems caused by acid rain.

2 Using map **C**.
   a) Describe the location of the major concentrations of sulphur and nitrogen oxides.
   b) i) Why do countries like Norway, Sweden and Canada want rapid decreases in the emissions of sulphur and nitrogen oxides?
     ii) Why are countries like Britain, Germany and the USA reluctant to reduce these emissions?

3 Two views are expressed in diagram **G**. Which of these views is likely to be supported by:
   i)   an industrialist
   ii) a coalminer
   iii) a conservationist?
   Give reasons, in each case, for your answer.

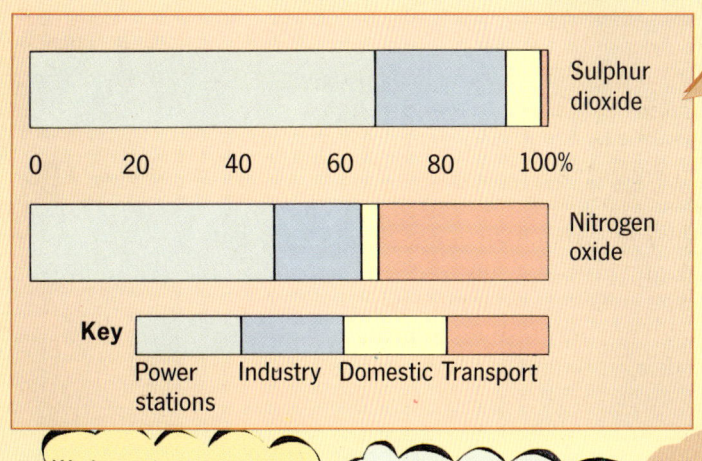

F

Sulphur dioxide

0   20   40   60   80   100%

Nitrogen oxide

Key

Power stations   Industry   Domestic   Transport

G

We have the technology to reduce acid rain and to manage our environment.

It will all cost a lot of money which few people or countries have. We will have to pay much more for our energy and cars.

Summary

Acid rain is a major form of atmospheric pollution. As it crosses international boundaries it creates many problems which can only be solved through international co-operation.

What are the characteristics of the tropical rainforests?

Tropical rainforest is the natural vegetation of places that have an equatorial climate (page 18). It provides the most luxuriant vegetation found on Earth (photos **B** and **C**). Over one-third of the world's trees grow here. There are thousands of different species with many yet to be identified and studied. As with all types of natural vegetation, the trees in the rainforest have had to **adapt** to the local environment. This means that they have had to adjust to growing in a climate that has constantly high temperatures and heavy rainfall, and an all-year-round growing season. Some of the ways in which the trees have adapted to the climate are shown in diagram **A**. The vegetation has also had to adapt to other local conditions such as soils, flooding and competition from other plants. Different plants also survive in their own microclimate (page 9), perhaps as an emergent needing to reach the sunlight, perhaps as a shade-lover on the forest floor. Each plant plays an important role in the forest ecosystem.

A

Height of trees which grow in **three layers**

40 m

Tallest trees called **emergents**

30 m

CANOPY

20 m

UNDER CANOPY

10 m

Lianas

Buttress roots

SHRUB LAYER

Ground level

How vegetation has adapted to the equatorial climate

- The trees can grow to over 40 metres in the effort to get sunlight

- The forest has an **evergreen** appearance due to the continuous growing season. This means that trees can shed leaves at any time, but always look green and in leaf

- The leaves have drip tips to shed the heavy rainfall

- Tree trunks are straight and branchless in their lower parts in their efforts to grow tall

- Lianas, which are vine-like plants, use large trees as a support to climb up to the canopy

- The forest floor is dark and damp. There is little undergrowth because the sunlight cannot reach ground level

- Dense undergrowth develops near rivers or in forest clearings where sunlight can penetrate

- Rivers flood for several months each year

- Fallen leaves soon rot in the hot, wet climate

- Large buttress roots stand above the ground to give support to the trees

Until recently few parts of the rainforest had been affected by human activity. Where it had, it was usually by groups of people clearing just enough land on which to grow crops for their small community. Often, in places like the Amazon forest, the land rapidly became infertile and the people had to move and make a new clearing. This method of farming, known as shifting cultivation, allowed the forest to re-establish itself. Re-established areas often have a thicker undergrowth as the initial clearance allowed more sunlight to reach the forest floor. More recently, human activity has led to vast areas of the rainforest being totally destroyed, a process known as **deforestation** (page 38). As large trees are destroyed, the habitat for other plants and wildlife is altered. Plants that cannot adapt quickly to the changed environment may die out.

Activities

1 Match up each of the eight descriptive points of the tropical rainforest in the list below with its correct number on diagram **D**.
   - buttress roots • main canopy • lianas
   - under-canopy • branchless trunks
   - little undergrowth • emergents • shrub layer

2 **a)** Why does rainforest vegetation grow so quickly?
   b) Why do some trees grow so tall?
   c) Why are buttress roots needed?
   d) Why is there so little undergrowth away from rivers?

3 **a)** Why did earlier human activity have little effect upon the tropical rainforest vegetation?
   b) Why are present-day human actions having a far greater effect?

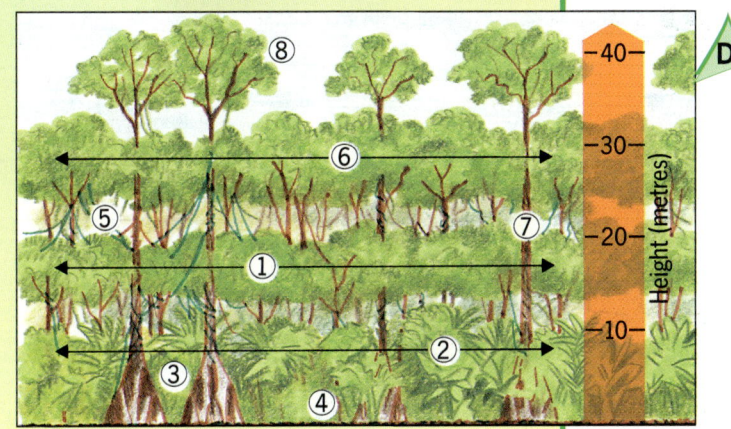

D

Summary The natural vegetation of the tropical rainforest has had to adapt to the hot, wet equatorial climate. It is now being increasingly affected by human activity.

What are the characteristics of the savanna grassland vegetation?

The savanna grassland, which often includes scattered trees (photos **B** and **C**), is the natural vegetation of places with a tropical continental climate (page 20). The vegetation forms a transition between the tropical rainforests and the hot deserts (map **D**, page 23). As with all types of natural vegetation, the plants growing here have had to **adapt** to the local environment. This means that they have had to adjust to a very warm climate which has a pronounced wet season, though the rainfall is often unreliable (page 26), followed by a very long dry season. Some of the ways in which the grass and trees have adapted to the climate are shown in diagram **A**. Apart from the major problem of water supply caused by the seasonal drought, the vegetation has also had to adapt to other local conditions such as soils, relief, and competition from other plants.

A

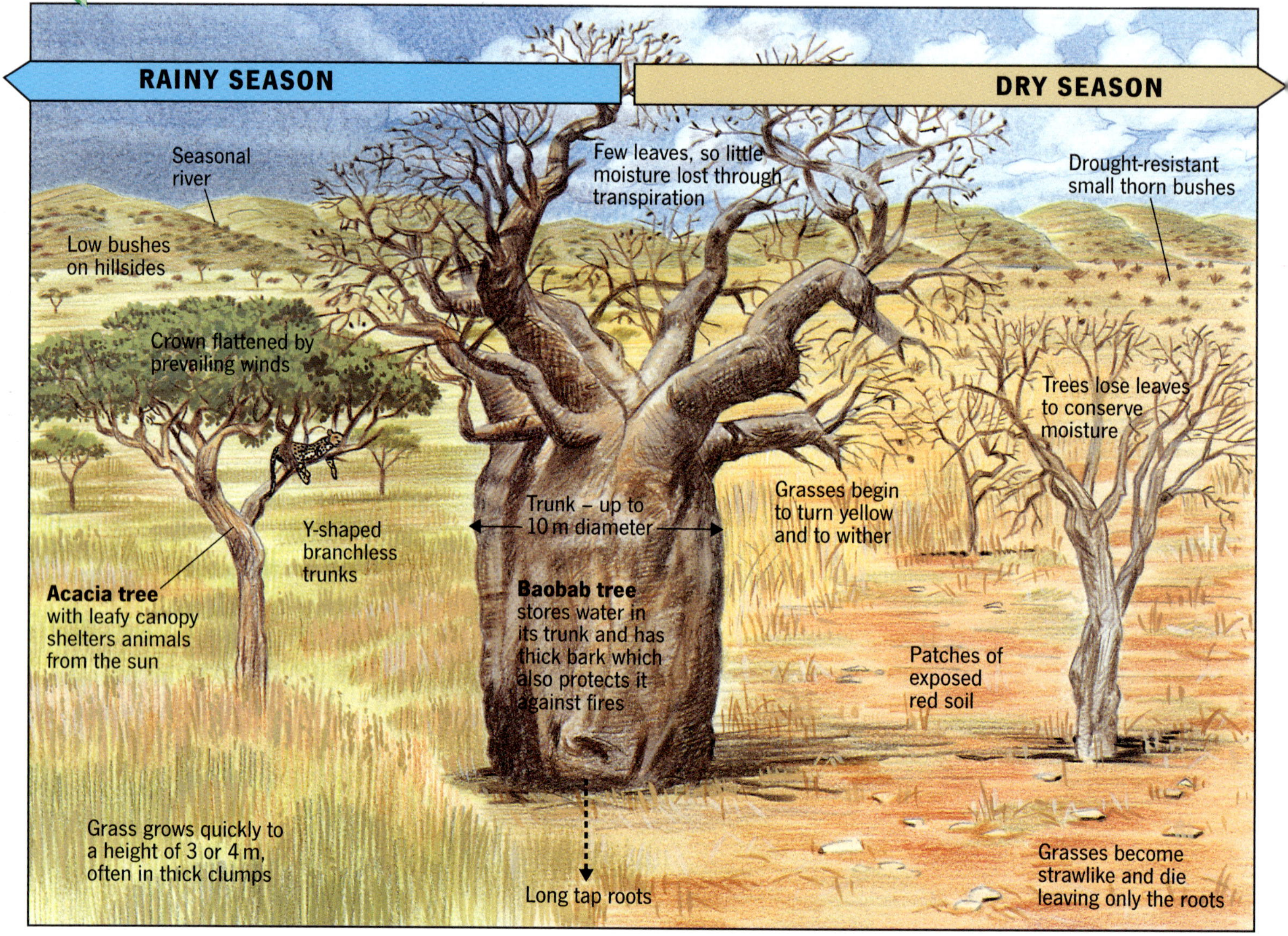

RAINY SEASON

DRY SEASON

Seasonal river

Low bushes on hillsides

Crown flattened by prevailing winds

Few leaves, so little moisture lost through transpiration

Drought-resistant small thorn bushes

Trees lose leaves to conserve moisture

Y-shaped branchless trunks

Trunk – up to 10 m diameter

Grasses begin to turn yellow and to wither

Acacia tree with leafy canopy shelters animals from the sun

Baobab tree stores water in its trunk and has thick bark which also protects it against fires

Patches of exposed red soil

Grass grows quickly to a height of 3 or 4 m, often in thick clumps

Long tap roots

Grasses become strawlike and die leaving only the roots

It has been suggested that the savanna grasses are not the natural vegetation of tropical continental climates. Rather they are the result of fires started either naturally or by human activity. Fires can result from either:
• lightning associated with convectional thunderstorms in the rainy season or

• cattle herders burning off the old grass during the dry season to encourage new shoots to sprout when the rains come.

The thick bark of the baobab tree (photo **B**) acts as a protection against fires.

B

Baobab tree

Recently many parts of the savanna grasslands, especially in Africa, which are near to the desert margins have suffered from drought and **desertification** (pages 48–49). The unreliable rainfall has caused vegetation to die. With insufficient grass for the large herds of wild and domestic grazing animals, the area suffers from **overgrazing** (page 49). As the human population increases, former nomadic tribes, like the Maasai in Kenya, find their traditional grazing grounds reduced in size as the land is settled permanently or is used to grow crops. This adds to overgrazing in the areas to which they are restricted. The increase in the human population has also meant that more trees and shrubs have to be cut for fuelwood or to create extra land for crops. With fewer trees and less grass to protect the land from the weather, the soil may be washed away during the rainy season or blown away during the dry season.

C

Acacia trees on the savanna grassland

Activities

1 Photo **C** was taken during the rainy season.
  a) Describe the appearance of the natural vegetation of the savanna grasslands during the rainy season.
  b) What differences will there be in the appearance of the natural vegetation during the dry season?
  c) Draw a baobab tree similar to the one shown in photo **B**. Add at least four labels to show how the tree has adapted to the climate.

2 Diagram **D** shows how the natural vegetation of parts of the savanna grasslands is being changed.
  a) Name three changes that are natural (not the result of human activity).
  b) Name four changes that are the result of human activity.
  c) Describe how these changes are altering the natural vegetation of the savanna grasslands.

Summary

The natural vegetation of the savanna grassland has had to adapt to a warm climate which has a wet and a dry season. It is being increasingly affected by human activity.

D

Drought for several years

Thunderstorm

Maasai herders

New houses

Collecting fuelwood

Herds of domestic cattle and goats

Large herds of wildebeeste, zebra and other wild herbivores

Newly planted maize

What are the characteristics of Mediterranean vegetation?

Mediterranean woodland and scrub (photos **B** and **C**) is the natural vegetation of places that have a Mediterranean type of climate (page 21). As with all types of natural vegetation, the plants which grow here have had to **adapt** to the local environment. This means that they have had to adjust to a climate that has hot, dry summers and mild, wet winters. Some of the ways by which the trees and shrubs have adapted to the climate are shown in diagram **A**. The vegetation has also had to adapt to other local conditions such as soils, relief, different rock types and competition from other plants.

The natural vegetation of the Mediterranean lands in Europe was woodland. Where this still exists the main trees are often evergreen oaks and pines (e.g. cork oak and Corsican pine). Where the woodland has been cut down, it has been succeeded by one of two types of scrub.

- **Maquis** is a dense tangle of undergrowth and grows on granite and other impermeable rocks.
- **Garrigue** is a less dense and lower-lying scrub which includes many aromatic plants such as rosemary and lavender. It develops on limestone and other permeable rocks.

A

Pine

Cypress

Cork oak

Some have thick bark as protection against the heat

Many have small, thin, waxy or leathery leaves to reduce moisture loss

LOW SCRUB

Sweet-smelling herbs

Rosemary

Very little grass. Too hot and too dry.

Lavender

Thyme

Quick life cycle to fit into the short growing season

Many plants have long roots to reach down to underground water

Rosemary can roll its leaves up tightly to reduce moisture loss

Due to human activities over many centuries, little of the natural Mediterranean woodland survives today. It has been changed as a result of several factors.

- **Deforestation** Some of the earliest civilisations (Greek) and empires (Greek and Roman) grew up on the shores of the Mediterranean Sea. Their inhabitants cleared many of the natural forests. They needed the space for farming and for settlement. Wood was needed for the construction of ships, the building of houses, and as a fuel for both cooking and warmth. Deforestation left the many steep mountainsides vulnerable to soil erosion during the heavy winter rains.
- **Grazing animals** Forests were unable to re-establish themselves as herds of sheep and, especially, goats ate the young shoots.
- **Fire** Forest fires were, and still are, extremely dangerous. The fires, often started deliberately during the long, dry summers, have added to the destruction of the forests and, more recently, human property.

B Mediterranean woodland

C Mediterranean scrub

Activities

1 Draw a simple diagram of a named Mediterranean tree (diagram **A**). Add three labels to show how it has adapted to the summer drought.

2 Using diagram **D**, describe the type of vegetation likely to grow on:
   a) hillside **X**
   b) hillside **Y**.

3 Describe three different human activities that have changed the natural vegetation of those places surrounding the Mediterranean Sea.

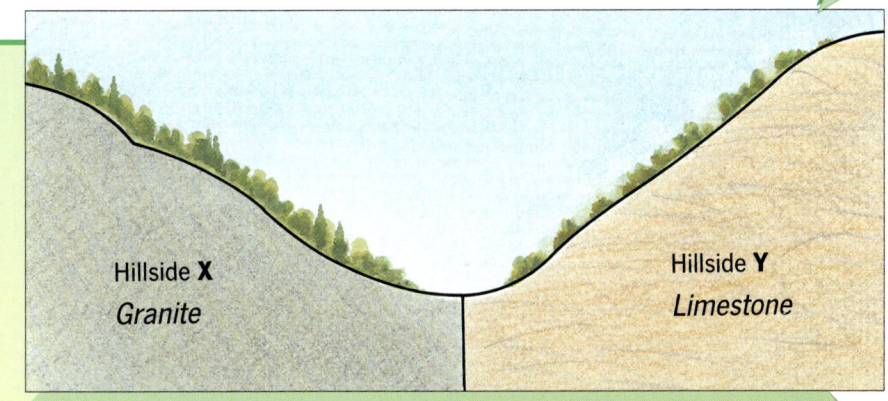

D

Hillside **X**
Granite

Hillside **Y**
Limestone

Summary The natural vegetation of places with a Mediterranean climate has had to adapt to a climate that has hot, dry summers and warm, wet winters. In countries surrounding the Mediterranean Sea, the vegetation has been changed over many centuries by human activity.

37

Deforestation – why are the rainforests being cleared?

Deforestation is the felling and clearance of forest land. Deforestation began in the Mediterranean lands (page 37) and north-west Europe many centuries ago. Today it is mainly taking place in those economically less developed countries that have tropical rainforests as their natural vegetation (page 33). The rapid clearances in recent years have made deforestation a key global environmental issue. Some estimates suggest that one-fifth of the Amazon forest was cleared between 1960 and 1990 (map **A**). Whereas in 1980 an area the size of Wales was possibly cleared, by 1990 the cleared area had increased more to the size of Great Britain (i.e. one hectare cleared every 2 seconds). The fastest clearances are still taking place in Brazil (graph **B**). Satellite photographs have shown that, on occasions, up to 5000 individual fires may be burning at the same time. These fires release carbon dioxide and smoke which pollute the atmosphere and reduce visibility (photo **C**). Although the rainforests may provide 'the most luxuriant vegetation found on Earth' (page 32), they are still a fragile environment which, once destroyed, is unlikely to be replaced.

A

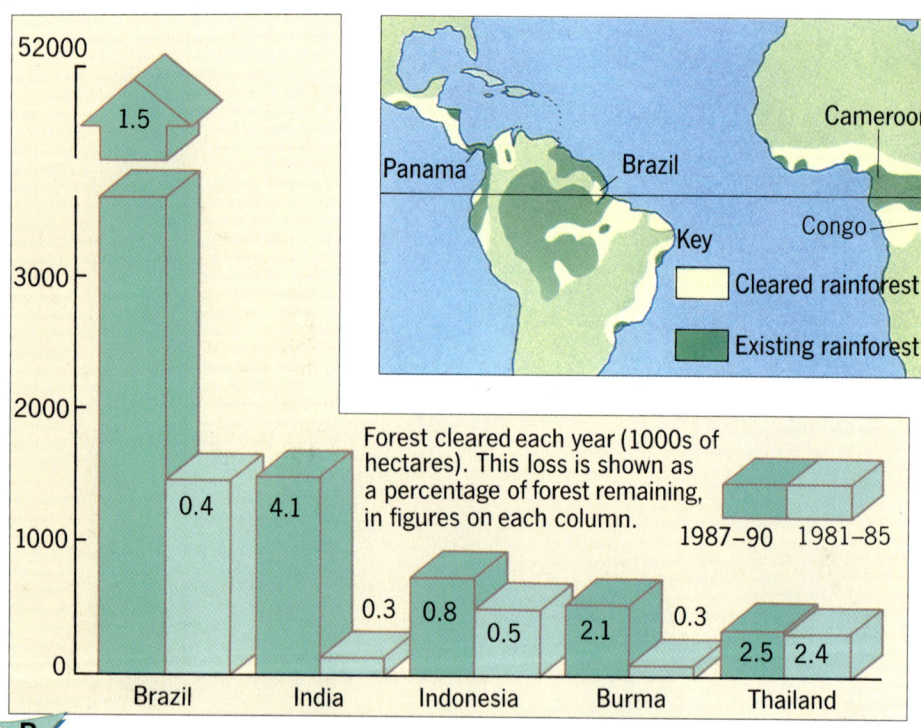

Key
- ☐ Cleared rainforest
- ▨ Existing rainforest

Forest cleared each year (1000s of hectares). This loss is shown as a percentage of forest remaining, in figures on each column.

1987–90   1981–85

Brazil	India	Indonesia	Burma	Thailand
1.5 / 0.4	4.1	0.3 / 0.8	0.5 / 2.1	0.3 / 2.5 / 2.4

B

Reasons for clearances

The Earth's remaining rainforests are under attack by a rapidly growing population, and an increasing demand by that population for natural resources. Deforestation can be the result of several types of activity (diagram **D**).

- Government policy, such as in Brazil where attempts have been made to resettle some of the country's many landless people.
- Transnational companies, which wish to grow cash crops, extract raw materials or develop energy on a commercial scale.
- Local people, who need more land on which to grow crops if they are to be able to feed themselves.

By 1990 plans had been made for a wide range of developments which would affect over 60 per cent of Brazil's remaining rainforest. At that time, less than 4 per cent of Brazil's rainforest was protected from development by law.

In late 1997, numerous uncontrolled fires in Indonesia led to severe pollution and poor visibility in several countries in South-east Asia, while in March 1998 uncontrolled fires in Brazil destroyed an area of rainforest the size of Belgium.

C   Amazon rainforest being burnt for cattle ranching

Activities

1 a) What is deforestation?
   b) Which parts of the world are experiencing most deforestation?
   c) Why is rapid deforestation taking place in those parts of the world?

2 a) Give eight reasons why the tropical rainforests are being cleared in countries like Brazil.
   b) Which of those reasons benefit:
      i)   local people
      ii) Brazil's government
      iii) transnational companies?

Summary

The effects of population growth and economic development have always put pressure on natural resources, especially forests. Today it is the tropical rainforests where deforestation is greatest.

Deforestation — what are the consequences?

Loss of wildlife

Many birds, insects, reptiles and animals rely upon trees for food or shelter. They die or are forced to move away if their habitat is destroyed.

Loss of medicines

Over half of our modern medicines come from the rainforests. These include painkillers and quinine (used to treat malaria). Recently one plant, a periwinkle, has proved successful in treating child leukaemia. Perhaps the rainforests may hold cures for cancer and AIDS. If they are cleared, we will never know!

Elimination of Indian groups and their way of life

Estimates suggest that 96 per cent of forest Indians have died since the arrival of Europeans in the sixteenth century. The majority died from Western illnesses to which they had no immunity (e.g. measles, influenza). Those remaining have been driven from their homes by the construction of roads, mines, reservoirs and cattle ranches (photo **A**). They have been forced to live on reservations which have few natural resources, and certainly none that are of value to the developers. In several parts of Brazil, Indians who have tried to resist being moved have been killed by developers.

Soil erosion

The forest canopy protects the soil by intercepting the heavy daily convectional rainfall. The tree roots help to bind the soil together and to reduce throughflow. Without the trees there is increased surface run-off which causes both soil erosion and more severe and frequent flooding.

Decrease in soil fertility

In order to live, trees take nutrients from the soil. Dead trees, and leaves shed from trees, rapidly decompose in the hot, wet climate. This allows the nutrients to be returned to the soil. This process is called the **humus**, or **nutrient, cycle** (diagram **B**). If trees are removed then the cycle is broken. Humus will not replaced and nutrients in the soil will be washed away (**leached**) by the heavy rain. Within three or four years the soil becomes infertile (diagram **C**). The forest Indians overcame this problem by moving home every few years (shifting cultivation).

Cattle ranchers, having cleared vast areas, now have to do the same – leaving large areas scarred and unusable. Former landless families, resettled here by the government, have seen the soil become too infertile to

Converting rainforest into land for cattle grazing in Brazil **A**

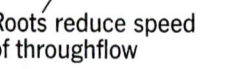
B Heavy daily convectional rainfall intercepted by tree canopy

Ground is protected from the heavy rainfall

Roots reduce speed of throughflow

Leaves provide humus

Humus cycle in an area **tropical rainforest**

Rich tree growth

Numerou fallen lea

Leaves c rapidly t form hu

Rich soil

Nutrients added to the soil

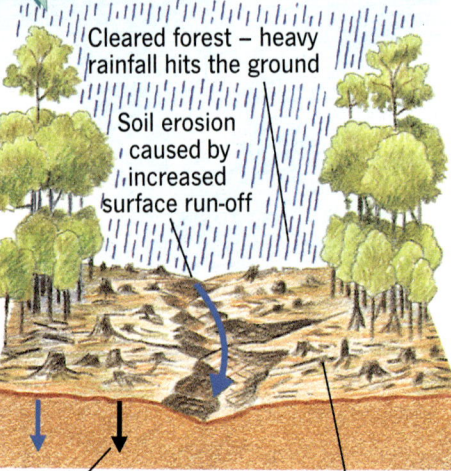
C

Cleared forest – heavy rainfall hits the ground

Soil erosion caused by increased surface run-off

Nutrients in soil washed downwards (leaching)

No fallen leaves to renew humus

The cycle after an area **forest has been cleared**

Poorer-quality vegetation. Soil erosion

Fewer tre and leave

Less hum

Soil becomes less fertile

Few nutrients add to soil. Others ar lost to plants through leaching grow sufficient food to feed themselves. Many have abandoned their new farms and moved to urban shanty settlements.

Decrease in hardwood

Only about one tree in twenty is of economic value to the timber companies, but their machinery, and falling timber, destroy many of the surrounding trees. As a result, some species, such as mahogany, greenheart and rosewood, are becoming endangered.

Carbon dioxide and oxygen balance

Deforestation means that there will no longer be trees to take in carbon dioxide nor to give out oxygen (page 42).

Minerals and hydro-electricity

The Brazilian rainforest includes two of the world's largest mining operations. The Carajas iron ore project (page 105) could lead to a mining and industrial complex the size of the

UK and France combined (photo **D**). Bauxite, used in the production of aluminium, is mined at Trombetas. These, and other, developments will rely on the building of up to 79 massive hydro-electric power schemes by the year 2010. These schemes will, in turn, involve the flooding of large areas of land. On a smaller scale, gold is being mined by nearly a million prospectors (photo **E**). These prospectors, many of whom work illegally, destroy vegetation by using high-pressure water jets and pollute water supplies with toxic mercury used in the mining process.

D Carajas iron ore mine, Amazon, Brazil

E Gold miners, Serra Pelade, Brazil

F

Loss of homes and land belonging to the Amazon Indians

Loss of trees for medicinal purposes

Decrease in soil fertility

Hardwoods becoming endangered

Loss of wildlife habitat

Increase in soil erosion

Forests, once felled, are burnt. This reduces oxygen given out by the trees

Land spoilt by mining activities or flooded for hydro-electricity

Activities

1 Diagram **F** suggests eight consequences of deforestation in Brazil. Describe how each affects the environment and the local community.

2 Deforestation is taking place so that the rainforests may be economically developed. Which of the following do you consider to be the more important?
   • Economic development
   • Rainforest conservation
   Give reasons for your answer.

Summary

Despite its apparent luxuriant vegetation, the rainforest is a fragile environment. There are fears that if deforestation for economic development continues at the same rate, the rainforest will soon be totally destroyed.

Deforestation — is there a need for international co-operation?

Deforestation is of international concern. The rainforests are a vital natural resource which provide a wide variety of products needed by all countries. Their destruction is not only losing these resources, it is also changing world climates.

- The burning of the rainforests, and the subsequent release of carbon dioxide (a greenhouse gas), is a major cause of global warming (page 28).
- A greatly reduced number of trees will mean a decrease in evapotranspiration. With less water vapour in the air, rainfall is expected to decrease (diagram **A**). Some scientists believe this could eventually turn places like the Amazon Basin into desert.
- Trees take in carbon dioxide and, through photosynthesis, give out oxygen (diagram **A**). It is estimated that nearly one-half of the world's supply of oxygen comes from trees in the Amazon Basin. It takes one large tree to provide enough oxygen for two people for one day, and 150 large trees to absorb the carbon dioxide produced by one small car.

A

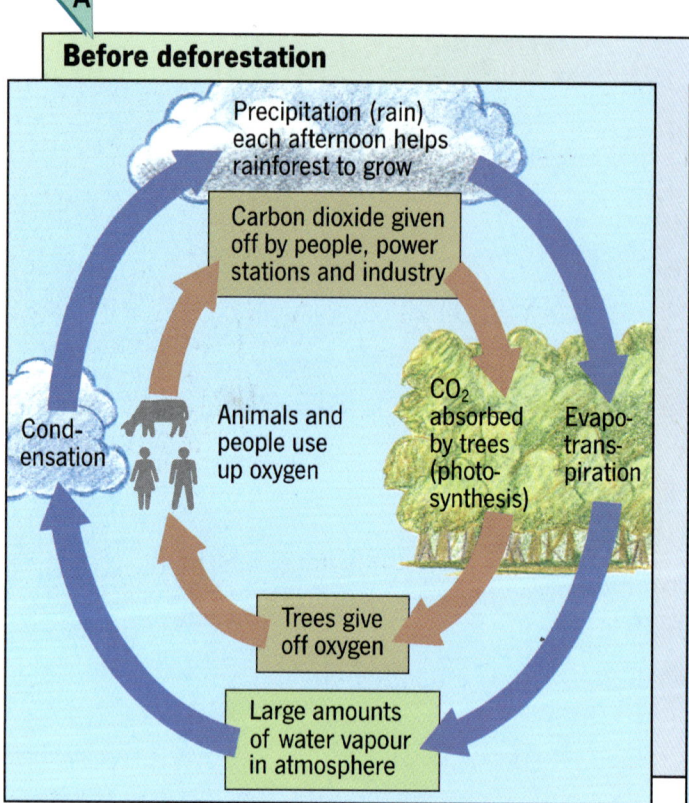
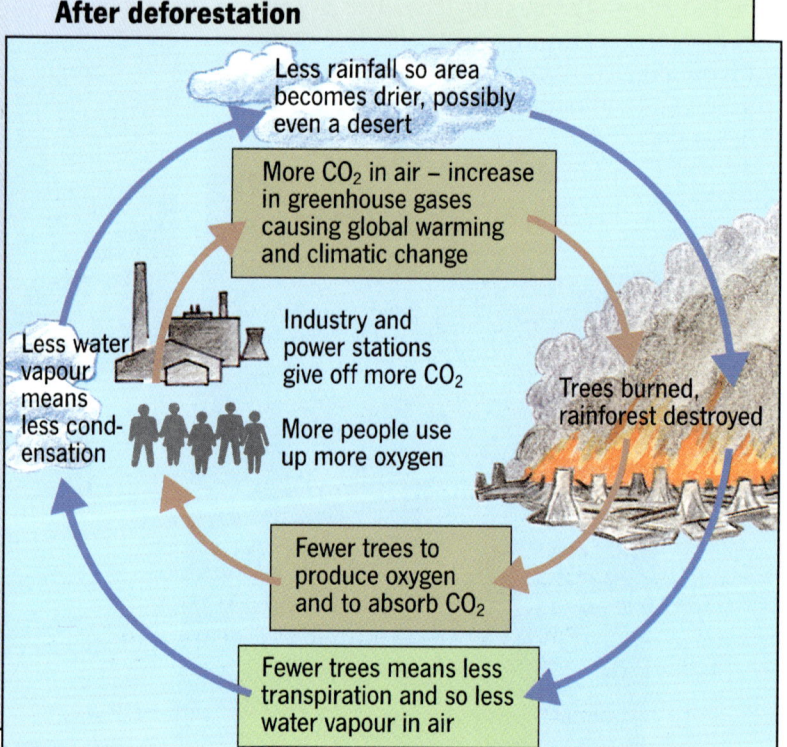

Before deforestation

Precipitation (rain) each afternoon helps rainforest to grow

Carbon dioxide given off by people, power stations and industry

Condensation

Animals and people use up oxygen

CO_2 absorbed by trees (photosynthesis)

Evapo-transpiration

Trees give off oxygen

Large amounts of water vapour in atmosphere

After deforestation

Less rainfall so area becomes drier, possibly even a desert

More CO_2 in air – increase in greenhouse gases causing global warming and climatic change

Less water vapour means less condensation

Industry and power stations give off more CO_2

More people use up more oxygen

Trees burned, rainforest destroyed

Fewer trees to produce oxygen and to absorb CO_2

Fewer trees means less transpiration and so less water vapour in air

There are two extreme conflicts of interest in the rainforest. On one hand there are those groups of people who wish to use the forest to make a quick profit. On the other there are those who wish to protect the forest and leave it exactly as it is. Caught in the middle are the people who actually live there. To them the forest is their home. They need to preserve the forest as well as being able to use its resources if they are to find work and improve their standard of living. The solution is to manage the forest in a **sustainable** way, using the resources carefully. Trees are a renewable resource, but only if they are used and managed carefully. At present nobody is taking responsibility for the rainforest. The forest is no longer managed in the traditional way by small-scale shifting cultivators, nor by government agencies or commercial companies. This leaves the forest open to illegal logging, mining and conversion to other land uses. Such an approach benefits nobody.

Diagram **B** suggests several proposed methods of managing the rainforest. Extract **C** quotes an example of an attempt to manage the rainforest in a sustainable way.

Emilio Sanchoma lives in the Amazon region of Peru where rapid deforestation is taking place. He is involved in a scheme aimed at managing the forest sustainably. A similar sustainable logging project in Mindanao in the Philippines is shown in photo **D**.

B

Create more National Parks and Forest Reserves similar to the Korup Park in the Cameroons (Africa).

Only give logging grants to transnational companies on the condition that they replant an equal number of trees as they fell.

Reduce international trade in such endangered hardwoods as mahogany.

Limit the mass burning of trees to reduce global warming and climatic change.

C

D

I was born in the rainforest and have lived here all my life. Like all rainforest people, I know how to harvest the forest sustainably to feed myself, my family and my tribe. I grow crops like rice to sell and other crops and fruit to eat. I also keep poultry and other animals. We use the plants of the rainforest for medicines.

As rainforest people we are worried about our own way of life and about the future of the planet. We have been trying to find better ways of using the forest. In our area, the Palcazú Valley, the government has given us title to the land. We have set up the Yanesha Forestry Co-operative to log the forest on a sustainable basis.

We clear-cut a strip of rainforest 20–50 metres wide, the same size as would be cleared if a large tree were blown down. It is wide enough to enable sunlight to penetrate the canopy and narrow enough for the plants to reseed themselves from the surrounding forest.

The trees are felled with chainsaws and then taken out by oxen onto a main logging road where they are loaded onto the co-op truck. The oxen don't damage the soil and surrounding vegetation and are less expensive than heavy machinery. We use every stick in the forest. Logs greater than 30 cm in diameter are sawn into lumber. Smaller logs between 5 and 30 cm are used for construction in our area. Smaller trees and odd-shaped scraps are made into charcoal and sold locally. We get 250 cubic metres of wood per hectare under this system, compared with a typical logger's yield of 3–5 cubic metres.

Source: Global Environment, *BBC/Longman*

Activities

1 Deforestation is an international problem. How is it affecting:
   a) global temperatures
   b) rainfall in equatorial areas
   c) the balance of oxygen and carbon dioxide in the atmosphere?

2 a) What is meant by the term 'to manage the rainforests in a sustainable way'?
   b) Describe one scheme that is trying to 'manage the rainforest in a sustainable way'.
   c) Why is it difficult to get international agreements that would enable the forests 'to be managed in a sustainable way'?

3 Divide your class into four groups. Each group should represent the views of one of the following:
   • the Brazilian government
   • an international logging company
   • a group of forest Indians
   • a conservation group.
Each group should take their turn to put forward their case for or against the development of the rainforest.

Summary

There is a need to balance the protection and the economic development of the rainforest. Sustainable development can only come about through international co-operation and management.

What causes soil erosion?

The first stage in the formation of soil is when physical and chemical weathering break down the underlying rock of a place into small particles. The second stage includes the addition of water, air (including oxygen), humus (material from decayed plants and animals) and living organisms (bacteria, worms). There are many different types of soil. They can vary in **depth**, **colour**, **texture** and **organic content** as well as in drainage, nutrients (humus) and acidity. Yet there is one thing that all soils have in common – the long period of time needed for them to form. Estimates suggest that, in Britain, it takes about 400 years for 1cm of soil to form, and between 3000 and 12 000 years for soil to become deep enough for farming. In contrast **soil erosion** can be very rapid. Several centimetres can disappear within minutes during a severe storm, while human mismanagement can cause soil to lose its fertility within a few years. Soil is a renewable source but, like water and trees, it needs careful management.

A

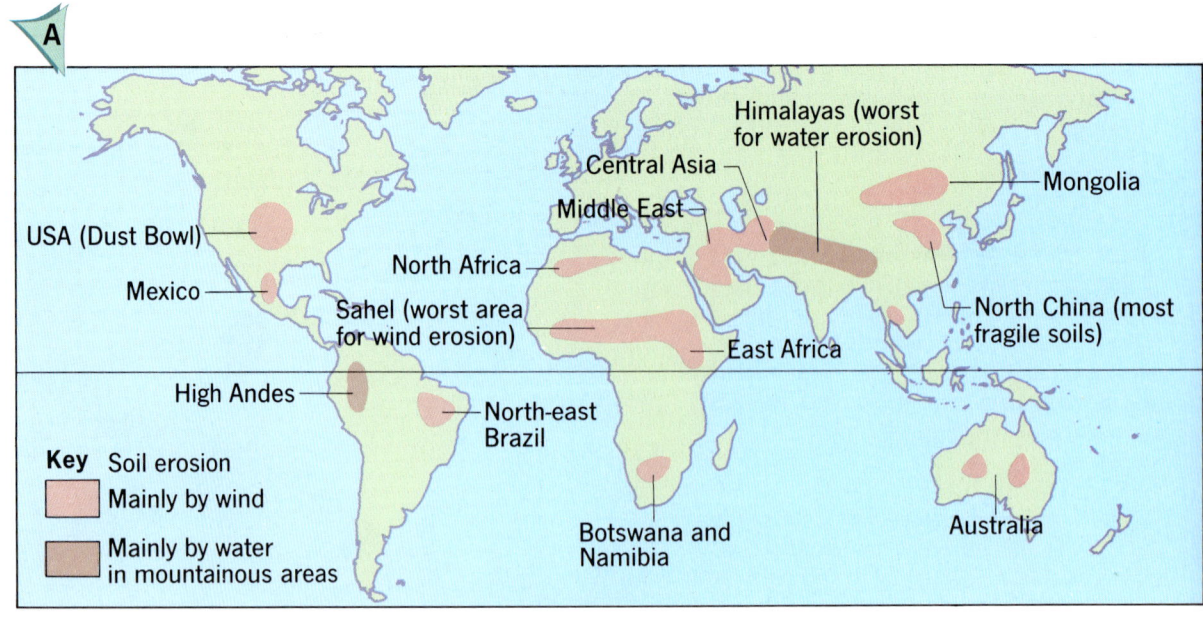

Key Soil erosion
Mainly by wind
Mainly by water in mountainous areas

USA (Dust Bowl)
Mexico
North Africa
Sahel (worst area for wind erosion)
High Andes
North-east Brazil
Central Asia
Middle East
Himalayas (worst for water erosion)
Mongolia
North China (most fragile soils)
East Africa
Botswana and Namibia
Australia

B

Soil erosion is a process by which soil is removed by the wind and running water. Soil erosion is not a major problem in places where there is permanent cover of grass or forest. It does become a problem when human activity removes this protective vegetation cover either to plough the land or through deforestation. If soil is left exposed to the weather it can be washed away during times of heavy rainfall or blown away when it dries out during times of drought. Map **A** shows those places most vulnerable to soil erosion.

- Where the land is mountainous with very steep slopes: one quarter of a million tonnes of topsoil are washed off the deforested mountain slopes of Nepal and northern India each year (extract **B**) only to be deposited into the Bay of Bengal.
- Where the climate includes a pronounced dry season and where annual rainfall totals are unreliable (page 26): when adverse human activity takes places in areas of unreliable rainfall, such as the Sahel countries in Africa, the resultant loss of soil and vegetation is known as **desertification** (page 48).

Much of the land has been deforested. The lower hillsides have been left almost bare of vegetation, and goats are busy eating what is left. It is not simply that the trees that once grew here cannot grow again, but that without its protective tree cover the soil itself is washed away. When the heavy monsoon rains come, both rain and earth are lost. Now, with the trees gone, the water runs quickly off the land, carving out new erosion channels and creating bare rock above and floods and landslides below. Great ravines are rapidly gouged out creating a man-made wilderness.

Adapted liberally from Nigel Nicolson, Himalayas, Time-Life Books

C

Diagram **C** shows the main causes of soil erosion. Most result from deforestation, overgrazing and overcultivation.

Steep slopes
e.g. mountainous areas in various parts of the world

Areas with unreliable rainfall
e.g. tropical continental/savanna grasslands

Tourism
Walkers enlarge footpaths. New runs for skiers.

Deforestation
a) Increases surface run-off and throughflow
b) Decreases interception and evapotranspiration

Silt (soil) blocks river. Increases flood risk and erosion of banks.

Overgrazing – Rearing too many animals in relation to amount of grass available

Heavy machinery
compacts ground, reducing infiltration

Burning grass
a) By people, to force new growth for grazing
b) By lightning strikes

Autumn ploughing
leaves soil unprotected during winter storms

Removing hedges or shelter belts to meet demand for fuelwood

Overcropping and monoculture
(Growing crops intensively, or a single crop year after year) – crop needed for export (cash) or to feed a growing population. Lack of manure – used as fuel instead of as fertiliser.

Ploughing up and down hill
creates channels down which rain-water can flow. Increases amount and speed of surface run-off.

- Washed downhill by water
- Moves slowly downwards under gravity

EXPOSED SOIL

- Washed away during wet season storms
- Blown away during dry season

Activities

1 a) How does soil form?
  b) How long does it take for soil to form?

2 a) Name two mountainous parts of the world where soil erosion is a serious problem.
  b) Give three possible causes of soil erosion in mountainous areas.

  c) Name two parts of the world with an unreliable rainfall.
  d) How can unreliable and seasonal rainfall be a cause of serious soil erosion?
  e) Give three possible causes of soil erosion in places with an unreliable rainfall.

Summary

It can take several centuries for soil to form but only a short time for it to be destroyed. Soil erosion, which is greatly accelerated by human activity, is most serious on steep-sided mountains and in places where the rainfall is unreliable.

45

What can be done to prevent or reduce soil erosion?

As the world's population continues to increase then presumably farmers are going to have to produce more food in order to feed the extra numbers. This can only be done if the soil is protected and carefully managed. Estimates suggest that by the year 2000, 20 per cent of land that was arable in 1985 will have been lost through erosion, desertification and conversion to non-agricultural uses.

By 2020 the same amount could again disappear. Although the loss is greatest in tropical economically less developed countries, it is by no means limited to those places. It is important that greater attempts are made internationally, similar to those described in case studies **A** to **D**, to reduce erosion and sustain productivity.

A

Terracing in Indonesia and the Philippines   Large areas of these two countries are covered in volcanic mountains which have steep slopes and fertile soil. Over 2000 years ago terraces, which resemble giant steps, were first built on many of the hillsides. Each terrace is flat and is fronted by a mud or stone wall known as a 'bund'. The bund traps both rainwater and soil. By allowing rainwater time to infiltrate into the ground, surface run-off and the removal of topsoil is prevented.

C

B

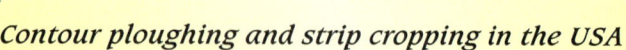

Contour ploughing and strip cropping in the USA
Contour farming is ploughing around hillsides rather than up and down the slope. By ploughing parallel to the contours, the furrows trap rainwater and prevent the water from washing soil downhill. Strip cropping is when two or more crops are planted in the same field. Sometimes one crop may grow under the shelter of a taller crop. It is harvested at a different time of year and uses different nutrients from the soil. Often the crops are rotated from year to year.

Animal welfare in Kenya   Large herds of cattle, goats, sheep and camels have long been considered a source of wealth and prestige in several African countries. Unfortunately quantity, rather than quality, has tended to result in overgrazing. The problem of overgrazing has increased partly because rainfall has become even less reliable and partly because of the rapidly growing population. Intermediate Technology, a British organisation, is working with local people in several parts of Kenya. In those areas it is helping to train one person from each village to become a 'wasaidizi' or animal care worker. By recognising and being able to treat basic animal illnesses, the wasaidizi is improving the quality of local herds. As the quality improves there should be less need for so many animals so that, hopefully, overgrazing will be reduced.

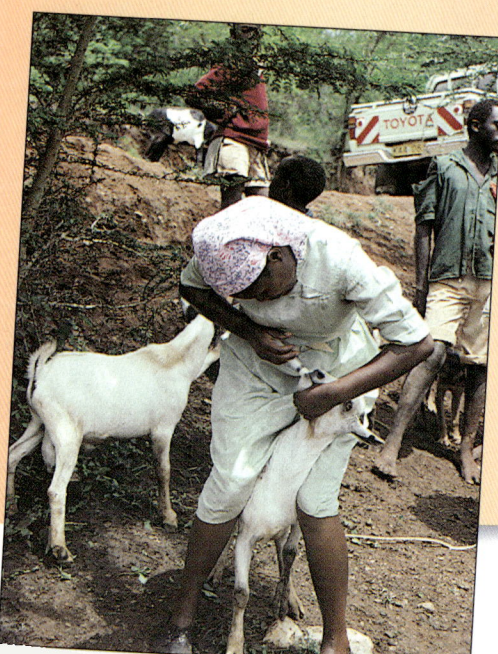

Stone lines ('magic stones') in Burkina Faso   This project, begun by Oxfam in 1979, uses appropriate technology, local knowledge and local raw materials. It involves villagers, of all ages and both sexes, collecting some of the many stones lying around their village. The stones are laid across the land to stop surface run-off following the all too rare heavy rainstorms. Water and soil are trapped. The water now has the time to infiltrate instead of being lost immediately through surface run-off. The trapped soil soon becomes deep enough for the planting of crops. Erosion is reduced and crop yields have increased by as much as 50 per cent. The only equipment needed is a simple level, developed by Oxfam, to help keep the lines parallel to the contours.

D

Activities

1 Diagram **E** shows several methods aimed at reducing soil erosion.
   a) Briefly describe each method.
   b) Which methods are appropriate to Britain?

E

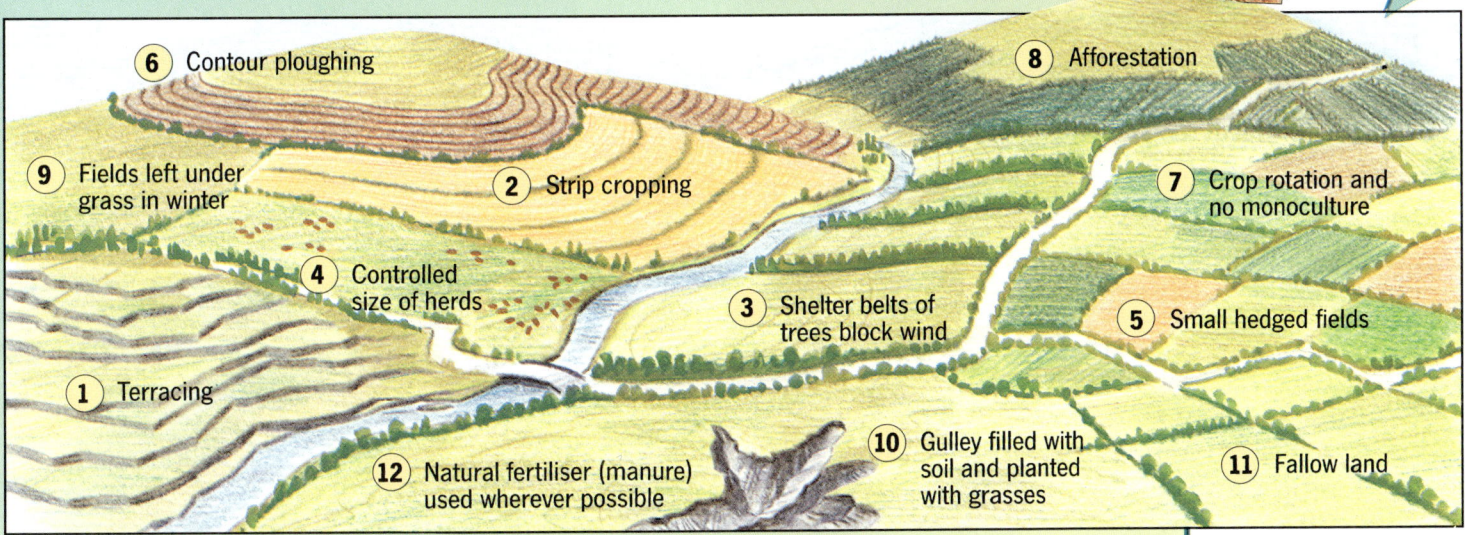

6 Contour ploughing

8 Afforestation

9 Fields left under grass in winter

2 Strip cropping

7 Crop rotation and no monoculture

4 Controlled size of herds

3 Shelter belts of trees block wind

5 Small hedged fields

1 Terracing

12 Natural fertiliser (manure) used wherever possible

10 Gulley filled with soil and planted with grasses

11 Fallow land

2 Figure **F** is a soil conservation poster used in Kenya. It was designed in cartoon form by a local artist who used local examples of afforestation, terracing and controlled grazing.
   a) What are the advantages of providing educational information in this way?
   b) Which methods of soil conservation are likely to be of most value to an economically developing country with unreliable rainfall and a growing population such as Kenya?
   c) Why is it often difficult for an economically developing country to introduce these methods?

F

Tueneze umuhimu wa kuhifadhi udongo wetu

Tell your friends about soil conservation

SAVE OUR SOILS

Ministry of Agriculture Soil and Water Conservation Branch

Summary

Soil is a renewable resource but only if it is managed carefully. All countries must make greater efforts if soil erosion is to be prevented and reduced so that soil productivity can be sustained.

What causes desertification?

'Turning land into desert' is the simplest of several definitions of desertification. Desertification occurs mainly in semi-arid lands which border the world's major deserts. Map **A** is often misinterpreted. It locates places that are **at risk** from desertification, **not** places where desertification has actually occurred. The area at greatest risk is the Sahel, a narrow belt of land extending across Africa and lying to the south of the Sahara Desert.

A

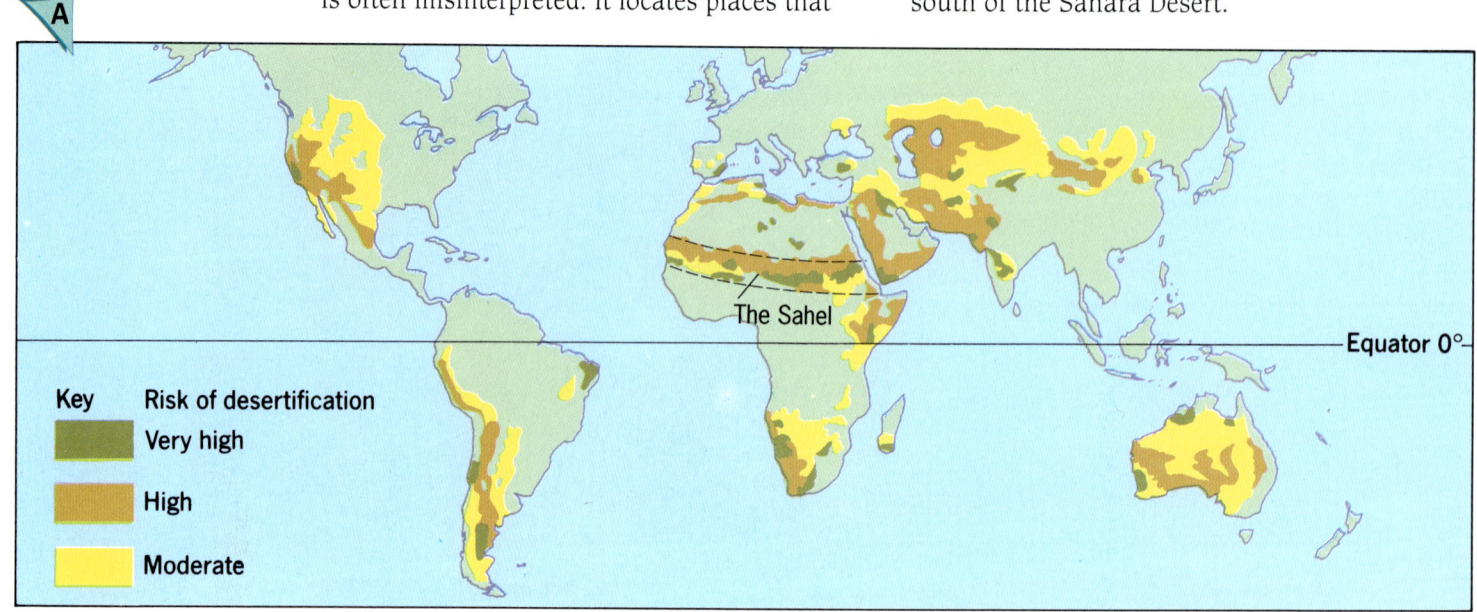

The Sahel

Equator 0°

Key **Risk of desertification**

Very high

High

Moderate

The causes of desertification are complex. They appear to result from a combination of climatic changes (e.g. decreased rainfall and global warming), and increased human activity and pressure upon the land (e.g. overgrazing, overcultivation and deforestation). How these factors may have contributed to desertification are shown on diagram **B**. During the 1980s it was claimed, and accepted, that the Sahara was advancing southwards at a rate of between 6 and 10 km a year. However, many claims were little more than estimates based upon short-term observations and were made at the height of one of Africa's worst ever recorded droughts. The drought, which began in the early 1970s, followed two wet decades (graph **C**).

B

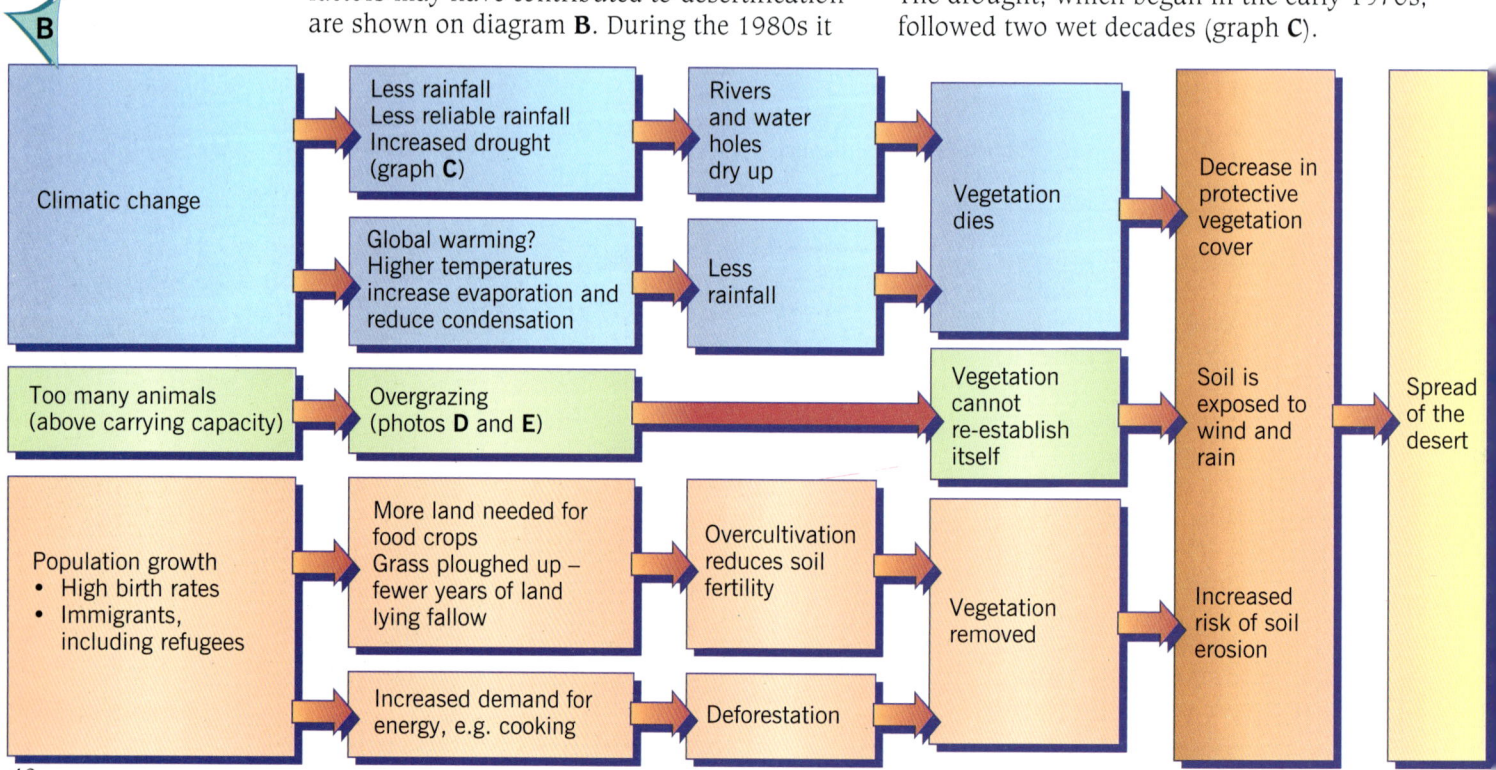

Climatic change

Less rainfall
Less reliable rainfall
Increased drought
(graph **C**)

Rivers and water holes dry up

Vegetation dies

Global warming?
Higher temperatures increase evaporation and reduce condensation

Less rainfall

Decrease in protective vegetation cover

Too many animals (above carrying capacity)

Overgrazing (photos **D** and **E**)

Vegetation cannot re-establish itself

Soil is exposed to wind and rain

Spread of the desert

Population growth
• High birth rates
• Immigrants, including refugees

More land needed for food crops
Grass ploughed up – fewer years of land lying fallow

Overcultivation reduces soil fertility

Vegetation removed

Increased risk of soil erosion

Increased demand for energy, e.g. cooking

Deforestation

During this wetter period farmers began to grow crops on land that had not been cultivated for several centuries, and to crowd larger herds of livestock onto smaller areas of pasture. When this was replaced by a much drier period it looked as if the land was being overcultivated and overgrazed. Within a few years over 100 000 people and millions of animals died. The initial investigations for those deaths and, later, for many more in Ethiopia, Sudan and Somalia, put the blame on desertification.

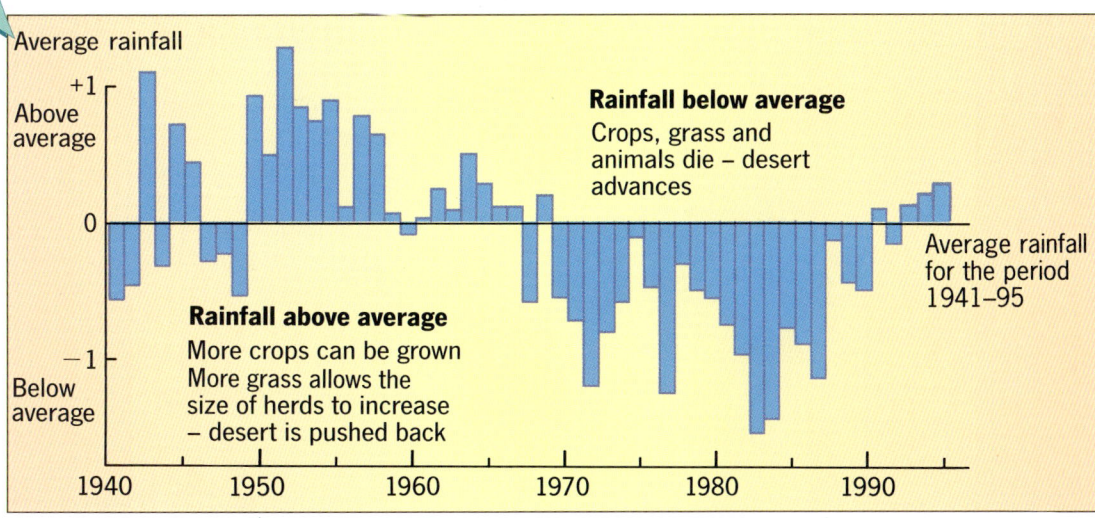

C

Average rainfall

+1
Above average

0

−1
Below average

Rainfall below average
Crops, grass and animals die – desert advances

Rainfall above average
More crops can be grown
More grass allows the size of herds to increase – desert is pushed back

Average rainfall for the period 1941–95

1940   1950   1960   1970   1980   1990

Recently the claim that the Sahara is advancing has been disputed. Evidence, based mainly on satellite images, does show annual changes resulting from variations in rainfall, but no permanent advance. This does not, of course, mean that the risk has disappeared. Hopefully the threat of desertification has increased people's awareness of the semi-arid lands as a fragile environment. Their boundaries are constantly changing as a result of variations in rainfall, and it is difficult to separate natural causes from human activity. (For example, is overgrazing a result of increased drought or increased human activity – photos **D** and **E**?) Regardless of whether desertification is already a major hazard or whether it is a future risk, one thing is certain: increased desertification is likely, as with all environmental issues, to result from people's misuse of natural resources.

D Goats, sheet and camels drinking at a well, Sudan

E

Overgrazed area, Burkina Faso

Activities

1 **a)** What is desertification?
   b) With the help of an atlas, name six Sahel countries.
   c) Desertification is blamed upon physical processes and human activity. Explain how the following might have combined to cause desertification:
   i) changes in rainfall and global warming
   ii) overgrazing, overcultivation and deforestation.

2 What recent evidence seems to contradict the claim that desertification is increasing?

Summary

Desertification in semi-arid lands may result from a combination of physical processes and human activity. Recent evidence suggests that, although the risks remain high, the increase in desertification may be less than was previously claimed.

► Why are wetland environments fragile? ◄

Key
- ▲ Wetland
- ● Selected Ramsar sites
- ■ Wildfowl and wetlands trust centres

Caerlaverock (Scotland)

N

Washington

Dee Estuary
Martin Mere
Humber Estuary
The Wash
Peakirk
Welney
Llanelli
Severn
Severn Estuary and Cardiff Bay
Slimbridge
Thames Estuary
Solent
Swale
Arundel
Chesil Beach
Chichester and Langstone harbours

0   100 km

Wetlands form a transition environment between land and water. As the water table is usually near to, or even at, the surface then the land is either permanently or seasonally covered with water. The water may be either slow-flowing, stagnant, brackish, fresh or salt. This produces several different types of wetland including coastal estuaries, river floodplains, freshwater marshes, peatlands and mangrove swamps. Most of Britain's largest remaining wetlands are in river estuaries (map **A**). Estuaries are places where salt and fresh water mix and where tidal action is important. As a result estuaries have developed a special ecosystem of their own (diagram **B**).

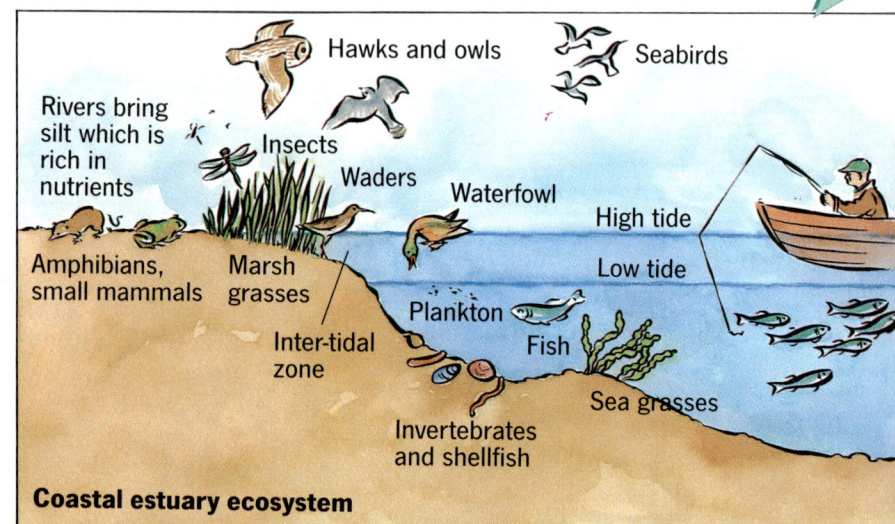

Hawks and owls   Seabirds

Rivers bring silt which is rich in nutrients

Insects

Waders

Waterfowl

High tide

Low tide

Amphibians, small mammals

Marsh grasses

Plankton

Fish

Inter-tidal zone

Invertebrates and shellfish

Sea grasses

Coastal estuary ecosystem

Why are coastal wetlands important?

Wetlands are among the world's most productive ecosystems (photos **C**, **D** and **E**). They:
- are often very fertile and can produce eight times more plant matter than the average field of wheat
- provide a life support system for a wide range of plants, birds, fish and insects
- provide a nursery for young fish and a winter feeding ground for birds
- help to filter pollution and sediment out of water
- slow down the speed of water and, since they can store excess water following storms, help to reduce the danger of flooding
- can provide jobs, especially in aquaculture (fish farming) and on nature reserves.

C Everglades National Park, Florida

D Mersey Estuary, Widnes

Why are many coastal wetlands under threat?

- Parts of wetlands have always been used for pasture farming and, if sufficiently well drained, can provide rich soil for crops.
- If water is extracted for domestic and industrial purposes then the water table will fall causing the land to sink. Floodbanks are needed where the land sinks below river or sea-levels.
- A falling water table can result in reeds and other plants dying and wildlife habitats being lost.
- There are an increasing number of tourists and tourist-related activities. Tourists disturb wildlife and their boats create waves which erode banks and destroy nesting grounds.
- There is increased pollution by diesel oil from pleasure boats or, from further upstream, run-off from farmland and waste from industry.

The greatest threat to all coastal wetlands is likely to come from the predicted rise in the world's sea-level resulting from global warming (page 29).

How can wetlands be protected?

Over 60 countries have now signed an international agreement called the Ramsar Convention. This Convention, first signed by several countries in 1971, is the oldest global conservation treaty (diagram **G**). International agreement is necessary as many wetlands extend across national boundaries. Since 1971 there has been a changed emphasis on the protection and use of wetlands (extract **F**).

E

The Camargue wetland is in the Rhône Delta in France. It is home to herds of white horses, thousands of flamingos and wintering, breeding and migrating wild birds. The wetland is threatened by housing developments, tourism, farming, drainage and industrial development.

WWF

F

Now, the value of a wetland as an example of a type characteristic of its region, or its value to a wide range of animals and plants, or even its socio-economic value to local communities, are all considered important. Parties must promote the conservation of sites, but this does not mean strict 'hands-off' protection. Provided the natural characteristics of the ecosystem are maintained, parties are encouraged to use Ramsar sites on a sustainable basis, and many more sites are exploited for the benefit of local people.

Worldwide Fund for Nature (WWF)

Activities

1 a) What are wetlands?
   b) Why is it considered important to protect wetlands and their ecosystems?
   c) How, according to diagram **G**, has the Ramsar Convention attempted to protect wetlands?

2 a) Make a copy of table **H** and complete it using information from these pages.
   b) If you had to develop a new wildfowl reserve, what:
      i) facilities would you provide to attract visitors
      ii) precautions would you take to ensure that the visitors did not harm the wildlife habitat?

G

Plan a sustainable use for wetlands

Encourage research into wetland ecosystems

Train people in wetland management

Develop a national policy on wetland conservation

Create nature and wildfowl reserves

Work with neighbouring countries on schemes which cross national borders

Threat to wetland ecosystem	Possible effects on wildlife and ecosystem

H

Summary

Wetlands are a fragile environment lying between land and water. They have developed a productive, but now a greatly threatened, ecosystem.

6 The European Union (EU)

▶ What are the patterns of tourism in the EU? ◀

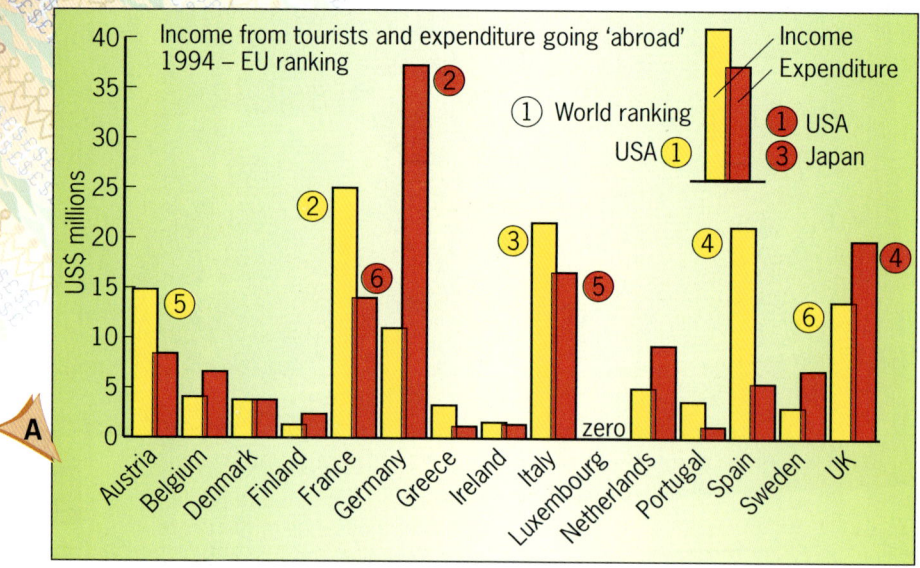

A Income from tourists and expenditure going 'abroad' 1994 – EU ranking

Article 2 of the Treaty of Rome (1957) gives the European Community (EC), now the European Union (EU) power to 'promote closer relations between the states which belong to it'. One way to achieve this is through tourism. Tourism, a labour-intensive industry, was believed to have provided 4 million jobs in 1980, and 9 million in 1995. If it reaches the predicted total of 13 million by the turn of the century, it will be the largest single employer in the EU. Yet, strangely, EU ministers do not appear to see tourism as a high priority.

Graph **A** shows how important tourism is to many countries within the EU. The 'southern' countries earn more from tourism than their residents spend abroad. The net 'gainers' tend to be the poorer countries in the EU (in Italy's case it is the poorest regions), and without tourism those countries would be even poorer. A major reason for Greece joining the EU was to increase its wealth from tourism. During the summer months more people visit Greece than actually live in the country permanently. Even so Greece, despite receiving many more visitors, does not receive as much income from tourism as does the United Kingdom. This is due to its lower standard of living (e.g. cheaper hotels and food).

Tourists who travel abroad for their holidays tend to look for places with one or more of the following: an attractive climate, spectacular scenery, specialist activities, a wide range of pastimes, night-life, cultural pursuits, health benefits or a low cost of living (map **B**). The resultant pattern showing the movement of tourists is, in most cases, from the north of the continent towards the south (diagram **C**).

B

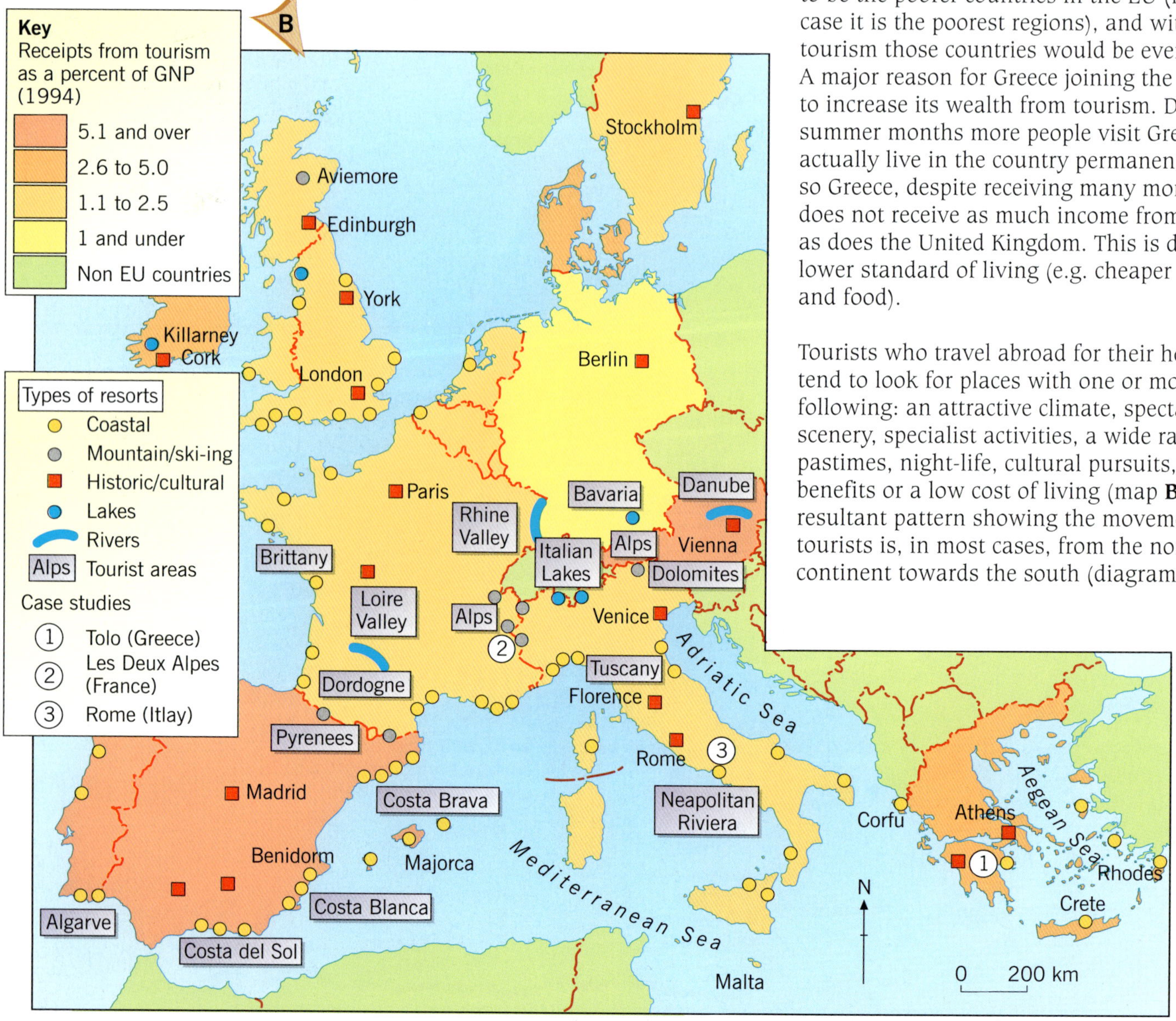

Key

Receipts from tourism as a percent of GNP (1994)

- 5.1 and over
- 2.6 to 5.0
- 1.1 to 2.5
- 1 and under
- Non EU countries

Types of resorts

- ● Coastal
- ● Mountain/ski-ing
- ■ Historic/cultural
- ● Lakes
- ～ Rivers
- Alps Tourist areas

Case studies

- ① Tolo (Greece)
- ② Les Deux Alpes (France)
- ③ Rome (Itlay)

Stockholm
Aviemore
Edinburgh
York
Killarney
Cork
London
Berlin
Paris
Bavaria
Danube
Rhine Valley
Italian Lakes
Alps
Vienna
Dolomites
Brittany
Loire Valley
Alps
Venice
Tuscany
Dordogne
Florence
Adriatic Sea
Pyrenees
Rome ③
Neapolitan Riviera
Madrid
Costa Brava
Corfu
Athens
Benidorm
Majorca
Aegean Sea
Rhodes
Costa Blanca
Crete
Algarve
Costa del Sol
Mediterranean Sea
Malta

N

0   200 km

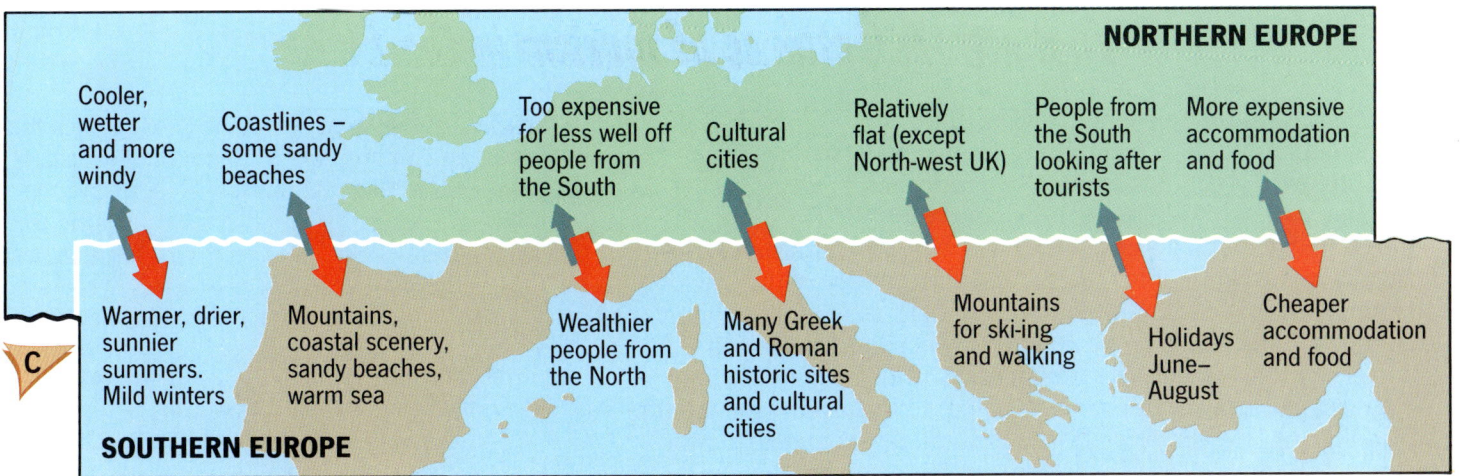

NORTHERN EUROPE

Cooler, wetter and more windy

Coastlines – some sandy beaches

Too expensive for less well off people from the South

Cultural cities

Relatively flat (except North-west UK)

People from the South looking after tourists

More expensive accommodation and food

SOUTHERN EUROPE

Warmer, drier, sunnier summers. Mild winters

Mountains, coastal scenery, sandy beaches, warm sea

Wealthier people from the North

Many Greek and Roman historic sites and cultural cities

Mountains for ski-ing and walking

Holidays June–August

Cheaper accommodation and food

C

EU tourism policies include:

- providing money from the European Regional Development Fund; this is used to encourage tourism in areas which have potential but have a low standard of living and a high unemployment rate, e.g. Mezzogiorno (southern Italy)
- encouraging craft industries and specialist activities to try to reduce regional and rural depopulation
- integrating cross-continental transport routes (the 'E' road and 'Eurail' networks)
- improving access to newly developing resorts and holiday areas (southern Greece)
- protecting the natural environment (beaches, seas and wildlife) and the cultural environment (ancient sites and historic buildings)
- improving tourist services and amenities, such as water and electricity supplies, sewerage; improvement safety in hotels; providing regulation camping and caravan sites
- removing, or in some cases reducing, border controls and customs checks (diagram **D**).

D

Border controls between some EU countries vanished in 1993. Passport checks became lighter throughout the EU.

There is a new blue channel at customs and millions of pages of customs forms have disappeared. Consumers can buy alcohol, tobacco and other products for personal use without limits.

A totally border-free Europe did not exist on 1 January 1993. Britain, Denmark, Greece and Ireland have retained some checks and controls.

New rules mean some qualifications are now recognised throughout the EU, making it easier for people to work abroad

Activities

1 a) Name five EU countries that receive more from foreign tourists than their own inhabitants spend in other countries.
   b) Describe the location within the EU of these five countries.
   c) Name five EU countries whose inhabitants spend more in foreign countries than they receive from tourists from other countries.
   d) Describe the location within the EU of these five countries.

E

	Country or region		
	1	2	3
Hot, dry, sunny summers; mild winters			
Sandy beaches, warm seas			
Ski-ing in winter; mountain climbing in summer			
Castles, cathedrals, ancient sites			
Earn most from tourism			
Cooler, wetter, less sunny			
More industry and so less attractive			
Fewer mountains; less opportunities for ski-ing			
Spend more on tourism than is earned			

2 a) Copy and complete table **E** by naming three countries which best fit each description.
   b) Draw a star diagram to describe five ways in which EU policy has affected tourism. Use these headings to help you:
   • Jobs • Transport • Environment
   • Services • Accommodation.

Summary

Tourism is one of the EU's most important sources of employment and income. It is most important to some of the poorer but warmer, drier and sunnier parts of southern Europe. EU policies have had a limited impact upon the continued development of tourism.

53

▶ A Greek coastal resort ◀

Tolo is located in the Peloponnese peninsula and to the south-west of Athens (map **A**). It has a long, sandy, sheltered and curving beach which stretches over 3 km between two rocky headlands.

In 1979 Tolo was still an unspoilt village with a linear shape. Many small shops selling local produce extended either side of the one long and narrow main street. The major occupations were farming (mainly fruit) and fishing. The only tourists were Athenians escaping in summer from the heat, noise and pollution of their city. Today Tolo is the largest resort in the Peloponnese. Landsketch **B** shows the natural advantages of Tolo and some of its added tourist amenities. It also gives some of the causes of pollution and conflict in the present resort. Tourism brings both benefits and problems.

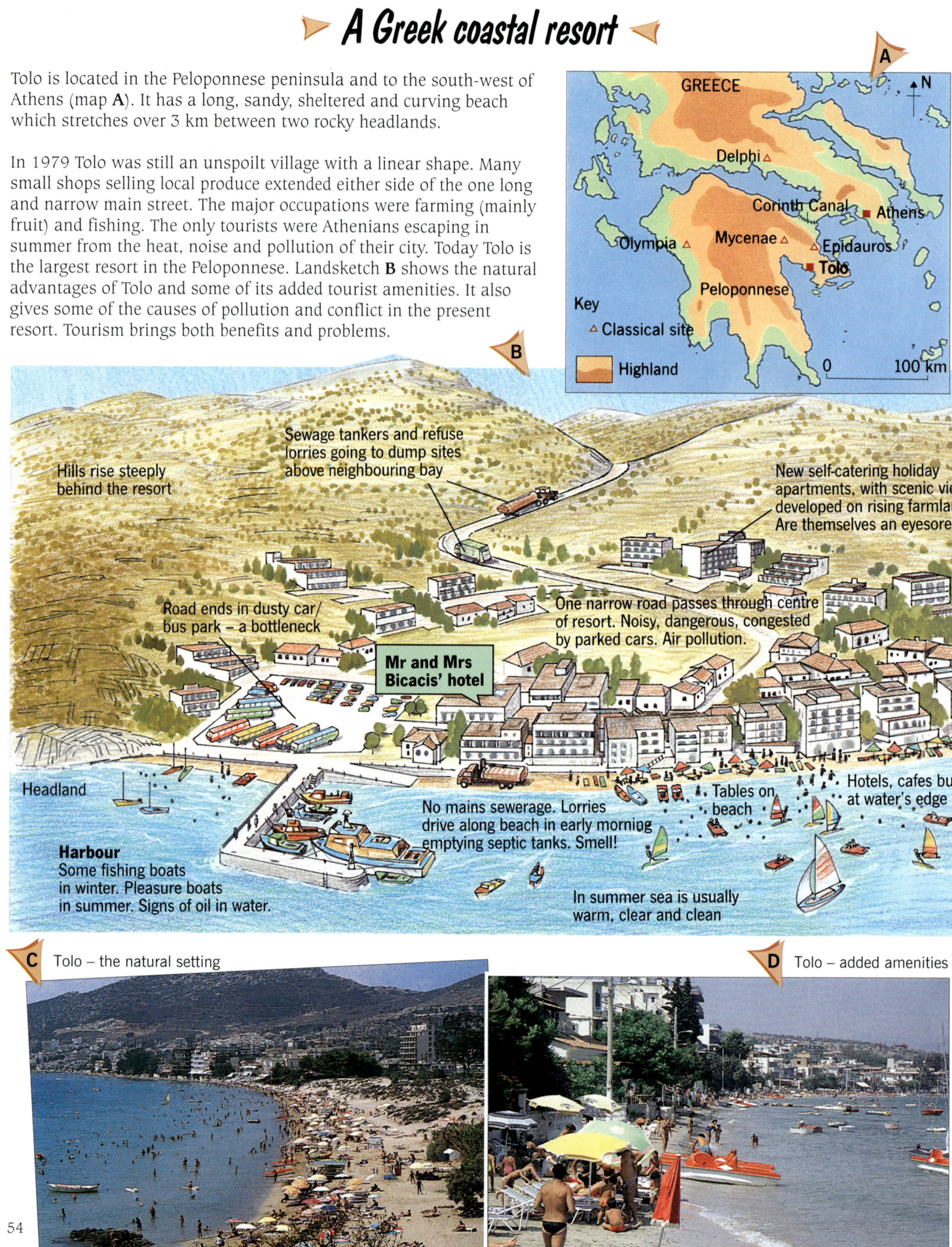

A

GREECE

Delphi △

Corinth Canal ■ Athens

Olympia △   Mycenae △   △ Epidauros

Peloponnese   ■ **Tolo**

Key

△ Classical site

Highland   0   100 km

B

Hills rise steeply behind the resort

Sewage tankers and refuse lorries going to dump sites above neighbouring bay

New self-catering holiday apartments, with scenic view developed on rising farmland Are themselves an eyesore.

Road ends in dusty car/bus park – a bottleneck

One narrow road passes through centre of resort. Noisy, dangerous, congested by parked cars. Air pollution.

Mr and Mrs Bicacis' hotel

Headland

Harbour
Some fishing boats in winter. Pleasure boats in summer. Signs of oil in water.

No mains sewerage. Lorries drive along beach in early morning emptying septic tanks. Smell!

Tables on beach

Hotels, cafes built at water's edge

In summer sea is usually warm, clear and clean

C Tolo – the natural setting

D Tolo – added amenities

Nikos and Katarina Bicacis

Mr and Mrs Bicacis live behind the hotel which they run together. As the holiday season is so short, Mr Bicacis also runs a farm 20 km away. Their working year is:

- **March** Hotel opens; very quiet.
- **May to August** The hotel is very busy and extra domestic help is needed. While tourists like the hot, dry weather, it does not help the farm where crops (mainly fruit) need to be watered each day.
- **September** Hotel is quiet.
- **October/November** Domestic staff are laid off. Repairs and redecorating jobs are done in the hotel.
- **December to February** Hotel is closed. This is the busiest time on the farm for oranges, the major crop.

Hot, dry sunny summers. Increased risk of water shortage for new hotels and apartments, and for farming. Winter rainfall is not sufficient to replace the water taken from ground in summer. Farmers get water from boreholes which are becoming salty.

Only one narrow road into resort. Busy in summer, noisy, little room to pass

New apartments built on farmland

Hotels, cafes, tavernas and craft shops all close for several months in winter

Former local shops turned into craft and souvenir shops. Tavernas and bars are noisy at night.

Remains of a Mycenaean settlement 3500 years old

Sand dunes

Thin sandy beach, now only 3 m wide as new hotels are built at the tideless water's edge

Sea and sand dunes polluted with litter from tourists

Sea full of swimmers, pedalos, windsurfers and yachts, all competing for the same space

Headland

Activities

1 a) Describe the appearance of Tolo in 1970.
 b) What natural advantages did Tolo possess to attract tourists?
 c) What amenities had been added by 1998 to attract more tourists to the resort?

2 Tourism can brings advantages and can create problems and conflicts. Use the information on these two pages to answer these questions.
 a) What advantages has tourism brought to Tolo?
 b) What problems has tourism created?
 c) What conflicts have been created between:
  • groups of local people
  • local people and tourists
  • groups of tourists?

Summary

People are attracted to Mediterranean resorts because of the hot, dry summer weather, the spectacular scenery and the added tourist amenities. Local residents, often poor by EU standards, see tourism as an opportunity to improve their standard of living even if it also changes their way of life and spoils their environment.

A French mountain resort

Les Deux Alpes is a purpose-built ski resort in the French Alps (photo **A**). It was originally two separate summer pasture areas which have been joined together by a long main road. The village is perched 1650 metres above sea-level on a sunny, rocky shelf. The only access from the valley below is by a narrow, steep road where the hairpin bends make driving difficult but a challenging stage for the annual 'Tour de France' cycle race. Behind the village, the Alps rise to almost 4000 metres, and there is access to both glacier and high-altitude ski-ing. Snow continues to lie, at higher altitudes, throughout the summer. This enables the village to attract walkers, climbers and those people who just wish to breathe the fresh mountain air or to admire the spectacular scenery.

As in any ski resort, numerous amenities have been added (landsketch **B**). Apart from a funicular railway, which goes under the Mont de Lans glacier to reach the highest runs,

there are 3 cable-cars, 2 gondolas, 15 chair lifts and 44 drag lifts. There are over 160 km of piste which include the widest possible range of difficulty. The resort itself consists of the main street which is lined with cafés, bars, discos and restaurants. Several hotels are located in the centre to be as near as possible to the ski-lifts and other amenities. Chalets offer cheaper accommodation and are sited on the edges of the village, further away from the main amenities. Les Deux Alpes has three sports and fitness centres, a swimming pool, a skating rink complex and a cinema.

Les Deux Alpes

A

B La Meije 3982 m

Glacier de la Girose

Glacier du Mont de Lans

Le Janori 3288 m

Tête de la Toura 2914 m

Pied Moutet 2339 m

C
H
H
H
H
H
H
H
C

Les Deux Alpes 1650 m

Key

— Chair lift   — Road

···· Gondola   **H** Hotel

++++ Funicular railway   **C** Chalets

Valley 1300 m

The French government has encouraged the development of ski resorts and the improvement of facilities in the Alps. Although ski-ing had become increasingly popular and affordable to a greater number of people since the 1960s, it was the early 1980s which proved to be the boom years for winter sports. Unemployment fell by 3 per cent in ski areas whereas in the rest of France it rose by 3 per cent. Younger people no longer had to leave the area to look for work. Tourists spent money not only in hotels and souvenir shops, but also on skis and ski clothing. Since the mid-1980s the number of tourists has decreased. This has been partly due to several mild winters during which there was a shortage of snow, and partly due to the economic recession in Europe. Resorts have also been affected by cheaper ski holidays in other countries and increased competition from new purpose-built ski centres within France.

National governments hope to increase employment, and property developers want large and quick profits. They have not always considered the effects that purpose-built ski resorts may have upon the environment or on the traditional way of life of local communities. Some of the resultant problems are summarised in table **C**.

C

Environmental impact
Deforestation of slopes for new and longer ski runs, and for new and expanding resorts
Loss of vegetation caused by ski-ing on thin snow
Visual pollution from ski-lifts and resorts built on hillsides
Less snow lower down makes skiers 'climb' higher onto fragile environments at higher altitudes
Acid rain killing vegetation in Alpine areas has been blamed on the huge increase in traffic

Social impact
Seasonal unemployment as most jobs are limited to the winter ski-ing season
Farmers and forestry workers have lost jobs as ski-ing takes over the area
Traditional way of life has changed due to increase in traffic and people
House prices rise and become too expensive for local people

D

Activities

1 **a)** What were the natural (physical) advantages of Les Deux Alpes as a ski resort? List your points under the two headings of 'Climate' and 'Relief'.
   b) What purpose-built amenities have been added to attract tourists to Les Deux Alpes?

2 Draw a simple sketch of photo **D**. On it label the following.
   a) Three physical advantages. (Think about climate, scenery and relief.)
   b) Three purpose-built amenities. (Think of accommodation, access and ski-facilities.)
   c) Three ways by which the local environment has, or may be, spoilt.

3 How can the building of a purpose-built ski-resort:
   a) be an advantage to local people
   b) create problems for local people and their environment?

Summary

Mountainous areas in Europe have become increasingly popular for winter sports. Both national and local governments have encouraged the growth of new ski resorts and improved facilities. The impact of purpose-built resorts upon local communities and the environment has not always considered.

An Italian cultural centre

The term **cultural**, taken in its widest sense, means learning about another country's civilisation and customs at a particular time in its history, e.g. Ancient Greece, Rome and Egypt. In this sense the term covers the development of religions and so includes places of religious pilgrimage, such as Rome. The term can also be applied, in a more narrow sense, to mean the creative activity and imagination of a group of people. This creativity includes the traditional arts such as painting, architecture, sculpture and music, as well as present-day fashions in, for example, clothes and food.

Television programmes, in particular, have made a greater number of people aware of other countries' lifestyles, both past and present. An increasing number of people in the economically more developed countries have become more wealthy and have longer and paid holidays, and transport has become faster and cheaper. As a result greater numbers have turned to 'cultural visits', and some combine these visits with the more traditional 'beach holiday' (e.g. visits to Thailand and Turkey).

Rome is one of many cultural centres in the EU. Tourists visit the city for many reasons.

Historical
Rome was the centre of the Roman Empire. Excavations have uncovered the remains of many buildings which date back to that time. At the centre of Roman life was the Forum (photo **A**) with its temples, triumphal arches, monuments and, later, Christian churches. Nearby is, perhaps, the most famous of Rome's ancient buildings – the Colosseum (photo **B**).

Religious
Within Rome is the independent state of the Vatican. The Vatican, dominated by the Cathedral church of St Peter's, is the residence of the Pope (photo **C**). Each year, and especially at the times of the major Christian festivals of Christmas and Easter, many Catholics make a pilgrimage hoping to receive the Pope's blessing.

B The Colosseum

C Cathedral church of St Peter's

Culture

Italy has, arguably, produced more famous artists than any other country. The Vatican Museum, one of many museums and art galleries within Rome, is visited by most tourists to the city. Probably the most famous part of the museum is the Sistine Chapel with its magnificent ceiling painted by Michelangelo. The nine panels (one is shown in photo **D**) took four years to paint.

Rome is full of statues and monuments dating from Roman times up to the present day. One popular tourist attraction is the Trevi Fountain (photo **E**). It is said that if you throw a coin into the fountain you are sure to revisit Rome. Rome is also noted for its architecture, especially its majestically designed piazzas (squares) and streets. More recently the city has become one of the world's leading fashion centres, and is renowned for its food and drink.

Large numbers of tourists are good for local economies. Yet while they bring in money and create jobs, the extra pressure that they put upon sites also creates many problems. There are often lengthy queues of people waiting to get into the Sistine Chapel, and flash photography is not allowed there or in art galleries because the bright light destroys the colours of the paintings. Some buildings in the Forum and parts of the Colosseum have had to be roped off to keep people from climbing over them. The many tourist buses and cars cause parking problems and add to traffic congestion. They also cause vibrations which affect the foundations of buildings and release chemicals which erode buildings and statues. Some sites are ruined visually by souvenir and refreshment stalls, and the litter left by tourists. Tourists, especially when wealthy, can also increase the cost of living for local people.

D Part of the ceiling of the Sistine Chapel

E The Trevi Fountain

Activities

1 a) If you decided to go on a cultural holiday, what sort of things would you expect to do and to see?
   b) Why is Rome a popular centre for a cultural holiday?
   c) Name a place (town or country) which you might like to visit for a short cultural holiday. Give reasons for your choice.

2 Draw a star diagram to describe some of the problems that might occur at Rome's most popular tourist sites.

Summary

Cultural holidays have become more fashionable as beach holidays have become less popular. Many people enjoy visiting places where the life-style is very different from their own. This increase in tourism has advantages but it also creates problems.

What are the patterns of migration in the EU?

Geographers look for patterns. In the case of migration they look to see if there are patterns of movement between places, or patterns of movement over a period of time. Map **A** shows recent migrations between countries in Europe and graph **B** shows when those movements took place. The most obvious patterns are described below.

- Between 1945 and 1973 when the countries of Western Europe had more job vacancies than they had workers. Britain and France encouraged people to move from the former colonies in the West Indies and North Africa. West Germany accepted large numbers of migrants from the poorer parts of south-east Europe and Turkey. For the migrants there was the main attraction of finding better-paid jobs, together with greater opportunities to improve their standards of housing and education.
- Around 1973 several West European countries introduced new laws which tried to control the number of

immigrants. Between 1973 and the late 1980s the need for extra workers in Western Europe decreased. Migrants were discouraged during times of economic recession (the early 1980s) when jobs were in short supply. During this time immigrants were often restricted to members of families already living and working in the receiving country.

- Since the late 1980s there has been a huge movement of voluntary migrants, mainly ethnic Germans, from Eastern Europe and what used to be the USSR. This movement peaked in late 1989 after the Berlin Wall was pulled down. The number of migrants has been considerably increased by asylum-seekers (refugees) forced by civil war to leave their homes in the former Yugoslavia. Graph **B** shows that over 70 per cent of this latest wave of migrants have tried to settle in the recently re-unified Germany.

A

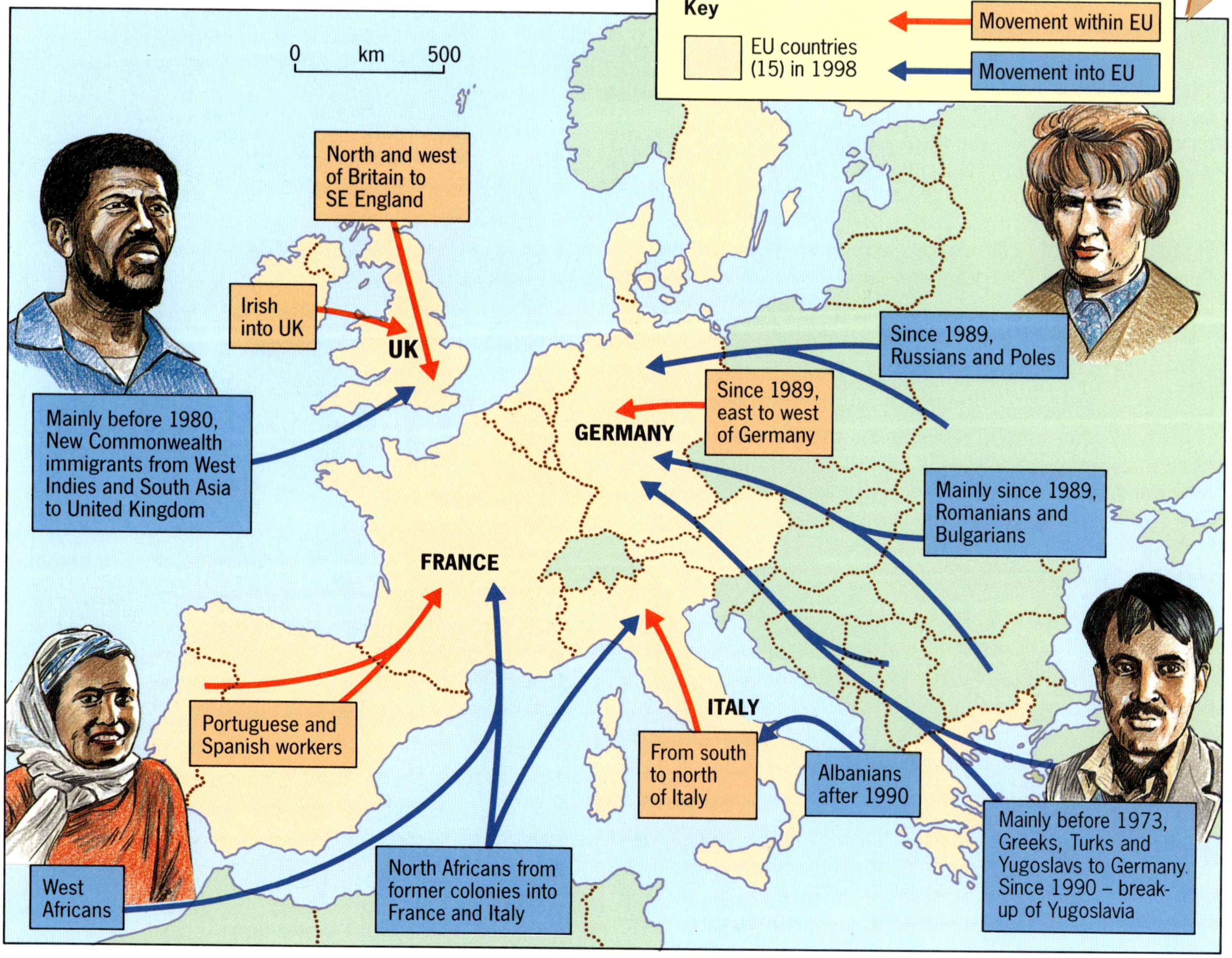

Key

EU countries (15) in 1998

→ Movement within EU

→ Movement into EU

0   km   500

North and west of Britain to SE England

Irish into UK

UK

Since 1989, Russians and Poles

Since 1989, east to west of Germany

GERMANY

Mainly before 1980, New Commonwealth immigrants from West Indies and South Asia to United Kingdom

Mainly since 1989, Romanians and Bulgarians

FRANCE

Portuguese and Spanish workers

ITALY

From south to north of Italy

Albanians after 1990

Mainly before 1973, Greeks, Turks and Yugoslavs to Germany. Since 1990 – break-up of Yugoslavia

West Africans

North Africans from former colonies into France and Italy

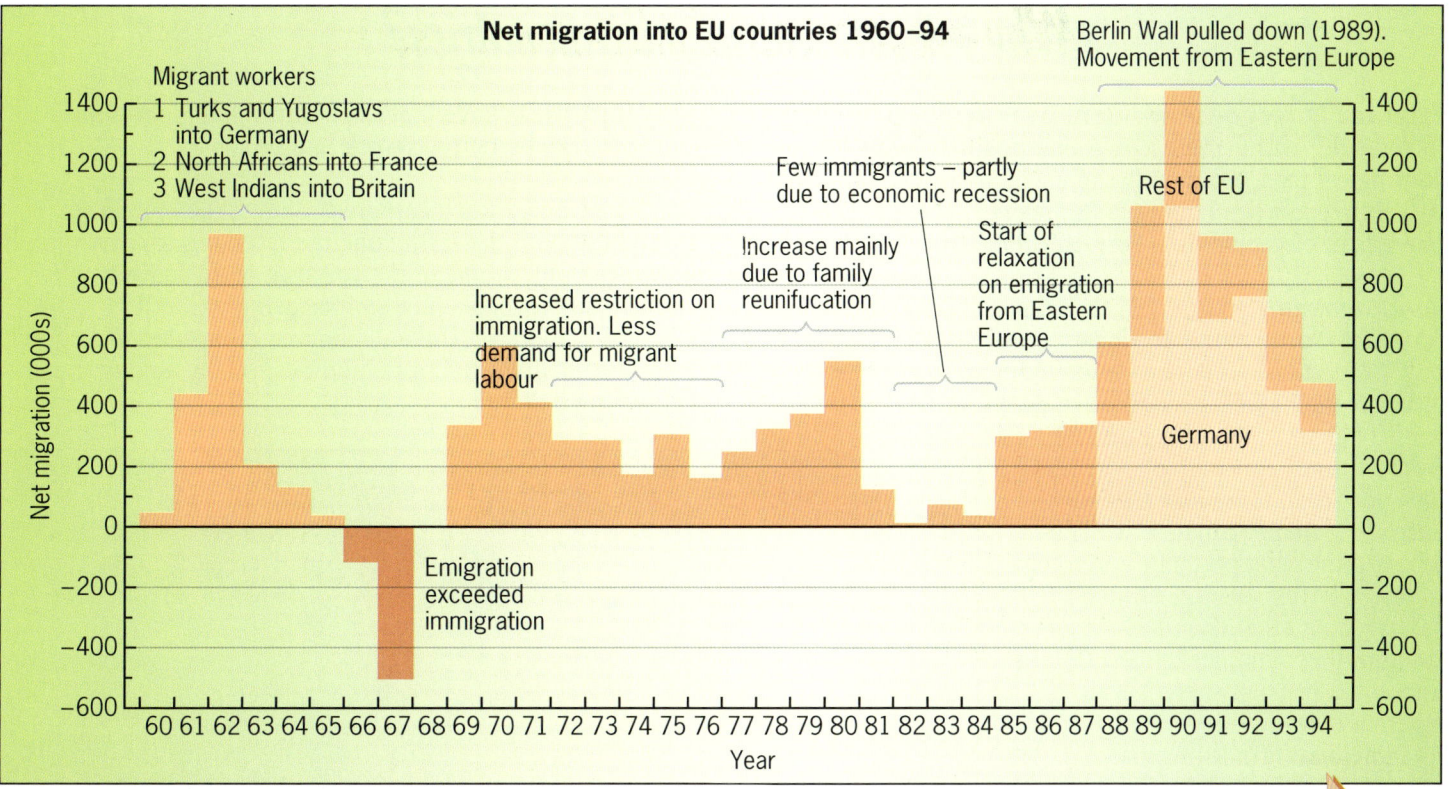

Net migration into EU countries 1960–94

Berlin Wall pulled down (1989). Movement from Eastern Europe

Migrant workers
1 Turks and Yugoslavs into Germany
2 North Africans into France
3 West Indians into Britain

Rest of EU

Few immigrants – partly due to economic recession

Increase mainly due to family reunifucation

Increased restriction on immigration. Less demand for migrant labour

Start of relaxation on emigration from Eastern Europe

Germany

Emigration exceeded immigration

Net migration (000s)

Year

B

Activities

1 Copy out and complete the sentences below by choosing the correct answer from the choice given in brackets.

- ◆ Britain and France received many immigrants from (former colonies/south-east Europe/Eastern Europe).
- ◆ For Britain this included (Turkey/the West Indies/North Africa) and for France (Turkey/the West Indies/North Africa).
- ◆ All these places were in (developed/developing) continents.
- ◆ Before 1973 most of West Germany's immigrants came from (the West Indies/ North Africa/south-east Europe and Turkey), especially the two countries of (the former USSR/Greece/Italy/the former Yugoslavia).
- ◆ Recently Germany has received many voluntary migrants from (Turkey/the former Yugoslavia/ Eastern Europe) and forced migrants from (Turkey/the former Yugoslavia/Eastern Europe).

2 The newspaper headlines in figure **C** give causes of migration into and between EU countries. Re-arrange the headlines in two columns headed:
   • Migration into the EU
   • Migration between EU countries.

3 Most migrants into the EU between 1945 and 1973 came from different places to those migrants who have arrived since the late 1980s.
   a) From which places:
       i) did most migrants come between 1945 and 1973
       ii) have most migrants come since the late 1980s?
   b) Give reasons why each group migrated.

C

Civil war in Yugoslavia

Germany, France and Britain short of skilled labour

Germany's laws allow in all refugees

France and Britain take in workers from their colonies

Portugal has lowest standard of living in EU

Berlin Wall pulled down

Russia allows residents to leave

High unemployment in Greece and Portugal

Germany, France and Britain short of unskilled labour

Summary

Early migrants into the EU were encouraged to come to find work. Later arrivals saw the move as a chance to join families or improve their standard of living. Many recent arrivals have come to escape political unrest and economic hardship in their home country.

61

▶ Why migrate between EU countries? ◀

Migrant Portuguese workers in France

In countries where there is a low standard of living and a shortage of jobs, groups of people will migrate to nearby, wealthier countries hoping to find work. One example is the movement of people from Portugal to France.

Conditions in Portugal Of the 15 present EU member countries, Portugal has the lowest standard of living. With only 38 per cent of its population living in towns, Portugal also has the highest proportion of people in Europe living in country areas and earning a living from the land. As rural jobs are less well paid than town jobs it is not surprising that Portuguese workers are paid the least per hour and receive the EU's lowest average annual salary. As in other farming communities, families tend to be large and, often because there is little machinery, work on the farm is hard. As individual farms are small, younger members of the family have to move to seek work elsewhere.

Many Portuguese have moved to France hoping to find temporary but better-paid work (map **A**).

When people migrate it can greatly affect the population structure of both the losing and the receiving country (graph **B**). It is usually people in the younger, more active age groups who move, leaving an increasingly elderly population at home. The much higher proportion of migrant males means divisions in families, especially among those with young children.

A

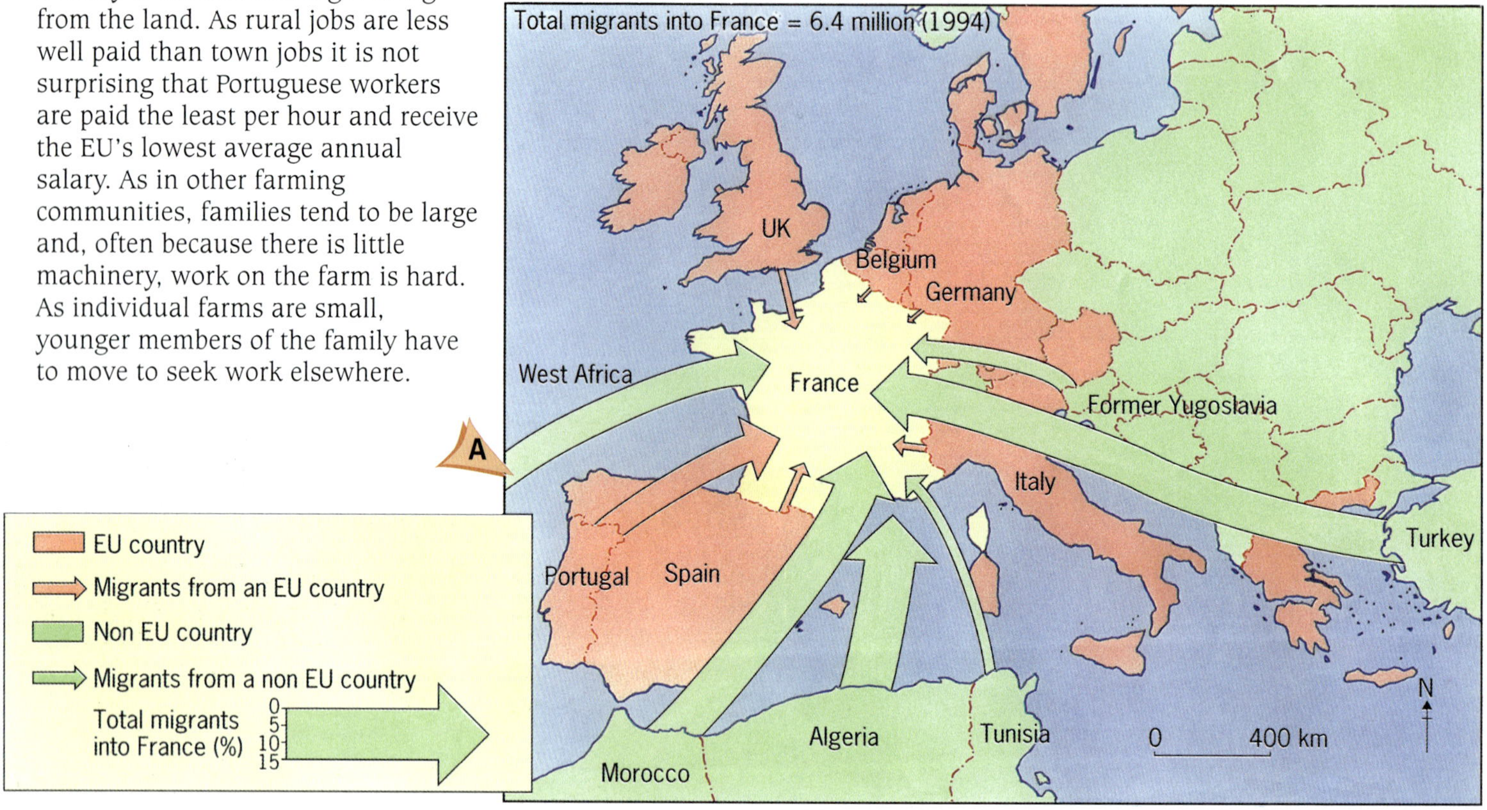

Total migrants into France = 6.4 million (1994)

UK
Belgium
Germany
West Africa
France
Former Yugoslavia
Italy
Turkey
Portugal
Spain
Algeria
Tunisia
Morocco

0   400 km

N

	EU country
	Migrants from an EU country
	Non EU country
	Migrants from a non EU country

Total migrants into France (%)   0 5 10 15

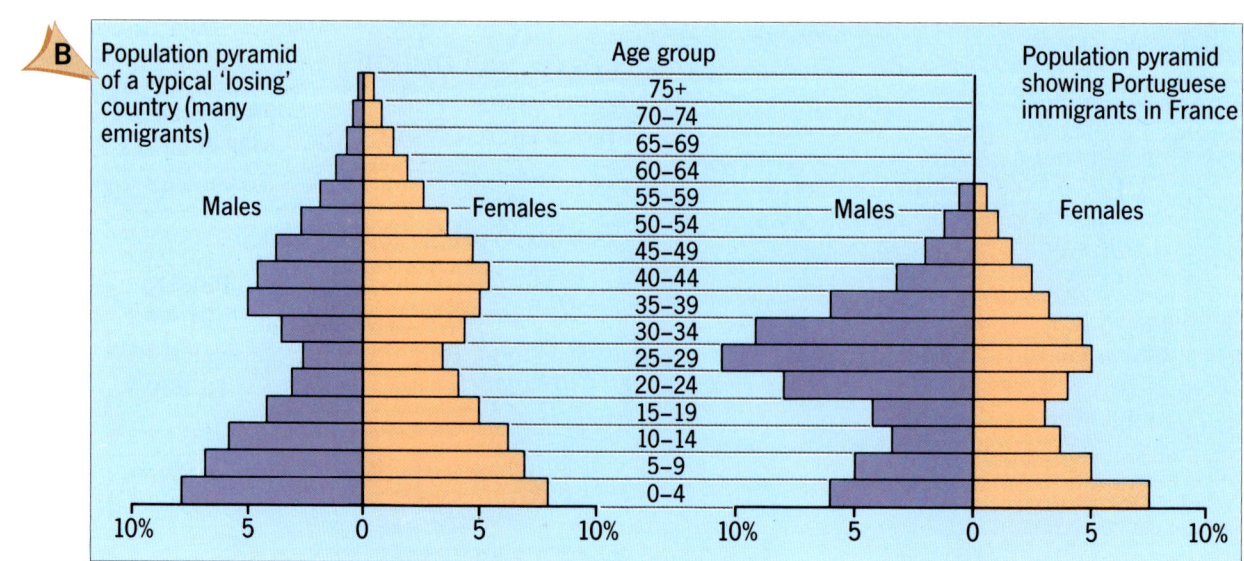

B

Population pyramid of a typical 'losing' country (many emigrants)

Age group

Population pyramid showing Portuguese immigrants in France

Males — Females

Males — Females

75+
70–74
65–69
60–64
55–59
50–54
45–49
40–44
35–39
30–34
25–29
20–24
15–19
10–14
5–9
0–4

10% 5 0 5 10%   10% 5 0 5 10%

Conditions in France As has already been mentioned (page 60) France had a shortage of workers after the Second World War. Workers from neighbouring poorer parts of southern Europe and North Africa were encouraged to move (map **A**). The largest number of these migrants came from Portugal. Many new Portuguese arrivals initially found work on farms, but soon turned to better-paid jobs in the construction industry, factories, hotels, restaurants, etc. By French standards these jobs often demanded long unsocial hours and were poorly paid (photo **C**).

The migrant Portuguese could, however, earn wages as much as five times higher than those paid at home. Yet it was a sacrifice. Many had to leave their families for several months at a time. They had to live with other workers often in crowded rooms in poor-quality government-built flats similar to those in photo **D**. Working conditions were often bad and a working day could last 18 hours. As the French had a high standard of living, much of the money the Portuguese earned went on accommodation, transport and cheap meals. What was left over was sent home. It was little use complaining about their conditions partly because of language problems and partly because many were illegal immigrants.

The position today It is becoming harder for migrant workers to find and keep jobs, especially as it tends to be the unskilled jobs that are lost first at a time of economic recession. Bad feeling towards migrant workers and those who have brought their families with them is growing. So far most resentment has been directed at the North Africans because of differences in language, culture and religion.

Activities

1 a) Rank in order the five places from which France has received most immigrants.
   b) What do you notice about the location of these places?

2 a) If you were Portuguese, what would be some of the:
   i) reasons why you might want to go to work in France
   ii) problems you might leave behind in Portugal?
   b) If you were French, what would be some of the:
   i) advantages of having Portuguese coming to work in your country
   ii) problems which you think the migrant workers may create?

Summary

Although the movement of workers from poorer countries to more wealthy countries has many advantages, it also creates many problems.

▶ Regional migration in the EU ◀

Most migrations take place between different regions **within** a country. People will move away from regions that have an unfavourable natural environment and few natural resources. People will move to those regions that have a lower relief, more favourable soils and climate, a better transport system, and more raw materials and job opportunities. Two adjacent regions in southern France are the Cevennes and Languedoc-Roussillon. The Cevennes is a mountainous area from which people move. Languedoc-Roussillon has the highest immigration rate of all the regions in the EU. Landsketch **A** gives some reasons for this regional movement.

A

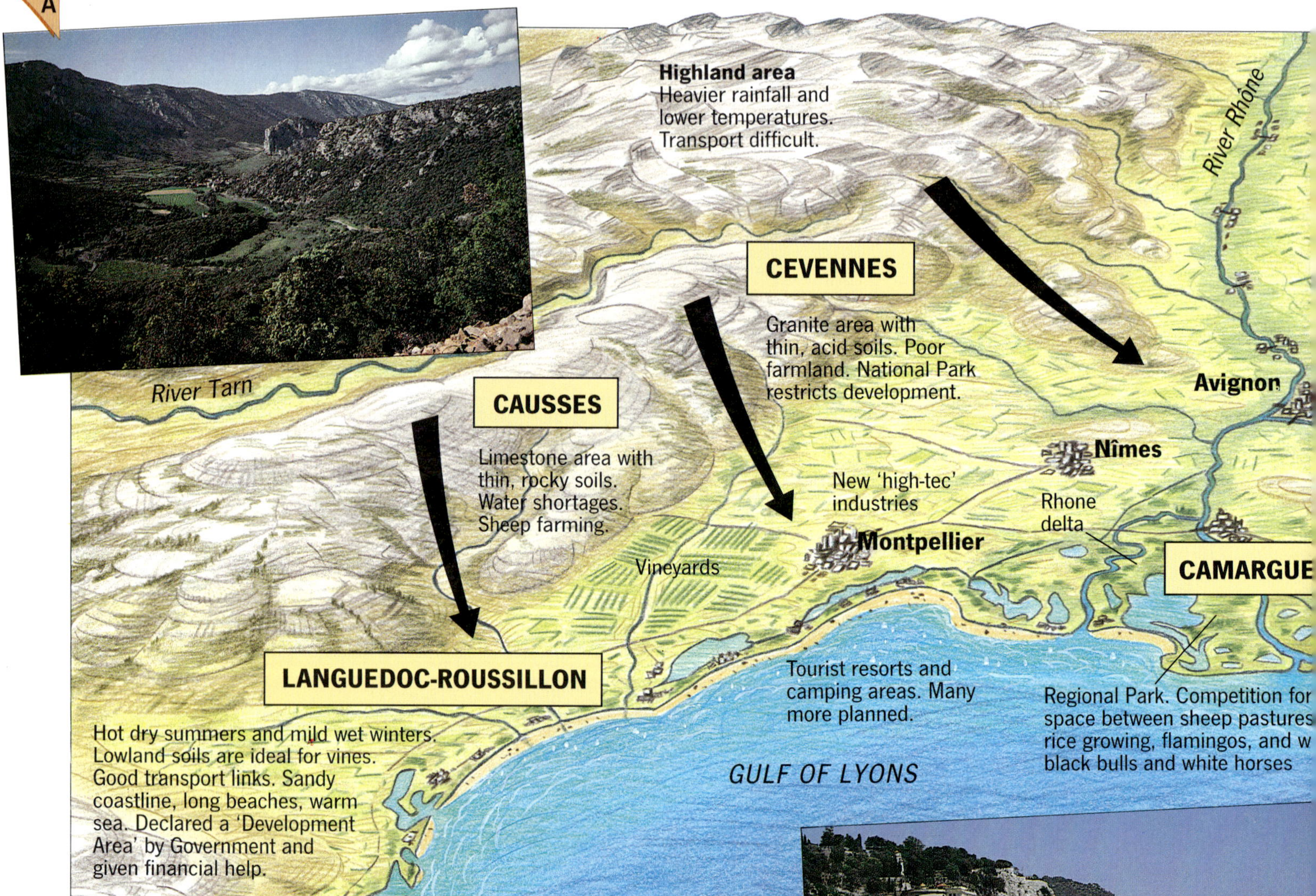

Highland area
Heavier rainfall and lower temperatures. Transport difficult.

River Rhône

CEVENNES
Granite area with thin, acid soils. Poor farmland. National Park restricts development.

Avignon

CAUSSES
Limestone area with thin, rocky soils. Water shortages. Sheep farming.

River Tarn

Nîmes

New 'high-tec' industries

Rhone delta

Montpellier

Vineyards

CAMARGUE

LANGUEDOC-ROUSSILLON

Tourist resorts and camping areas. Many more planned.

Regional Park. Competition for space between sheep pastures, rice growing, flamingos, and w black bulls and white horses

GULF OF LYONS

Hot dry summers and mild wet winters. Lowland soils are ideal for vines. Good transport links. Sandy coastline, long beaches, warm sea. Declared a 'Development Area' by Government and given financial help.

Perpignan

Beach at Nice, Côte d'Azur

Activities

1 a) Why do some people like living in the Cevennes?
   b) Why do other people move away from the Cevennnes?
   c) Why are so many people moving into Languedoc-Roussillon?

2 What effect will these population movements have on each region?

► Seasonal migration in the EU ◄

Seasonal movement is when people move home for part of the year. Two regions in France where this occurs are the High Alps and the Camargue-Côte d'Azur (map **B**). For many centuries farmers in this area have taken their sheep from winter pastures in the flat Camargue district of the Rhône delta to summer pastures in the High Alps. Although this type of farming, known as **transhumance**, is dying out, it is being replaced by another type of seasonal movement – tourism. In winter the snow of the High Alps attracts many skiers. In summer it is the hot, dry weather of the Côte d'Azur that becomes the magnet for many visitors. Landsketch **B** gives some reasons for these seasonal movements.

B

River Durance

HIGH ALPS

Ski-ing in winter. New resorts are using up sheep pastures. Some tourists in summer. New roads have been built.

DURANCE VALLEY

In June sheep are taken to Alpine pastures. Originally this was a month's walk, but sheep are now moved in double-decker lorries. Lorries cause congestion on narrow roads twice a year. Transhumance is in decline and pastures are being lost. Rural areas are too isolated for young people and there are better-paid jobs in the cities.

Nice

In October sheep are brought down to the Camargue. It has mild, wet winters which are good for grass. The land is flat and there are few tourists. Summers are too hot and dry for grass to grow.

Cannes

COTE D'AZUR

Rocky headlands.
Sandy or rocky beaches.
Hot, dry summers.
Good harbours.
Large hotels and restaurants.

Marseille

Toulon

Activities

1 **a)** What is transhumance?
   b) Why are sheep taken to the Camargue in winter and to the High Alps in summer?
   c) Why do so many people visit the High Alps in winter?
   d) Why do so many people visit the Côte d'Azur in summer?

2 What effect will these seasonal movements have upon each of the two regions?

Summary

Whether or not migration is between countries, between regions or at different times of the year, it has considerable effects upon the different regions involved.

▶ *What are the alternative policies to migration in the EU?* ◀

The United Nations (UN) claim that '80 million people have left their homes for economic, political, environmental or other reasons – often embarking on precarious new lives'. Although the vast majority of these moves have been made in and between developing countries, the EU now has 8 million immigrants, a number that is growing rapidly.

Migrants into the EU

Most early arrivals were **economic migrants**. These were people looking for work in the hope of improving their standard of living, e.g. North Africans moving to France and Turks moving to West Germany. Many more recent migrants have been seeking asylum (safety). If asylum-seekers can prove that they are escaping from political, racial or religious persecution at home then they are granted the dubious status of being **refugees** (e.g. Bosnians into Germany). The UN define people who are forced to move within their home country as **displaced**

persons (e.g. ethnic cleansing in the former Yugoslavia). The largest proportion of migrants today are **illegal immigrants** who enter a country without permission (e.g. West Africans dumped in the sea two or three kilometres off the coast of Italy or Spain, who then try to swim ashore).

Until the 1990s most EU countries had a fairly liberal policy on immigration. However, there is a changing attitude amongst members for several reasons.
- Growing numbers of immigrants coming from Eastern Europe and the former USSR.
- Fears that immigrants pose a domestic threat (extracts **A** and **B**).
- Increasing numbers of illegal immigrants.

Some of these views and changes in legislation are expressed in diagram **C**.

A

Turks in Germany

January 1993

A Turkish spokesperson said, 'We have lived here for years yet we are still without representation and feel cut off from German life. We are seen as aliens which makes us an easy target. Germans have a negative attitude to people who look and think differently.' In reply a German claimed, 'Some Turks may have lived here since arriving as "guest workers" in the 1960s but only 1 per cent have taken out German citizenship. They refuse to apply as it would mean giving up Turkish nationality. They do not want to be German.'

In the boom years of the 1960s and 1970s, the lack of political rights was, in the eyes of most Turks, compensated for by relatively good wages. Even if they were not treated as equals, the Turks were tolerated by most West Germans who recognised that they did the menial jobs they themselves would not do. Since the economic problems resulting from German re-unification, Turks have been increasingly lumped with asylum-seekers and other refugees and accused of draining resources and 'taking' jobs. Groups of extremists have burnt Turkish property and have been responsible for several murders. In response the majority of Germans have reacted with large anti-racist marches.

B

November 1992

North Africans in France

Until recently North African migrants, though never encouraged to integrate socially, existed peacefully with the French and tensions were few. However, as unemployment has continued to rise then accusations have been made that the North Africans are taking jobs from the French. They are also feared for their very high birth rate and their alien customs. Muslim extremists have encouraged strikes of Arab workers and discouraged young women and new immigrants from adopting French customs. Trouble finally broke out in several large urban areas. Here the immigrants live in high-rise ghettos where they are shunned and despised by the French. Race riots and the growth of an extreme French racist political party has shocked many young French people into launching a campaign of support and solidarity for the young North Africans in their country.

C

United Kingdom: We have a quota system which restricts entry to a proportion of people from various countries but it is weighted against New Commonwealth immigrants. We will allow genuine refugees from places like Bosnia to enter if they can prove that their lives would be in danger if they were sent home – but not economic migrants just wanting jobs. Those refugees we do accept may be sent to 'quieter' parts of Britain like Cumbria. We fine airlines that bring in people without a valid passport or entry visa. We are also worried about the abolition of border controls between EU countries – it could let in terrorists and drug dealers.

France: Since 1974 only those rejoining their families have been allowed entry. We offered money to migrants to tempt them to be repatriated. Very few accepted and some who did just took the money, went home and then returned! We are now being swamped by illegal immigrants or those who come with 'tourist visas' and stay. In future migrants will get a 'transit (passing through) visa'.

EU IMMIGRATION POLICY GROUP

Italy: As so many Italians have emigrated it was right that we, in return, allowed free entry to all immigrants. But we have had so many problems with refugees and illegal immigrants that people from North Africa and Turkey will only be admitted if they have a valid passport.

EU Commissioner: We must try to halt illegal immigration; plan legal immigration; help the social integration of future immigrants. We may have to restrict entry to people with certain skills that are lacking in the EU.

Germany: We have had an open door policy to all migrants. However, since accepting nearly 2 million ethnic Germans from Eastern Europe and the former USSR, and 0.6 million legal refugees from the former Yugoslavia, we are having to revise our ideas. Many Germans feel we have already accepted too many.

Activities

1 What is the difference between economic migrants, refugees and illegal immigrants?

2 Why is the increase in population movement into the EU causing concern among several member countries?

3 **a)** Why are individual EU countries such as Britain, France, Germany and Italy looking for new immigration policies with stricter controls?

   b) Why is it important for the EU to have a common immigration policy?

   c) What do you think should be the EU's policy towards immigration?

Summary

As the number of migrants, both legal and illegal, into the EU increases, individual governments are changing their policies and putting pressure on the EU itself to produce a 'common' immigration policy.

▷ Paris – a changing city ◁

Paris is the capital of France and one of the world's great cities. With a population of about 9.3 million it is the largest city in Europe and one of the fastest-growing capitals in the Western world. Situated on the River Seine at the centre of the fertile Paris Basin in the north of France, it is ideally located to develop as a city in its own right. It is also well placed to influence the rest of the country and to develop links with Europe and the wider world.

This ideal location has resulted in Paris growing much faster than other cities in France. Lyons and Marseilles, the second and third largest, have populations of just over a million each and are much less important than Paris. Indeed Paris

has come to dominate France in a way that is perhaps unusual for rich and developed nations where influence is generally shared more equally around the country. Diagram **A** gives some reasons for Paris's growth and increased influence.

Although continued growth and success had made Paris very prosperous, it became obvious by the mid-twentieth century that serious problems were emerging which were becoming a major threat to the city itself and France as a whole. Most of these problems were a consequence of the city being allowed to grow haphazardly and without any planning. Some of the problems are shown in diagram **B** below.

A

Paris – a city of growth

- Capital of France since the tenth century
- Centre for French industry from the mid-nineteenth century
- Employs 20% of the French labour force and provides a third by value of the nation's exports
- Is the focus of the country's major roads, autoroutes and railways
- Is at the hub of national and international air routes
- Is one of Europe's main tourist centres
- Is at the centre of France's main agricultural region, the Paris Basin
- Has port facilities on the navigable River Seine to handle imports and exports
- Attracts migrants from other parts of France and Europe looking to improve their quality of life

B

Paris – a city with problems

- Rapid population growth due to rural depopulation, the arrival of migrant workers and a rise in the birth rate
- Poor-quality housing with many people living in cramped and overcrowded slum conditions
- An inadequate transport system with massive road congestion and inefficient public transport
- Old-fashioned factories badly located in inner city locations
- High labour costs making industrial growth difficult (30% above national average)
- High pollution levels from transport and industry
- Depressed growth in other parts of France because of an over-emphasis on Paris

Activities

1 Draw a star diagram like the one below to show at least six reasons for the growth of Paris.

2 Describe the problems of Paris using the headings from drawing **D** below.

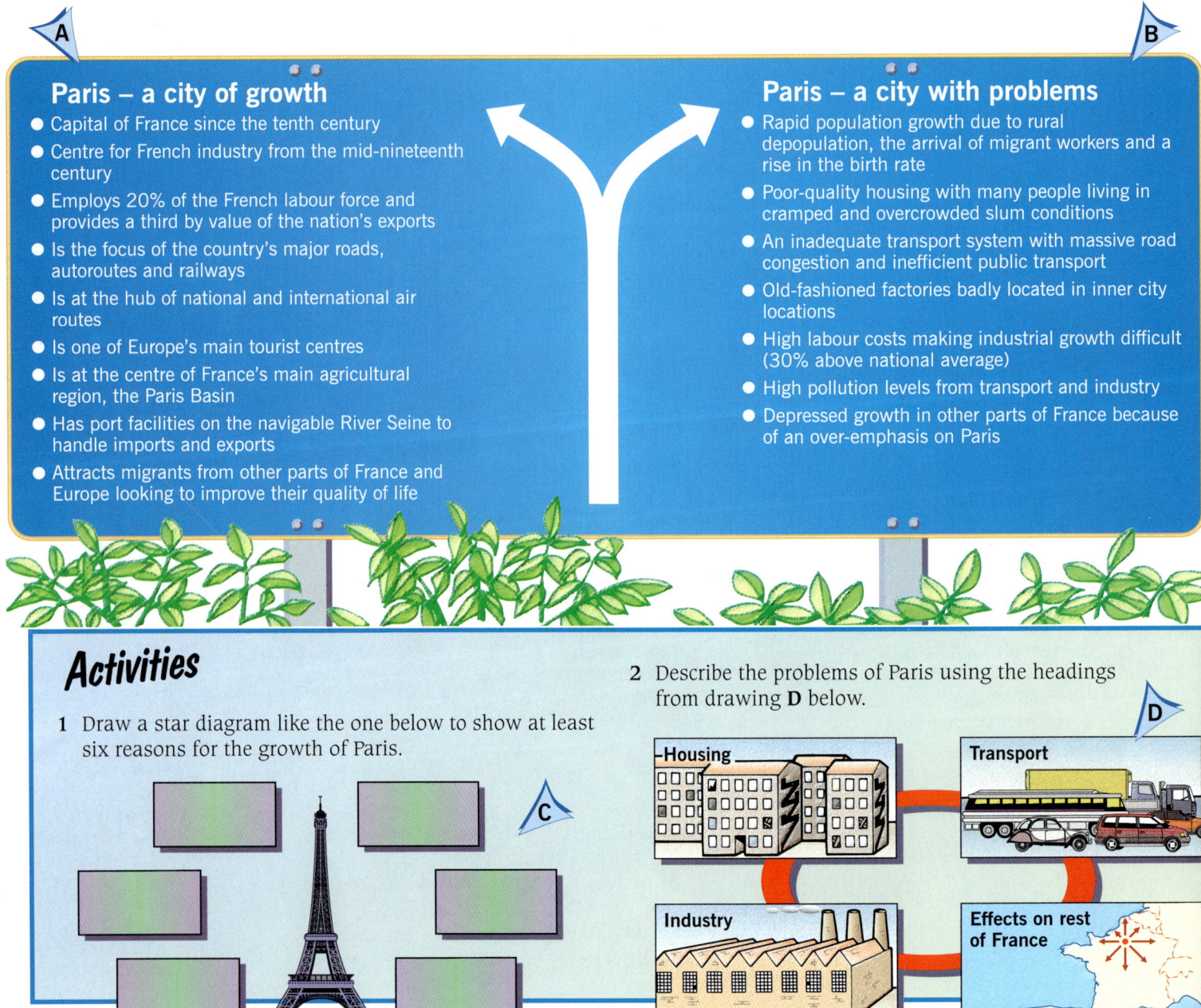

C

D

Housing

Transport

Industry

Effects on rest of France

Since the 1960s the urban development of Paris has been more controlled and greater care has been taken in appreciating the needs of the rest of France. This has been done by careful planning and the introduction of a series of development plans. These plans have had two principal objectives. The first is to implement structural change to the city itself, and the second is to relocate and decentralise some city-based activities to other areas of Paris and to less developed parts of France. The main points covered by the plan are shown in map **E**.

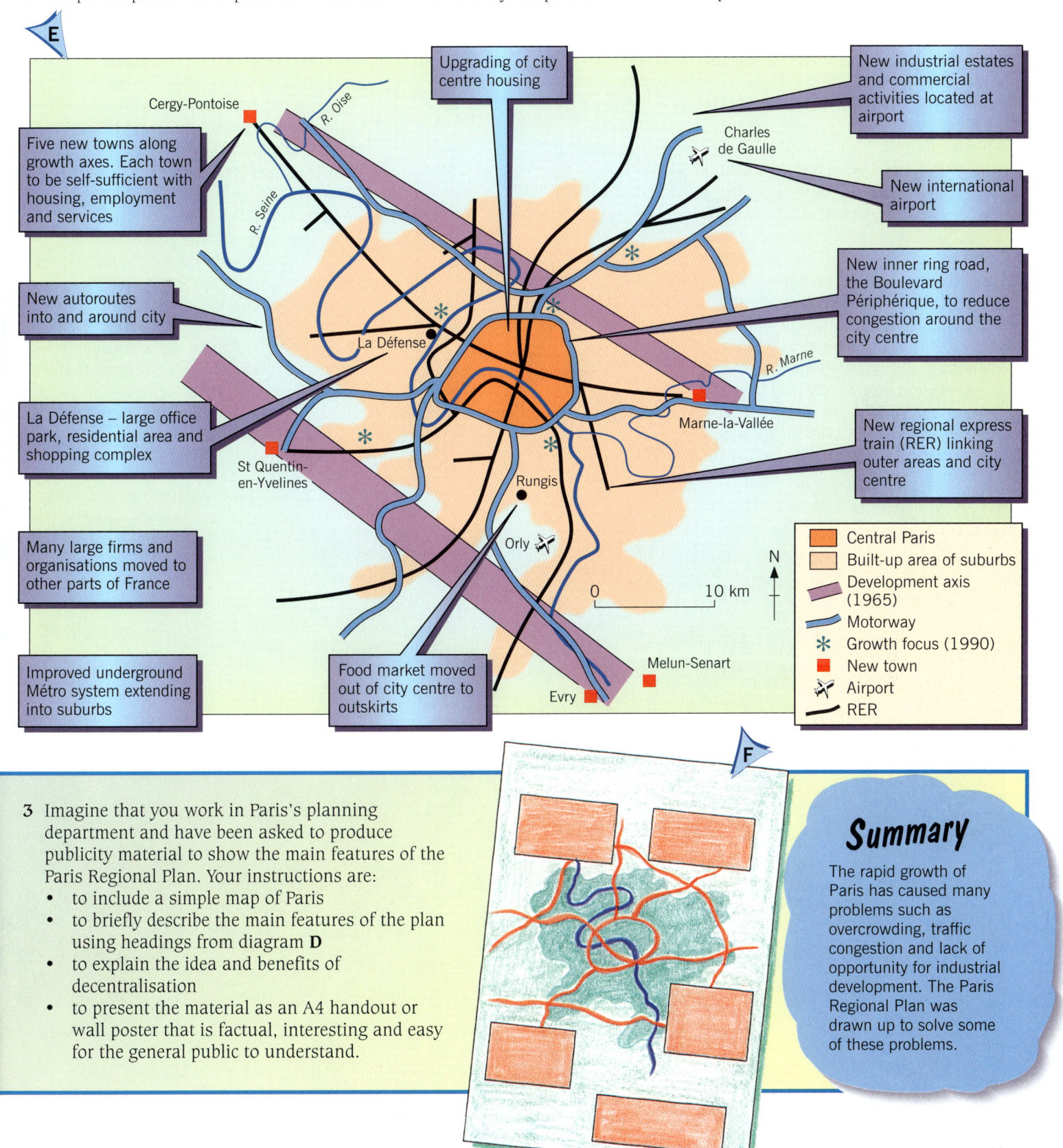

E

Upgrading of city centre housing

New industrial estates and commercial activities located at airport

New international airport

New inner ring road, the Boulevard Périphérique, to reduce congestion around the city centre

New regional express train (RER) linking outer areas and city centre

Five new towns along growth axes. Each town to be self-sufficient with housing, employment and services

New autoroutes into and around city

La Défense – large office park, residential area and shopping complex

Many large firms and organisations moved to other parts of France

Improved underground Métro system extending into suburbs

Food market moved out of city centre to outskirts

Cergy-Pontoise

R. Oise

R. Seine

Charles de Gaulle

La Défense

R. Marne

Marne-la-Vallée

St Quentin-en-Yvelines

Rungis

Orly

Melun-Senart

Evry

	Central Paris
	Built-up area of suburbs
	Development axis (1965)
	Motorway
*	Growth focus (1990)
■	New town
✈	Airport
—	RER

N

0   10 km

3 Imagine that you work in Paris's planning department and have been asked to produce publicity material to show the main features of the Paris Regional Plan. Your instructions are:
   • to include a simple map of Paris
   • to briefly describe the main features of the plan using headings from diagram **D**
   • to explain the idea and benefits of decentralisation
   • to present the material as an A4 handout or wall poster that is factual, interesting and easy for the general public to understand.

F

Summary

The rapid growth of Paris has caused many problems such as overcrowding, traffic congestion and lack of opportunity for industrial development. The Paris Regional Plan was drawn up to solve some of these problems.

▷ *How can urban renewal reduce pressure on cities?* ◁

An important aim of the **Paris Regional Plan** was to reduce pressure in the central areas of the city and to improve facilities in the suburbs. This was to be done by a process of **decentralisation** whereby people and jobs were to be moved out of the city centre and relocated in purpose-built developments either in the suburbs or further out on the edge of the city.

One of the grandest and most prestigious projects has been **La Défense**, a huge modern development located some 8 km north-west of the city centre. Whilst the spectacular skyscrapers are the most obvious feature of La Défense, included in the scheme are new houses, shops, offices, industries, cultural facilities and leisure opportunities – indeed all the requisites of modern living and sound economic growth. The project is one of **urban renewal** with a new, well-planned, self-contained development replacing what was once a run-down suburban area of Paris.

Tour Sans Fin
425 m

Tour Eiffel
321 m

B

Whilst La Défense has attracted some criticism for its somewhat modern and perhaps stark architecture, the development is considered by most people to be an enormous success. In particular it has become a focus for economic development, providing a centralised business district for Paris which had previously been missing, and helping reduce the need for people to use the city centre. It has also solved the problem of urban decay and decline in the area as well as becoming a home and place of work for thousands of Parisians who, by all accounts, are more than satisfied with their new surroundings and excellent public transport system.

Future developments include underground motorways and the world's most slender skyscraper, the cylindrical glass and concrete Tour Sans Fin (diagram **B**).

- ○ Contains more than 40 tower blocks
- ○ An expected population of 60 000 people
- ○ Employment for more than 80 000 people
- ○ Total of 200 000 workers in La Défense and surrounding area
- ○ One of the largest shopping centres in Europe
- ○ Has become a major tourist attraction

A ▷ La Défense

- ○ Contains over 15% of all Paris offices
- ○ Over 9400 old buildings demolished
- ○ Linked by express railway and underground metro to city centre
- ○ Easy access to new motorway system
- ○ One of Europe's most futuristic projects

La Défense has been called 'America in Paris' because of its spectacular skyscrapers and modernistic architecture. At the centre of the development is the Grande Arche, an enormous high-tech office block that was opened on 14 July 1989. It quickly became the busiest tourist location in France with over 900 000 visitors taking the lift to the roof for an aerial view of Paris.

C

The Grande Arche – La Défense

Activities

D

1 **a)** What is meant by decentralisation?
  b) How can decentralisation help reduce pressure and congestion in central Paris?

2 Look at cartoon **D**. For each of the people, suggest a reason why they may be attracted to La Défense.

3 Make a larger copy of table **E** and show how La Défense has been successful by giving an example for each aim.

Company director   City centre resident   Unemployed worker

La Défense

4 Choose three items from table **E** and explain how they may help reduce pressure and congestion in the central areas of Paris.

E

Aims of the scheme	Successes
Re-house people from central Paris	
Provide jobs away from the centre	
Improve public transport	
Link to national road system	
Provide out-of-town shopping	
Build additional office space	
Clear old buildings and derelict land	
Attract visitors and tourists	

Summary

La Défense is a new and exciting development located in the suburbs of Paris. Through careful planning it has successfully reduced dependence on the city centre and become a major business, commercial and residential centre in its own right.

How can new towns reduce pressure on cities?

One way of relieving pressure in large cities and at the same time improving living conditions for people is to build **new towns**. New towns are designed for modern living and if successful can encourage people and jobs to relocate from the busy city centre into the outskirts. Around Paris there are now five new towns, each with a present population of between 100 000 and 200 000. Each town is self-contained with residential areas, shopping centres, leisure activities and employment opportunities making them as independent from central Paris as possible.

One of these towns is Marne-la-Vallée, located 13 km east of Paris and built around 26 small villages. The plan for the new town is based on a modern transport system and will eventually cover an area of 15 000 hectares, making it larger than the city of Paris itself. To cope with this enormous size, the area has been divided into four sectors, each providing a mix of facilities but developing an identity and character of its own. The first two sectors are largely complete and most work is now taking place in Sector 3. The final completion date is 2020.

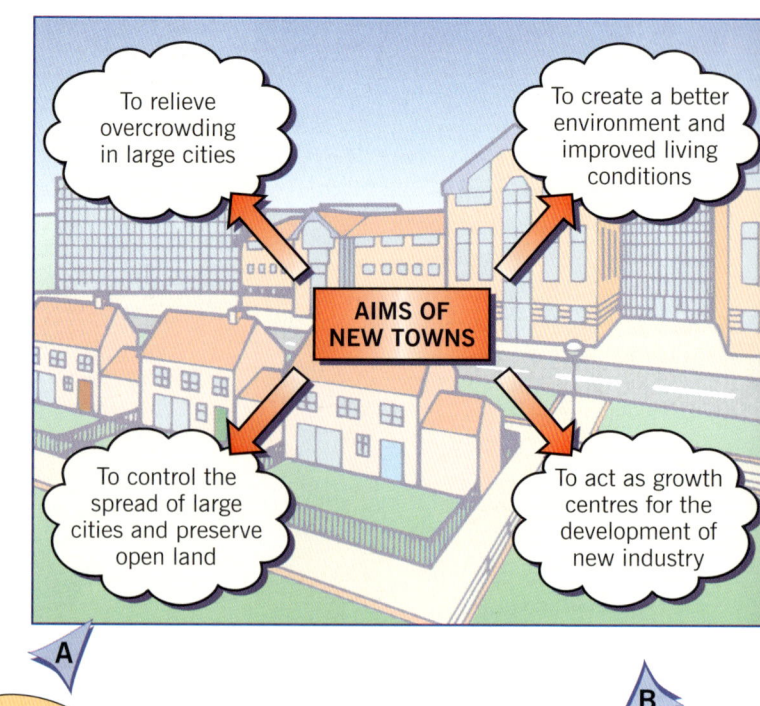

To relieve overcrowding in large cities

To create a better environment and improved living conditions

AIMS OF NEW TOWNS

To control the spread of large cities and preserve open land

To act as growth centres for the development of new industry

A

B

Housing has always been a top priority here and we think that we now have housing to suit the needs of everyone. At present our population is about 200 000 but it is forecast to reach 300 000 by the year 2020. Many people have moved here from the slum clearance areas of central Paris.

We have a great variety of industrial and commercial enterprises in our town. These have helped provide jobs for local people and laid the foundation for future economic growth and prosperity in the Paris region. Some of the firms have relocated from central Paris.

Marne-la-Vallée new town

Key

- Built-up area
- Water
- Woods and parks
- TGV
- RER
- Motorway

River Marne

N

0   5 km

RER

Disneyland Paris

A4

← PARIS

A104

TGV

Sector	1	2	3	4
	Noissy-le-Grand	**Val Maubuée**	**Val de Bussy**	**Val d'Europe**
	Business sector	Market centre	Technological growth pole	Tourism and leisure

Marne-la-Vallée has been designed as a garden town with vast areas of parkland, forest and open space. Attracted by this 'green' environment, good communications and easy access to the city, French and international companies have been drawn to the area. In 1997 there were over 5300 new companies employing more than 100 000 people.

Housing has been carefully thought out, with a variety of homes being built to suit the needs of both the rich and the poor. Most of the cheaper accommodation is in the west and located close to industrial areas so that workers have only short distances to travel. The more expensive housing is towards the east around Val de Bussy.

Recent surveys have shown that most people living in Marne-la-Vallée are generally content with their new town and that their living conditions have improved. In addition, only a small proportion of the population now commute to Paris and this has helped reduce overcrowding and congestion in the central areas.

Our modern transport system is one of the best in Europe. Local journeys are served by the rapid express train (RER) and a good road system. For the Paris region and the rest of France we have new motorways and the high-speed train (TGV). Then just 20 minutes away are two international airports with flights to worldwide destinations.

Our town is a pleasant place in which to live and has plenty of leisure facilities. We have large areas of woodland and parks as well as 35 lakes. Even the embankments along the River Marne are landscaped for recreation. The huge Disneyland Paris theme park is located here and most of the business parks offer a wide range of leisure activities.

Activities

1 List the main aims and benefits of new towns. Give at least six.

2 Draw a diagram like **C** to show the main features of Marne-la-Vallée. Try to write about 20 words for each heading.

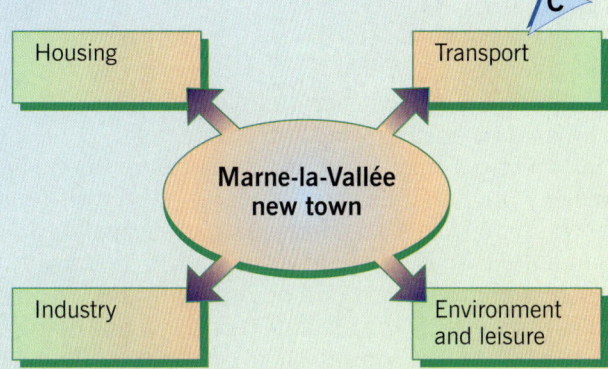

C

Housing — Transport

Marne-la-Vallée new town

Industry — Environment and leisure

3 The people listed in diagram **D** all work or live in central Paris. For each one suggest why they might like to move to Marne-la-Vallée.

D

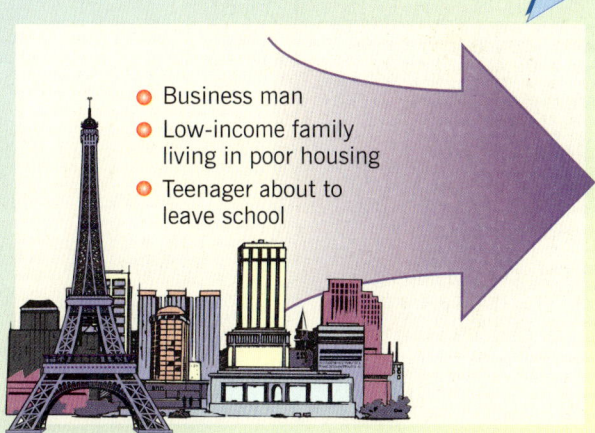

- Business man
- Low-income family living in poor housing
- Teenager about to leave school

4 Do you think that the aims of Marne-la-Vallée, to improve living conditions and reduce pressure on central Paris, have been achieved? Give reasons for your answer.

Summary

Marne-la-Vallée is a well-planned and self-contained new town which provides good living conditions for its inhabitants. Its success has encouraged people and businesses to move out of Paris and so reduce problems in the city centre.

What are the land use and main occupations in the Ile de France?

The Ile de France is the third smallest in area out of France's 22 political regions. However, with a population of 10.6 million, it has the country's highest population density (diagram **A**). Almost one-fifth of the total French population live in this region, which includes the city of Paris.

Land use

The central part of the Ile de France consists of the urban area of Paris which is continuously taking up larger amounts of land. Apart from the expansion of the city itself and the creation of five new towns (map **B**), many outlying villages are becoming increasingly suburbanised. These settlements are linked to Paris by an increasing number of major roads and railways. The major land use for most of the remainder of the region is forest and agriculture. The forests, mainly natural beech and oak, initially formed part of large estates (e.g. Fontainebleau and the Chevreuse Valley). They are now protected by the state and provide places of recreation for urban dwellers. Agriculture is both intensive and commercial. Surrounding Paris are numerous smallholdings providing fresh market garden produce. The south-west of the region merges into the wheat-growing area of Beauce. Between the rivers Seine and Marne is the dairy farming *pays* (district) of Brie, which gives its name to an internationally well-known cheese.

The employment structure for the region shows that most people work in either the secondary or tertiary sectors (diagram **A**). The vast majority of these jobs are found within Paris itself (map **B**).

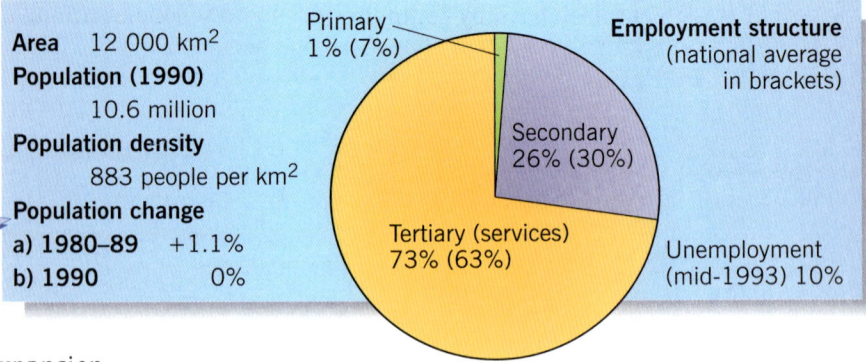

A

Area	12 000 km²
Population (1990)	10.6 million
Population density	883 people per km²
Population change	
a) 1980–89	+1.1%
b) 1990	0%

Employment structure (national average in brackets)

Primary 1% (7%)
Secondary 26% (30%)
Tertiary (services) 73% (63%)
Unemployment (mid-1993) 10%

B

Industry Centre for French industry. Four main groups:
- engineering, especially manufacture of cars – Renault-Saab and Peugeot-Citroën employ over 100,000 workers at their large Paris plants
- electrical goods including electronics, computers and other new high-technology industries
- chemicals, e.g. pharmaceuticals and cosmetics
- consumer goods, e.g. clothing, footwear and furniture

Service industries Shops, restaurants, schools and hospitals. Twelve universities with 35% of the total number of France's students.

Route centre Junction of main autoroutes (motorways) and TGV routes. Two international airports. River routes.

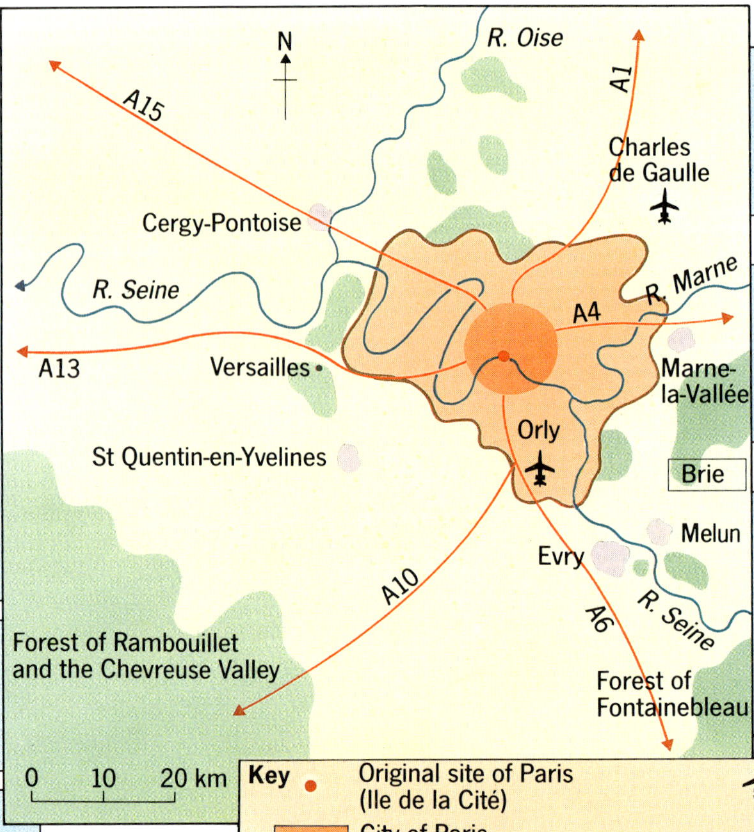

Commercial and financial centre Banks, insurance companies and the stock exchange

Regional and national governments Government administration employs over 330 000 people

Tourist centre Historic buildings (Eiffel Tower, Arc de Triomphe); cathedrals (Notre Dame); art galleries (Louvre); museums; opera; entertainment and restaurants

N

R. Oise
A15
A1
Charles de Gaulle
Cergy-Pontoise
R. Marne
R. Seine
A4
A13
Versailles
Marne-la-Vallée
Orly
Brie
St Quentin-en-Yvelines
Melun
Evry
A10
A6
R. Seine
Forest of Rambouillet and the Chevreuse Valley
Forest of Fontainebleau

0 10 20 km

Key
- Original site of Paris (Ile de la Cité)
- City of Paris (Paris ville)
- Built-up area of Greater Paris
- Motorways (autoroutes)
- International airport
- New towns
- Woods and forests
- Farmland

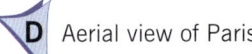

Settlement

Most of the settlements, including Paris and its new towns, are nucleated. A more linear pattern of settlement, inhabited by commuters, has developed along many of the main roads which lead into the capital. Many younger people still migrate to Paris. This is because the city, being the capital and industrial centre of the country, offers the best career opportunities as well as providing the most and the best-paid jobs. However, an almost equal number of people are moving out of the city to try to escape from the problems of overcrowding, traffic congestion, high land prices, and air and noise pollution. Although attempts have been made to create jobs in the new towns, many people still have to commute to Paris for work.

D Aerial view of Paris

C Palace of Versailles

Activities

1 **a)** What proportion of people living in the Ile de France are employed in each of the primary, secondary and tertiary sectors?
   b) What are the three main types of land use in the Ile de France?

2 **a)** What are the main types of primary activity in the Ile de France?
   b) What are the main types of secondary activity (industry) found in Paris?
   c) Why does Paris have a high percentage of tertiary (service) jobs?

3 Photo **E** is a Landsat image of the Ile de France. It covers the same area as that shown on map **B**. Using the photo and the map, name the following:
   a) Rivers ①, ② and ③.
   b) Urban area ④.
   c) New towns ⑤, ⑥, ⑦, ⑧ and ⑨.
   d) Airports ⑩ and ⑪.
   e) Forest areas ⑫ and ⑬.
   f) The economic activity shown by the pinkish/red squares.

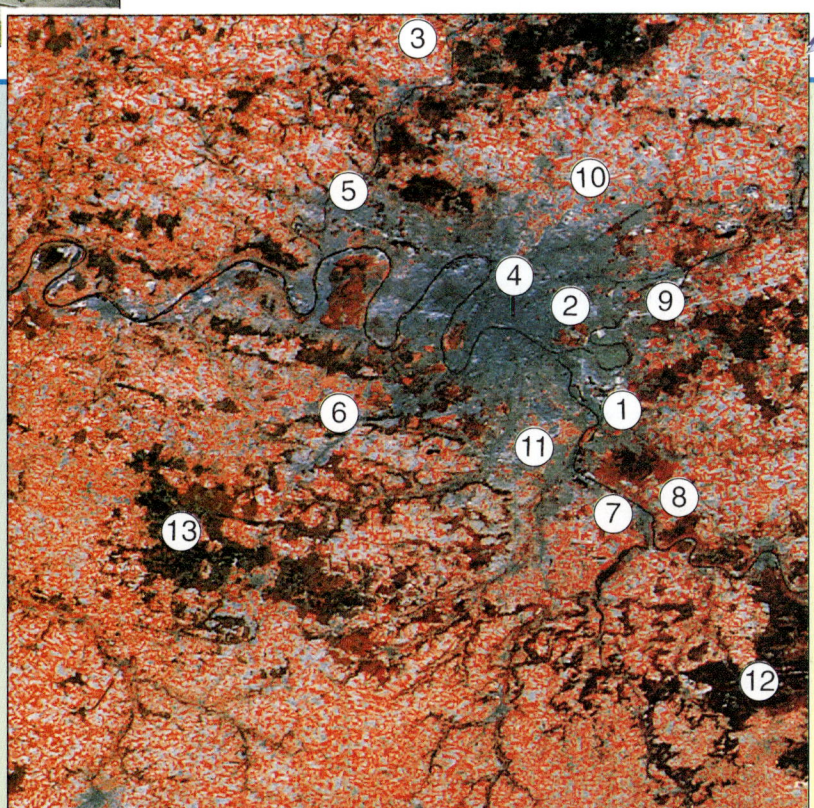

E

Summary

The Ile de France is the richest and most densely populated region in France. Paris and its surrounding towns cover much of the land. Most of the remainder is either left as forest or is used for farming.

▷ *What causes industrial decline?* ◁

The city of Lille lies 300 km north-east of Paris and close to the border with Belgium. It is the fourth largest urban area in France and is at the centre of one of the country's most important industrial regions. Like most industrial areas, the Lille region has seen many changes over the years. For a time at the end of the nineteenth century it was one of Europe's most successful regions. Gradually, however, in the first half of the twentieth century, the region slipped into decline as resources ran out, industries closed and unemployment became increasingly common. Since the 1960s determined efforts have been made to encourage industrial growth and improve the region's economy. This cycle of growth, decline and regrowth is typical of many older industrial communities and causes many problems for planners and residents alike.

Early growth

The Lille region's early success was based on mining the local reserves of coal and iron ore. Later, with the help of a good transport network and a large labour force, the area developed into a major manufacturing region. Engineering industries were the first to arrive. They grew up close to the coal and iron reserves in the south-east of the region. These were followed by factories making textiles and using coal to power the machinery. The textile industry was centred in and around Lille itself and based on the traditional crafts of the area. By 1900 a large number of other industries had developed and the Lille region had become one of the most densely populated and prosperous in the whole of France.

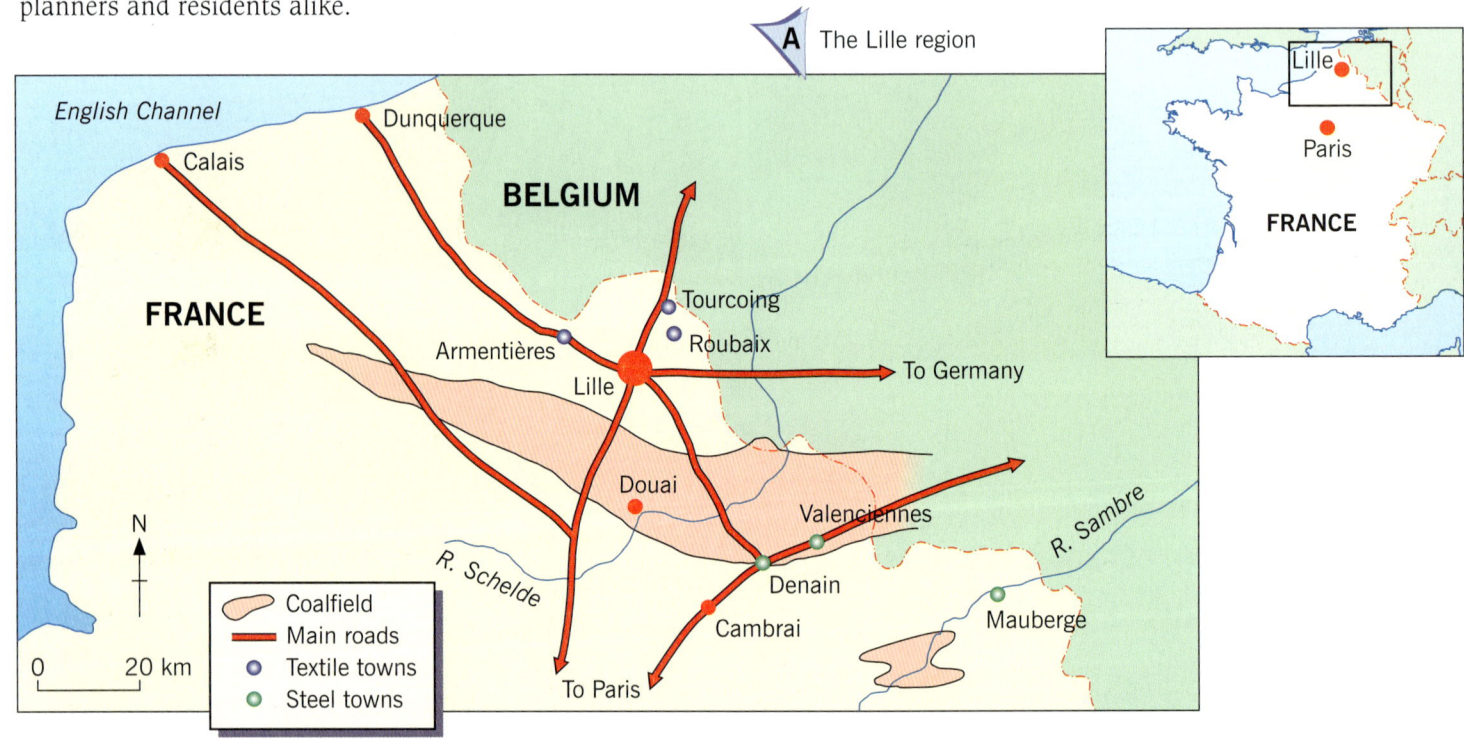

A The Lille region

Activities

1 **a)** Make a larger copy of the flow diagram **C**.
  b) Complete the diagram by adding the information in the list to the correct boxes.

- Near to a large coalfield
- Iron and steel works
- Many jobs available
- Local deposits of iron ore
- Large labour force
- Increase in population
- Coal and iron ore mining
- Engineering industries
- Textile factories
- Good transport network
- Greater prosperity

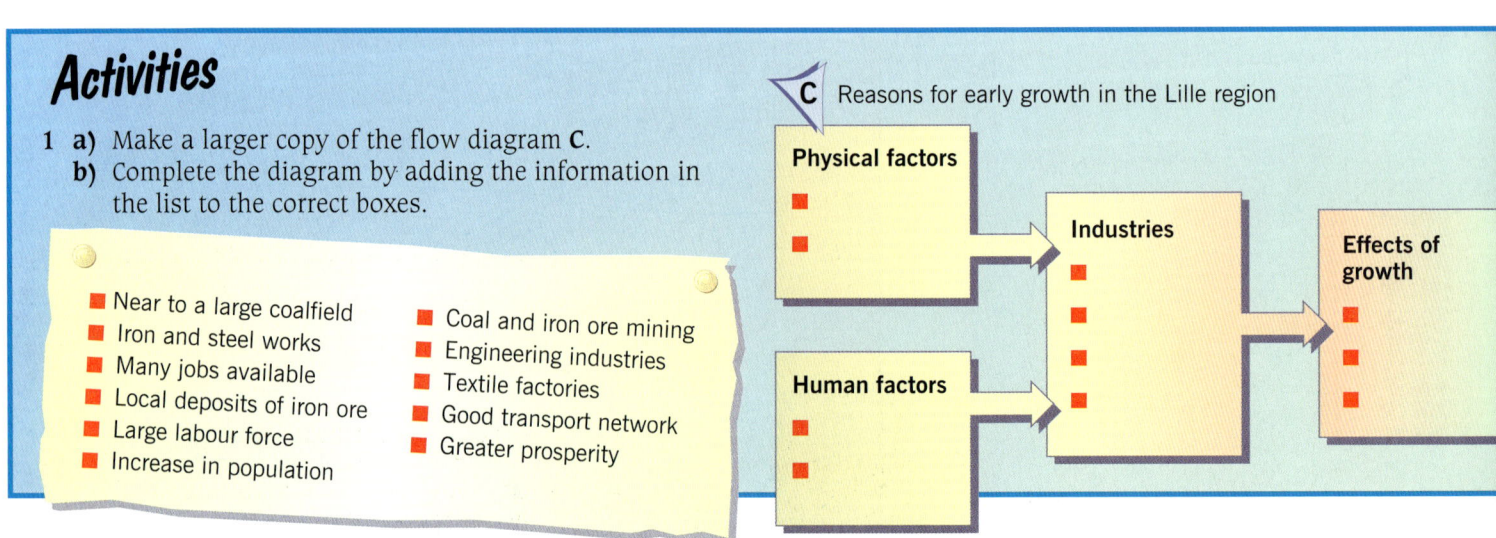

C Reasons for early growth in the Lille region

Later decline

In 1939, with coal production at a peak and manufacturing industries competing well in world markets, the Lille region was a success story. By 1950, however, the picture had changed dramatically with the rapid decline of traditional industries. All around the region were disused coalmines, old buildings and derelict factories. With that came unemployment and a deterioration in living standards. Some of the reasons for this decline are shown in diagram **B**.

B

Going down	Dropping off	Moving out

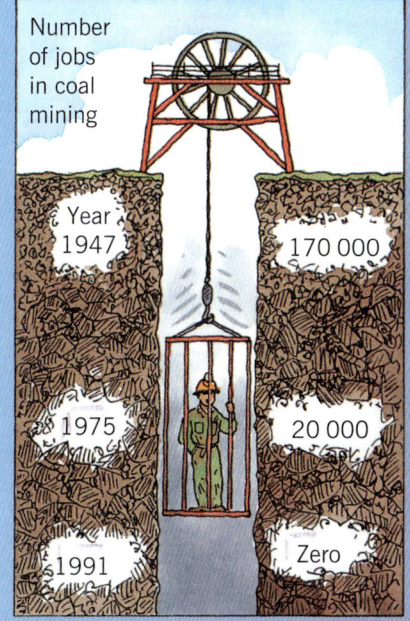

Going down
- Coal reserves running out
- High labour costs
- Steelworks closures reduce market for coal
- Nuclear energy replaces coal power
- Outdated methods increase production costs
- Cheaper imported coal available

Dropping off
- Lack of money for modernisation
- Inefficient methods raise production costs
- Cheaper steel produced abroad
- Local coal and iron ore in short supply
- Steelworks move to better sites on the coast

Moving out
- High labour costs make pricing uncompetitive
- South and East Asia produce cheaper goods
- Lack of funding for new machinery and factories
- Loss of market to newly industrialised countries

2 **a)** Make a larger copy of table **D**.
   b) Complete the table using examples from each industry. Not all the boxes will be filled. Some may have more than one example.

3 Choose one of the industries and write a newspaper article of about 100 words explaining the causes of its decline. Give your article a short, interesting headline.

 D Causes of industrial decline in the Lille region

	Mining	Steelmaking	Textiles
Exhaustion of resources			
Increased costs			
Loss of markets			
Competition			
Lack of investment			

Summary

The Lille region was once one of Europe's most prosperous areas. Industrial decline in the region has largely been due to the running out of resources and uncompetitive production methods.

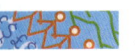

▷ *What helps industrial growth?* ◁

In the late 1960s a plan was produced by the French government to regenerate growth in the Lille region. It was to be financed by a number of agencies including the EC (as it then was) which officially classified the region as 'an area of industrial decline'. By 1997 a total of £28.7 million had been invested in the area, of which the EU had contributed £5.74 million.

Much of the money that poured in was spent on cleaning up the region and making it a more pleasant place in which to live and an attractive location for new industries. Some of the changes already in place are shown in diagram **A**.

The main aim of the plan, however, was to make Europe the foundation for the region's growth and to market Lille as the Eurometropolis and 'crossroads of Europe'. To do this, priority was given to improving its transport links with Paris and other industrial centres throughout Europe, as well as supporting projects with an obvious European emphasis. Some of these are shown in figure **B**.

B

- At the hub of northern Europe's new motorway system.
- The route centre for France's high-speed train, the TGV.
- A stop on the Eurostar network with links to Britain through the Channel Tunnel.
- Euroteleport: a collection and distribution point for satellite information, telecommunications data and cable TV throughout Europe.
- The Eurolille complex: modern offices, accommodation, shopping and the Eurostar/TGV interchange station providing access to markets all over Europe.

 **A** Regeneration of the Lille region

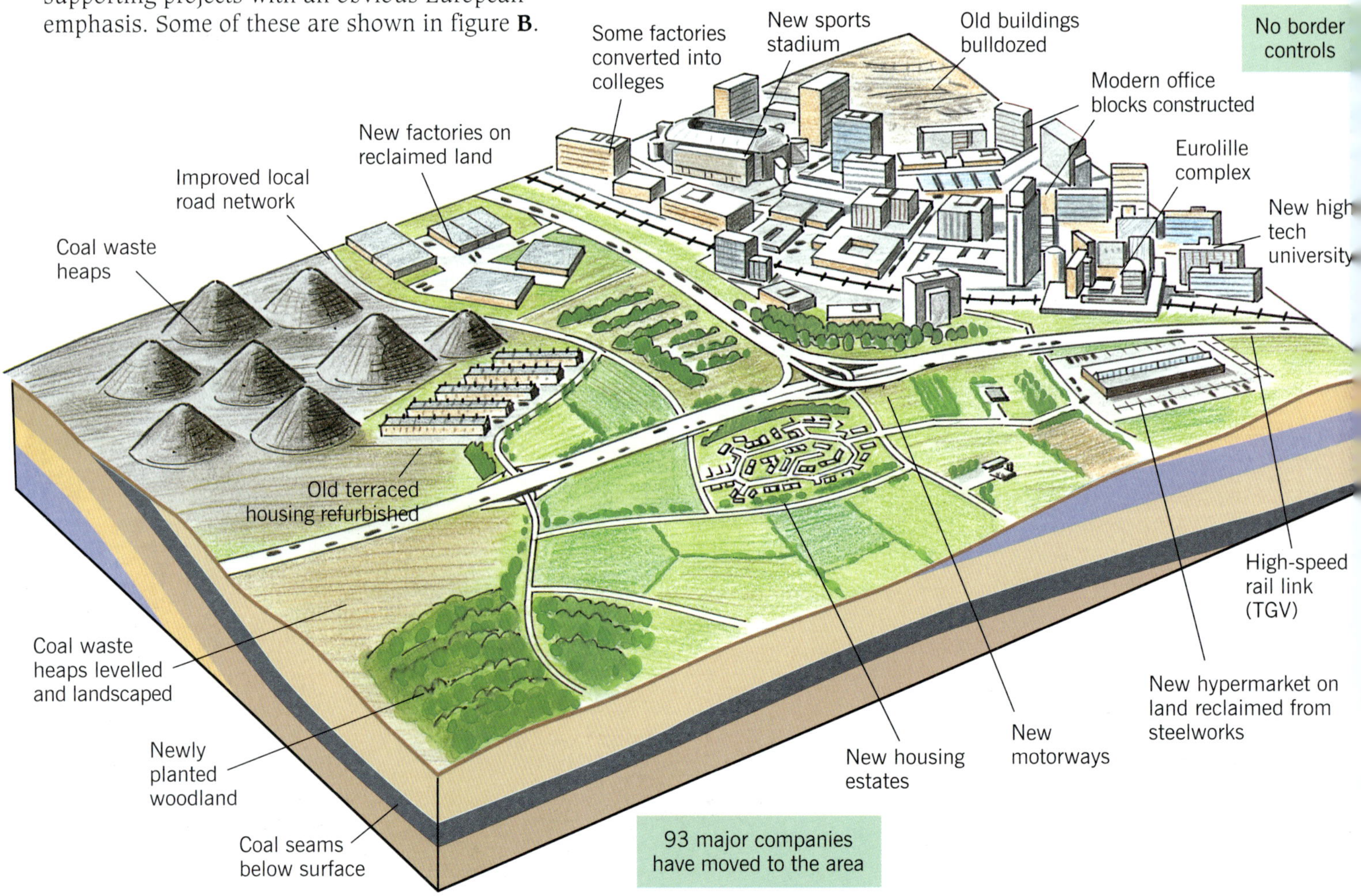

No border controls

Some factories converted into colleges
New sports stadium
Old buildings bulldozed
Modern office blocks constructed
Eurolille complex
New high tech university
New factories on reclaimed land
Improved local road network
Coal waste heaps
Old terraced housing refurbished
Coal waste heaps levelled and landscaped
Newly planted woodland
Coal seams below surface
New housing estates
New motorways
New hypermarket on land reclaimed from steelworks
High-speed rail link (TGV)

93 major companies have moved to the area

C Eurostar

The Lille region now has many advantages for industrial growth. There is a large and skilful workforce available, there are new factories and offices ready for immediate occupation, financial support is available to new firms, and the region has become the centre point of Europe's rapidly developing transport system. As well as this, there is new housing, a pleasant working environment and a liveliness to the region that makes it attractive to local people and newcomers alike.

There are still problems, however. Unemployment is above the national average, many areas are still in need of redevelopment, and the recent migration of Africans into the region has caused a degree of social unrest. Nevertheless, whilst recovery may not yet be complete, the area has made great progress to becoming a boom region again after so many years of decline.

D Europe's high-speed rail routes (times from Lille)

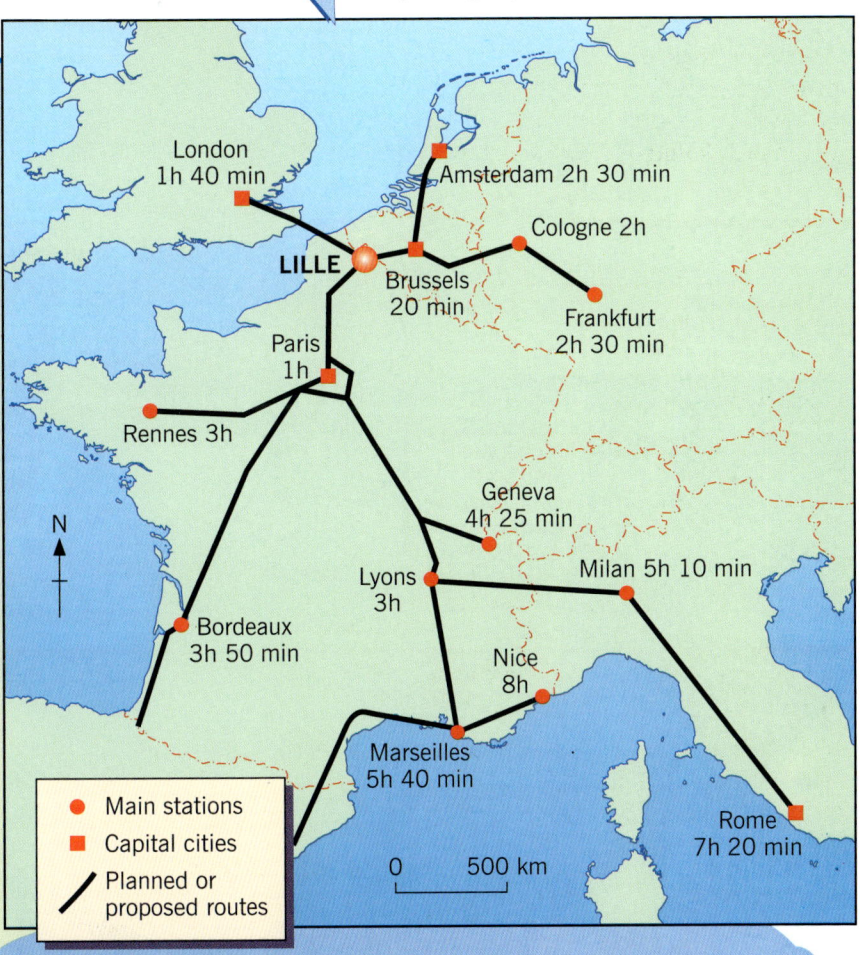

London 1h 40 min
Amsterdam 2h 30 min
Cologne 2h
LILLE
Brussels 20 min
Frankfurt 2h 30 min
Paris 1h
Rennes 3h
Geneva 4h 25 min
Lyons 3h
Milan 5h 10 min
Bordeaux 3h 50 min
Nice 8h
Marseilles 5h 40 min
Rome 7h 20 min

N

● Main stations
■ Capital cities
╱ Planned or proposed routes

0   500 km

Activities

1 From information in figure **B**, describe how, in terms of transport and communications, Lille has become the 'crossroads of Europe'.

2 Study diagram **A**. List the changes that have happened in the Lille region under the headings given below.

Transport	Factories and offices	Education	Leisure and environment

3 Look at map **D**.
   a) Name the European capitals that may be reached from Lille by high-speed train.
   b) Which cities are within three hours' travelling time of Lille?
   c) How many countries are on the high-speed rail network?

4 Draw a star diagram to show at least six advantages of the Lille region for industrial growth.

Summary

Recent industrial growth in the Lille region has largely been achieved by improving the environment, developing transport links and establishing the area as a major European centre.

▷ What are the general features of the USA? ◁

Physical features

Most of the USA, together with the state of Alaska, lies on the North American Plate. This plate borders the:

- Pacific Plate at the San Andreas Fault in California – the location of major earthquakes
- Juan de Fuca Plate in the north-west of the country – where Mount St Helen's erupted in 1980
- Pacific Plate off the south coast of Alaska – the location of several active volcanoes, the island arc of the Aleutians, and frequent earthquakes.

Between the high, young fold mountains of the Rockies and the lower, older mountains of the Appalachians lies the huge drainage basin of the Mississippi–Missouri.

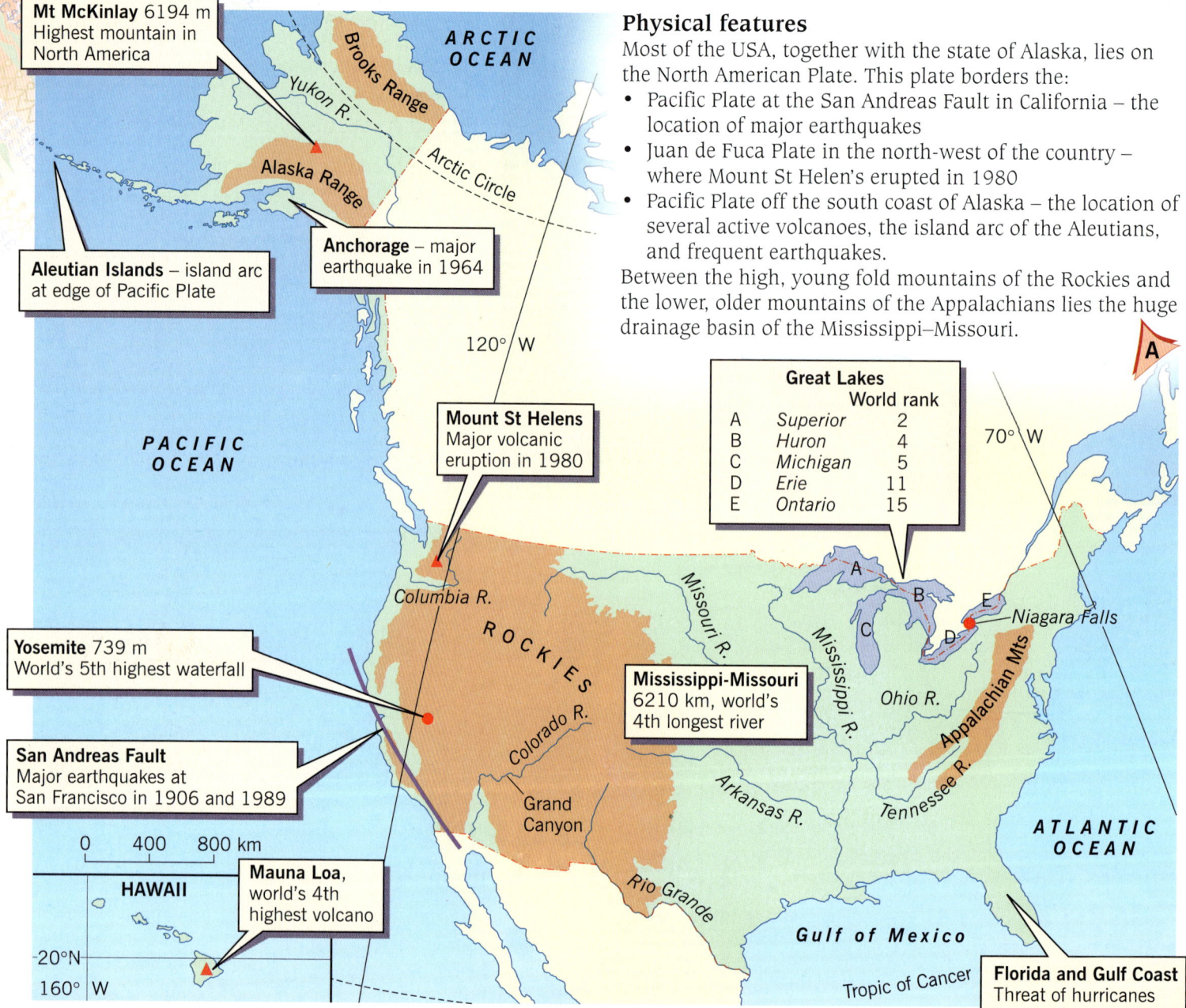

Mt McKinlay 6194 m
Highest mountain in North America

ARCTIC OCEAN

Brooks Range

Yukon R.

Arctic Circle

Alaska Range

Aleutian Islands – island arc at edge of Pacific Plate

Anchorage – major earthquake in 1964

120° W

Mount St Helens
Major volcanic eruption in 1980

70° W

Great Lakes

		World rank
A	Superior	2
B	Huron	4
C	Michigan	5
D	Erie	11
E	Ontario	15

A

PACIFIC OCEAN

Columbia R.

ROCKIES

Missouri R.

Niagara Falls

Yosemite 739 m
World's 5th highest waterfall

Mississippi-Missouri
6210 km, world's 4th longest river

Mississippi R.

Ohio R.

Appalachian Mts

San Andreas Fault
Major earthquakes at San Francisco in 1906 and 1989

Colorado R.

Grand Canyon

Arkansas R.

Tennessee R.

ATLANTIC OCEAN

0   400   800 km

HAWAII

Mauna Loa, world's 4th highest volcano

Rio Grande

Gulf of Mexico

20°N

160° W

Tropic of Cancer

Florida and Gulf Coast
Threat of hurricanes

Activities

1 a) What is the approximate distance across the USA from the west coast to the east coast?
   b) Between which two lines of latitude does most of the USA lie?
   c) Between which two lines of longitude does most of the USA lie?
   d) How is the difference in latitude likely to affect the climate of the USA (remember that Alaska and Hawaii are part of the USA)?

2 This activity is likely to be revision. Find out why:
   a) earthquakes occur in California
   b) Mount St Helen's erupted in 1980
   c) volcanic eruptions and earthquakes occur in Alaska.

3 a) What is meant by the term 'Mississippi–Missouri drainage basin'?
   b) Where is the source of the Missouri?
   c) Name three tributaries of the Mississippi.
   d) What landform is found at the mouth of the Mississippi River?

Human features

Although the USA has the world's third largest population after China and India, it is spread out unevenly across an area that is exceeded in size only by Russia, Canada and China. As a result, the average population density is only 28 persons per km² – a density exceeded by 161 other countries. Almost 80 per cent of this population live in urban areas and there are 36 cities with a population of more than 1 million.

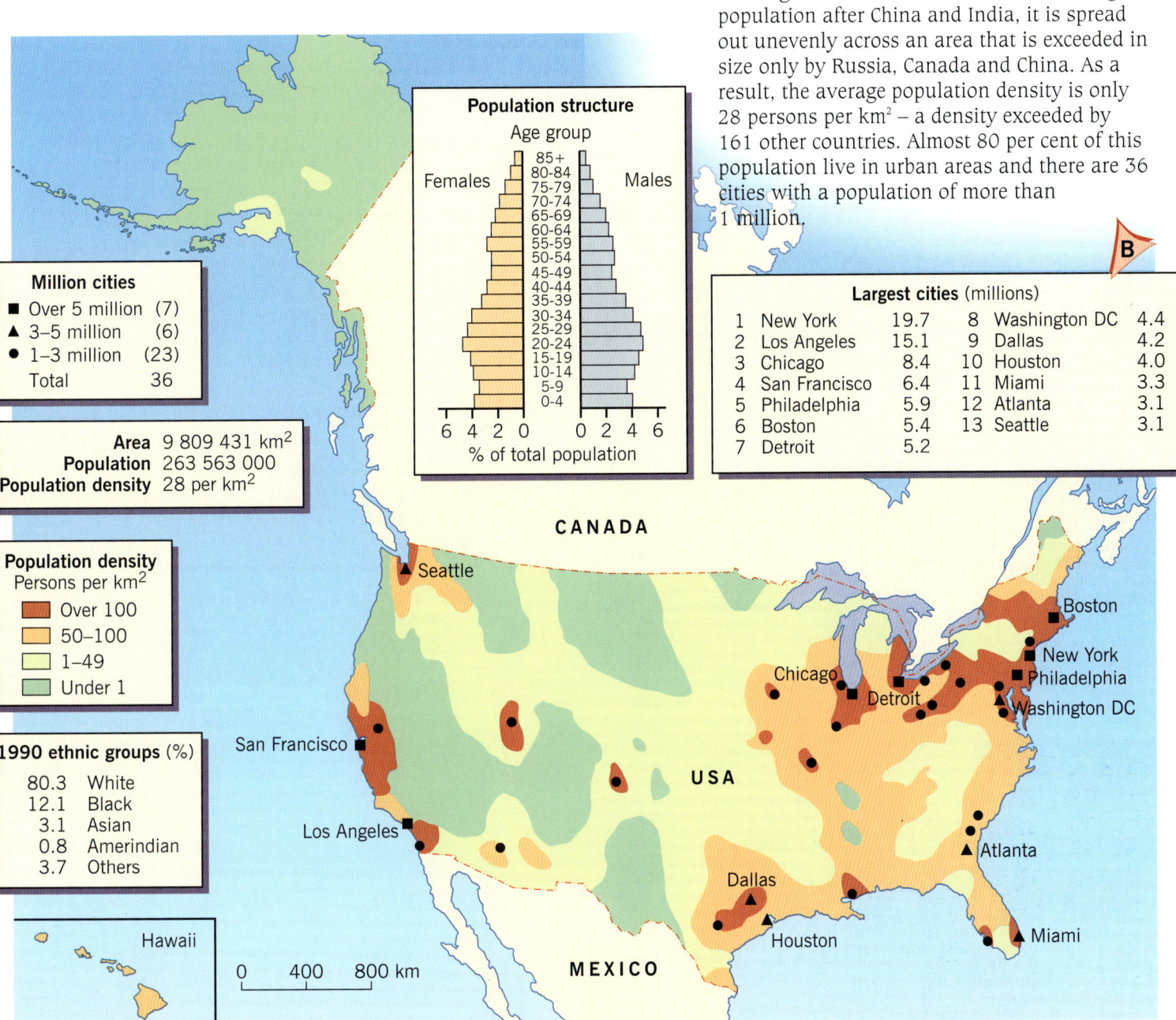

Million cities

- ■ Over 5 million (7)
- ▲ 3–5 million (6)
- ● 1–3 million (23)
- Total 36

Area 9 809 431 km²
Population 263 563 000
Population density 28 per km²

Population density
Persons per km²

- Over 100
- 50–100
- 1–49
- Under 1

1990 ethnic groups (%)

80.3	White
12.1	Black
3.1	Asian
0.8	Amerindian
3.7	Others

Population structure
Age group
Females — Males

85+, 80-84, 75-79, 70-74, 65-69, 60-64, 55-59, 50-54, 45-49, 40-44, 35-39, 30-34, 25-29, 20-24, 15-19, 10-14, 5-9, 0-4

6 4 2 0   0 2 4 6
% of total population

Largest cities (millions)

1	New York	19.7	8	Washington DC	4.4
2	Los Angeles	15.1	9	Dallas	4.2
3	Chicago	8.4	10	Houston	4.0
4	San Francisco	6.4	11	Miami	3.3
5	Philadelphia	5.9	12	Atlanta	3.1
6	Boston	5.4	13	Seattle	3.1
7	Detroit	5.2			

0 400 800 km

B

Activities

1. **a)** What is meant by the term 'population density'?
   b) Name two areas in the USA that have a high population density.
   c) Name two areas in the USA that have a low (sparse) population density.
   d) What is meant by the term 'million city'?
   e) How many million cities are there in the USA?

2. This activity is likely to be revision. Find out why:
   a) the two areas that you named in **1b)** have a high population density
   b) the two areas that you named in **1c)** have a low population density.

3. What evidence does the population structure graph on map **B** give about the USA's:
   a) birth rate, death rate and life expectancy
   b) natural increase (growth rate in population)?

▶ What are the USA's sources of energy? ◀

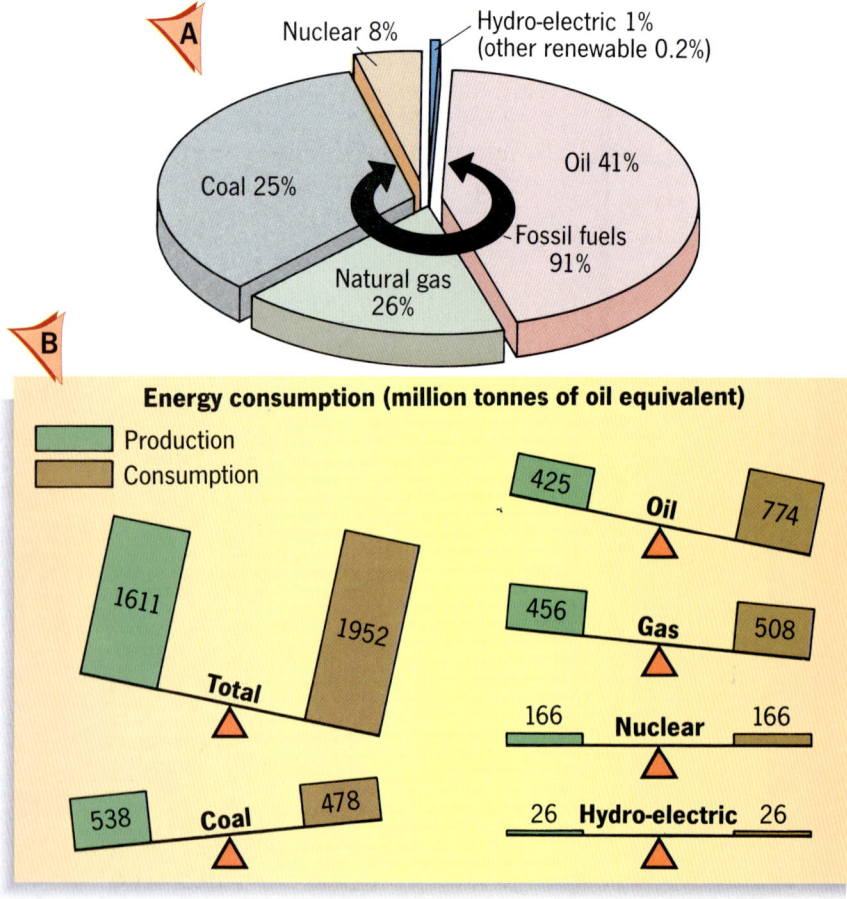

A

Nuclear 8%
Hydro-electric 1%
(other renewable 0.2%)
Oil 41%
Fossil fuels 91%
Coal 25%
Natural gas 26%

B

Energy consumption (million tonnes of oil equivalent)

Production
Consumption

1611 — Total — 1952

538 — Coal — 478

425 — Oil — 774

456 — Gas — 508

166 — Nuclear — 166

26 — Hydro-electric — 26

The USA is the world's largest consumer of energy (24.6 per cent of the world's total). In 1990 each American used the same amount of energy as 2 people living in the EU, 10 people in South America, 13 people in Asia and 25 people in Africa. Fortunately for the USA, it has large and varied energy resources. It also had the capital and technology to develop these resources. In 1990 it was, after Russia, the world's largest producer of energy (19.4 per cent of the world's total). The USA has used its own energy resources, as well as those of other countries, to develop industry and to reach a high standard of living.

Coal, oil and natural gas provide over 90 per cent of the USA's total energy requirements (graph **A**). A large proportion of these fuels are used to generate electricity. They are fossil fuels which, once burnt, cannot be used again. Most of the remainder of the country's energy requirements are provided by nuclear power. Nuclear power uses uranium which, although not a fossil fuel, is also a non-renewable resource. The USA also has a wide range of renewable resources which include hydro-electric, geothermal, wind, wave and solar power. However, these have only been developed in local areas and, with the exception of hydro-electricity, do not yet make any major contribution to the national power supply.

Non-renewable sources of energy (map C)

Coal, which provided 85 per cent of the USA's energy needs in 1900, still supplied 25 per cent in 1992. The oldest coalmining areas lie in the Appalachian Mountains and to the south of the Great Lakes. Since the 1970s coalfields have been developed near to the Rocky Mountains. Coal in these western states is strip-mined on the surface, by giant excavators. This coal is easier and cheaper to produce and, because it has a lower sulphur content, causes less pollution when burnt. However, this coal has to be transported further to cities, increasing transport costs, and gives off less heat when burnt. The USA produces sufficient coal for considerable amounts to be exported (diagram **B**).

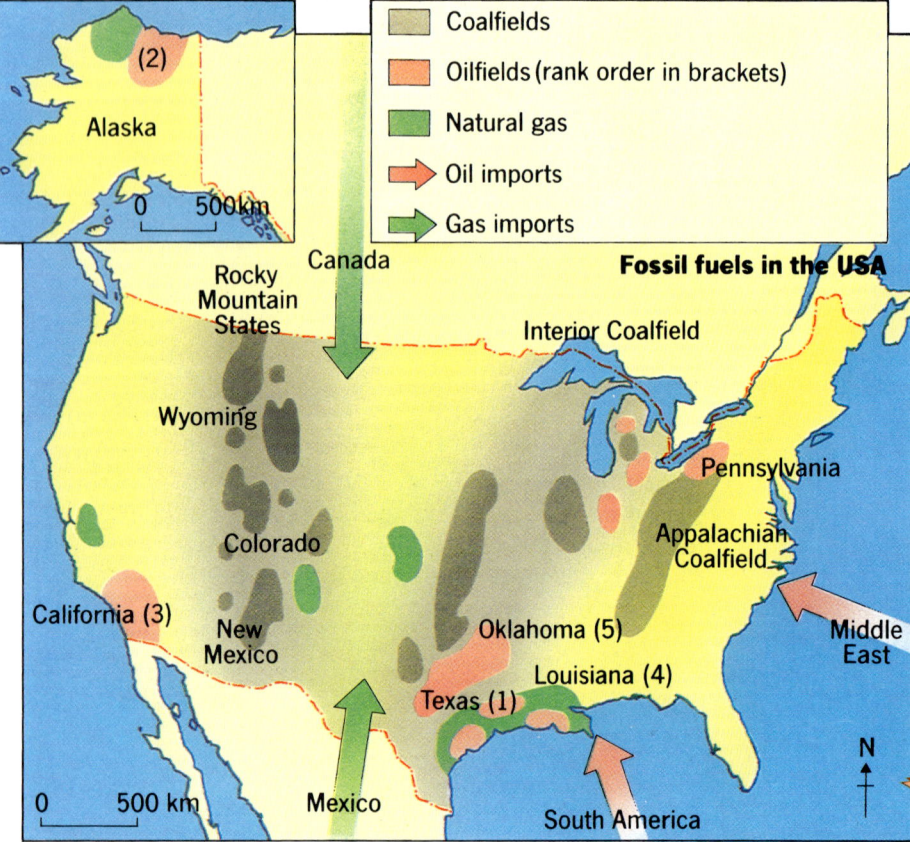

Coalfields
Oilfields (rank order in brackets)
Natural gas
Oil imports
Gas imports

Fossil fuels in the USA

Alaska (2)
0 — 500km

Canada
Rocky Mountain States
Interior Coalfield
Wyoming
Pennsylvania
Colorado
Appalachian Coalfield
California (3)
New Mexico
Oklahoma (5)
Middle East
Louisiana (4)
Texas (1)
Mexico
South America
0 — 500 km

N

C Fossil fuels in the USA

Oil is the USA's most important source of energy. Although the USA is the world's second largest producer of crude oil, it consumes far more than it produces (diagram **B**). The gap has to be filled by importing oil from the Middle East (a major reason for America's involvement in the Gulf War) and South America. Although the USA has large oilfields in Texas, southern California and Alaska, reserves are dwindling. Attempts have been made, since the mid-1970s, to reduce the dependency upon oil in order to conserve the country's remaining reserves and to reduce the cost of oil imports.

Natural gas is an increasingly popular source of energy as it is clean, efficient and easy to move by pipeline. Like oil, the USA consumes more natural gas than it produces and pipelines have been built to import gas from Mexico and Canada. The USA hopes to develop new gasfields off Alaska and in the Gulf of Mexico.

During the 1970s, nuclear power was regarded as the solution to the USA's energy problem. By 1993 nearly 120 nuclear power stations were operating, mainly along the Atlantic coast and in California. However, since the accident which caused the closure of the Three Mile Island power station in 1979, and following earthquakes in California, opposition to this form of energy has grown considerably.

Renewable sources of energy (map D)

Hydro-electricity is the only form of renewable energy that has been developed in the USA. Even so, it is largely limited to the Tennessee, Colorado, Columbia and St Lawrence Rivers. Many parts of the USA either have insufficient water or are too distant from urban and industrial centres. Large wind farms are being developed in California and solar power is being used in the sunnier south-west of the country. There appears to be a potential to develop geothermal power in California and wave power off several coasts.

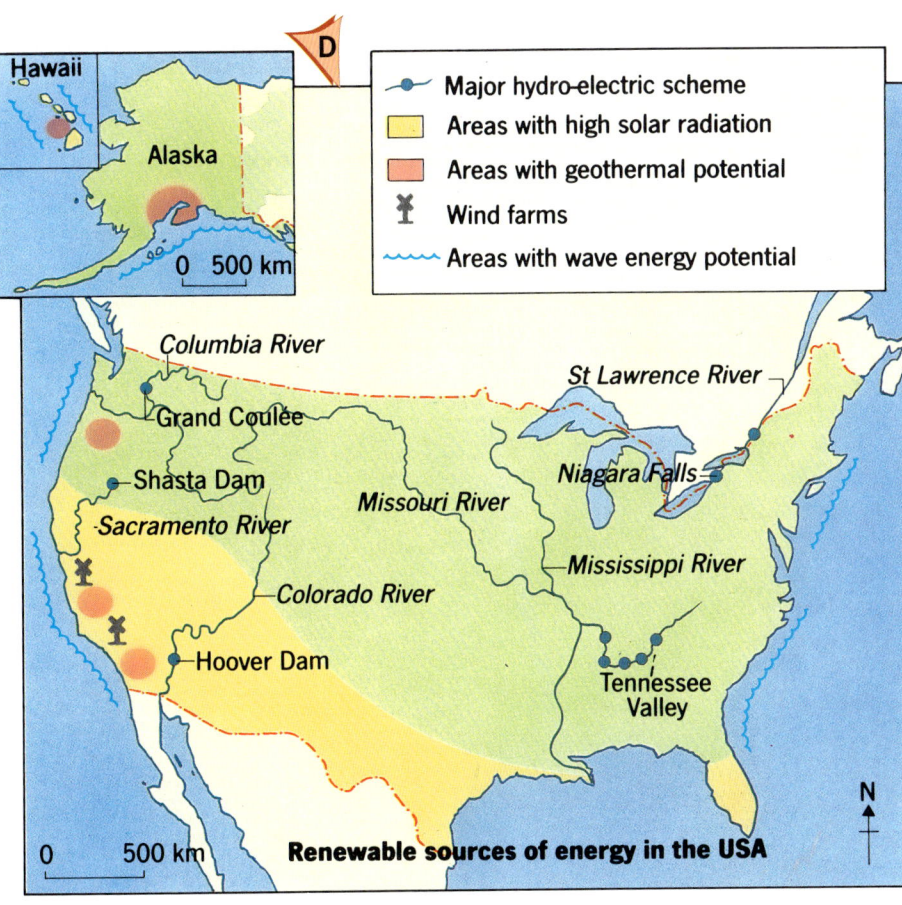

D

- ●— Major hydro-electric scheme
- ▨ Areas with high solar radiation
- ▨ Areas with geothermal potential
- ⅄ Wind farms
- ∿ Areas with wave energy potential

Hawaii

Alaska

0   500 km

Columbia River
Grand Coulee
Shasta Dam
Sacramento River
Missouri River
St Lawrence River
Niagara Falls
Colorado River
Mississippi River
Hoover Dam
Tennessee Valley

0   500 km   **Renewable sources of energy in the USA**

N

Summary

The USA is the world's second largest producer of energy and its largest consumer. Over 90 per cent of the country's energy requirements come from fossil fuels. As consumption exceeds production then significant amounts of oil and natural gas have to be imported.

Activities

1 Draw a percentage bar chart to show the types of energy used in the USA.

2 Make a larger copy of table **E**. Complete it by using the following instructions.
   a) List the five types of energy used by the USA. Put them in rank order, the highest first.
   b) For each type of energy say if it is renewable, a fossil fuel, or neither.
   c) Name places in the USA where each type of energy can be found.
   d) Name countries (if any) from which the USA has to import some of this type of energy.

3 a) Why does the USA rely upon fossil fuels for most of this energy?
   b) What types of renewable energy are available to the USA?
   c) Why do renewable sources only contribute 1 per cent of the USA's total energy production?

E

Types of energy (rank order)	Renewable energy, fossil fuel or neither	Location in the USA	Countries from which energy is obtained

➤ *Where did early industry locate in the USA?* ◀

Early industries in the USA located in the north-east of the country. The main areas were New England and a region extending from the Great Lakes to the Atlantic coast (map **A**). In 1900 this part of the USA had over 70 per cent of manufacturing jobs and was referred to as the **manufacturing belt**. Industries, such as iron and steel, heavy engineering and car assembly, located here for these reasons.

A

Industrial areas in the USA

- Many immigrants from Europe arrived and settled here. They brought with them industrial and business skills.
- The rapid growth in population, due to natural increase and immigration, led to both a large local market and a large supply of labour (workforce). In time the labour supply became increasingly skilled, especially in industries such as car manufacturing.
- The area was rich in raw materials such as coal and iron ore which gave rise to a large iron and steel industry (map **B**).
- Sources of energy were available. Fast-flowing rivers were initially used to turn waterwheels in New England. In the manufacturing belt coal and, later, oil were available locally.
- Transport developed along rivers or on the Great Lakes. The Atlantic coast faced Europe with which the region established trade links. Water transport has always been the cheapest method of moving bulky goods.
- The wealth generated by selling goods overseas enabled the region to invest in new technology and to produce a wider range of products at competitive prices.

Over a period of time the ideal site for the location of steelworks changed (map **B**).

B The development of the iron and steel industry

Key
- Iron ore field
- Coalfield
- Limestone
- Major steel area
- ┼┼┼ Movement of iron ore and coal on land
- ← Movement of iron ore by ship
- ← Movement of coal by ship
- ── Canal

Lake Superior

Mesabi

Duluth

Marquette

CANADA

St Lawrence Seaway

Iron ore from Labrador (Canada)

Lake Ontario

Lake Huron

Buffalo

USA

Lake Michigan

Detroit

Lake Erie

New York

Chicago

Gary

Toledo

Cleveland

Youngstown

Pittsburgh

Sparrows Point

Iron ore from Canada

Interior coalfield (Illinois)

Pennsylvania coalfield

West Virginia coalfield

Iron ore from Venezuela and Brazil

N

0   km   300

① The first iron and steel works were located on coalfields: Pittsburgh, Youngstown. Rivers and lakes were used to transport iron ore and coal.

② Duluth exported iron ore and received coal in the returning ships. Great Lakes are ideal for transport of heavy materials in bulk.

③ 'Break of bulk' ports developed on lakesides. Coal and iron ore had to change transport, so logical to build steelworks at places like Chicago, Gary, Detroit, Cleveland, Buffalo.

④ US iron ore supplies ran short. Iron ore imported from Canada and South America. Steelworks built on tidal, coastal sites (e.g. Sparrows Point).

Detroit – the centre for car production

Detroit was near to local steelworks and the many smaller factories which produced the component parts needed for car assembly. It also had easy access to energy supplies. Nearby was a large labour force, both skilled and unskilled. In time the industry became increasingly mechanised, although this meant repetitive work. Car companies expected high productivity and standards for the wages paid. Detroit was centrally placed for the assembly of car parts and the sale of vehicles. It was also in a good position to export surplus cars to overseas markets. There was plenty of space on which to build the large car factories and room for later expansion (photo **D**). Even so, Detroit became the centre for cars partly due to a chance, because Henry Ford just happened to live there.

Since the 1970s, many of the major industries in the manufacturing belt have declined. This has partly been due to a fall in demand for such products as iron and steel, heavy engineering and motor vehicles and partly because modern factories have been located in places with a more attractive environment and climate (the Sunbelt – page 86). As factories have closed and people have migrated away from the region, the manufacturing belt has been renamed the **rustbelt**. In 1990 less than 35 per cent of manufacturing jobs were found in this region.

C Steelworks at Baltimore – coastal location

D General Motors Hamtramck Assembly Plant, Detroit

Activities

1 a) Where was the so-called 'manufacturing belt' in the USA?
  b) Draw a star diagram to show six advantages for early industry locating in the manufacturing belt.
  c) How important were sources of energy in the growth of industry in the manufacturing belt?

2 a) The ideal locations for iron and steel works in the manufacturing belt have changed over a period of time. Explain why each of the places named in diagram **E** became important for the production of iron and steel.
  b) What advantages did Detroit have which enabled it to become the world's leading producer of cars?

Pittsburgh → Duluth → Cleveland → Sparrows Point **E**

Summary

Sources of energy were only one reason why industries such as iron and steel, heavy engineering and car assembly became important in the manufacturing belt of the USA.

Why has modern industry changed location in the USA?

Many modern industries are said to be **footloose**. The term 'footloose' means that, unlike older industries, firms have a relatively free choice of where to locate and are not tied to being near to raw materials. As many of these newer industries provide services for people, they are best located near to large markets where people are likely to buy, or use, the products. Usually both the component parts and the finished product are light in weight and so they can easily be transported by road and air. Americans, with their high standard of living, increasingly want to live and work in a more pleasant environment. A pleasant environment includes plenty of open space, attractive scenery, leisure amenities, modern services and an agreeable climate. The result has been that, since the 1970s, firms and people have been moving away from the manufacturing/rustbelt to the **sunbelt** (table **A**).

The term 'sunbelt' was originally applied to five states in the south-west of the USA where population and economic growth rates were far in excess of the national averages (map **B**). The rapid growth of high-technology (sunrise)

industries and their good job opportunities attracted many younger people from the depressed industrial (sunset) areas of the north and east. The term 'sunbelt' is now often applied more widely to include all states in the south and south-east of the country.

A

Seven fastest-growing states 1980–92		Seven slowest-growing states 1980–92	
(percentage growth of population)			
Nevada	+66.9	West Virginia	–7.2
Alaska	+46.3	Iowa	–3.8
Arizona	+41.1	North Dakota	–2.9
Florida	+38.3	Wyoming	–1.0
California	+30.5	Pennsylvania	+1.1
Texas	+24.3	Illinois	+1.6
Georgia	+24.0	Michigan	+1.7

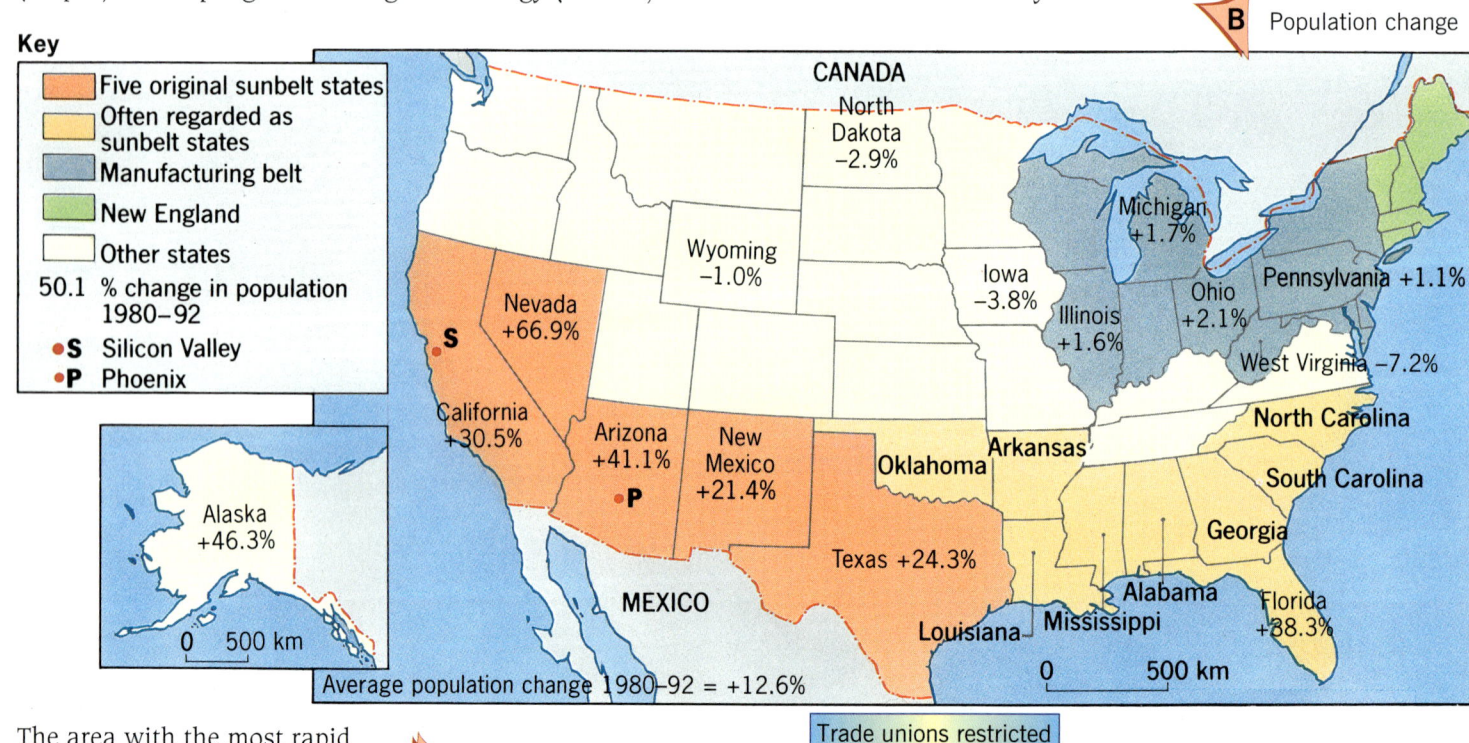

B Population change

Key
- Five original sunbelt states
- Often regarded as sunbelt states
- Manufacturing belt
- New England
- Other states
- 50.1 % change in population 1980–92
- ●S Silicon Valley
- ●P Phoenix

Average population change 1980–92 = +12.6%

C Advantages of the sunbelt
- Trade unions restricted
- Sunbelt states impose low taxes
- Plenty of cheap land available
- Good road and air links with the rest of the USA and the world
- Climate – under 200 mm rain, plenty of sunshine
- Plenty of modern services (new shops, schools, hospitals) and leisure amenities
- Attractive scenery throughout the region – mountains, Californian coast, Grand Canyon
- Investment from overseas
- Skilled labour from the north. Unskilled labour from Mexico.
- Lower wages

The area with the most rapid population increase has been Phoenix in Arizona. Here the population increased by 55 per cent between 1970 and 1980 and by 54 per cent between 1980 and 1992. The attractions of Phoenix for both industry and people are given in diagram **C**.

The greatest concentration of high-technology industry in the USA is Silicon Valley to the south of San Francisco in California (map **D** and photo **E**). The area produces over 25 per cent of America's microelectronics, computers, and scientific instruments. As elsewhere in California, Silicon Valley has many firms connected with the aerospace and defence industries.

Why does high-technology industry locate in Silicon Valley?

◆ Near to major road systems (internal transport) and airports (international trade).
◆ Plenty of space for development and future expansion.
◆ Near to large cities (markets and a skilled workforce) yet far enough away for land values to be lower than in urban areas.
◆ Near to universities which include some of the most advanced scientific and technological centres in the world.
◆ Clean and quiet industries do not pollute an attractive environment and a pleasant climate.

Two factors could slow down the movement of people and industry to the sunbelt. The first is the problem of water supply. Many parts of the region have a desert climate with little, or unreliable, rainfall. Already many places rely upon water being piped vast distances. The second is the uncertain future of the aerospace (high costs) and defence (reduced military spending) industries.

D

To Sacramento   0   20 km

N

Golden Gate Bridge
Bay Bridge
Oakland
San Francisco
Coast Range
San Francisco Bay
Highway 5

Key
— Highways
✈ Airports
▢ Urban area
- - - San Andreas Fault

Santa Cruz Mountains
Redwood City
Silicon Valley
Palo Alto
To Los Angeles
Highway 280

E

Silicon Valley

Activities

1 a) Make a larger copy of map **F**.
  b) Name the original five sunbelt states (labelled **A** to **E**).
  c) Name, with the help of an atlas, the six cities (numbered **1** to **6**).
  d) Name the two sea areas (labelled **X** and **Y**).

2 You are the managing director of a small, but expanding, computer firm in Pennsylvania. Make a list of reasons why you decide:
  a) not to expand your factory in Pennsylvania
  b) to have a new factory built in one of the sunbelt states.

• City (1)
State (A)

B
1
A
3
2
C
4
D
5
E
6
X
Y

F

Summary

Many firms and people have left the old manufacturing belt of the USA and moved south-westwards into the sunbelt. Firms have moved as new footloose high-technology industry is no longer tied to raw materials. People have moved as they prefer to live and work in a more pleasant environment.

How has industry affected the environment of the USA?

As the USA developed its industries it gave little thought as to how this would affect the environment. By the 1970s water supplies and the air had become severely polluted. This began to cause serious health problems for people and was posing a threat to the existence of wildlife. The worst affected areas were around the Great Lakes and in the manufacturing belt. These places had high population densities, many large industries and thermal power stations and an increasing number of cars.

Water pollution

Figure **A** is an extract describing conditions around the southern shores of Lake Erie 30 years ago. It was estimated that the pollution was caused by over 1000 chemicals being released into, or finding their way to, the Great Lakes. These came from steel works (page 84), the petroleum industry, paper mills and car assembly plants. Since then attempts have been made to clean up the Great Lakes and polluted rivers (map **B**). Despite big improvements, the pollution of earlier years cannot be cleaned up overnight. Indeed recent investigations have shown that major breeding problems exist, with a decline in the fertility of fish, mammals, reptiles and birds in the Great Lakes area. The number of alligators in Florida has also declined. It is believed that certain industrial chemicals, together with pesticides, are turning male alligators into females. As water is sometimes taken from rivers and treated before its domestic use, then this may also explain a decrease in human fertility. Map **B** also shows the worst polluted sea areas which surround the USA.

A

n the Great Lakes region of North America, various pollutants have made Lake Erie a 'dead lake'.

One of the nation's most polluted streams, Ohio's Cuyahoga, became so covered with oil and debris that in July 1969 this river caught fire in Cleveland's factory area, damaging two railway bridges. Along this six-mile stretch, before emptying into Lake Erie, the river receives the wastes of steel mills, chemical factories and meat-rendering plants, and other industries. Just upstream, Cleveland and Akron discharge inadequately treated sewage. And from hinterland farms drain phosphate- and nitrate-rich fertilisers and poisonous pesticides.

The Cuyahoga flows into Lake Erie, mixing with effluent from the Detroit River. The flow, rich in nutrients, stimulates growth of algae. As the overfertilised algae die and decompose, oxygen essential to fish life is depleted.

Lake Erie is said to be 'too thick to drink, too thin to plough'.

B

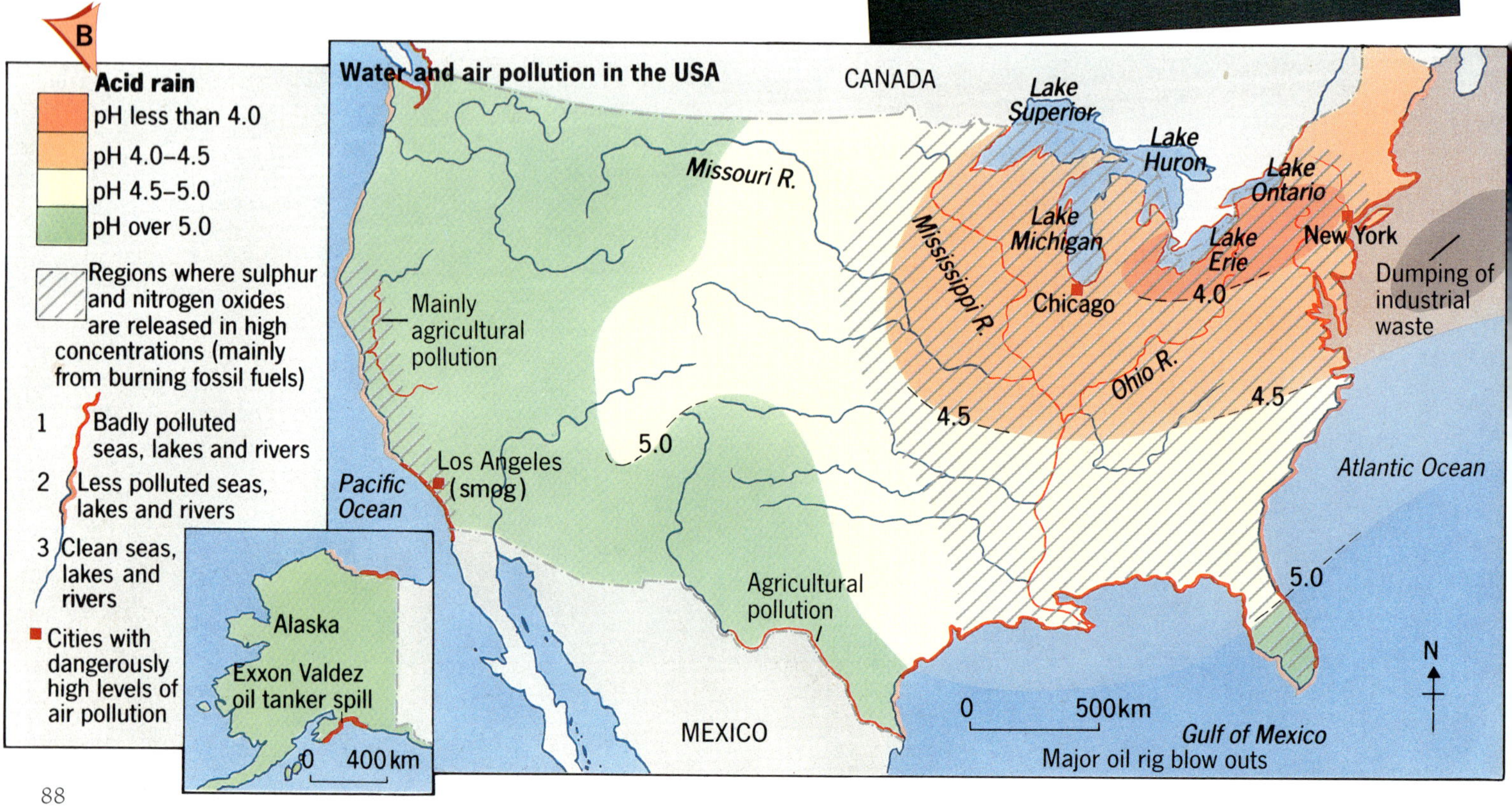

Water and air pollution in the USA

Acid rain
- pH less than 4.0
- pH 4.0–4.5
- pH 4.5–5.0
- pH over 5.0

Regions where sulphur and nitrogen oxides are released in high concentrations (mainly from burning fossil fuels)

1 Badly polluted seas, lakes and rivers

2 Less polluted seas, lakes and rivers

3 Clean seas, lakes and rivers

■ Cities with dangerously high levels of air pollution

CANADA

Lake Superior
Lake Huron
Lake Ontario
Lake Michigan
Lake Erie
New York
Missouri R.
Mississippi R.
Chicago
4.0
Ohio R.
4.5
4.5
Dumping of industrial waste
Atlantic Ocean
5.0
Mainly agricultural pollution
5.0
Los Angeles (smog)
Pacific Ocean
Agricultural pollution
5.0

Alaska
Exxon Valdez oil tanker spill
0   400 km

0   500km

MEXICO

Gulf of Mexico
Major oil rig blow outs

N

Air pollution

The burning of fossil fuels in factories, thermal power stations and by motor vehicles releases sulphur dioxide and nitrogen oxide (photo **C** page 85). It is these pollutants that cause acid rain (page 30). Acid rain destroys forests, kills fish and plant life in lakes, increases acidity in soils and wears away buildings. Most of the pollutants that contribute to acid rain in North America are released in the manufacturing belt of the USA. However, due to the prevailing westerly winds, the greatest effects are felt by places lying to the east (map **B**).

Smog is a second type of air pollution. It is a thick fog which contains pollutants released from the burning of fossil fuels in factories and thermal power stations and from fumes released by car exhausts. In Los Angeles smog can be expected on up to 300 days in a year. Fog forms when warm air from the land meets cold air from the Californian Current (page 25). Fog is worst when the wind blows from the sea in summer (diagram **C** and photo **D**). As the sea is cooler than the land at this time of year, the wind blowing from it is also cold (page 9). The cold air undercuts the warmer air to give a **temperature inversion**. Normally the temperature of the air decreases with height (page 9), but during a time of temperature inversion a layer of warm air lies on top of the cold air. Smog forms because smoke and exhaust fumes cannot rise above the inversion and so become trapped. Smog causes breathing difficulties and makes eyes sting. It can be fatal to people with asthma, bronchitis and other severe breathing problems.

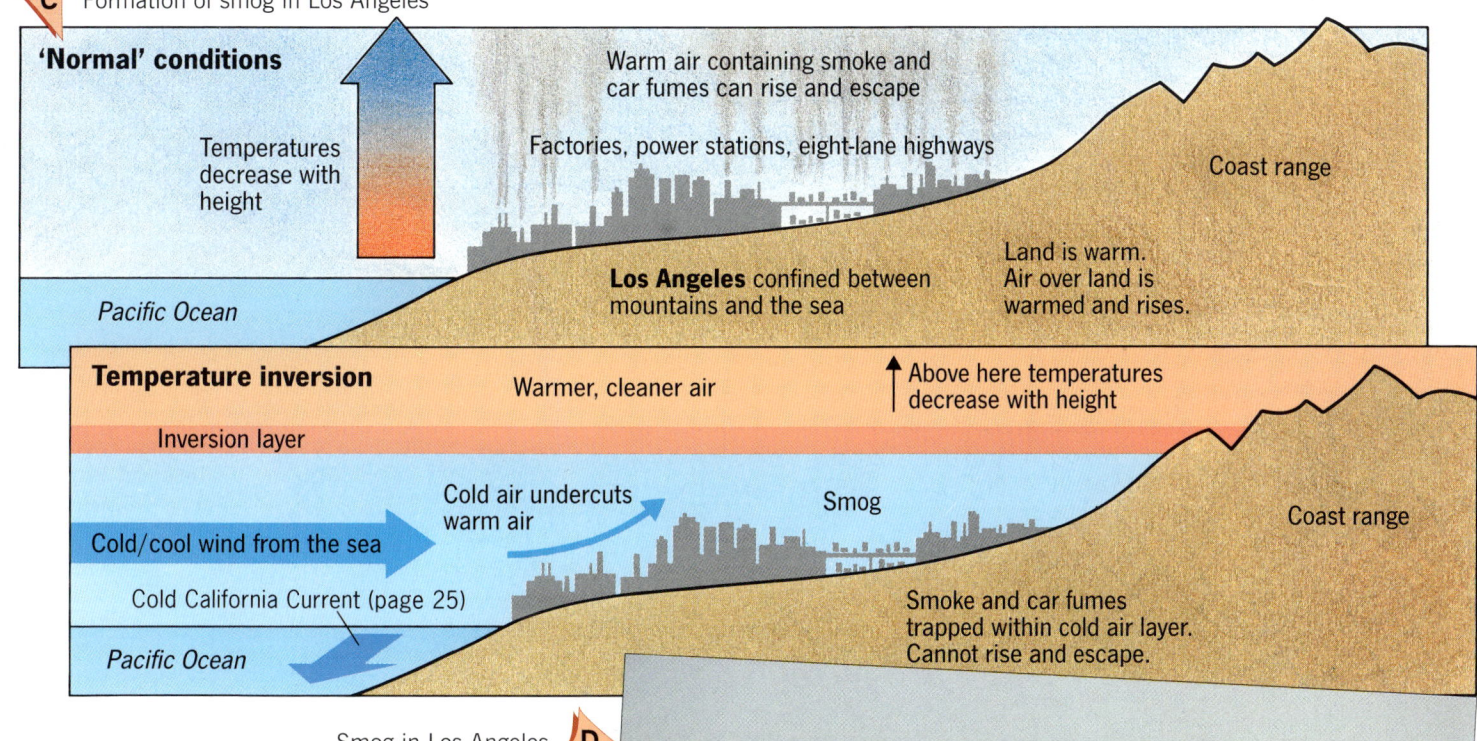

C Formation of smog in Los Angeles

'Normal' conditions

Warm air containing smoke and car fumes can rise and escape

Temperatures decrease with height

Factories, power stations, eight-lane highways

Coast range

Los Angeles confined between mountains and the sea

Land is warm. Air over land is warmed and rises.

Pacific Ocean

Temperature inversion

Warmer, cleaner air

Above here temperatures decrease with height

Inversion layer

Cold air undercuts warm air

Smog

Coast range

Cold/cool wind from the sea

Cold California Current (page 25)

Smoke and car fumes trapped within cold air layer. Cannot rise and escape.

Pacific Ocean

Smog in Los Angeles **D**

Activities

1 a) What were the main causes and effects of pollution in Lake Erie 30 years ago?
   b) What is the latest concern believed to be caused by industrial chemicals being released into lakes and water supplies?

2 a) Which part of the USA is the major contributor to acid rain?
   b) Why are the worst effects of acid rain not always experienced in this part of the USA?
   c) What is smog?
   d) What are the causes and effects of smog in Los Angeles?

Summary The rapid growth of industry caused serious water and air pollution in parts of the USA. The task of cleaning up the environment, which takes a long time and costs a lot of money, is difficult so long as fossil fuels are burnt and the number of cars increases.

▷ Why are there variations in economic prosperity in the USA? ◁

Economic growth is rarely evenly distributed. Growth becomes concentrated in a few favoured locations leaving other places relatively poor and underdeveloped in comparison. This can be seen at different levels – in a city, in a region, in a country and between countries.

Core–periphery model

The most prosperous and developed part of a country is called the **core**. The core is likely to contain the capital city, the chief port and the major industrial areas (diagram **A(a)**). As the core continues to grow and to develop it will attract other industries and services such as banking, insurance and government offices. As levels of capital and technology increase, the region will be able to afford schools, hospitals, shopping centres, a modern transport system and better-quality housing. These 'pull' factors encourage people to migrate from the surrounding rural areas. Often the level of wealth and development decreases with distance from the core so that the poorest areas are towards the **periphery** of the country (diagram **A(a)**). In the periphery jobs will be few in number, poorly paid, relatively unskilled and mainly in the primary sector. Services and government investment are usually limited. These 'push' factors force many people to migrate out of the area.

As a country develops economically, industry and wealth begin to spread out. Initially a second core region will develop (diagram **A(b)**), followed by several secondary core regions (diagram **A(c)**). This results in a decline in the dominance of the original core. Although wealth will now be more evenly spread around the country, there will still be periphery areas which are less well off.

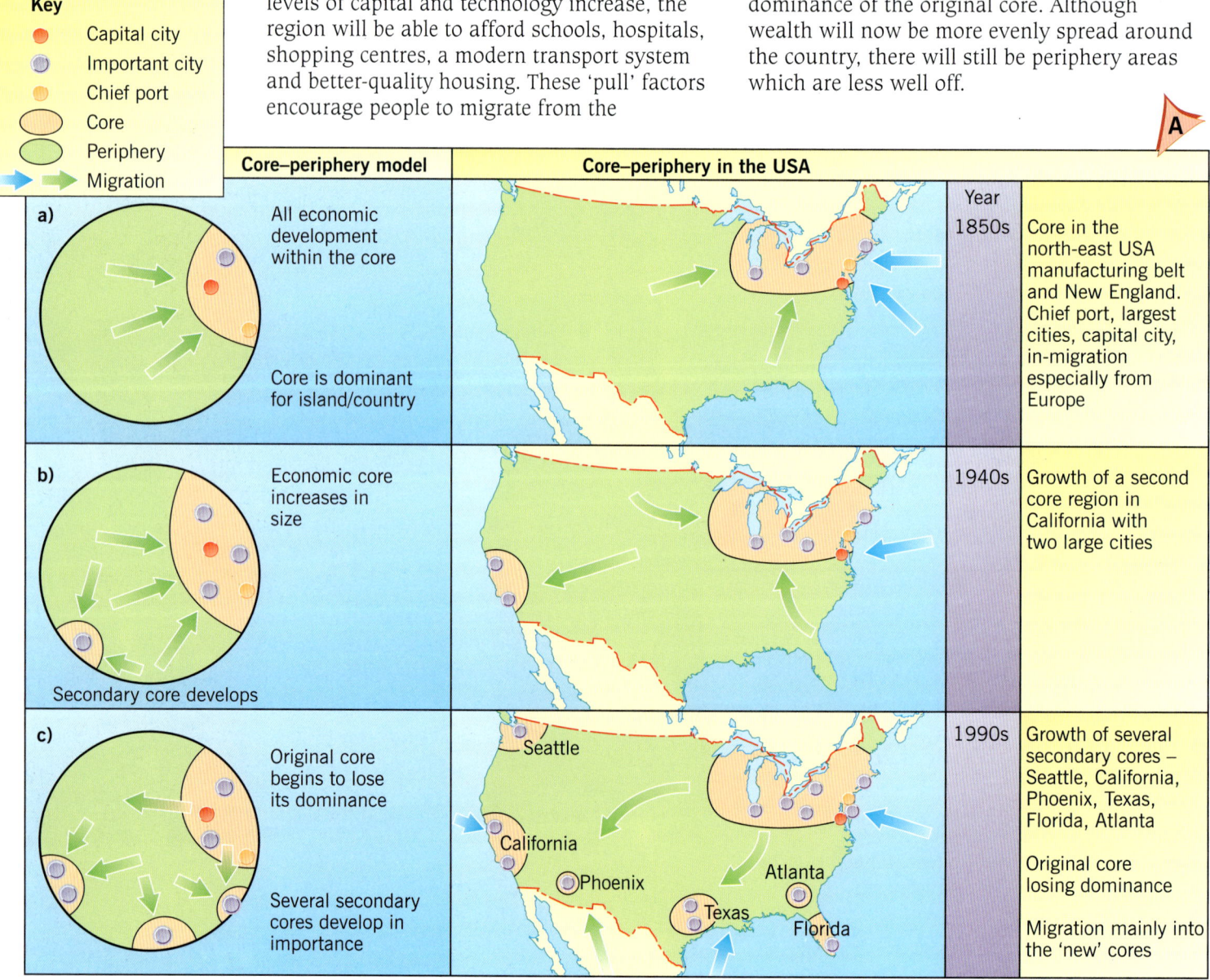

Key
- 🔴 Capital city
- 🔵 Important city
- 🟠 Chief port
- ⬭ Core
- 🟢 Periphery
- ➡ Migration

Core–periphery model		Core–periphery in the USA	Year	
a)	All economic development within the core		1850s	Core in the north-east USA manufacturing belt and New England. Chief port, largest cities, capital city, in-migration especially from Europe
	Core is dominant for island/country			
b)	Economic core increases in size		1940s	Growth of a second core region in California with two large cities
	Secondary core develops			
c)	Original core begins to lose its dominance	Seattle	1990s	Growth of several secondary cores – Seattle, California, Phoenix, Texas, Florida, Atlanta
	Several secondary cores develop in importance	California Phoenix Atlanta Texas Florida		Original core losing dominance

Migration mainly into the 'new' cores |

A

Variations in wealth and development in American cities

You may have a perception that, if you were a wealthy American, you would probably live in somewhere like Miami (Florida) or Los Angeles (California). Perhaps your ideal 'home' is a mansion next to the film stars who live in Malibu (hoping it will not be destroyed by forest fires or landslides!). It is possible, however, that you have an alternative perception. You may think of Miami as a place where foreign tourists are mugged and sometimes killed, while Los Angeles is a city where severe riots take place.

Los Angeles, like many other large American cities, has two faces (diagram **B**). One face shows an economic development which has resulted in an exceptionally high standard of living (photo **C**). The other face shows extreme poverty with severe social, economic and environmental problems (photo **E**). The gap, in wealth, between the two faces is extremely wide. The distance, in kilometres, between them is very small (map **D**).

B

Well-off areas (shaded green on map)

Ninety per cent of people are white. The average annual income is over $84 000 per family. Many houses are large, with swimming pools and spacious gardens. Many families employ servants. There is easy access to the beach and to services such as shops, schools and hospitals. Most families have two or more cars.

Least well-off areas (shaded orange on map)

Fewer than 15 per cent of the people are white. In some districts 70 per cent are black and in others 70 per cent are Hispanic (mainly from Mexico). The average annual family income is $6700. Housing is poor and overcrowded. People live in run-down tenements which lack basic amenities. An increasing number are homeless and sleep on the streets. Unemployment is high (50 per cent among black people). There are high rates of crime (gang warfare, drug dealing) and racial tension. There is also a high rate of migration of Hispanics from Mexico, many of whom enter the country illegally.

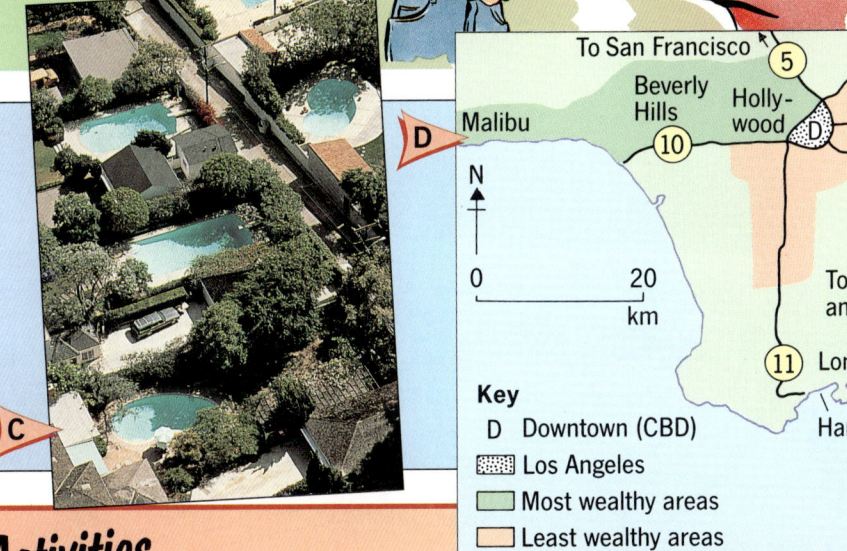

C

D

Map key:
- **D** Downtown (CBD)
- Los Angeles
- Most wealthy areas
- Least wealthy areas

To San Francisco
Malibu — Beverly Hills — Hollywood — State highways
To San Diego and Mexico
Long Beach — Harbour
0 — 20 km
N

E

Activities

1 Explain, with the help of a simple diagram, the meaning of the terms 'core' and 'periphery'.

2 **a)** Copy and complete the table below to show how the core region in the USA showed the characteristics of the model.
   b) Which was the second core region to develop in the USA?
   c) How does the core–periphery model help to explain the differences in the economic development of the USA in the 1990s?

3 Describe the differences in wealth and development in Los Angeles under the following headings.
   • Racial groups
   • Family income
   • Housing
   • Employment
   • Social/living conditions

Summary

Wealth and economic development are never evenly spread out. The core–periphery model can be used to try to explain the causes and consequences of uneven development in either a country or a city.

Location	Two industrial regions	Capital city	Chief port	Three other major cities	Immigration from

9 Brazil, a more economically developed country
▶ How have the Brazilian Amerindians adapted to the environment? ◀

The tropical rainforest of Brazil is home to numerous Amerindian tribes. However, their numbers have declined rapidly since the arrival of the first Europeans and recent so-called attempts to 'develop' the region. Those Amerindians who remain still:

- have a daily life-style which hardly alters from year to year
- live in harmony with their environment. Their housing, clothing, diet, transport and way of life are affected by the equatorial climate (page 18), the tropical rainforest (page 32), and the rivers of the Amazon drainage basin.

The Tukano

Several small tribes are grouped together to form the larger Tukano tribe. The Tukano tribe live in an isolated part of north-west Brazil, near to the border with Colombia. It is this isolation from the outside world that has enabled the Tukano to preserve their way of life and their culture. Although small in stature (men are usually less than 170 cm and women 150 cm), the Tukano are very strong and are not affected by the high humidity. Families rarely have more than two or three living children. The men are usually named after forest birds, the women after forest plants and flowers.

Houses

The Tukano live in large communal houses called malocas (photo **A**). Each maloca is built in a clearing in the forest, maybe many kilometres from the next maloca, and can only be reached by river (diagram **B**). The Tukano's maloca has a rectangular shape and often measures over 40 metres in length, 20 metres in width and 12 metres in height. It is built from local forest materials. The main wooden supports, made from trunks of large hardwood trees, are bound together by lianas (page 32). Large palm leaves, and sometimes flattened tree bark, are woven to form a thatch for the roof and walls. The door for the men is at the front and the door for the women is at the rear (diagram **C**).

Inside, the central front area is used by the men and is the focal point for ritual life, political meetings and entertaining visitors. The area surrounding the four central posts is used for dancing.

The rear central part of the maloca is where the women spend most of their days, usually in preparing cassava (page 94). Palm leaves are also used for screens which divide the sides at the rear of the house into a series of compartments, one for each family. Hammocks are strung across each compartment. Weapons for hunting and tools for clearing the forest lie against the walls, while ripening fruit and freshly caught fish hang from the roof. The men tend to store their few possessions in wooden boxes while the women keep theirs in baskets.

A A Tukano maloca

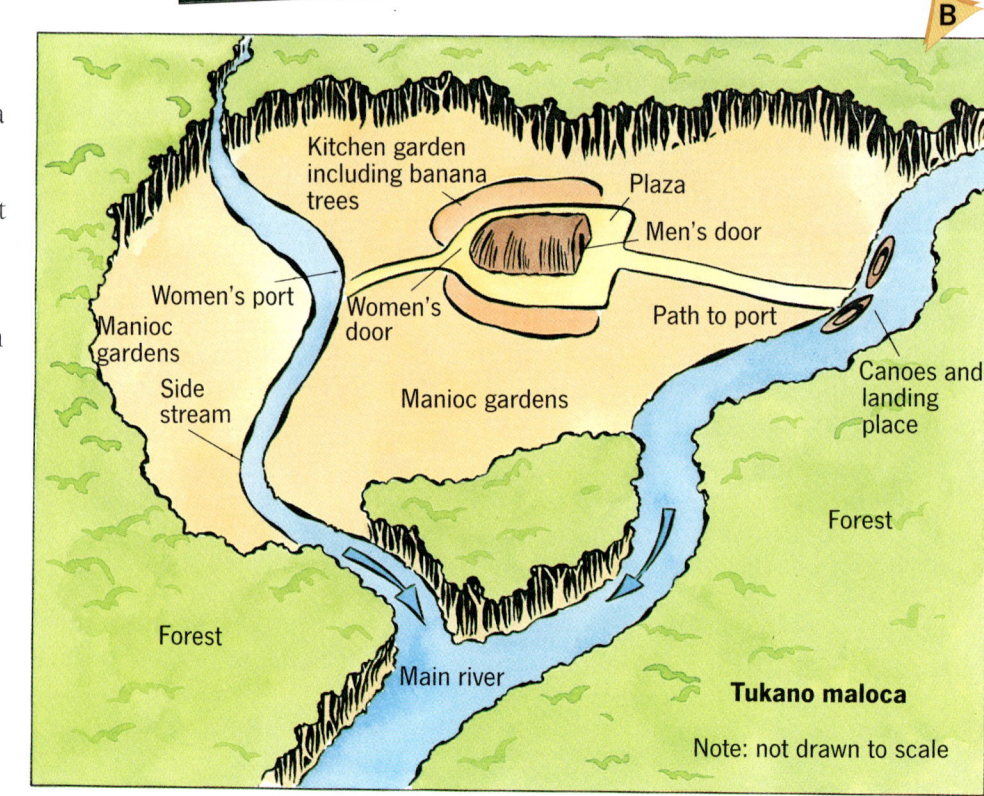

Kitchen garden including banana trees

Plaza

Men's door

Women's port

Women's door

Path to port

Manioc gardens

Side stream

Manioc gardens

Canoes and landing place

Forest

Forest

Main river

Tukano maloca

Note: not drawn to scale

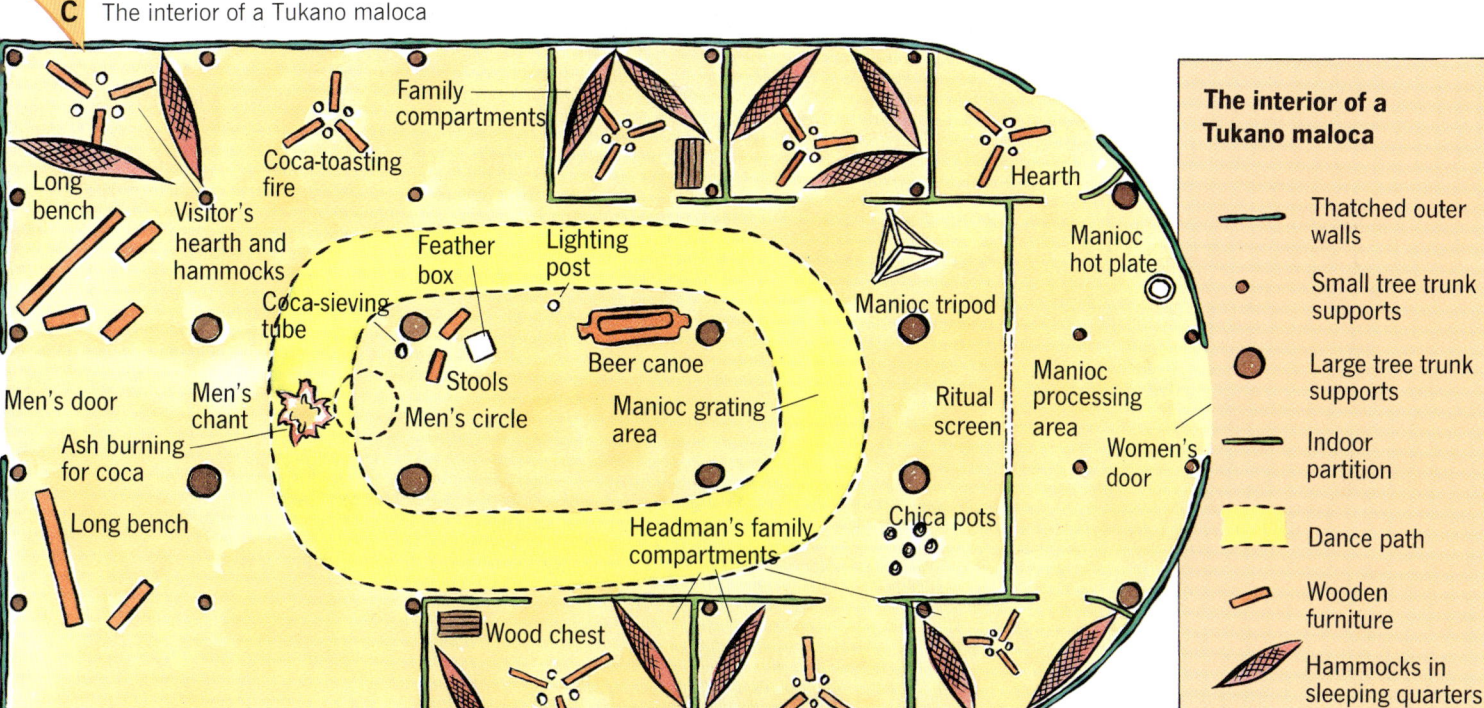

C The interior of a Tukano maloca

Family compartments
Coca-toasting fire
Long bench
Visitor's hearth and hammocks
Feather box
Lighting post
Coca-sieving tube
Beer canoe
Stools
Men's circle
Manioc grating area
Men's door
Men's chant
Ash burning for coca
Long bench
Wood chest
Headman's family compartments
Chica pots
Hearth
Manioc hot plate
Manioc tripod
Ritual screen
Manioc processing area
Women's door

The interior of a Tukano maloca

──	Thatched outer walls
∘	Small tree trunk supports
●	Large tree trunk supports
──	Indoor partition
▱	Dance path
▬	Wooden furniture
◊	Hammocks in sleeping quarters

Dress

As the Tukano live in a hot, wet climate, traditional clothing was a loincloth. Women and girls wear their hair long while men and boys have theirs cut short. Both sexes paint their faces with a red powder obtained by boiling the leaves of a vine. Women accentuate their hair and jaw lines with a black dye obtained from another plant. At dances, further dyes are applied and ornaments are added. The most elaborate item of clothing is the head-dress which often incorporates macaw, egret and parrot feathers (photo **D**).

D Tukano Indian wearing a ceremonial head-dress

Activities

1 **a)** Where do the Tukano tribe live?
  b) How have they managed to preserve their traditional life-style?

2 **a)** What is a maloca?
  b) Draw a sketch of a maloca. Add labels to show its size and the materials used to build it.
  c) Either draw a plan or write a short account to describe the inside of a maloca.

Summary The climate and vegetation of the Amazon rainforest affects the housing and clothing of the people who live there.

How has the environment affected the Amerindians' daily life?

Jobs and diet

The daily life of the Tukano Indians is described in table **A**. The men and women have different but clearly defined roles. The men are responsible for clearing new areas of forest for farming, and they hunt for food. The women do all the farming (photo **B**), except for the collection of coca and tobacco leaves. Most of their time, however, is spent preparing and cooking cassava bread which is made from the manioc plant (photo **D**).

 A

Time of day	Men		Women
Early morning	Wash in river.		Up before dawn. Light fires since it is quite cool. Collect water from river.
Breakfast	Cassava bread, juice, leftovers from previous night. Men and women eat separately.		
Morning	*Either:* (a) Clear new area of forest using machetes and axes to fell trees. Trees burnt to produce fertiliser.	(b) Hunting expedition for fish or meat (tapir, monkey, parrot). Use spears, bows and arrows and blowpipes.	Take manioc baskets to the chagras (fields). Weed crops (grow rapidly in hot wet climate). Collect some maize, pineapples, bananas. Uproot manioc (a plant used to prepare cassava). Plant/collect yams, beans and peppers. Plant manioc in ash.
Lunch	Cassava bread (eaten at all meals), fresh fruit (bananas, pineapples).		
Afternoon	(a) Short rest in heat of the day. Collect coca and tobacco leaves (the only male farming job done once the land is cleared). Make baskets and strings of beads, smoke.	(b) May still be on hunting expedition, especially if looking for meat.	Wash freshly collected manioc, dirty pots and children, in the river. Spend most of afternoon preparing cassava bread – manioc is grated, the resultant pulp is sieved through baskets, water is added and then the pulp is squeezed through a cassava press to separate the tapioca starch from a poisonous juice (used by the men in hunting). The starch is flattened and cooked to make cassava bread. Young girls make pots.
Evening meal	Cooked fish and/or meat, freshly cooked vegetables and cassava bread and juice.		
Evening	Drink chicha (home-made beer) and chew coca leaves (gives hallucinations), play musical instruments (panpipes, drums). Many rituals and festivals with drinking and dancing.		Supervise younger children. Time spent separate from the men until evening or (when allowed to) join in specific festivals.

B

(Left) An area of forest cleared for farming by the Tukano, known as a chagra

C

(Right) Man weaving a basket for sieving manioc

 C

Transport

Travel by the Tukano is almost entirely on water. Although they travel on foot through the rainforest on hunting expeditions, dug-out canoes are used to go further afield, either to fish or to trade with other tribes. Like most other forest tribes, the Tukano have evolved their own methods of making canoes. A large tree is felled. A 7 metre section is cut, its bark removed and the log is left for several weeks to dry. Using an azador, a curved hoe-like blade, the outside of the log is shaped and the centre is cut out (photo **E**), making sure that the sides are not cut too thin. The final process is to gently burn the sides.

Why is the traditional Amerindian way of life changing?

The Tukano, like most other Amerindian tribes, are **shifting cultivators**. They clear small areas of forest for their malocas and chagras. As the cleared area no longer has a protective tree cover, humus in the soil cannot be replaced and the heavy rainfall is not intercepted by leaves and branches. Within four or five years nutrients in the soil are washed away (leached) and the land becomes infertile. The forest Indians overcame this problem by moving their home every few years. Recently, large areas of rainforest have been cleared for commercial reasons (pages 38–39). These clearances, known as deforestation, have had a dramatic effect upon the lives of people, wildlife and the environment of the rainforest (pages 40–43). The number of Indians has declined rapidly, their freedom to move around the forest has been curtailed, and their daily way of life (culture) has been altered.

D Woman preparing cassava bread from the sieved manioc

E A Tukano Indian and canoe

Activities

1 a) Describe the daily life of a Tukano man and a Tukano woman.
   b) How is daily life of the Tukano affected by:
      i)   the landscape
      ii) weather
      iii) wealth?
   c) Why is transport on water so important in the lives of the Tukano?

2 a) Briefly describe the traditional way of life of the Tukano.
   b) Why is it claimed that this 'traditional way of life was in harmony with the environment'?

Summary The daily life of people living in the Amazon rainforest was related to, and was affected by, the environment and location of the region. This traditional way of life is being altered by recent changes in human activity.

What are the main physical features of Brazil?

We have already seen that it is often physical factors that determine:

- **population distribution** – i.e. where people live
- **population density** – i.e. why some places are crowded while others have few people living there.

Physical factors include climate, natural vegetation, relief, soils and natural resources (raw materials). These two pages describe the physical features of Brazil. Pages 98 and 99 show how these features have influenced the distribution of population in that country.

A

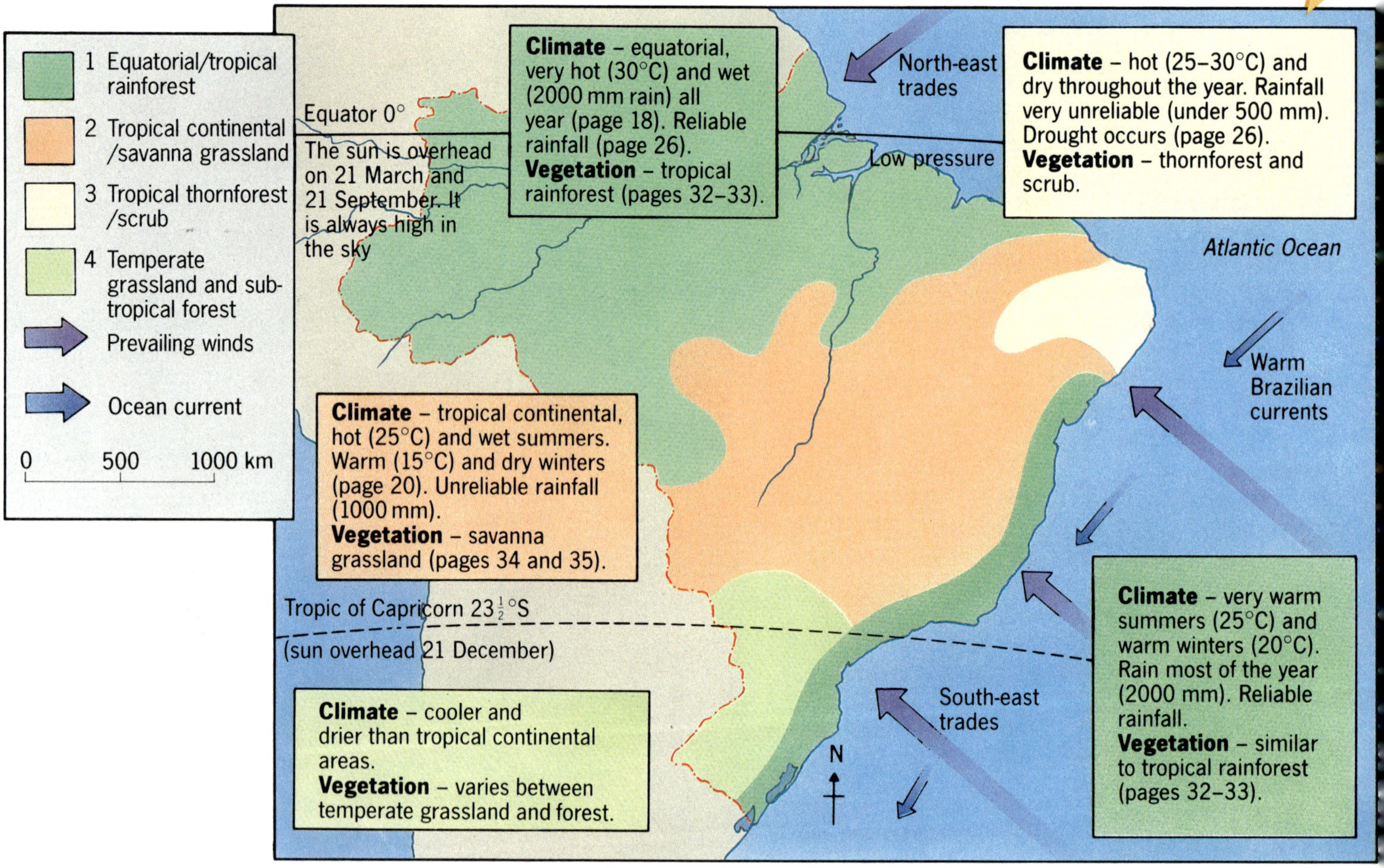

Key

1 Equatorial/tropical rainforest

2 Tropical continental /savanna grassland

3 Tropical thornforest /scrub

4 Temperate grassland and sub-tropical forest

→ Prevailing winds

→ Ocean current

0   500   1000 km

Equator 0°

The sun is overhead on 21 March and 21 September. It is always high in the sky

Climate – equatorial, very hot (30°C) and wet (2000 mm rain) all year (page 18). Reliable rainfall (page 26).
Vegetation – tropical rainforest (pages 32–33).

North-east trades

Low pressure

Climate – hot (25–30°C) and dry throughout the year. Rainfall very unreliable (under 500 mm). Drought occurs (page 26).
Vegetation – thornforest and scrub.

Atlantic Ocean

Climate – tropical continental, hot (25°C) and wet summers. Warm (15°C) and dry winters (page 20). Unreliable rainfall (1000 mm).
Vegetation – savanna grassland (pages 34 and 35).

Warm Brazilian currents

Tropic of Capricorn 23½°S

(sun overhead 21 December)

Climate – very warm summers (25°C) and warm winters (20°C). Rain most of the year (2000 mm). Reliable rainfall.
Vegetation – similar to tropical rainforest (pages 32–33).

South-east trades

N

Climate – cooler and drier than tropical continental areas.
Vegetation – varies between temperate grassland and forest.

B

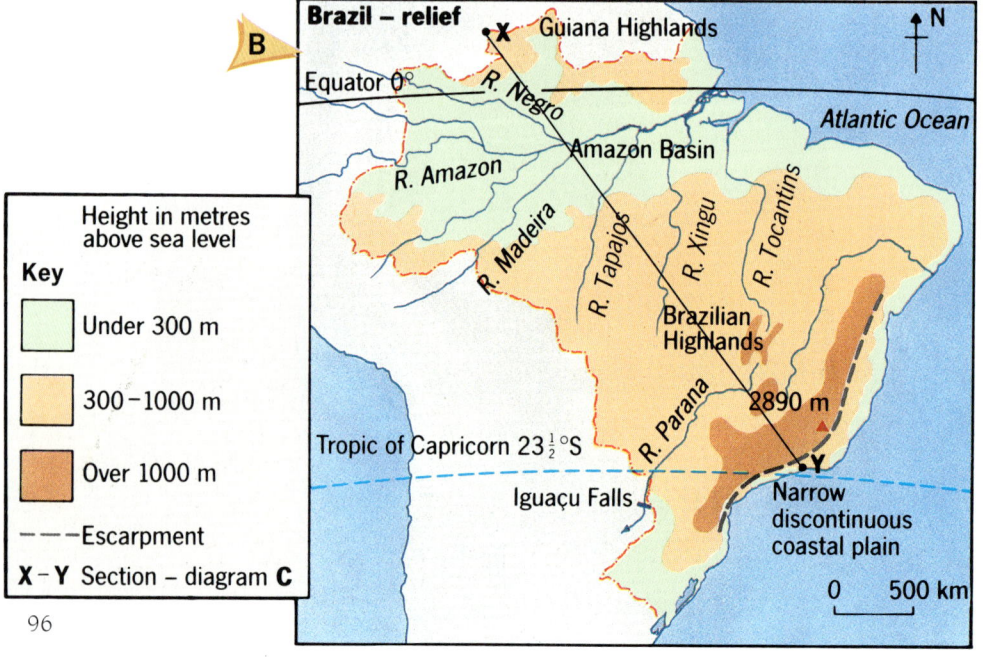

Brazil – relief

N

Equator 0°

Guiana Highlands

R. Negro

Amazon Basin

R. Amazon

R. Madeira

R. Tapajós

R. Xingu

R. Tocantins

Atlantic Ocean

Brazilian Highlands

R. Parana

2890 m

Tropic of Capricorn 23½°S

Iguaçu Falls

Narrow discontinuous coastal plain

Key

Height in metres above sea level

Under 300 m

300–1000 m

Over 1000 m

– – – Escarpment

X – Y Section – diagram C

0   500 km

Map **A** briefly describes the major differences in the climates and vegetation of Brazil. Most of the country experiences either an equatorial climate (page 18) with tropical rainforest vegetation (pages 32–33) or a tropical continental climate (page 20) with savanna grassland vegetation (pages 34–35). Remember that climate is related to latitude and distance from the sea (page 8); prevailing winds and relief (page 9); ocean currents (page 24); and to different types of rainfall (pages 10 and 11) and its reliability (page 26).

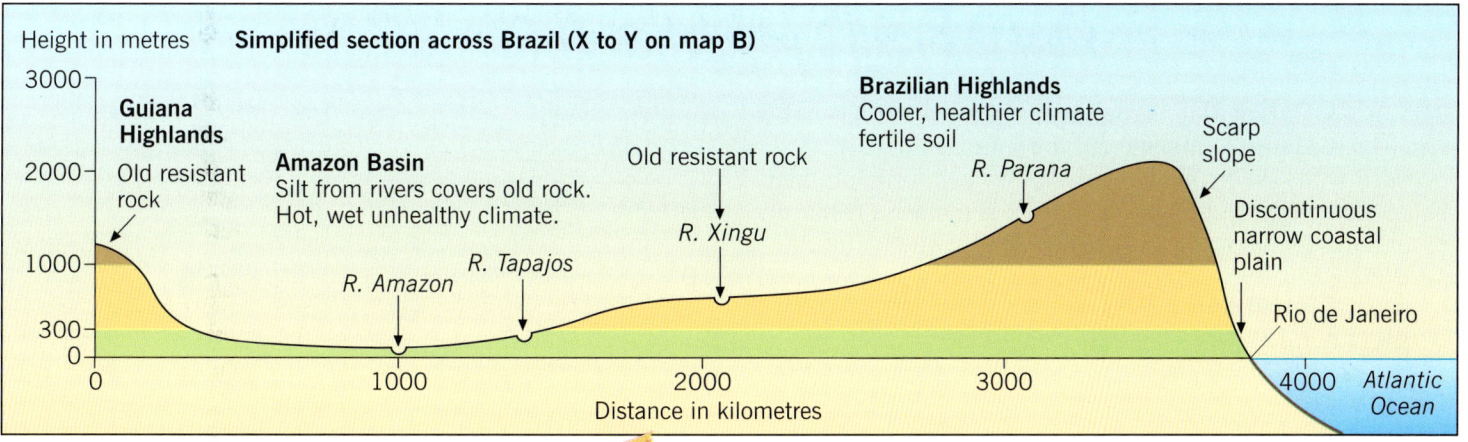

Simplified section across Brazil (X to Y on map B)

Height in metres

Guiana Highlands — Old resistant rock

Amazon Basin — Silt from rivers covers old rock. Hot, wet unhealthy climate.

R. Amazon

R. Tapajos

Old resistant rock

R. Xingu

Brazilian Highlands — Cooler, healthier climate fertile soil

R. Parana

Scarp slope

Discontinuous narrow coastal plain

Rio de Janeiro

Atlantic Ocean

Distance in kilometres

C

Map **B** and diagram **C** have both been simplified. Map **B** shows the relief of Brazil (highland and main rivers). Diagram **C** is a cross-section taken from the north-west of the country to the south-east (X–Y). Remember that while most people living in Britain usually choose to live in flat, low-lying areas, in the tropics people often prefer to live in highland areas where the climate is both cooler and more healthy.

People, in whichever country they live, are attracted to places that have considerable natural resources. Natural resources include fertile soils, mineral deposits and energy supplies. Map **D** shows the location of the more important natural resources in Brazil. The first natural resources to be utilised in Brazil were in the south-east. It is only during the last three decades that many more mineral deposits have been discovered and, like several of the energy supplies, developed. Most of this recent development has occurred in the Amazon rainforests (page 41).

Brazil – natural resources

N   0   1000 km

Recent exploitation of gold and silver

Amapa – manganese

Trombetas – bauxite

Pitinga – tin

Tucurui HEP station

R. Amazon

Carajas – iron ore and, nearby, gold

Hydro-electric (HEP) potential

Lead

Gold

Salvador Small oilfield

Minas Gerais (oldest mining area) – iron ore, manganese, gold, precious stones including diamonds

Itaipù HEP station

Copper
Coal

Atlantic Ocean

Mineral	World rank	% total
Iron ore	2	16.2
Diamonds	3	14.6
Tin	3	14.2
Manganese	3	11.4
Bauxite	4	8.3
Gold	7	3.3
(1993)		

D

Key

Forest products

Energy

Minerals

Rich soils

Activity

Map **E** has been simplified to show four different regions in Brazil.
a) Make a copy of table **F** and complete it by using the information given on these two pages.
b) Which of the regions do you consider to have the:
 i) most
 ii) least physical advantages?
 Give reasons for your answers.

E

F

Region	Map number	Climate	Vegetation	Relief and drainage	Soils	Water supply	Energy	Minerals
Amazon Basin								
Brazilian Highlands								
North-east Brazil								
East coast								

Summary

The distribution of population within a region, country or continent is often influenced by physical factors which include climate, vegetation, relief, soils and natural resources.

How is Brazil's population distributed?

Brazil's population, like that of every other country, is not evenly spread out. Some parts of the country are very crowded while others have relatively few people living there. This uneven distribution of population is mainly a result of:

- migration – the movement of people into and within the country
- physical conditions – the influence of climate, relief and raw materials (pages 96–97).

The movement of people into Brazil

The present inhabitants of Brazil are descended from four main groups of people who arrived in the country from different directions (map **A**). The Amerindians of the Amazon Basin are believed to have originated in eastern Asia and migrated to America along with the Incas (Andes), Aztecs (Mexico) and the North American Indians. The Portuguese, who ruled Brazil for several centuries, were the first Europeans to arrive. Most of the Portuguese were young males, many of whom married black slaves brought from Africa. The present population is derived from several ethnic groups and mixed marriages. Brazil is proud of its racial harmony and relative lack of discrimination and prejudice.

Differences in physical conditions

Brazil is the fifth largest country, by area, in the world. It is bigger than the whole of Europe (excluding Russia). In a country of this size there is a wide range of physical conditions. Sometimes these are positive and attract people to an area. Sometimes they are negative and discourage settlement. Map **B** shows a simple distribution pattern in

A

> Amerindians from Eastern Asia – about 1200 years ago
> 1492 – estimated 6 million
> 1992 – estimated 0.2 million

> After 1500, many Portuguese settled along the north-east coast, and later along the south-east coast

> Most settled in the rainforests of the Amazon Basin

> Equator

> Central areas received few immigrants

> 1600–1850 African slaves mainly coastal areas

> Early 20th century – man Japanese settled in São Paulo

> After 1850 an increasing number of Italians, Spaniards and Germans settled in the south-east, often in the Brazilian Highlands

N

0   500 km

Brazil. The most densely populated areas are in the south-east of the country. Population decreases rapidly towards the north and west where the density is sparse.

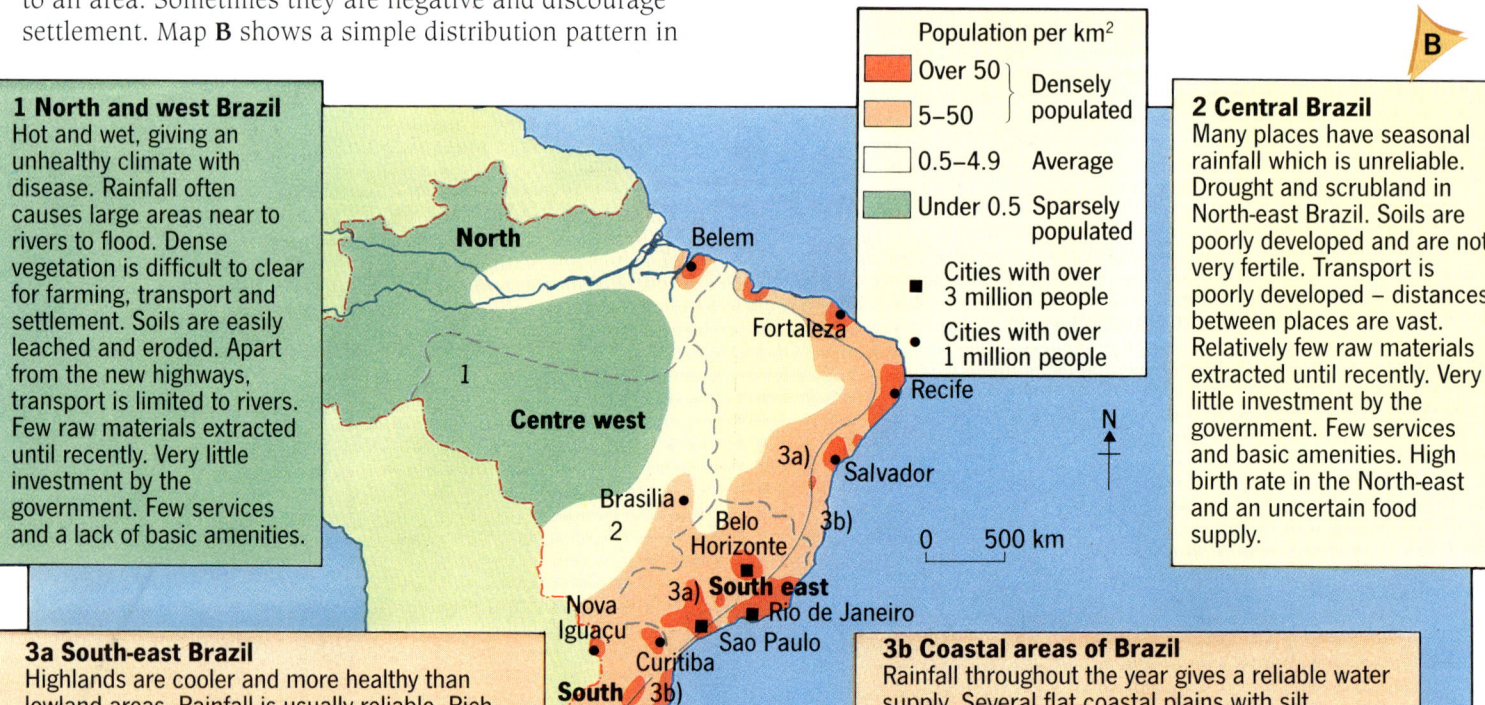

B

Population per km²
- Over 50 — Densely populated
- 5–50 — Densely populated
- 0.5–4.9 — Average
- Under 0.5 — Sparsely populated
- ■ Cities with over 3 million people
- ● Cities with over 1 million people

1 North and west Brazil
Hot and wet, giving an unhealthy climate with disease. Rainfall often causes large areas near to rivers to flood. Dense vegetation is difficult to clear for farming, transport and settlement. Soils are easily leached and eroded. Apart from the new highways, transport is limited to rivers. Few raw materials extracted until recently. Very little investment by the government. Few services and a lack of basic amenities.

2 Central Brazil
Many places have seasonal rainfall which is unreliable. Drought and scrubland in North-east Brazil. Soils are poorly developed and are not very fertile. Transport is poorly developed – distances between places are vast. Relatively few raw materials extracted until recently. Very little investment by the government. Few services and basic amenities. High birth rate in the North-east and an uncertain food supply.

3a South-east Brazil
Highlands are cooler and more healthy than lowland areas. Rainfall is usually reliable. Rich terra rossa soils are ideal for growing coffee. Many minerals – iron ore, gold, precious stones. Transport networks are well-developed. Much government investment. Many services and amenities. Major industrial areas around São Paulo and Belo Horizonte.

3b Coastal areas of Brazil
Rainfall throughout the year gives a reliable water supply. Several flat coastal plains with silt deposited by rivers. Natural harbours developed as ports to receive immigrants and for trade. Much government investment. Many services and amenities. Port industries (Rio de Janeiro) and tourism (Rio and Salvador, the old Portuguese capital).

Recent movements of population

In Brazil, as in all economically developing countries, there has been a rapid movement of people from the countryside to the towns and cities (diagram **C**). The result of this rural-to-urban migration has been the increase in urbanisation (graph **D**) and the associated problems of urban growth. There have been smaller movements away from the south-east due to:

- the Brazilian government's decision to create Brasilia as the country's new capital city in 1952; at that time the area around the chosen site was virtually uninhabited
- the development of mineral resources and energy supplies at such places as Carajas, Trombetas and Tucurui (page 97), and the government's attempts to settle landless farmers in the Amazon Basin (page 98).

> São Paulo and Rio de Janeiro have big, modern buildings which include hospitals, shops, cinemas and universities

> The North-east of Brazil has one of the highest birth rates in the world. The average family size is eight people. There are too many of us to find jobs on the farms

> Drought and poor soils mean we cannot grow enough food to feed ourselves and so we have to move to the city

> We are farmers but many of us do not own any land, and if we do the plots are very small

> We have learned some skills at school but we cannot use them in our local village

> It is not far to the city so we can get work there and still visit our village

C

Activities

1 **a)** Which groups of immigrants to Brazil came from:
   i) eastern Asia before AD 1400, ii) Africa,
   iii) Europe, iv) Asia during this century?

  b) In which parts of Brazil did each of these four immigrant groups settle?

2 Make a copy of map **D**. Complete it to show why places in the south-east of Brazil are more densely populated than places in the north and west of the country, by adding descriptions to the headings for **each** area.

3 **a)** i) Why have so many people from rural areas in Brazil moved into towns and cities?
   ii) What was Brazil's urban population in 1940, 1970 and 1990?

  b) How was the building of Brasilia meant to encourage people to move inland and away from the south-east coast?

  c) What two recent developments have encouraged people to move into the Amazon Basin?

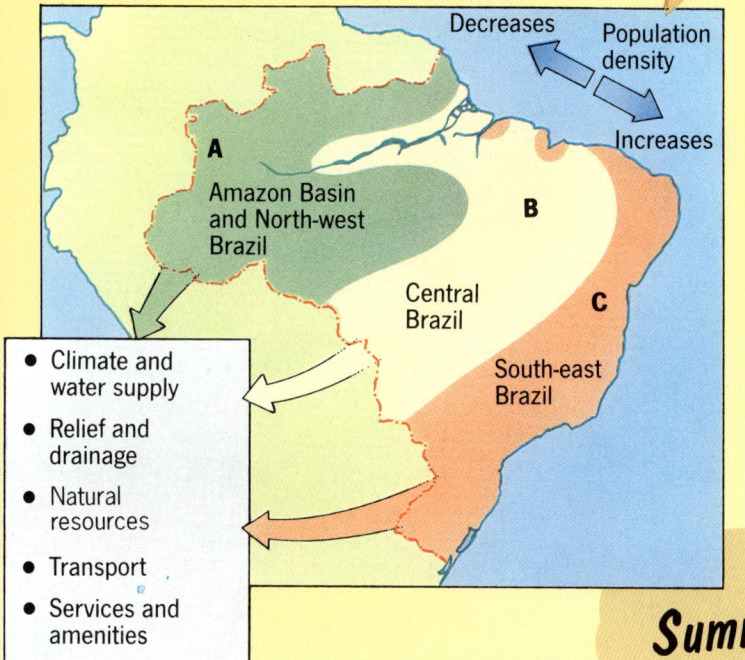

D

- Climate and water supply
- Relief and drainage
- Natural resources
- Transport
- Services and amenities
- Government help

E

People living in urban areas (%)

Year	%
1940	32
1950	40
1960	42
1970	56
1980	68
1990	77
2000 (est)	82

Summary The distribution of population in Brazil has mainly been influenced by physical factors and migration both into and within the country.

► Does Brazil have the characteristics of a developing country? ◄

We are all aware of different levels in development between places. We can see differences within in a British city, between regions in the United Kingdom and the European Union, and between countries across the world. Perhaps the sharpest contrast in development made by people is when they place the countries of the world into one of two groups with the result that each country is said to be either 'economically more developed' or 'economically less developed'. The placing of a country in either of these two groups depends upon certain characteristics. These characteristics include:

- economic factors which explain the wealth of a country, e.g. gross national product (GNP – page 122), the development of industry and the level and type of trade
- social factors which describe the standard of living and quality of life in a country, e.g. population growth, health care and education.

Unfortunately, when considering these characteristics it is all too easy to generalise and to build up a **negative**, and often incorrect, **perception** of an economically developing country (diagram **A**). We often only hear about these countries through the media during times of a major disaster such as drought or civil war. When the disaster passes and conditions in the country improve, it is 'forgotten' as it is no longer considered to be 'news-worthy'. Perception is often very different from reality.

Brazil is grouped with the economically less developed countries, but is it one of them? How does it measure up to the characteristics of an economically developing country as listed in diagram **A**? How does it compare with other countries in the world (table **B**)?

A

Poor transport · Export primary goods and import manufactured goods giving trade deficit · Rapid population growth · High infant mortality rates · High birth rates · Poor housing · High death rates · Low rate of adult literacy · Poor diet · Low GNP – a 'poor' country · Low level of energy consumption · Most people find work in primary activities with few in secondary or tertiary jobs · Many people per doctor and few hospitals · High proportion of population live in rural areas and few in urban settlements · Short life expectancy

B

1994	GNP (US$)	Birth rate	Death rate	Infant mortality rate	Population under the age of 15 (%)	Life expectancy	People in primary jobs (%)	Energy consumption per person	Urban dwellers (%)	People per doctor	Adult literacy	Trade balance
Japan	31 450	12	8	5	19	79	7	474	78	780	99	Surplus
USA	24 750	14	9	8	21	76	2	1074	78	520	99	Deficit
France	22 360	13	10	7	20	76	6	543	73	540	99	Deficit
UK	17 970	14	12	8	19	76	2	540	90	650	99	Deficit
Mexico	3750	27	5	36	37	70	23	189	76	2010	87	Deficit
Brazil	3020	26	8	57	36	66	25	81	79	1660	81	Surplus
Egypt	660	31	9	57	40	61	41	70	45	970	49	Deficit
India	290	31	10	88	36	60	62	35	28	3690	50	Deficit
Kenya	270	47	10	64	50	61	81	11	28	7870	75	Deficit
Bangladesh	220	41	14	108	44	53	59	8	19	7810	36	Deficit

Twelve characteristics of development are listed in table **B**. Of these twelve, Brazil appears to fall into the category of 'economically less developed' on four occasions, into 'economically more developed' on three and is borderline between them on the remaining five (diagram **C**). Indeed when it comes to trade, Brazil has had a surplus since 1982. This means that it has earned more money from exporting its raw materials and manufactured goods to other countries than it has spent on imports. In 1994, the date of the figures in table **B**, Brazil and Japan were the only countries to show a trade surplus. In contrast the USA, UK and France all had, like the economically less developed countries, a trade deficit. It is often difficult, and misleading, therefore, to label a country as being either economically 'more developed' or 'less developed'.

Brazil experienced a so-called 'economic miracle' in the 1960s and 1970s. During this time it developed large-scale industries, began to utilise its energy resources and increased its GNP. However, just as economic development is not even across the world, neither is it within a country. Although Brazil's 'economic miracle' created many new industrial jobs in the country, its benefits were mainly confined to the government, large businesses and overseas transnationals. The improvement in economic wealth was not shared equally between all the regions and people within the country (pages 102 and 103), while the money borrowed to pay for new developments has left Brazil deep in debt (pages 104 and 105).

Level of development	Where does Brazil fit?
Least economically developed countries	No similarities
Below average economically	Birth rate. Infant mortality rate. Population under the age of 15. Energy consumption
Average economic development	GNP. Life expectancy. People per doctor
Above average economically developed countries	People in primary jobs (%). Adult literacy
Most economically developed countries	Death rate. Urban dwellers (%). Trade balance

C

D

E

Activities

1 Diagram **A** makes fifteen points. Explain why each point is characteristic of an economically less developed country.

2 Table **B** gives twelve differences in the level of development between ten selected countries. Using this, and table **C**:
 a) list the characteristics which Brazil shares with countries which are said to be
  i) economically less developed
  ii) economically more developed.
 b) Why is it often difficult to label a country as being either 'economically more developed' or 'economically less developed'?

3 a) Write down the first ten things you think of about Brazil. These are likely to be your perceptions of the country.
 b) Which of these perceptions are negative (bad) points and which are positive (good) points?
 c) Photos **D** and **E** were both taken in Rio de Janeiro.
  i) How does photo **D** confirm the often negative perceptions of an economically less developed country?
  ii) How does photo **E** show that there are also many positive characteristics about economically less developed countries?

Summary Individual countries have different levels of economic development and so are referred to as being either economically 'more' or 'less' developed. While Brazil is commonly regarded to be part of the 'less developed' world, it shows several characteristics usually associated with 'more developed' countries.

Why has economic development in Brazil been uneven?

Economic development is rarely evenly distributed whether it be in a city or at a regional, national or international level. Growth and wealth become concentrated in a few favoured locations (the **core**) leaving other places relatively poor and underdeveloped in comparison (the **periphery**)(page 90). In the case of a country, the core is likely to contain the most jobs (usually in the secondary and tertiary sectors), the most developed transport system, and the best housing and services. It is also likely to have the highest standard of living. In most countries the level of prosperity and economic development decreases rapidly with distance from the core (diagram **A**). The poorest regions are therefore usually found towards the periphery of the country. Mainly due to a lack of jobs (other than those in the primary sector), people will migrate from the more 'rural' periphery regions to the more urbanised, industrial core.

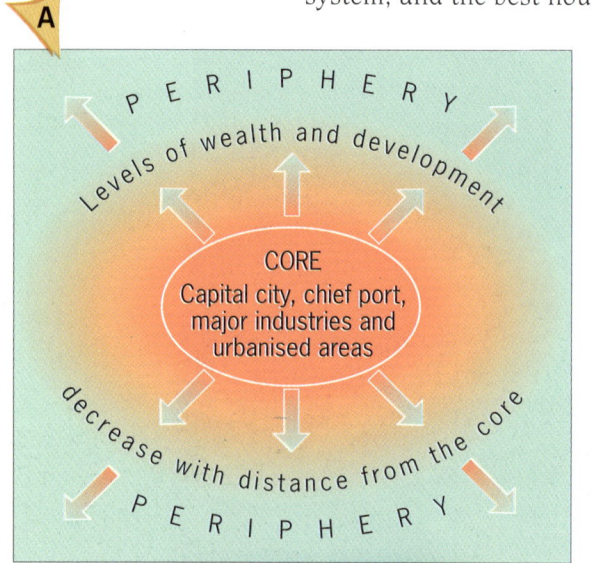

A

PERIPHERY

Levels of wealth and development

CORE
Capital city, chief port, major industries and urbanised areas

decrease with distance from the core

PERIPHERY

B

North

North-east

Recife

Brazil's national border

Centre-west

Salvador (capital before 1793)

Brasilia (capital since 1960)

South-east

Belo Horizonte

São Paulo

Rio de Janeiro (capital 1763–1960)

South

N

0   1000 km

Key

North = Region

Core

Periphery

C São Paulo

D Favelas in Salvador

Regional imbalance in Brazil

During the early years of Portuguese colonial rule, the North-east became the wealthiest region of Brazil (map **B**). Its wealth was based on plantation crops, especially sugar cane. Salvador (Brazil's first capital) and Recife grew as ports exporting sugar and receiving large numbers of European immigrants together with slaves brought from Africa. However, it has been the South-east region where – and especially since 1950 – industrialisation, urbanisation and the creation of jobs and wealth have been the most rapid. Today the North-east has 30 per cent of Brazil's population but only 14 per cent of the country's wealth compared with the South-east where 42 per cent of the population now live and which has 64 per cent of the nation's wealth. The South-east is therefore the core region in Brazil (photo **C** and fact file **E**) with the North-east, together with the North, forming the periphery (photo **D** and fact file **F**).

Fact file E
South-east Brazil – the core

The initial development of the South-east was centred on coffee growing (São Paulo), gold and diamond prospecting (Minas Gerais) and the export of these products through the natural port of Rio de Janeiro. Real growth followed with the mining of iron ore, the production of steel, and the manufacture of ships and cars. Hydro-electricity, produced locally, and oil, imported and refined at Rio, provided the necessary supply of energy. The region has become Brazil's centre of commerce, education, administration, transport and culture. The prospect of more and better-paid jobs, a more reliable food supply, improved services (schools and hospitals) and the perception of the 'bright city lights' have all acted like a magnet to attract many people who previously lived in the surrounding rural areas. The region has received most government and foreign investment and, despite the large number of people living in favelas and on the streets, has the highest standard of living in the country.

Factfile F
North-east Brazil – the periphery

Most people are subsistence farmers or landless sharecroppers who farm the land for someone else and in return receive a share of the produce. The soils, once used to produce plantation crops, are now mainly exhausted and eroded. The poor soils and frequent drought mean that crop yields are often insufficient to feed the local population. Where soils are better, the crops grown are usually for export (sugar cane and cocoa) rather than for home consumption. The high birth rate and lack of natural resources mean that the region is overpopulated. Although there is one large hydro-electric power station in the region (Paulo Afonso), energy supplies are insufficient for domestic use or the development of industry. The lack of government and foreign investment has meant that transport systems and industry have not developed and services have not been provided. The lack of jobs, services and a guaranteed food supply has meant the migration of thousands of people from the region. Many have moved to the South-east, a few have been resettled in the North.

E

F

Activities

1 The core region has the greatest level of urbanisation in a country together with the most industries and services. With reference to table **G** give:
   a) one piece of evidence that more people live in urban areas
   b) two pieces of evidence that there is more industry
   c) three pieces of evidence that health care (services) is better
   d) one piece of evidence that education is better
   e) two pieces of evidence that there are better household amenities
   f) two pieces of evidence that the standard of living is higher in South-east Brazil (the core) than in North-east Brazil (the periphery).

2 a) Why is the South-east of Brazil more economically developed than the North-east of Brazil?
   b) Is it true that all of South-east Brazil has a high standard of living?

Brazil	South-east	North-east
Population density	63 per km²	25 per km²
Birth rate	22	48
Infant mortality rate	49	109
Life expectancy	63	48
People per doctor	875	2150
Adult literacy (%)	72	39
Brazil's industrial production (%)	56	16
People employed in industry (%)	70	10
Brazil's energy consumption (%)	71	13
Urban dwellers (%)	84	47
With electricity (%)	82	15
Clean water (%)	64	23
Car ownership (%)	66	10

G

Summary

Wealth and economic development are rarely spread out evenly. Parts of South-east Brazil are as well-off as many economically more developed countries. Other parts of South-east Brazil have, like the North-east, a very low standard of living.

► How has internal investment affected Brazil's economic development? ◄

Economic development and growth needs capital and technology, two commodities that are not readily available to economically less developed countries. Development, therefore, has to rely upon assistance either in limited amounts from their own government or, as is more usual, from overseas. Brazil's government, together with the Bank of Brasil, helped to build the state-owned steelworks at Volta Redonda and to form the state-controlled Petrobras petroleum company. These early schemes were expensive and tended to concentrate industrial expansion in the South-east at the expense of other parts of the country.

Brasilia

Many Brazilians expressed concern over the speed of economic development and population and urban growth in a triangular area which was bounded by São Paulo, Rio de Janeiro and Belo Horizonte. This growth led to an increasing gap in wealth between the South-east and other Brazilian regions. In 1952 the Brazilian Congress agreed to create a new capital city. The site chosen was uninhabited, was almost equidistant from all the regional capitals and was 1200 kilometres inland from the existing capital of Rio de Janeiro. Building work began in 1957 and Brasilia was inaugurated as capital in 1960. The main hope was that Brasilia would lead to the opening up of the more central parts of the country and so spread out more evenly Brazil's economic growth. Although Brasilia's population had reached 1.9 million by 1990, its economy was based on commerce and administration rather than industry (photo **A**). Many top business people and politicians still prefer to live in Rio de Janeiro or São Paulo and to commute to work during the week. Brasilia, a city built for the motorist, has become the focus for new roads which lead away in all directions.

Regional development

During the mid-1960s the Brazilian government set up five regional development agencies. One of these, SUDAM, became responsible for developing Amazonia and improving its social and economic conditions. The agency realised that the region could not be developed without improved accessibility and so, in 1968, it financed a route through the rainforest for the Trans-Amazonia Highway (photo **B**). This, and later highways, became a 'growth corridor' along which landless farmers from the North-east region (page 103) were re-settled as 'colonists'. Although the colonists were given land to farm (photo **C**), the settlement programme has not been a success. The traditional method of farming in the rainforest had been shifting cultivation (page 95). This was because, once the forest had been cleared, the heavy rain soon leached and eroded the soil (page 40). While the Amerindian shifting cultivators could then move to a new site in the forest, the 'colonists' could not. Consequently as crop yields fell and feelings of isolation grew, many colonists abandoned their new farms and moved to the large urban centres on the coast and in the South-east.

A Brasilia

B The Trans-Amazonia Highway

In 1975 the Brazilian government introduced a Second National Development Plan called, in this region, **Polamazonia**. Fifteen 'growth poles' were created in the region (map **E**). At each growth pole the government, often with help from transnational companies, invested large sums of money to try to generate economic activity. The hope was that as each centre developed, growth would extend outwards into the surrounding areas. Developments have included highways, a free port, mining (iron ore and bauxite – photo **D**), agriculture (cattle ranching), industry (timber and steel) and the production of hydro-electricity (map **E**). As always with development schemes, there are advantages and disadvantages. Polamazonia is credited with creating many new jobs, generating wealth for many Brazilian-owned companies and helping the country to achieve a trade surplus (page 107). It has also been blamed for destroying large areas of rainforest and the traditional Amerindian way of life.

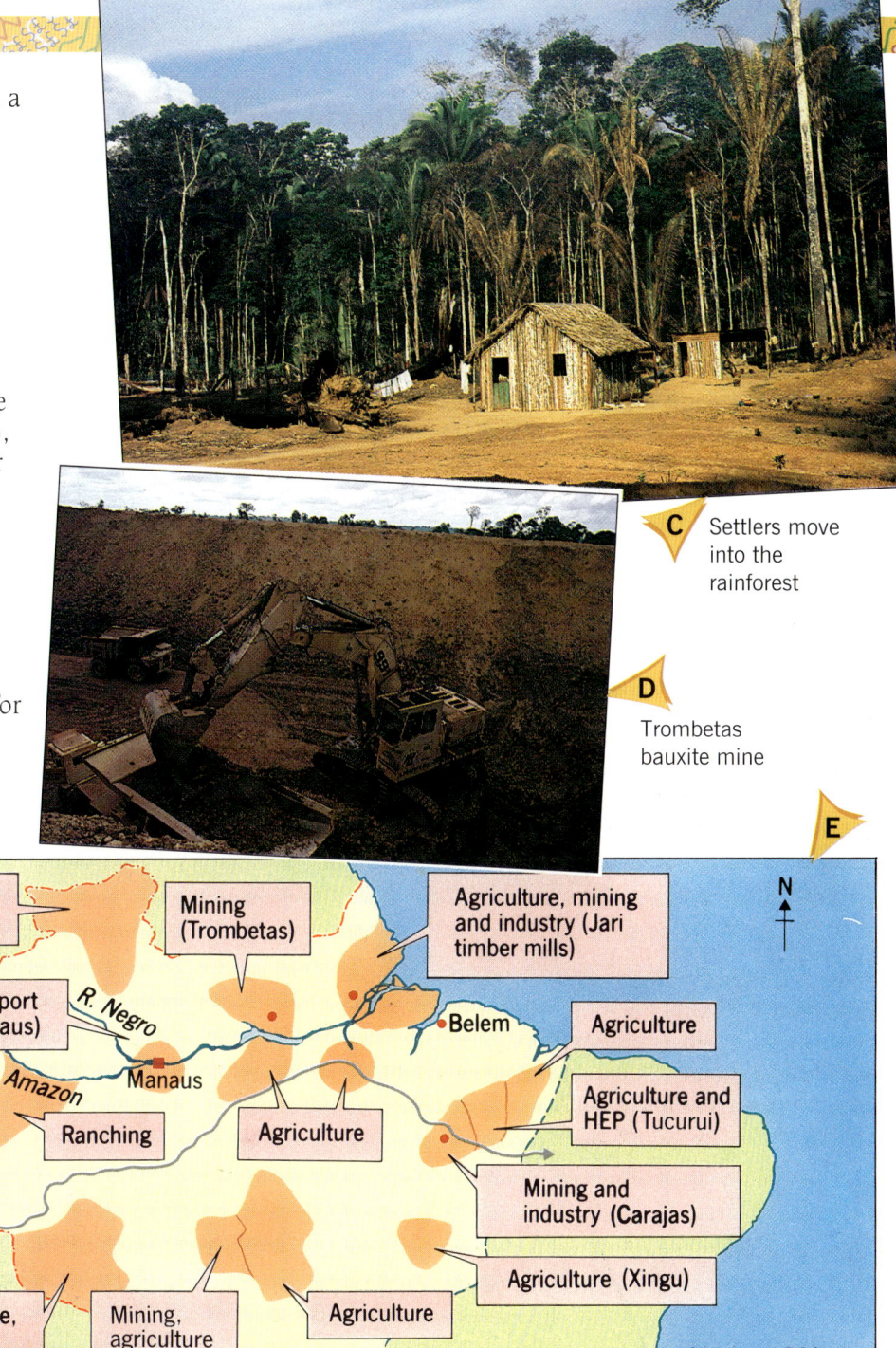

C Settlers move into the rainforest

D Trombetas bauxite mine

E

Brazilian border
SUDAM's border
Polamazonia projects

Free port – an area where goods can be made or assembled without payment of import or export duties

Trans Amazonia Highway

HEP – Hydro-electric power

Agriculture and mining
Mining (Trombetas)
Agriculture, mining and industry (Jari timber mills)
Free port (Manaus)
R. Negro
Belem
Agriculture
R. Amazon
Manaus
Agriculture and HEP (Tucurui)
Ranching
Agriculture
Mining and industry (Carajas)
Agriculture (Xingu)
Ranching
Agriculture, mining and HEP
Mining, agriculture and HEP
Agriculture

N

0   500 km

Activities

1 a) Why was there a need for development in other regions in Brazil, apart from the South-east?
   b) Give three reasons why the Brazilian government created the new capital of Brasilia.

2 a) What was SUDAM?
   b) Why were growth corridors created? How successful have they been?

   c) What were the main aims of Polamazonia?
   d) Describe five different types of economic development which have taken place under Polamazonia. In what ways have these developments been successful and what problems have they created?

Summary

The amount of government (inward) investment can greatly influence the speed and type of economic development of an economically developing country.

▶ *How has foreign investment affected Brazil's economic development?* ◀

Many economically developing countries have come to rely upon aid. Aid is the giving of resources by one country, or an organisation, to another country. Aid can include money, goods, food, technology and people. Developing countries may seek aid for several reasons:

- To try to improve their standard of living – although this type of aid is often spent on prestigious schemes (e.g. hydro-electricity schemes) which benefit relatively few people within the country.
- To pay off trade debts – as most developing countries do not make enough money from their exports (usually primary products) to pay for their imports (usually manufactured goods).
- Following disasters – many developing countries are prone either to natural disasters (e.g. drought and earthquakes) or to human-induced disasters (e.g. desertification and civil war).

The three main types of aid are described in diagram **A**. Unfortunately the giving of aid is complicated and controversial, because it often does not benefit the country or the people to whom it is given.

After 1964, foreign banks and transnational companies perceived that Brazil had a huge potential for industrial growth. Foreign banks became increasingly prepared to loan money to the Brazilian government, while transnational companies invested money in developing the country's mineral reserves, energy resources and industry (photo **B**). Both the banks and the transnational companies assumed that, as Brazil developed economically, they would get their money back and make a handsome profit. These loans and investments have had mixed effects upon the Brazilian economy. The Brazilian government, using bank loans, has financed several successful state companies, including Petrobras and Telebras, while transnationals, especially those connected with oil and cars, have created jobs and wealth (table **C**). However, although Brazil has become the most industrialised and one of the better-off economically less developed countries, it has done so at the expense of creating a huge national debt (graph **D** and extract **E**).

Bilateral aid is when one country gives resources directly to another country. It is usually given 'with strings attached' which gives the donor some control over the recipient. E.g. the recipient **must** buy manufactured goods from the donor. Recipient countries usually fall deeply into debt.

A

Multilateral aid is given by international organisations such as the World Bank or EU Development Fund. Often these organisations, based in 'rich' countries, hold back if they disagree with the economic or political system of the recipient country.

Voluntary aid is given by organisations such as Oxfam, Action Aid and Intermediate Technology. There are no political ties. Money is spent on sustainable, small-scale projects more appropriate to the needs and technology of recipient countries.

During the 1980s Brazil had to borrow more money just to repay interest rates on earlier loans. At the same time economic growth and the creation of wealth was not evenly distributed between regions and people (pages 102–103). As in many economically developing countries, the gaps between the rich and the poor and between the core and the periphery have grown more rapidly than in the economically developed world.

C

Rank	Company	Field of business	Ownership
1	Petrobras	Petroleum	Brazil
2	Pao de Açucar	Supermarkets	Brazil
3	Shell	Petroleum	UK/Netherlands
4	Telebras	Telecommunications	Brazil
5	Texaco Brazil	Petroleum	USA
6	Volkswagen do Brasil	Cars	Germany
7	Esso Brasileira	Petroleum	USA
8	Sousa Cruz	Beverages, tobacco	UK
9	Vale do Rio Dole	Mining (Carajas)	Brazil
10	Mendes Junior	Machinery	Brazil
11	General Motors	Cars	USA
12	Copersucar (fuel for cars)	Sugar, alcohol	Brazil

B

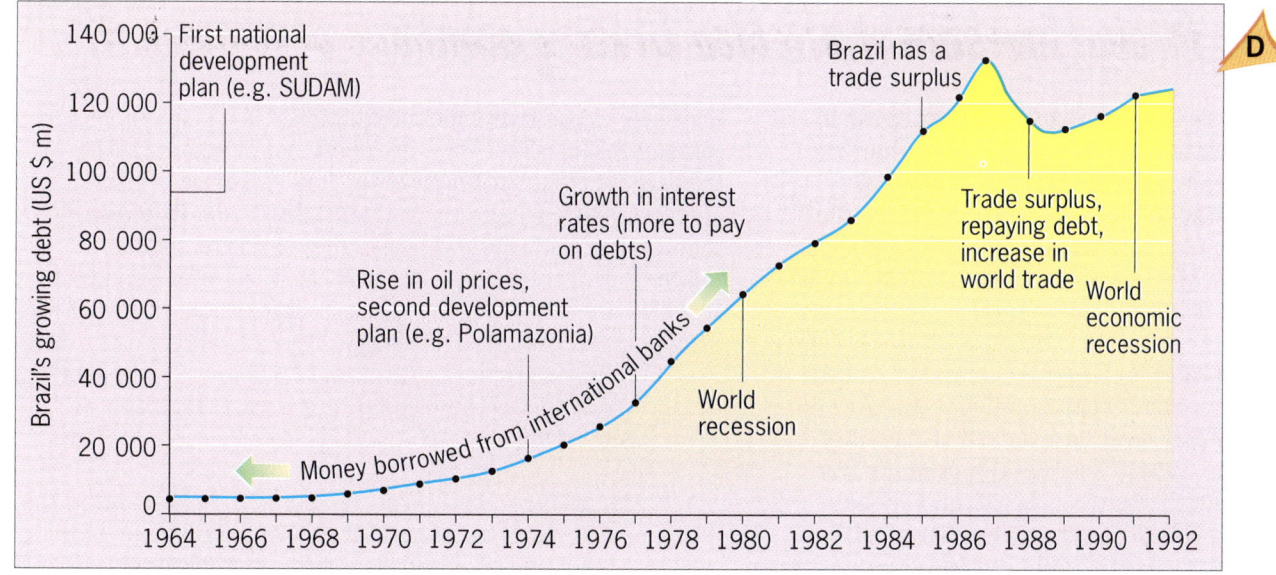

Graph D. Brazil's growing debt (US $ m):
- First national development plan (e.g. SUDAM)
- Rise in oil prices, second development plan (e.g. Polamazonia)
- Money borrowed from international banks
- Growth in interest rates (more to pay on debts)
- World recession
- Brazil has a trade surplus
- Trade surplus, repaying debt, increase in world trade
- World economic recession

Economic miracle and international debt

Between 1964 and 1974 the military government, supported by the USA, developed policies to make Brazil prosperous and powerful. During this period, known as the 'economic miracle', landless peasants, used as cheap labour, made this aim seem a possibility. European and American banks encouraged this economic growth by offering large loans with low interest rates. These were used to finance ambitious, often ill-founded, industrial and agricultural projects. Transnational companies set up industries but most of their profits were taken out of the country.

Imports of cheap oil helped this process of economic expansion, but, in the mid-1970s, oil prices rose steeply, so increasing import bills. As a result of Western government policies, interest rates on the loans increased and the prices for Brazil's exports on the world market fell. Rich countries limited the amount of Brazilian manufactured goods that they imported. All these pressures were outside the control of the Brazilian government. Brazil tried to bridge the gap between earnings and debt payments by borrowing more money over short periods, but this increased the government's debts even further. Today, Brazil's external debt has now reached $US119 billion, with little possibility of full payment.

Source: Brazil Country Profile, *ActionAid*

Activities

1 a) Why do many economically developing countries seek aid?

b) What are the differences between bilateral, multilateral and voluntary aid?

c) Which of the three types of aid do you consider to be the best for the receiving country? Give reasons for your answer.

2 a) Why were foreign banks prepared to make loans, and transnational companies to invest in Brazil after 1964?

b) How has Brazil benefited from these loans and investments?

c) What problems have resulted from these loans and investments?

d) Why did Brazil's debt increase rapidly between 1974 and 1986?

e) Although Brazil has had a trade surplus since 1986 (graph **F**), why has it been unable to reduce its debt?

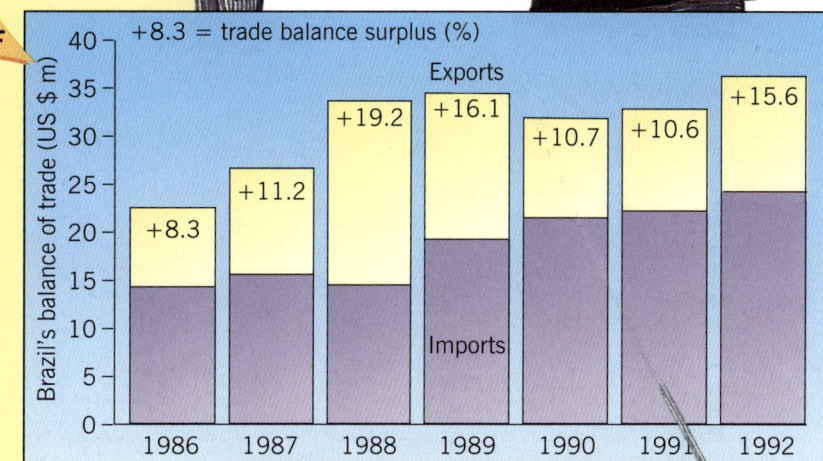

Graph F. +8.3 = trade balance surplus (%). Brazil's balance of trade (US $ m). Exports / Imports.
- 1986: +8.3
- 1987: +11.2
- 1988: +19.2
- 1989: +16.1
- 1990: +10.7
- 1991: +10.6
- 1992: +15.6

Summary

Brazil needed foreign loans and investment to stimulate economic development. Economic growth has, however, led to a large national debt and an increasing gap between Brazil's rich and poor.

10 Bangladesh, a less economically developed country

◀ How have rivers formed Bangladesh? ◀

The Ganges and Brahmaputra are two of the longest rivers in the world. Together they drain an area more than six times the size of Britain, and they flow through five different countries. Having flowed almost 90 per cent of their course, the two rivers eventually join in Bangladesh and are joined by the Meghna, another great river which has its source some 800 km to the north-east.

The **drainage basin** of these rivers includes some of the wettest places in the world, in the Himalayas and Assam. The mean annual rainfall over Bangladesh alone ranges from 1250 mm in the west to over 5500 mm in the north-east. Most of the rain falls between April and September, the rest of the year being relatively dry. When this rainfall is compared with London's annual total of just 610 mm spread fairly evenly through the year, it becomes clear just how wet the area is and how much water the rivers have to cope with. Indeed the total **peak flow** or **discharge** of the rivers as they approach the sea is about three times greater than that of the mighty Mississippi as it flows past New Orleans and into the Gulf of Mexico.

The size of the rivers means that there is considerable erosion, transportation and deposition of material. The country of Bangladesh owes its very existence to these processes and most of it is a giant **delta** and **floodplain** containing over 250 rivers and thousands of smaller streams and waterways. Huge amounts of **silt**, sand and pebbles are carried by the rivers and deposited in the delta area to form islands. The largest, Bhola Island, was formed just 600 years ago and is already 80 km long. Estimates suggest that the silt deposits in this area of the delta are over 2000 metres deep.

Each year as the rivers flood, the islands, mainland and the streams and channels around them constantly change their shape. This situation provides a very unstable environment for human occupation and land use in a country that is one of the poorest and most densely populated in the world (diagram **A** page 126).

A The Ganges–Brahmaputra–Meghna drainage basin

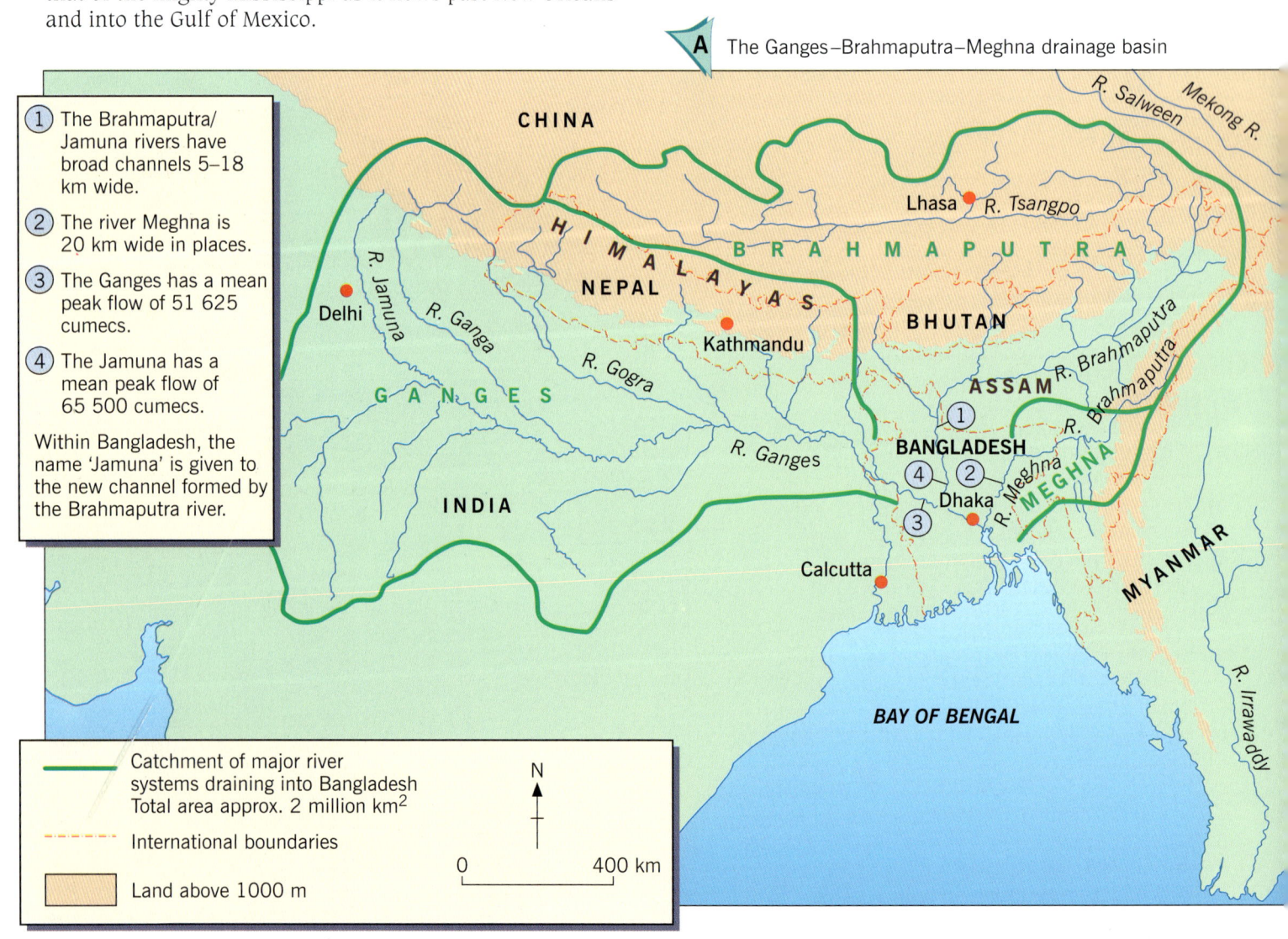

① The Brahmaputra/Jamuna rivers have broad channels 5–18 km wide.

② The river Meghna is 20 km wide in places.

③ The Ganges has a mean peak flow of 51 625 cumecs.

④ The Jamuna has a mean peak flow of 65 500 cumecs.

Within Bangladesh, the name 'Jamuna' is given to the new channel formed by the Brahmaputra river.

Catchment of major river systems draining into Bangladesh Total area approx. 2 million km²

International boundaries

Land above 1000 m

0   400 km

N

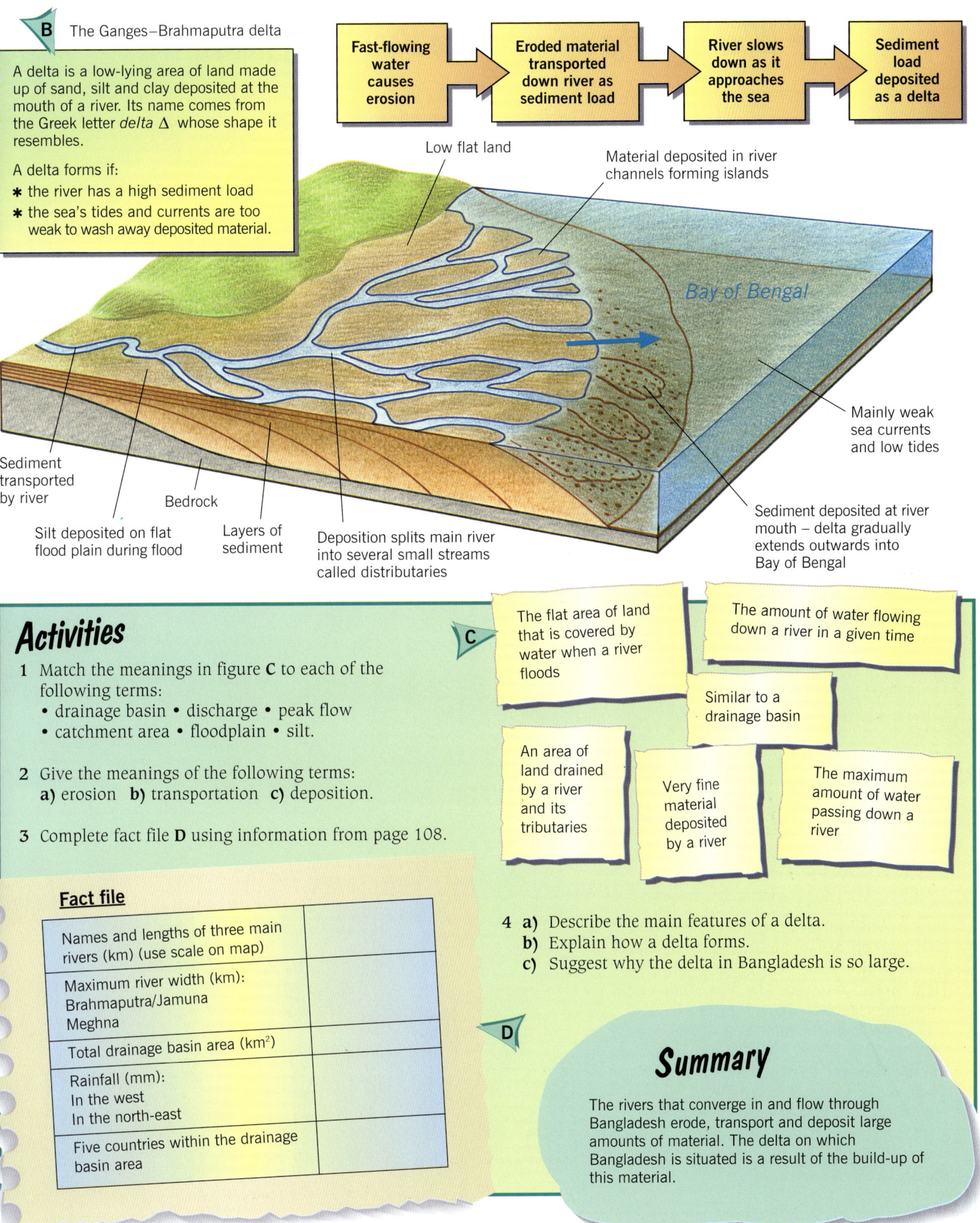

B The Ganges–Brahmaputra delta

A delta is a low-lying area of land made up of sand, silt and clay deposited at the mouth of a river. Its name comes from the Greek letter *delta* Δ whose shape it resembles.

A delta forms if:
* the river has a high sediment load
* the sea's tides and currents are too weak to wash away deposited material.

| Fast-flowing water causes erosion | Eroded material transported down river as sediment load | River slows down as it approaches the sea | Sediment load deposited as a delta |

Low flat land

Material deposited in river channels forming islands

Bay of Bengal

Mainly weak sea currents and low tides

Sediment transported by river

Silt deposited on flat flood plain during flood

Bedrock

Layers of sediment

Deposition splits main river into several small streams called distributaries

Sediment deposited at river mouth – delta gradually extends outwards into Bay of Bengal

Activities

1 Match the meanings in figure **C** to each of the following terms:
   • drainage basin • discharge • peak flow
   • catchment area • floodplain • silt.

2 Give the meanings of the following terms:
   a) erosion **b)** transportation **c)** deposition.

3 Complete fact file **D** using information from page 108.

C

The flat area of land that is covered by water when a river floods

The amount of water flowing down a river in a given time

Similar to a drainage basin

An area of land drained by a river and its tributaries

Very fine material deposited by a river

The maximum amount of water passing down a river

4 **a)** Describe the main features of a delta.
   b) Explain how a delta forms.
   c) Suggest why the delta in Bangladesh is so large.

D

Fact file

Names and lengths of three main rivers (km) (use scale on map)	
Maximum river width (km): Brahmaputra/Jamuna Meghna	
Total drainage basin area (km²)	
Rainfall (mm): In the west In the north-east	
Five countries within the drainage basin area	

Summary

The rivers that converge in and flow through Bangladesh erode, transport and deposit large amounts of material. The delta on which Bangladesh is situated is a result of the build-up of this material.

What were the effects of the Bangladesh floods?

In August and September of 1988 the worst floods in living memory hit Bangladesh. The effects were disastrous . . .

The floods were devastating to the country. They covered 80 per cent of the land and affected two-thirds of the population. Over much of the country only the tops of the trees and buildings could be seen. The water in Dhaka, the country's capital, was 2 metres deep and covered 75 per cent of the city. The electricity supply was cut off for several weeks and there was no safe drinking water because the wells were flooded and the water in them polluted.

A

B

Estimates suggested that over 7 million homes were destroyed and at least 25 million people made homeless or stranded. The official death toll was 2379 although many more were simply reported missing and unaccounted for. Many people drowned but there were also deaths from diseases such as cholera and dysentery. Some people even died from snake bites as the snakes took refuge on the rooftops along with people escaping the flood.

C

Both during and after the floods there were shortages of food and medicine. Two million tonnes of rice, a quarter of the normal crop yield, were destroyed. Most of the jute, sugar cane and vegetable crops were also lost, as well as up to half a million cattle and poultry. Thousands of kilometres of roads, a third of the railways and the international airport at Dhaka were all flooded. Many bridges were also destroyed. This destruction of the communications network meant that it was impossible to deliver emergency food and medical help to those in need.

D

Flooding happens in Bangladesh every year. It is part of the normal way of life for our people. To a large extent we have planned the country's settlements, communications and land use to cope with this situation and to minimise problems.

Normal flooding does have some good effects. Every year the flooding rivers deposit layers of silt, a rich fertile soil, that enables up to three crops of rice a year to be grown by farmers. The floods replenish fish stocks in the lakes and ponds and refill wells and groundwater supplies.

Major damage and problems only occur when floods are unexpected or particularly intense. We call these abnormal floods. In such a low-lying country as ours, an extra metre of flood height can be disastrous.

Abnormal floods can destroy our crops, buildings and roads, cause the displacement or evacuation of millions of people, and disrupt business, industry and public services. The overall cost of the 1988 flood was more than $1.1 billion.

Our country is very poor and we cannot afford to prepare properly for a flood disaster. The effects of flooding are therefore a lot worse than they would be for a rich country.

E Damage due to abnormal floods, 1971–88

Year	Loss of human life	Loss of livestock (thousands)	Loss of rice production (thousand tonnes)	Houses totally/partially damaged (thousands)
1971	120	2	285	229
1974	1987	46	800	6165
1975	15	n/a	93	19
1976	54	n/a	682	89
1984	553	76	2147	536
1987	1657	65	2036	2536
1988	2379	172	2922	7179

n/a = not available

Activities

1 Look at table **E**.
   a) What is meant by an 'abnormal flood'?
   b) List the four most damaging floods. Give them in order, the worst first.
   c) Briefly describe the problems caused by the 1974 floods.
   d) What made the 1988 flood so much worse than any of the other floods?

2 Look at photos **A**, **B** and **C**. Make a list of the problems caused by flooding in each photo. Which of these would be long-term problems?

3 **Barsha** is an important word in Bangladesh. It means 'beneficial flood'. Describe the benefits that a barsha may bring to the country.

4 Describe the effects of flooding in Bangladesh by writing a paragraph for each of the newspaper headlines in figure **F**. Include facts and figures where possible.

F

Bangladesh devastated by worst flood of all

Death toll soars as millions made homeless

Starvation and disease hit Bangladesh

Transport links broken as floods drown country

Summary

In all the world, Bangladesh is probably the nation most affected by floods. Although normal flooding may bring some benefits, the impact of abnormal floods is usually disastrous. Extreme poverty and a large, densely packed population increase the suffering and make planning for future disasters difficult.

What are the causes of flooding in Bangladesh?

Apart from a few hills in the north and south-east, Bangladesh is flat as far as the eye can see. Most of the country is less than 6 metres above sea-level and with very high rainfall and two great rivers flowing across it, it is no surprise that flooding is a regular event.

The flood hydrograph **A** shows why flooding due to heavy rainfall and overflowing rivers is confined to only a few months of the year. This is the time of the **monsoon**, a period of heavy rain blown in from the Indian Ocean by warm, moist south-easterly winds. The monsoon arrives every year at about the same time, and shortly after its arrival Bangladesh receives its normal annual flood.

As we have seen, however, the real problem in Bangladesh is the increasing frequency of abnormal floods and the devastating effect that these have on the country. Some possible causes of the 1988 flood are shown in diagram **B**.

A Flood hydrograph for Dhaka and the Ganges

Rainfall (mm)
0
100
200
300
400
500
River discharge (thousand cumecs)
0
5
10
15
20
25
30
35
40
45
50
J F M A M J J A S O N D

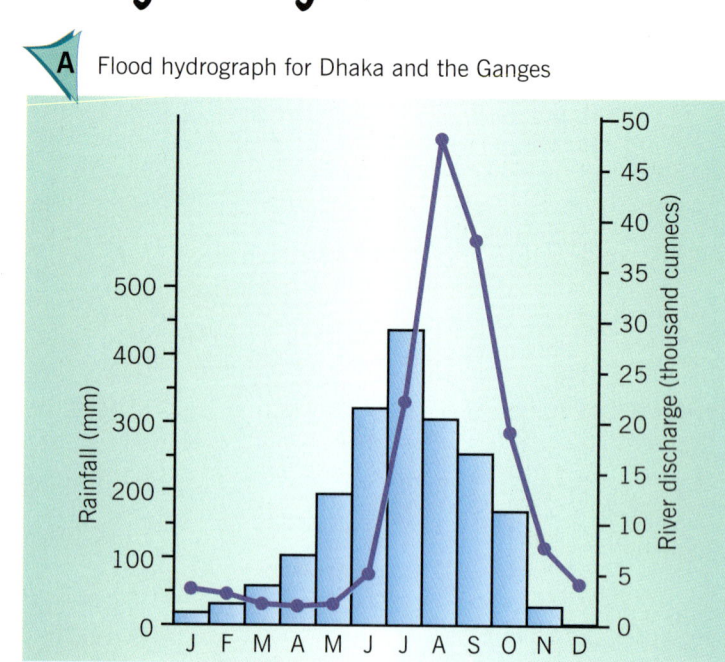

B Causes of flooding in Bangladesh

Rivers filled to overflowing by exceptionally heavy rain over the enormous catchment area.
Melting snow
Deforestation in Nepal and Tibet has probably increased surface run-off and added to deposition downstream.
The heavy rainfall caused all three rivers to have their peak flow at the same time. In years of normal floods the Brahmaputra peaks a month before the Ganges.
The building of embankments upstream has resulted in more of the discharge reaching the delta area.
80% of Bangladesh is a huge floodplain and delta. It is flat, low-lying and easily flooded.
TIBET (China)
NEPAL
R. Ganges
BHUTAN
Patna
INDIA
R. Brahmaputra
Calcutta
Dhaka
R. Meghna
N
Bay of Bengal
The river has been dammed in India. This has reduced flow in the dry season and increased deposition. The silt now blocks the river channels
Poorly maintained embankments leak or give way completely.
High tides and storms in the Bay of Bengal happened at the same time as the flood.
Large areas of Bangladesh are flooded by extremely heavy monsoon rain falling on the land.
Rivers have been blocked and their channels made shallower by the deposition of silt.

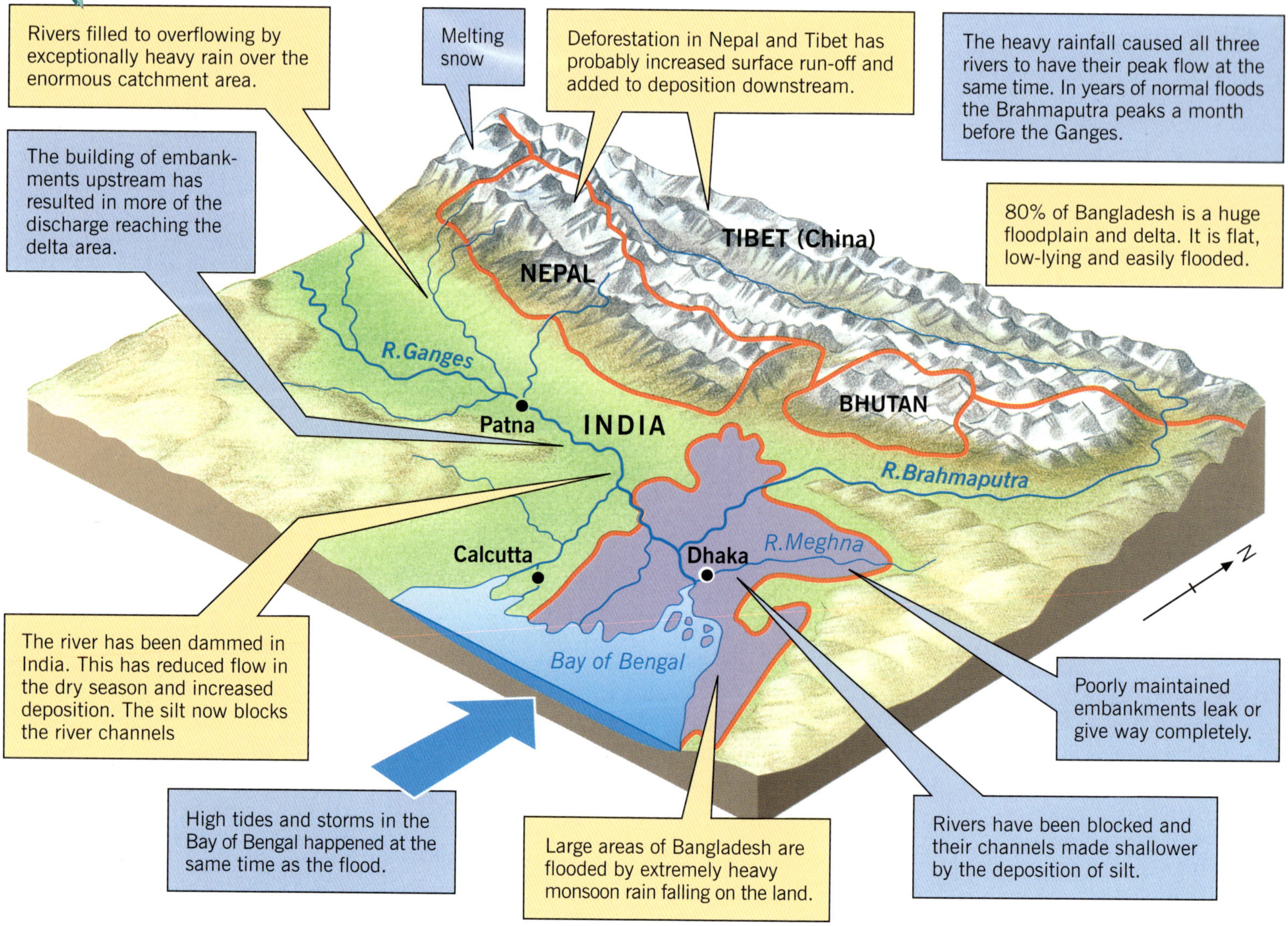

The build-up of silt contributes greatly to flooding in Bangladesh. Every year some 2.5 billion tonnes of it is deposited in the delta area. Silt forms as the river erodes and breaks up rock and soil. It is then carried downstream by the river and deposited when the load is too much to be carried. This gradually blocks the channel and raises the river bed, causing the river to overflow its banks more easily. This is a natural process and has been happening for thousands of years in the Bangladesh area.

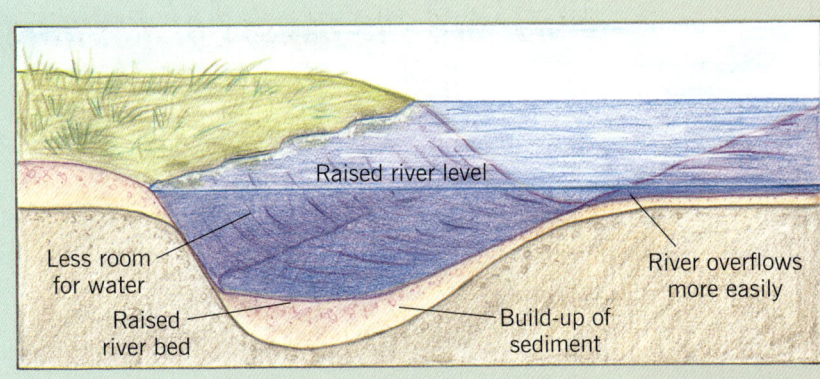

C

Raised river level

Less room for water

Raised river bed

Build-up of sediment

River overflows more easily

Concern has been voiced recently that human activities such as embankment construction, dam building and deforestation have increased the amount of silt being deposited and so added to the severity of flooding.

The question of deforestation is hotly debated. Some researchers claim that Bangladesh floods result mainly from snowmelt and run-off in the Himalayas in the spring and early summer topped up by heavy rain across the floodplain. The massive clearance of forest, they say, has increased run-off and erosion rates, caused more silt to be deposited downstream and resulted in higher levels of flooding. Many

people argue strongly against this theory. They say that information on the forest areas of Nepal is unreliable and that there is probably more forest cover now than there was a century ago.

This is one of the problems for Bangladesh. It can be very difficult to decide exactly what the causes of severe flooding are and therefore even more difficult to do something about it.

D Deforestation – the impact on flooding

1 Removal of forest cover (deforestation)

More load reaches the floodplain and delta

Channel beds raised

Soil easily washed off bare slopes

Rainfall runs quickly over surface into rivers

Channels silt up with increased load

4 Increased discharge in rivers

8 Risk of serious flood increased

Activities

1 Look at graph **A**, the flood hydrograph.
   a) What is the rainfall for July?
   b) What is the discharge in August?
   c) Which four months are the wettest?
   d) Which four months have the highest discharge?
   e) Describe the link between the pattern of rainfall and the river discharge.

2 List the possible causes of flooding using the headings below.

Possible causes of flooding	
Natural	Human

3 Put the information in figure **D** into the correct order. Three boxes have been done for you.

4 Explain why it may be difficult to identify the causes of floods.

Summary

Flooding in Bangladesh is a combination of several factors. The main ones include heavy rain, a large catchment area, low-lying land and the build-up of silt in river channels. It is sometimes difficult to decide exactly what the causes are.

◀ Can Bangladesh be protected from floods? ◀

The Plan

In 1989 the government of Bangladesh began working with several international agencies to produce a Flood Action Plan (FAP). This huge scheme contained 26 action points which together, it was hoped, would provide a long-term solution to the country's serious flooding problem.

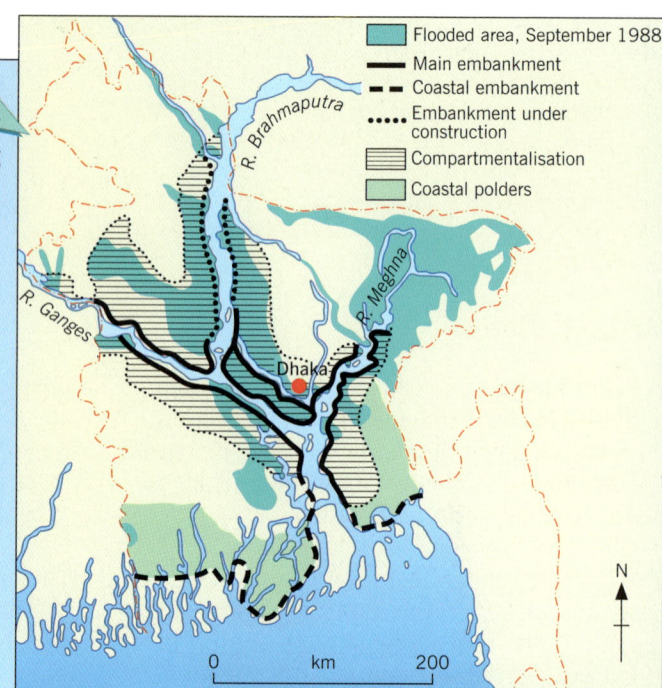

A Managing flooding in Bangladesh

Legend:
- Flooded area, September 1988
- Main embankment
- Coastal embankment
- Embankment under construction
- Compartmentalisation
- Coastal polders

R. Brahmaputra, R. Ganges, R. Megna, Dhaka

0 km 200

N

Shelters and warning systems

- Build 5000 flood shelters in the areas most at risk. These are cheap and easy to construct and would provide a place of safety for almost everyone.
- Improve the flood forecasting system using satellite and computer technology.
- Prepare flood disaster management plans which provide early warning and clear, effective instructions as to what people should do before, during and after a flood.

Dams

- Build dams to control river flow and hold back the monsoon rainwater in reservoirs. These would be concentrated in Bangladesh but the plan could be extended to India and Nepal. The water would be used for irrigation and generating electricity. The cost would be more than £500 million.

Chauba Dam, India

The Problems

The Flood Action Plan has not been welcomed by everyone and indeed has attracted considerable criticism internationally as well as from within Bangladesh itself. Many people are concerned about the unknown effects of such a large scheme and are worried that a shortage of money will result in only the urban areas being protected, leaving the very poor rural inhabitants still at risk.

B

The embankments will trap rainwater and make the flooding worse.

How can we provide solutions if we don't really know the causes?

Dam construction could increase the build-up of silt and make flooding worse.

Flood control

Divide the land into compartments and control water flow through a system of channels by sluice gates and water pumps. In the dry season water can be moved to farming areas requiring irrigation. Before the monsoon, water would be drained away to leave room for the floodwaters.

Embankments

Complete and strengthen the embankments along all main river channels to a height of up to 7 metres. More than 7500 km of embankment is already in place but repairs, heightening and new building would cost over $6 billion. This scheme should prevent serious flooding from river overflow.

Activities

1 What are the main aims of the Flood Action Plan?

2 Draw up a table like the one below to describe the main points of the Flood Action Plan.

Proposal	Description	Good points	Bad points

3 Which of the proposals do you think will be:
   a) the cheapest
   b) the most expensive
   c) the most successful in reducing the flood risk?
   Give reasons for your answers.

4 Why is it harder to reduce the flood risk in economically less developed countries like Bangladesh than in economically more developed countries like the USA?
(*Clues:* funding, materials, workforce, organisation, equipment, expertise.)

Summary

There is no easy solution to Bangladesh's flooding problem. The enormous size of the problem, the extreme poverty of the country, and the difficulty of identifying the exact causes of flooding make the task almost impossible. The Flood Action Plan tries to give protection from disastrous floods whilst still retaining the benefits of normal flooding. Not everyone agrees with the plan.

What is farming like in Bangladesh?

Flooding causes many problems for Bangladesh but it also brings benefits. The **silt** deposited by the rivers forms what is recognised as potentially the most productive agricultural land in the world. With good soil, warm conditions throughout the year and an abundance of rainfall, it is not surprising that Bangladesh is an agricultural country with the vast majority of people involved in **subsistence farming** and food production.

The main crops grown are rice, wheat, tea, sugar cane and a variety of fruits and vegetables including banana, lime, coconut and aubergine. Jute, a fibrous plant which is used for sacking and the backing of carpets, has for many years been the country's main export earner. This is now in rapid decline as synthetic materials have begun to take over the market.

Farming in Bangladesh is very closely **adapted** to the environment. Because of seasonal flooding, fertile soil, and high rainfall and humidity, rice is the principal crop. It covers about 80 per cent of the agricultural land and with its high nutritional value can provide up to 90 per cent of the country's total diet.

Improved technology and the introduction of new strains of rice now make it possible to grow three rice crops each year. Two crops are grown in the wet April to late October period whilst if irrigation is available, a third may be grown in the dry season between November and February. To enable farmers to achieve this, three groups of rice have been developed. These are **boro**, **aus** and **aman** and each has been adapted to seasonal differences in temperature, day-length and depth of flooding. For example, aus matures in less than 90 days and is suitable for relatively dry conditions, whilst deep-water aman can lengthen its stem with rising floodwater and so is used successfully in the wet season.

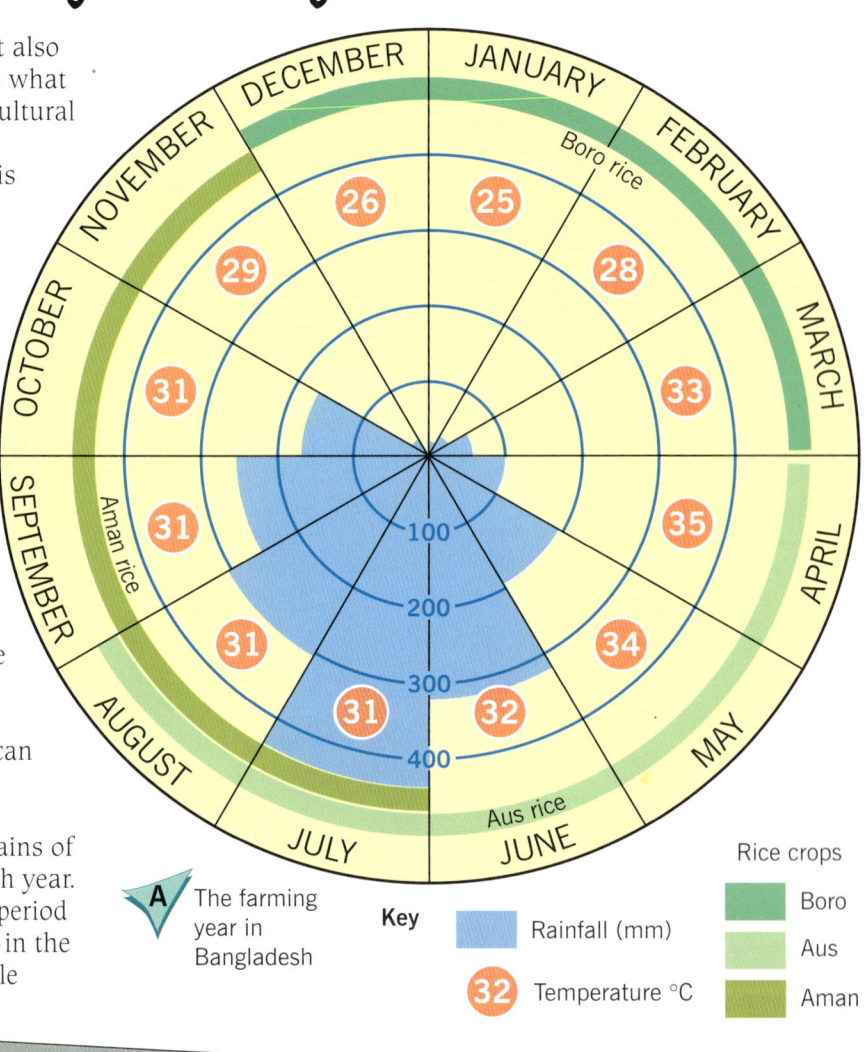

A The farming year in Bangladesh

Key

Rainfall (mm)

32 Temperature °C

Rice crops
Boro
Aus
Aman

B Rice cultivation in Bangladesh

Crop yields have improved so much in recent years that Bangladesh is now self-sufficient in rice and almost so in wheat. This has helped the country to make progress in providing food for its rapidly growing population.

The poorer farmers still have a very difficult life, however. Land ownership is probably the biggest problem. Over 60 million people have a maximum of 0.2 hectares each or are landless (0.2 hectares is about the size of a football pitch penalty area). Until the distribution and ownership of land is more fairly organised, there is little hope for these people. It is not surprising that many of them are leaving farming and heading for cities such as Dhaka in the hope of improving their chances in life in the urban areas.

C Some problems for farmers in Bangladesh

We are **subsistence** farmers – we produce just enough food for the family and have nothing spare to sell.

Serious flooding can destroy all of the crops as well as the family home

There are three classes of farmer:

The rich and powerful **landowner** who controls the land and makes the decisions. Half of all the land is owned by just 6% of the population.

The **sharecropper** who pays rent to the landowner for use of the land in produce not cash. A failed crop can leave a farmer in severe debt.

The **labourer** who works for the landowner for a wage. This is usually temporary, seasonal work and is extremely low-paid. These people are very poor and increasingly insecure.

The poorest of us live on the newly formed land which is in most danger from floods.

Many of our laws seem to benefit the rich rather than the poor.

Very few of us have access to any farm machinery and many of us don't even have a plough, never mind farm animals to pull it.

Activities

1 Look at diagram **A**.
   a) i) Name the wet season months.
       ii) What type of rice is grown at this time?
       iii) Explain how rice has been adapted for the wet season.
   b) i) Name the dry season months.
       ii) What type of rice is grown at this time?
       iii) Explain how technology has helped rice growing in this season.

2 a) Make a larger copy of diagram **D**.
   b) Write a sentence for each box to explain how year-round rice cultivation is successful in Bangladesh.

3 Write a paragraph to describe the physical features and farming methods shown in photo **B**.

4 List the problems of farm labourers in Bangladesh using the headings below.

Problems for farmers	
Physical (natural)	*Human*

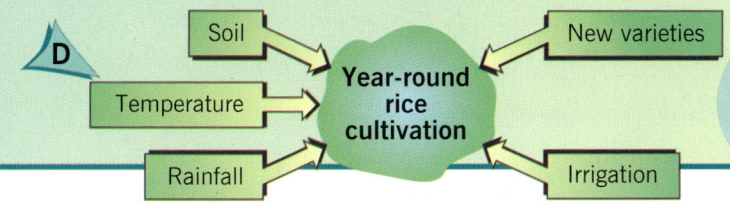

D

Soil → Year-round rice cultivation ← New varieties
Temperature → Year-round rice cultivation
Rainfall → Year-round rice cultivation ← Irrigation

Summary

The soils and climate of Bangladesh are ideal for farming. Food production has increased recently with the introduction of new technology and better rice varieties. Life for most farmers is very hard and it is difficult for them to improve their conditions.

▶ *What is Dhaka's land use?* ◀

As we have seen, towns do not grow in a haphazard way but tend to develop recognisable shapes and patterns (pages 68 and 69). Each town is unique but similar patterns of land use may be shared with other urban areas. These patterns can be shown more simply as **urban land use models**. Cities in the economically developing world have different patterns of land use to those in the developed world. This is largely because their history, traditions and economic conditions are very different. Land use in Dhaka is typical of such cities.

Dhaka is the capital and largest city in Bangladesh. It is also one of the fastest-growing cities in the world and is expected to have a population of over 11 million by the year 2000. Its rapid growth is a result of both **rural-to-urban migration** and higher than average birth rates in a city where young adults make up a large proportion of the migrants.

The rapid influx of people, most of them extremely poor, has caused many problems for Dhaka and has resulted in the development of enormous areas of slum housing called **bustees**. Bustees are built in areas which have little economic value and are unsuitable for farming,

industry or quality housing. These places are often unhealthy marshlands or areas most likely to flood. Most of the bustees are located on the outskirts of the city. They consist of rough shelters and lack basic amenities such as clean water and sewage systems.

Dhaka city centre is a mixture of modern and traditional buildings. Some are in good condition but many are in serious need of repair. Although there are few private cars, the streets are teeming with people, overcrowded buses and cheap rickshaw taxis – small three-wheeled vehicles that are either pedalled or powered by a small engine.

The richer people mainly live close to the city centre in modern, good-quality housing. The houses generally have large gardens and even swimming pools. Many have housemaids and security guards. Houses here are protected from flooding by the Flood Action Plan. Most of the inhabitants work in well-paid jobs in the nearby city centre.

C Typical urban land use model for a city in the economically less developed world

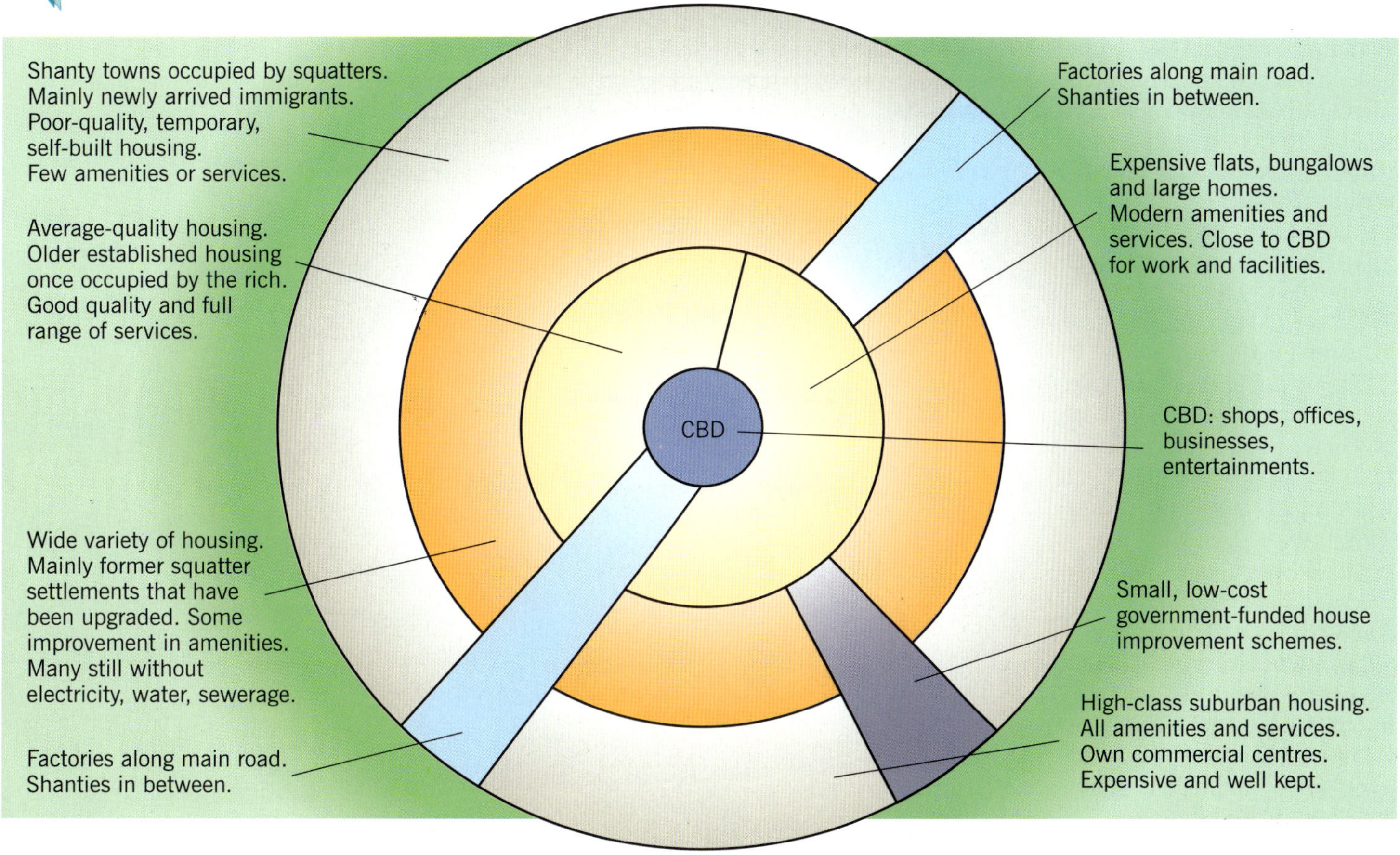

Shanty towns occupied by squatters. Mainly newly arrived immigrants. Poor-quality, temporary, self-built housing. Few amenities or services.

Average-quality housing. Older established housing once occupied by the rich. Good quality and full range of services.

Wide variety of housing. Mainly former squatter settlements that have been upgraded. Some improvement in amenities. Many still without electricity, water, sewerage.

Factories along main road. Shanties in between.

CBD

Factories along main road. Shanties in between.

Expensive flats, bungalows and large homes. Modern amenities and services. Close to CBD for work and facilities.

CBD: shops, offices, businesses, entertainments.

Small, low-cost government-funded house improvement schemes.

High-class suburban housing. All amenities and services. Own commercial centres. Expensive and well kept.

Activities

1 **a)** What is an urban land use model?
   b) What is meant by rural-to-urban migration?
   c) What is a bustee?

2 **a)** Make a copy of transect **D**.
   b) Using diagram **C**, label the different residential land uses along the transect. Give your transect a title.
   c) Make another copy of transect **D** and this time label the residential land uses using diagram **E**. Give your transect a title.
   d) Describe the differences between the two transects.

CBD
Edge of city

D

3 Describe and suggest reasons for the location of poor-quality shanty housing.

4 **a)** Describe the location of high-quality housing in cities of the less developed world.
   b) Describe the main features of this housing.

E Simplified urban land use model for a city in a developed country

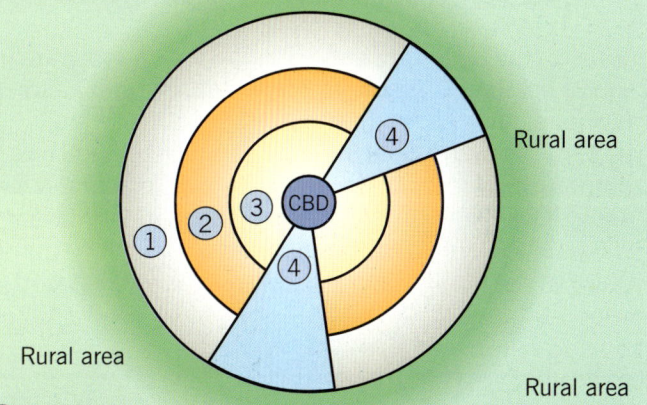

Rural area

Rural area

Rural area

CBD

① Modern, high-cost private housing
② Medium-quality housing
③ Mainly older, low-cost, poorer-quality housing
④ Industries along transport routes

Summary

It is possible to recognise patterns of land use and functional zones within a city. Cities in economically less developed countries have developed different patterns from those of older settlements in developed countries.

119

⊳ *What is it like to live in the slums?* ⊲

The problems . . .

A

In 1961 half a million people lived in Dhaka, but the population is increasing so rapidly that by 2005 this figure is expected to top 15 million. The new arrivals are mainly landless peasants forced by flood, debt and sheer population pressure to leave the countryside and head for the big city, where most end up in the shanty-town slums to suffer further hardship and a bleak future.

The slum areas of Dhaka are called **bustees**. Here, people live in cramped and crowded conditions with little hope of access to basic amenities such as electricity, gas, clean running water, toilets or mains sewerage. Their homes are typically one-roomed dwellings made of bamboo, coconut leaves, mud and cardboard in which a whole family has to live, eat and sleep.

Many of the slums are located in the lowest-lying areas where flooding is common. The building of embankments has made the situation worse in some of these areas as they prevent rainwater from draining away. In these places it is not unusual for the floods to last for up to five months. Sometimes the water almost reaches the roofs of the shelters, and simple platforms have to be built so that families can survive above the dirty polluted water. At this time, makeshift boats are used to move from place to place.

Few shanty-town dwellers are educated and there is little chance of them obtaining a job, earning regular money and so improving their living conditions. A small number work as rickshaw drivers but the work is hard and very poorly paid. Others complete menial tasks, help on building sites, collect rubbish to sell cheaply at the market . . . or simply beg.

Activities

B

1 **a)** Explain Dhaka's rapid population growth.
   b) What factors cause people to leave the countryside and move to the city?

2 What is a shanty town and which people live in them?

3 Make a larger copy of sketch **B** showing life in the shanty towns. Complete it by adding the answers to the questions.

a) What amenities are lacking?

b) What are the houses made from?

c) Why are many shanties located in low-lying areas?

d) Why have embankments been built?

e) What problems have the embankments caused?

f) How do the people cope with flooding?

g) What jobs do people living in shanties do?

h) Why is getting a job a problem?

... and possible solutions

Bangladesh is such a poor country and the problems of the slum areas are so enormous that it is virtually impossible to provide a successful solution. Many international organisations and governments give aid to Bangladesh in order to help improve conditions but it can be difficult to ensure that aid goes to the right places and helps those most in need. Nevertheless, progress is being made in some areas.

Water for washing, cooking and drinking comes from streams and stagnant ponds. Unclean water is a major health hazard, responsible for serious infections such as diarrhoea and typhoid. Much effort is now being put in, particularly by aid organisations, to provide slum dwellers with a safe water supply. This is usually done by drilling a borehole and fitting a simple hand pump that requires no servicing.

Self-help housing – under this scheme the council provides basic amenities such as water, electricity and sewerage to an area. They also make available at a low price, building materials such as breeze-blocks and roofing tiles, and a plot of land on which to build. The advantages of self-help schemes are that they are simple, require no advanced technology or machinery and are relatively cheap.

C

One of the slum-dwellers' biggest problems is debt and an inability to start up small businesses because of a total lack of money. A new **loan system** has recently been introduced which helps people overcome this problem. The loans are very small-scale and typically may be used to purchase a set of scales for use in a market shop to sell rice to local people. The scheme has enjoyed much success and so far it has been rare for the loan not to be paid back.

Good as these schemes may be for some of the shanty-town dwellers, much more still needs to be done. Unfortunately the local authorities in Dhaka just cannot keep pace with the continuous and large numbers of new migrants, and so the problems continue.

4 **a)** What is a self-help housing scheme?
   b) Which of the features in diagram **D** will be:
      i) bought by the shanty-town dweller
      ii) provided by the local authority?
   c) From the diagram, list the four most important features of a self-help house. Give reasons for your answer.
   d) Why are many types of low-cost, self-help housing not much help to people who live in shanty towns?

5 Briefly describe three other ways in which life in a shanty town may be improved.

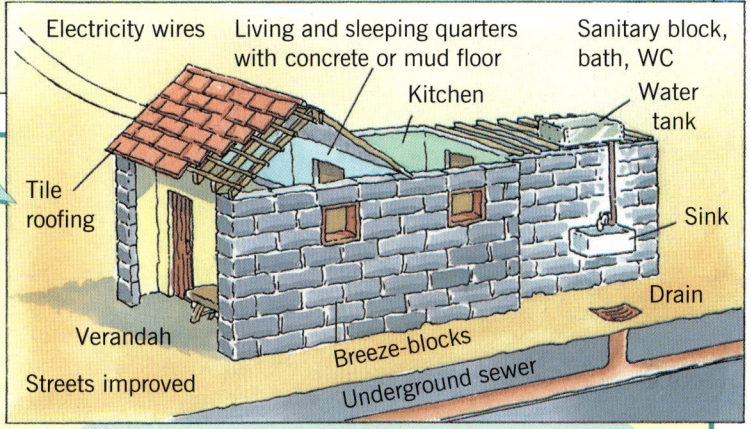

D

Electricity wires Living and sleeping quarters with concrete or mud floor Sanitary block, bath, WC Kitchen Water tank Tile roofing Sink Drain Verandah Breeze-blocks Streets improved Underground sewer

Summary Migration from rural areas has caused the formation of many shanty towns or slum areas. The people living in these places face many hardships and a bleak future. Improving life in the shanty towns is very difficult.

11 World development and trade

▷ What are the characteristics of development? ◁

Geographers are concerned with:
- differences in levels of development between places, both within and between countries
- mapping these differences to see if there are recognisable patterns in development
- trying to explain why these differences have occurred, and how they may be evened out.

The term 'development' has been defined, and is interpreted, in many different ways. It is difficult for geographers, and other groups of people, to find methods of measuring development. The traditional, and easiest, method of comparing development is by measuring the 'wealth and economic growth' of a region or country. The wealth of a country is measured in terms of its GNP (**gross national product**). The GNP per capita is the total value of goods produced and services provided by a country in a given year divided by the number of people living in that country.

GNP is given in US dollars (US$) to allow easy comparisons to be made between countries. Table **B** on page 100 includes the GNP for 10 countries at different levels of economic development. It shows that in 1994 every person in the UK, regardless of their age, would have received US$ 17 970 had the wealth created in the UK been shared out evenly. In the real world, wealth is never shared out evenly and so GNP hides differences in wealth within cities and between regions.

Map **A** shows how, based on GNP, the world can be divided into two economic groups.
- The **economically more developed** countries, which have the highest GNP, include the richer, more industrialised nations of the 'North'.
- The **economically less developed** countries, with the lowest GNP, include the poorer, less industrialised nations of the 'South'.

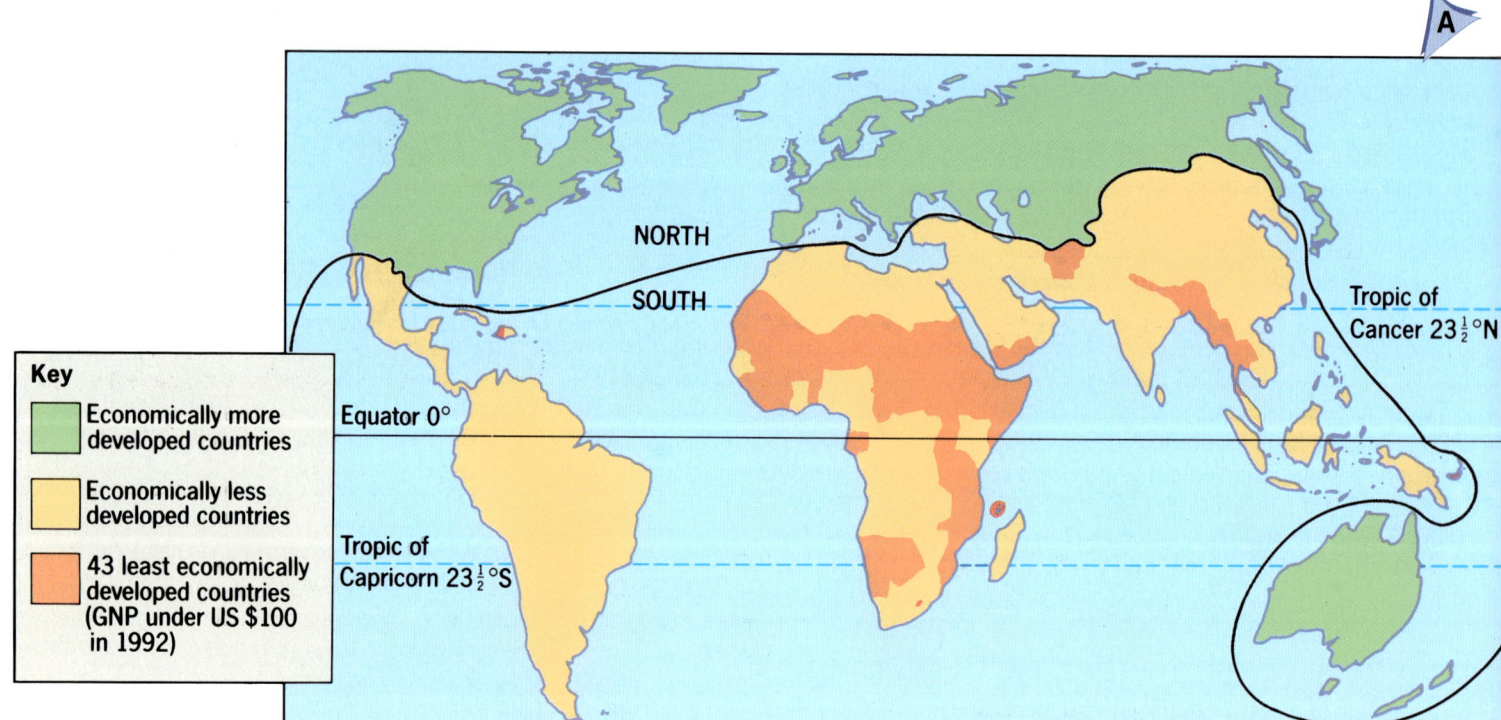

A

Key

■ Economically more developed countries

□ Economically less developed countries

■ 43 least economically developed countries (GNP under US $100 in 1992)

NORTH
SOUTH
Equator 0°
Tropic of Capricorn 23½°S
Tropic of Cancer 23½°N

To many people living in a Western, industrialised country such as the UK, economic development has been associated with a growth in wealth. This suggested that the GNP of a country had to increase if the standard of living and quality of life of its inhabitants was to improve. More recently the meaning of the term 'development' has been widened to include various social, health and educational indicators. However, as shown in diagram **B**, and in table **B** on page 100, these indicators are themselves usually dependent upon the wealth of a country. Economically less developed countries are perceived, when compared with economically more developed countries, as having smaller volumes of trade and a trade deficit; more jobs in the primary sector and fewer in the secondary and tertiary sectors; higher birth, death and infant mortality rates; a shorter life expectancy; a lower level of literacy; and relatively few doctors per size of the population.

B

		Developing countries	*Developed countries*
Jobs	Number of jobs in the primary, secondary and tertiary sectors, expressed as a percentage	Most jobs in primary sector (highest percentage in farming). Relatively few in secondary and tertiary sectors.	Few jobs in the primary sector. Larger number in the secondary sector. Highest percentage in the tertiary sector.
Trade	Volume (amount), value and type of trade	Small in volume and value. Mainly raw materials (minerals and foodstuffs which are cheap to buy).	Large volume and value. Mainly manufactured goods (expensive to buy).
Population	*Birth rate* – number of births per 1000 people *Death rate* – number of deaths per 1000 people *Infant mortality rate* – number of babies out of every 1000 born alive who die before the age of one *Life expectancy* – age a person born in a country can expect to live	High birth rate (falling). Relatively high death rate (falling). High infant mortality rate (falling slightly). Short life expectancy (increasing).	Low birth rate (steady). Low death rate (steady). Low infant mortality rate (steady). Long life expectancy (increasing).
Health	Number of people to every doctor	Few doctors, nurses and hospitals. Each doctor may have several thousand patients.	More doctors, nurses and hospitals. Each doctor may have only several hundred patients.
Education	*Level of literacy* – the percentage of adults able to read and write	Insufficient money for full-time education. Low percentage of literate adults, especially among women.	Full-time education. High percentage of literate adults including women.

Activities

1 a) What do you understand by the term 'development'?
b) Why is development hard to define?
c) What is gross national product (GNP)?
d) What is the GNP for each of the USA, the UK, Brazil, Kenya and India?
e) Why do the USA and the UK have a higher GNP than Kenya and India?
f) Describe the location and distribution of the economically less developed countries.

2 Name six indicators, other than GNP, which can be used to show differences in levels of development between regions and countries.

Summary

GNP is the most frequent method used to show differences in development between places. Development can also be measured using social, health and educational indicators.

Is there a link between GNP and development?

Many of the characteristics (page 122) applied to economically less developed countries are often linked to their GNP. How justifiable and accurate are these statements? For example, do birth and infant mortality rates decrease and does life expectancy increase as the GNP (wealth) of a country increases? It is possible, by using a **scattergraph**, to see whether there is a close link, or relationship, between GNP and the various characteristics of development.

Table **A** gives three variables. These variables are the GNP, life expectancy and the birth rate for ten selected countries which are at different stages of economic development. The resultant graphs shows a scatter of ten crosses to which a 'best fit line' has been added. The resultant best fit line does not pass through all of the points on the graph, but it has been drawn as close as possible to all of them. The closer the scatter of crosses to a straight line, the closer is the relationship between the two variables.

If, as in the first graph, the best fit line goes from the bottom left to the top right then the relationship, or correlation, between the two variables is said to be **positive** (diagram **B(a)**). This means that 'as the GNP (one variable) of a country increases then so too does the life expectancy (the second variable)'.

If, as on the second graph, the best fit line goes from top left to bottom right then, while there is still close relationship between the two variables, this time the correlation is said to be **negative** (diagram **B(c)**). This is because 'as the GNP (one variable) increases then the birth rate (the second variable) decreases'.

Occasionally a scattergraph may show one or more points to lie a long way from the best fit line (diagram **B(d)**). These points are called 'anomalies' because they do not fit with the usual trend or pattern. Usually there is a specific reason for an anomaly. For example, a country may have a higher than expected birth rate as religious beliefs may be contrary to birth control.

A

| Country | Variables | | |
	GNP (US$)	Life expectancy	Birth rate
Japan	31 450	79	12
USA	24 750	76	14
France	22 360	76	13
UK	17 790	76	14
Mexico	3750	70	27
Brazil	3020	66	26
Egypt	660	61	31
India	290	60	31
Kenya	270	61	47
Bangladesh	220	53	41

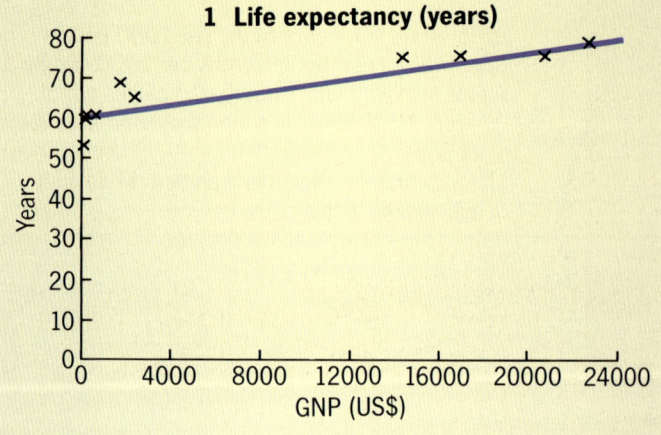

1 Life expectancy (years)

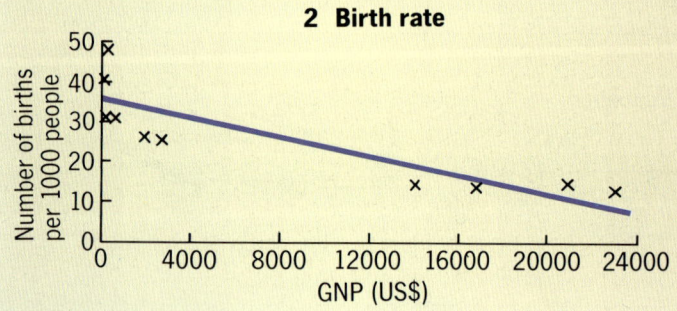

2 Birth rate

Types of correlation between two variables

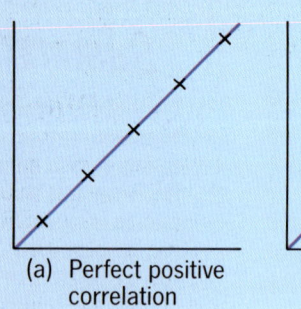

(a) Perfect positive correlation

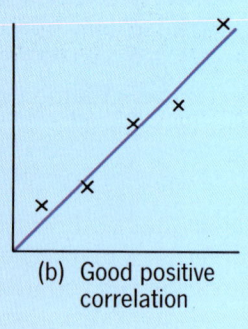

(b) Good positive correlation

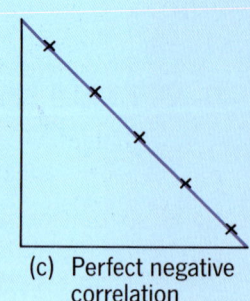

(c) Perfect negative correlation

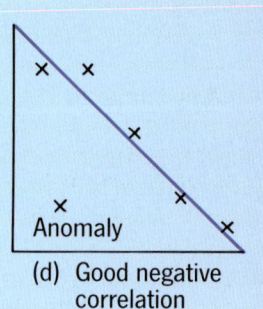

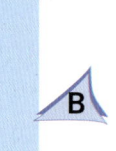

Anomaly

(d) Good negative correlation

B

Development and literacy

Table **B** on page 100 gave the adult literacy rates for ten countries at different stages of economic development. It does not need a scattergraph to see the close positive relationship between the two variables of adult literacy and GNP. The higher the GNP the greater the number of adults who can read and write, since low levels of literacy are both a cause and a consequence of poverty. However, adult literacy figures, especially those for the less economically developed countries, hide the fact that literacy rates for women are usually much lower than those for men. Map **C** shows that female literacy rates are lowest in Africa, where women have spent on average only one year at school, and in southern Asia. Some of the explanations for Africa's low literacy rates are given in figure **D**. How the education of women helps a country to develop is described on page 129.

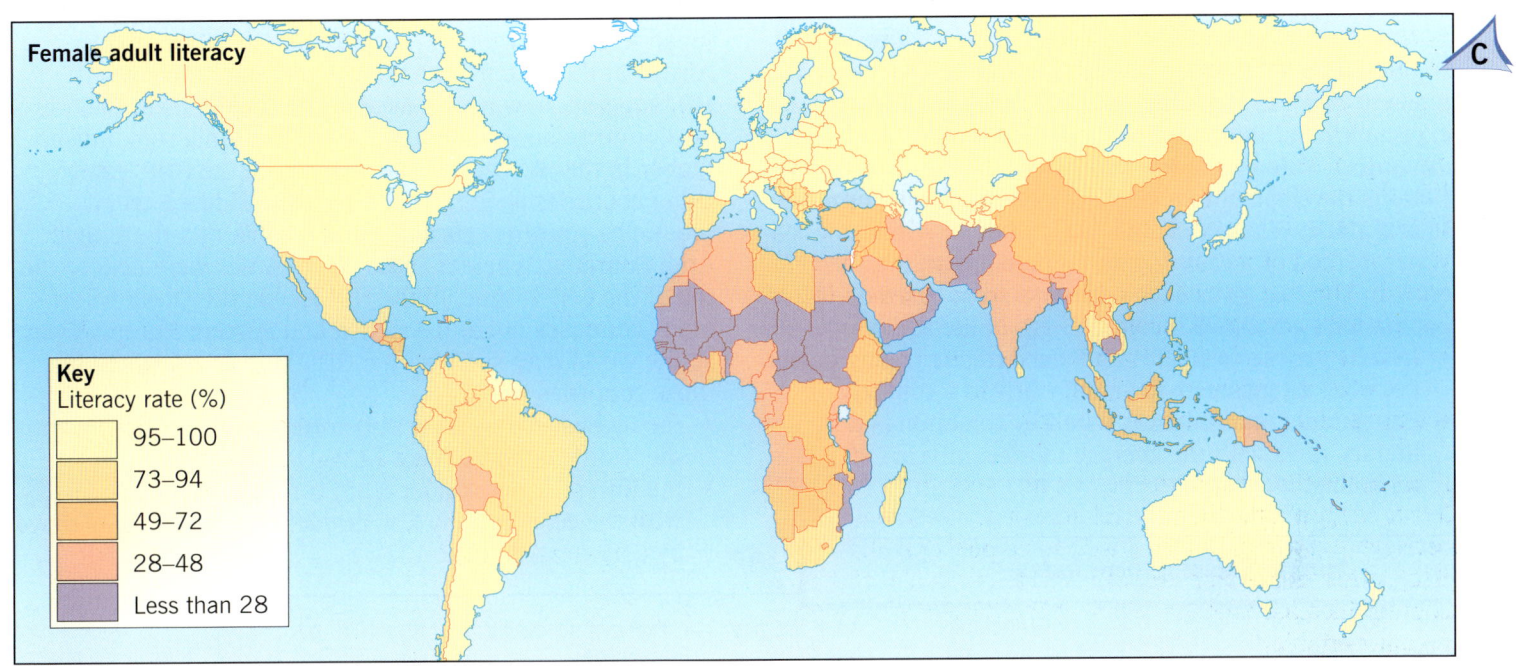

Female adult literacy **C**

Key
Literacy rate (%)

- 95–100
- 73–94
- 49–72
- 28–48
- Less than 28

D

Women are responsible for family care. The majority are also unpaid farmers who have to collect water and fuelwood, and do the cooking. This leaves little time for education. In countries like Ghana and Kenya many sustainable appropriate technology schemes are run by women.

The Islamic male-dominated cultures of North Africa see the role of women as limited to work in the home. Consequently education is though to be unnecessary. South of the Equator, women are so occupied in farming and trading that they are prevented from gaining an education. This is due to the constraints of poverty, time and tradition.

Activities

1. **a)** Draw a scattergraph to show any possible relationship between GNP and the percentage of people employed in agriculture. The figures are in table **B** on page 100.
   b) Is the relationship (correlation) positive or negative? Explain what this means.

2. **a)** What is the relationship between GNP and illiteracy?
   b) Why are female illiteracy rates so high in Africa?

Summary

Scattergraphs show relationships between variables, e.g. GNP and life expectancy, birth rates and the numbers employed in agriculture.

How can development be measured other than by GNP?

It has already been pointed out that GNP provides the easiest method of measuring, and the simplest way to compare, different levels of development (page 122). However, it is increasingly argued that the term 'development' has a wider meaning than just 'wealth'.

During the 1980s the Overseas Development Council (ODC) suggested the physical quality of life index (PQLI). This index replaced GNP (an economic measure) with literacy rates, life expectancy and infant mortality (three social/welfare measures). This was followed, in 1990, by the United Nations Development Programme's **Human Development Index' (HDI)**. The UN claims that human development is a better method of measuring development than income growth. The HDI gives each country a score based on its population's combined income, length of life and education.

- Income per capita (GNP) is adjusted to purchasing power, i.e. what an income will actually buy in a country.
- Educational attainment is found by combining adult literacy rates with the average number of years of schooling.

- Life expectancy is regarded as the best measure of a country's health and safety.

Each variable is given a score ranging from 1 (the best) to 0 (the poorest). The HDI is the average score, also ranging from 1 to 0, of the three variables. The latest UN figures put Japan at the top with a score of 0.993 and Guinea (West Africa) at the bottom with a score of 0.045 (table **A**). The HDI suggests how poor a measure of development GNP can be. Countries such as Sri Lanka and Tanzania rank much higher in the HDI league than they do in the GNP league. Other countries do less well, especially Middle East oil-producing countries such as Saudi Arabia and the United Arab Emirates. Whereas these oil countries were near to the top of the GNP league, in the HDI league they rank below many countries in Latin America and Eastern Europe. Even so the world map showing the HDI (map **C**) reveals that those countries with:

- the highest scores (over 0.9) correspond very closely with the 'North' (map **A**, page 122)
- the lowest scores (under 0.25) correspond equally closely with the economically less developed countries as defined by GNP (map **A**, page 122).

A

Human Development Index					
Rank order	Country	Life expectancy at birth (years)	Adult literacy rate (%)	Years of schooling (average)	Real GNP per capita (PPP$*)
1	Japan	78.6	99.0	10.7	17 616
2	Canada	77.0	99.0	12.1	19 232
3	Norway	77.1	99.0	11.6	16 028
4	Switzerland	77.4	99.0	11.1	20 874
5	Sweden	77.4	99.0	11.1	17 014
6	USA	75.9	99.0	12.3	21 449
7	Australia	76.5	99.0	11.5	16 051
8	France	76.4	99.0	11.6	17 405
9	Netherlands	77.2	99.0	10.6	15 695
10	United Kingdom	75.7	99.0	11.5	15 804
12	Germany	75.2	99.0	11.1	18 213
22	Italy	76.0	97.1	7.3	15 890
23	Spain	77.0	97.5	6.8	11 723
37	Russian Federation	69.3	94.0	9.0	7 968
48	Poland	71.8	96.0	8.0	4 237
53	Mexico	69.7	87.6	4.7	5 918
70	Brazil	65.6	81.1	3.9	4 718
84	Saudi Arabia	64.5	62.4	3.7	10 989
101	China	70.1	73.3	4.8	1 990
124	Egypt	60.3	48.4	2.8	1 988
129	Kenya	59.2	49.1	2.7	1 921
132	Pakistan	57.7	34.8	1.9	1 862
134	India	59.1	48.2	2.4	1 072
142	Nigeria	51.5	50.7	1.2	1 215
147	Bangladesh	57.8	35.3	2.0	872
170	Burkina Faso	48.2	18.2	0.1	618
171	Afghanistan	42.5	29.4	0.8	714
172	Sierra Leone	42.0	20.7	0.9	1 086
173	Guinea	43.5	24.0	0.8	501

*Purchasing power parity in US dollars All figures are from 1990

B

Top developing nations (overall ranking)

1 Barbados (2)
2 Hong Kong (24)
3 Cyprus (27)
4 Uruguay (30)
5 Trinidad and Tobago (31)
6 Bahamas (32)
7 South Korea (33)
8 Chile (30)
9 Costa Rica (42)
10 Singapore (43)

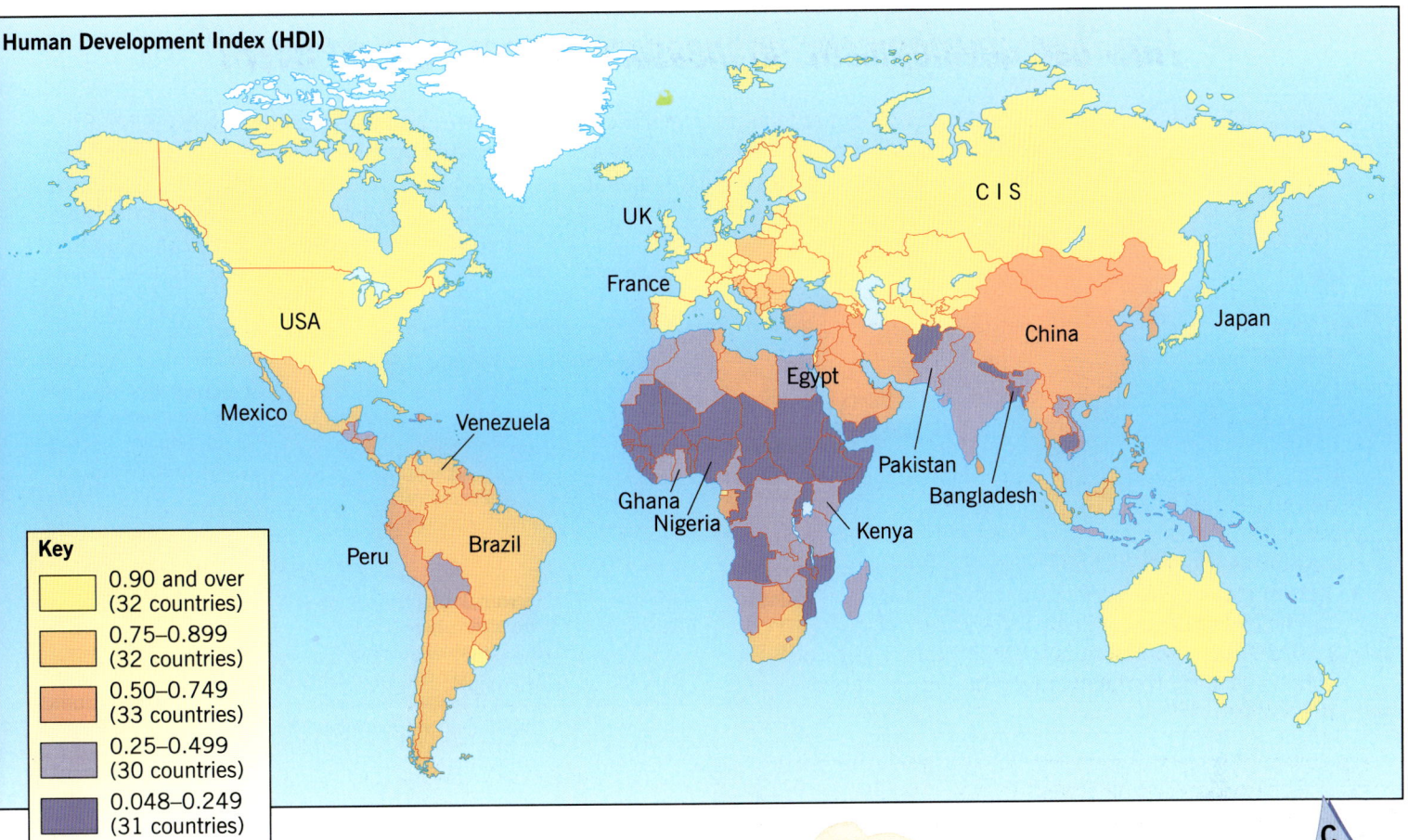

Human Development Index (HDI)

UK
France
USA
Mexico
Venezuela
Peru
Brazil
CIS
Egypt
China
Japan
Pakistan
Bangladesh
Ghana
Nigeria
Kenya

Key

	0.90 and over (32 countries)
	0.75–0.899 (32 countries)
	0.50–0.749 (33 countries)
	0.25–0.499 (30 countries)
	0.048–0.249 (31 countries)

C

The HDI can also be used to expose inequalities within a country as well as inequalities between countries. For example, when the HDI is calculated for black people in the USA, it gives them a similar score to people living in Trinidad (table **B**).

The HDI is not without its critics who claim that the index should also include a measure of human rights and freedom. The UN has responded by arguing that human freedom is difficult and too volatile to measure. The HDI will serve its purpose if it shows where poverty is worst, and if it stimulates debate about where aid, trade and foreign debt reduction should best be focused.

D

Activities

1 a) Why did the United Nations suggest the Human Development Index (HDI)?

b) Which three variables are used to determine the HDI?

c) How is the HDI worked out?

d) In what ways is the Human Development Index a better guide to development than the more traditional use of GNP?

2 a) Describe carefully the location of those countries with an HDI of:

i)   over 0.9

ii) between 0.5 and 0.9

iii) under 0.5.

b) How do these locations compare with a map showing GNP (page 122)?

Summary

The Human Development Index (HDI) has extended the meaning of development to include real income, education and life expectancy. Even so there are considerable similarities between the GNP and HDI maps.

Are there recognisable stages in economic development?

Rostow was an economist who proposed a model for economic growth. Remember that a model is a method of showing reality, which is often complex, in a more simplified and generalised way. Rostow claimed that all countries had the potential to develop economically. However, before a country can become as developed as Japan or the USA, it will have to pass through a sequence of stages (diagram **A**) which are described in diagram **B**.

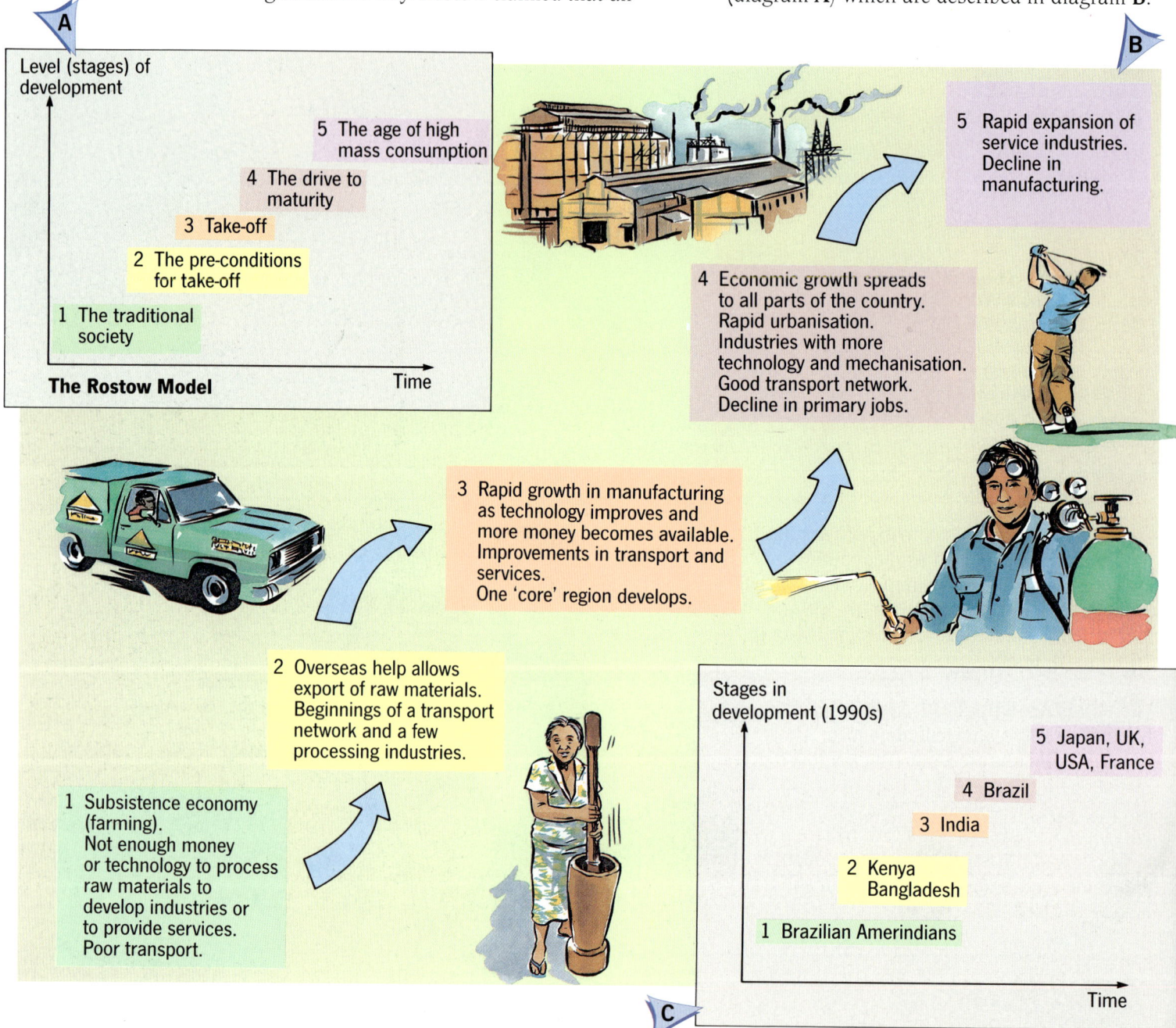

A

Level (stages) of development

5 The age of high mass consumption

4 The drive to maturity

3 Take-off

2 The pre-conditions for take-off

1 The traditional society

The Rostow Model

Time

B

5 Rapid expansion of service industries. Decline in manufacturing.

4 Economic growth spreads to all parts of the country. Rapid urbanisation. Industries with more technology and mechanisation. Good transport network. Decline in primary jobs.

3 Rapid growth in manufacturing as technology improves and more money becomes available. Improvements in transport and services. One 'core' region develops.

2 Overseas help allows export of raw materials. Beginnings of a transport network and a few processing industries.

1 Subsistence economy (farming). Not enough money or technology to process raw materials to develop industries or to provide services. Poor transport.

C

Stages in development (1990s)

5 Japan, UK, USA, France

4 Brazil

3 India

2 Kenya Bangladesh

1 Brazilian Amerindians

Time

Rostow's model, like other models, is open to criticism. He claimed that each country needed an injection of money before 'take-off' could begin. However, it is now recognised that, despite financial aid, many countries are unlikely to become industrialised and economically developed. This may be due to a combination of a lack of raw materials, capital and technology as well as a rapid growth in their population. Diagram **C** suggests, using Rostow's model, the stage of development reached by a selection of countries.

How can the quality of life in economically developing countries be improved?

Two methods by which economically developing countries may try to improve their quality of life is to raise their standards of education, especially for women, and to extend appropriate technology.

Education Education can develop skills which can increase productivity in agriculture, industry and commerce. It can also raise self-confidence which allows people to try out new ideas. It is important that women are given the same educational opportunities as men (photo **D**). Agriculture is the backbone of the economy in most of the economically less developed countries, and women are responsible for up to 70 per cent of the farm work. Education of women also leads to improvements in diet and hygiene, two factors that can reduce illness and improve health. It is an accepted fact that as female literacy increases, the birth rate and family size decrease.

Appropriate technology Intermediate Technology is a British charitable organisation which works with people in economically less developed countries. It helps people, especially in rural areas, to acquire the tools and techniques needed if they are to work themselves out of poverty. Intermediate Technology helps people to meet their basic needs in food, clothing, housing, farm equipment, energy and employment. It uses local knowledge, and adds to this by providing technical advice, training, equipment, and financial support to help people to become more self-sufficient and independent. The ideal is for local people to earn a surplus, however small, which can be invested in their subsistence farms and small-scale businesses (photo **E**). Most of Intermediate Technology's projects are in response to local groups which are often, especially in Africa, run by women. Such projects should be sustainable and appropriate to the technology of the country involved.

D Schoolgirls in Zimbabwe

E Women in Kenya unloading stoves from a kiln after firing

Summary

Rostow's model suggests that a country has to pass through several stages before it becomes economically developed. The best opportunity for poorer countries to develop seems to lie with improved education and the use of appropriate technology.

Activities

1 **a)** Draw a diagram to show the five stages of development in the Rostow model.
   b) Describe the level of development at each stage.
   c) At approximately which stage of development would you place the following countries: Italy, Ethiopia, Egypt, Mexico, Germany, China, Nigeria and Hong Kong?

2 **a)** Explain the importance of the following quotation: 'The need to educate women to the same level as men is seen by many as the greatest single way in which development can be encouraged'.
   b) What are the aims of Intermediate Technology (IT)?
   c) Why is its support often more valuable to an economically developing country than large loans given by the World Bank or a developed country?

▷ *How has trade affected development?* ◁

No country can provide everything that its inhabitants will want or need. To provide these needs a country has to **trade** with other countries. It has to buy (**import**) things that it is either short of, or which can be produced more cheaply elsewhere. These items may include foodstuffs, energy resources and manufactured goods. In order to buy these goods, a country will have to sell (**export**) things of which it has a surplus, or which it can produce more cheaply than other countries. Ideally a country hopes to have a **trade**

surplus. This means that it earns more money from the goods it exports than it has to spend on imports. A country with a trade surplus will become richer and can use the extra money to provide services and to widen its industries. Unfortunately it is impossible for every country to have a trade surplus. Those that have a **trade deficit** will remain poor, and will have insufficient money to develop new industries or to provide services. A country with a trade deficit spends more on imports than it earns from exports.

A

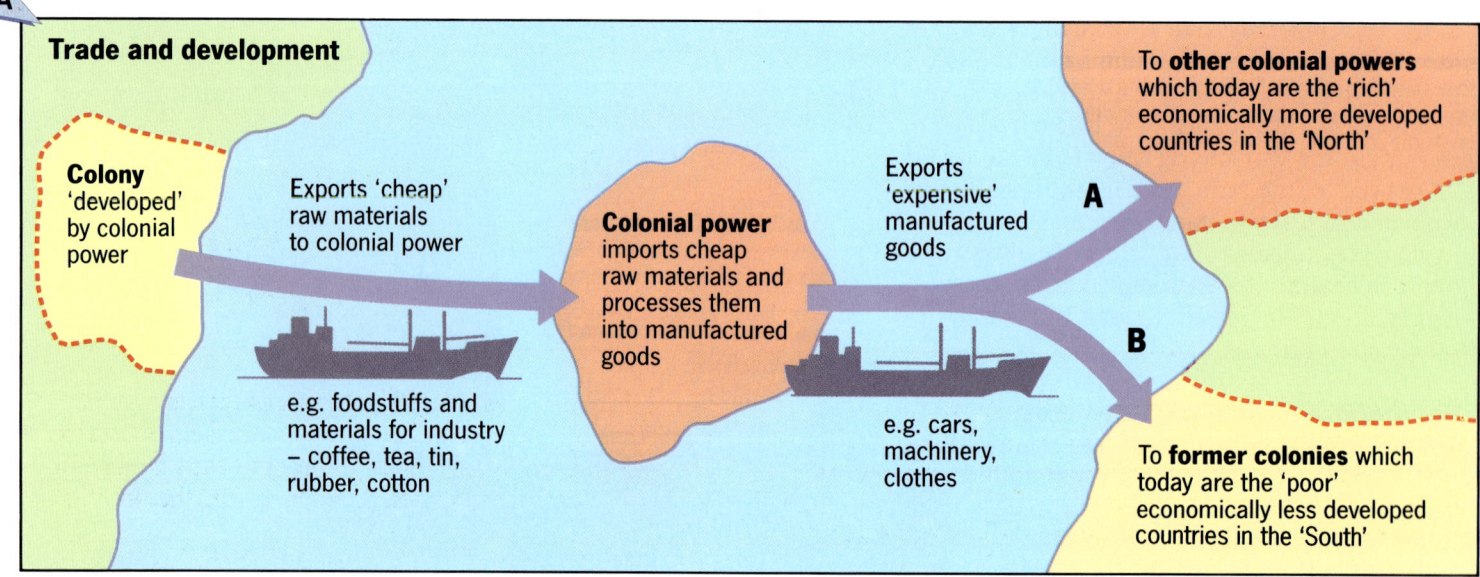

Trade and development

Colony 'developed' by colonial power

Exports 'cheap' raw materials to colonial power

e.g. foodstuffs and materials for industry – coffee, tea, tin, rubber, cotton

Colonial power imports cheap raw materials and processes them into manufactured goods

Exports 'expensive' manufactured goods

e.g. cars, machinery, clothes

A

B

To **other colonial powers** which today are the 'rich' economically more developed countries in the 'North'

To **former colonies** which today are the 'poor' economically less developed countries in the 'South'

World trade grew rapidly during colonial times. It was the richer countries in the 'North' which became the colonial powers. They 'developed' colonies in the 'South'.

Colonies provided raw materials (primary goods) for the colonial powers (diagram **A** and photo **B**). The colonial powers then either consumed these materials or processed them into manufactured goods. Many of the manufactured goods were then sold back to the colonies (photo **C**). The prices of primary goods are low in comparison with those of manufactured goods. The result has been:

- a trade deficit for the former colonies, leaving them as the economically less developed countries of the 'South'
- a trade surplus for the former colonial powers, enabling them to become the economically more developed countries of the 'North'.

B

C

Egypt
Oil and cotton 83%

Cuba
Sugar 77%

Honduras
Bananas 76%

Ghana
Cocoa 80%

Nigeria
Oil 99%

Kenya
Tea and coffee 52%

Laos
Timber 76%

Bangladesh
Jute 51%

Zambia
Copper 87%

Countries where one or two products are more than half of all exports

D

Map **D** shows another problem faced by developing countries. Many of them, especially in Africa, rely heavily upon just one or two commodities to provide jobs at home and income from exports. When prices and demand for these products are high then the income earned by exporting them is also high. However, prices for primary goods are often fixed and kept low by the developed countries. Demand is more likely to fluctuate as it usually depends upon economic conditions in the developed countries. The economy of a developing country will therefore be seriously affected if:

- a crop or mineral is over-produced
- there is a decline in demand for a product, especially at times of world economic recession
- a rival producer sells the item more cheaply
- there is a crop failure or a mineral is used up.

Developing countries still have the largest percentage of their workforce in agriculture. However, farmers are often forced to grow crops for export, in order to earn money for the country, rather than to grow crops to feed themselves.

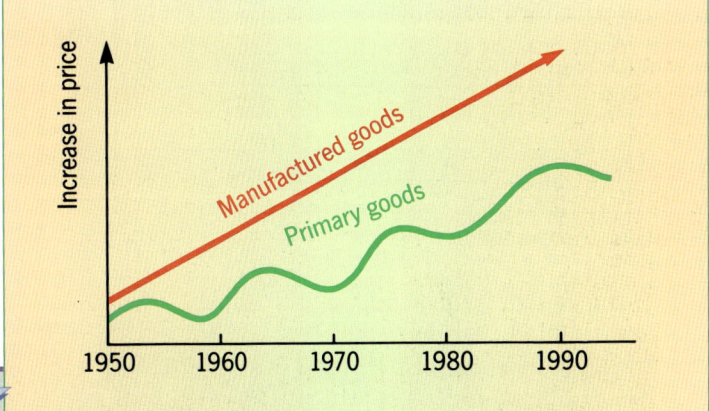

E

Activities

1 a) What is the difference between a trade surplus and a trade deficit?

b) What types of goods are exported by countries in the:
  i) South
  ii) North?

c) i) How does diagram **E** help to explain why the gap between rich and poor countries is getting wider?
  ii) Give four reasons for the price drop in primary products since 1990.

2 a) Name six countries that rely heavily upon the export of one or two commodities.

b) Why do countries that depend mainly on one or two exports:
  i) usually have a trade deficit
  ii) find it difficult to improve their standard of living and quality of life?

Summary Countries trade to try to share out resources and to earn money. Countries that only export raw materials do not develop as quickly as countries that export manufactured goods.

How do government policies affect international trade?

Trade between countries has become increasingly complex and competitive. All countries strive to improve their volume of trade and value of exports and to reduce their dependency upon imports. Trade is seen as a major way for a country to improve its standard of living and, as a result, the quality of life of its inhabitants.

Many countries have grouped together to try to improve their trade balance. The trade balance is the difference between the cost of imports and the value of exports. By joining together, countries form **trading blocs** (map **A**). The UK is a member of one of these blocs, the European Union (EU). One of the first aims of the EU was to try to improve trading links between member countries. This was achieved by eliminating customs duties previously paid on goods moved between member countries. This lowered the price of those goods making them cheaper and more competitive against goods from non-EU countries. Also, as the number of EU member countries has grown, so too has its internal market. The larger the internal market the greater the number of potential customers.

Map **B** shows that trade is not shared out equally between countries. Whereas the EU, the USA and Japan together are responsible for 62 per cent of the world trade total, the developing countries together only account for 20 per cent. Differences in trade are another reason why the gap in development between the rich countries and the poor countries continues to widen.

A

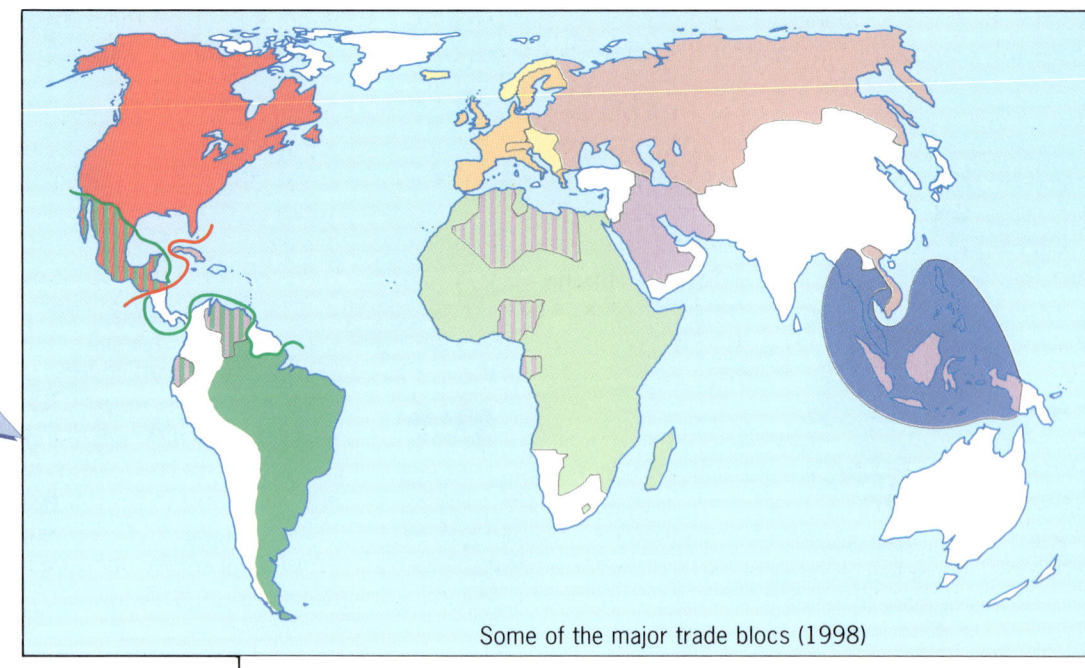

Some of the major trade blocs (1998)

EU	European Union	NAFTA	North American Free Trade Association
EFTA	European Free Trade Association		Mercosur
COMECON	Council for Mutual Economic Aid (formerly)	ASEAN	Association of South East Asian Nations
OPEC	Organisation of Petroleum Producing Countries	OAU	Organisation of African Unity

B

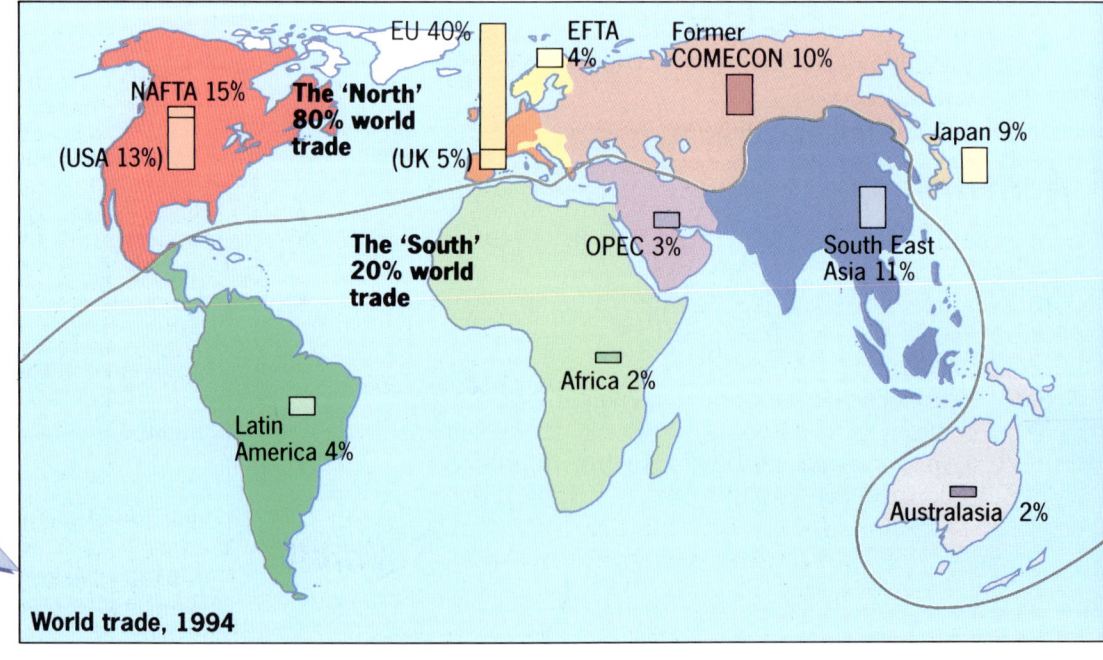

NAFTA 15%
(USA 13%)
The 'North' 80% world trade
EU 40%
EFTA 4%
Former COMECON 10%
(UK 5%)
Japan 9%
The 'South' 20% world trade
OPEC 3%
South East Asia 11%
Latin America 4%
Africa 2%
Australasia 2%

World trade, 1994

In an ideal world there should be free trade between all countries. Free trade is when governments neither restrict nor encourage the movement of goods. In the real world of today, this rarely happens. Virtually all governments, and especially those of economically more developed countries, are involved in regulating overseas trade. This is done by creating trade barriers which, governments hope, will protect jobs and industries within their own country. The most common methods of affecting the levels and patterns of international trade are through **tariffs** and import **quotas**. The years of negotiations leading up to the GATT trade agreement of December 1993 (page 135) were centred on trying to remove trade restrictions. Economists claimed such an agreement would increase world trade, create more jobs and, even more so in the poorer countries, raise standards of living.

Tariffs, quotas, cartels and international commodity agreements

Tariffs are taxes or customs duties paid on imports. The exporter has to pay a percentage of the value of the goods to the importer. Importers sometimes add tariffs just to raise money, but usually it is to put up the price of imported goods so that they become more expensive and therefore harder to sell. Tariffs can therefore either reduce the cost of imports (helping the trade balance) or protect similar home-made goods.

Quotas limit the amount of goods which can be imported. At present, quotas tend to be restricted to primary goods and so work against the economically less developed countries.

Cartels occur when countries group together to set fixed prices for their product. Tariffs, quotas and cartels all work in favour of the 'rich' countries.

International commodity agreements, in contrast, are made by developing countries. They are made in an effort to stabilise prices and demand for individual primary commodities. The best known of these agreements was that made in 1960 by a group of oil-producing countries which called themselves OPEC (map **A**). Other agreements have been made on commodities such as coffee, tin, cocoa and rubber.

Activities

1 **a)** Map **C** shows four trading blocks. For each trading bloc give:
   i)   its initials   ii) its name in full
   iii) the names of three member countries.
   b) Give two reasons why countries group together to form trading blocs.

2 Diagram **D** shows the volume of trade between the EU, the USA and Japan.
   a) What percentage of world trade is shared by the EU, the USA and Japan?
   b) Of the three, which has a:
   i)   trade surplus with the other two
   ii) trade surplus with one and a trade deficit with the other
   iii) trade deficit with the other two?

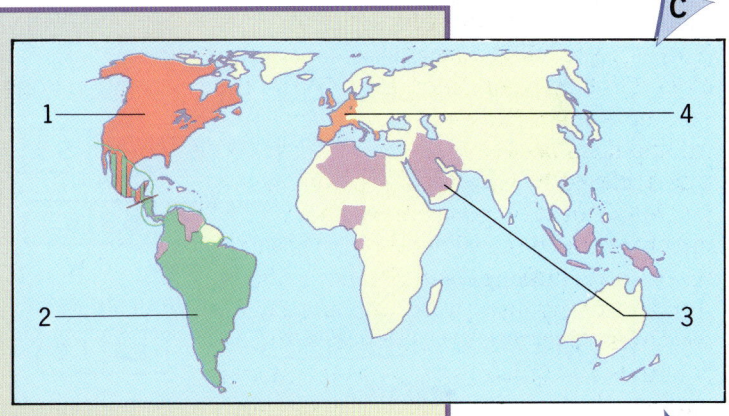

C

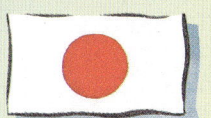

| USA to Japan 48.6 | EU to Japan 28.9 | Japan to EU 53.9 |
| USA to EU 98.1 | EU to USA 97.4 | Japan to USA 90.0 |

D

Exports in US$ billion (1993)

3 Study figure **E**.
   a) What are:
   i)   tariffs   ii) quotas?
   b) How do tariffs and quotas work in favour of rich countries and against poor countries?
   c) What can poor countries do to try to increase their value of trade?

E

You have most of the world's trade, yet you impose tariffs and quotas to prevent us from selling our goods

We must protect our jobs and industries by limiting your cheap imports

Economically less developed countries 20% of world trade

Economically developed countries 80% of world trade

Summary Governments try to influence patterns of international trade by grouping together to establish trading blocs and by imposing tariffs, quotas and international commodities agreements.

What are some of the recent trends in international trade?

The Pacific Rim

The term 'Pacific Rim' has been applied to the earthquake and volcanic belt which surrounds the Pacific Ocean. Increasingly it is also being used to refer to that part of the world which has seen, since the 1980s, the most rapid economic growth. This growth has also extended to international trade (map **B** page 132).

Taken in its widest sense, the Pacific Rim includes all countries that surround the Pacific Ocean and its adjacent seas (map **A**). Countries such as Singapore and South Korea are widely accepted as being part of the rim although neither faces directly onto the Pacific. Likewise not all countries in the rim have experienced a rapid growth in GNP and trade. Although growth has, so far, been limited to a few countries, commentators seem to agree that the balance of trade is shifting from the Atlantic to the Pacific. Some of the recent trends in trade within the Pacific Rim are listed on page 135.

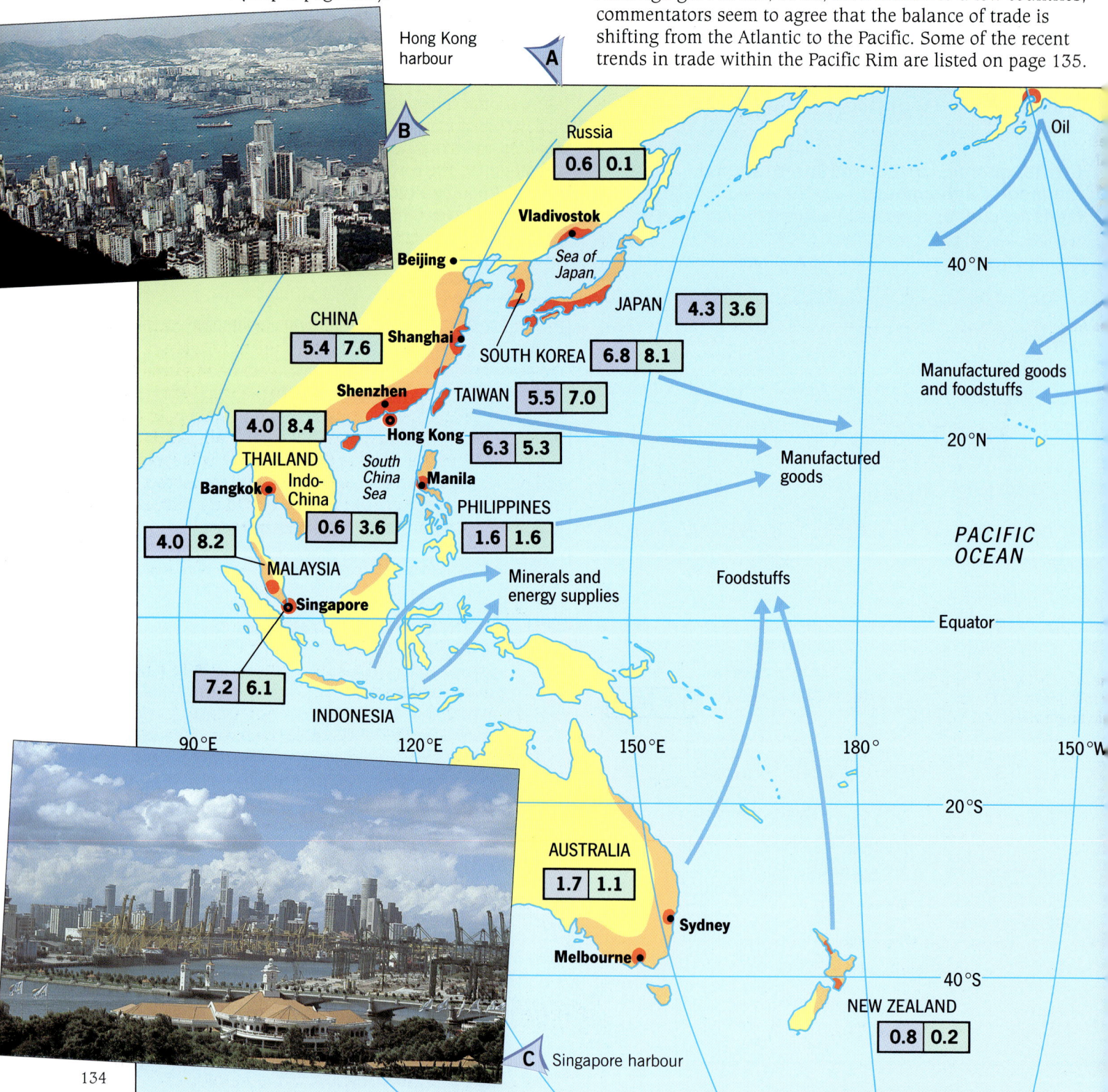

Hong Kong harbour

Singapore harbour

- Growth has been concentrated within a few countries and has not extended to much of Latin America or to parts of mainland Asia.
- Japan and the western USA experienced a rapid growth between 1950 and 1980 but since then the rate of growth has slowed.
- The countries with the fastest-growing economies since 1980 are Hong Kong (photo **B**), Singapore (photo **C**), Taiwan and South Korea. They are threatening the former supremacy in the Pacific region of Japan and the USA.
- In other countries growth is limited to core areas, e.g. Bangkok in Thailand, Manila in the Philippines, Shenzhen in China, and Kuala Lumpur and Penang in Malaysia.

- Most Asian countries lack the raw materials and energy resources needed for industry. Their trade therefore consists of importing these goods and exporting manufactured goods. This gives them a healthy trade balance surplus.
- The USA shares more trade with Asia than it does with its traditional trading partners which now belong to the EU.
- Four of the world's six busiest ports are within the Pacific Rim.

General Agreement on Trade and Tariffs (GATT)

The Uruguay round of the GATT negotiations began in 1986. The main hope was to create one large world free trade area which would replace the various protectionist blocs. Although some 150 nations were involved in the negotiations, most of the arguing and decision-making was made by the G7 (Japan, Italy, France, Germany, UK, USA and Canada). The two major disputes were between:
- the USA and the EU over farm subsidies
- Japan and the remainder over tariffs since Japan discriminated against exports from other countries yet was free to export cars and electrical equipment to the rest of the world.

During most of the negotiations the developing countries, to whom free trade is essential if they are to be allowed to sell their goods to developed countries, were often forced to watch events as spectators. It was perhaps only because all of the G7 leaders had to urgently improve their political image at home, that an agreement was finally reached in December 1993. The hope is that free trade will speed up the end of the world's economic recession, create more jobs and increase the volume of world trade. It is likely that, as usual, the developed countries will benefit the most.

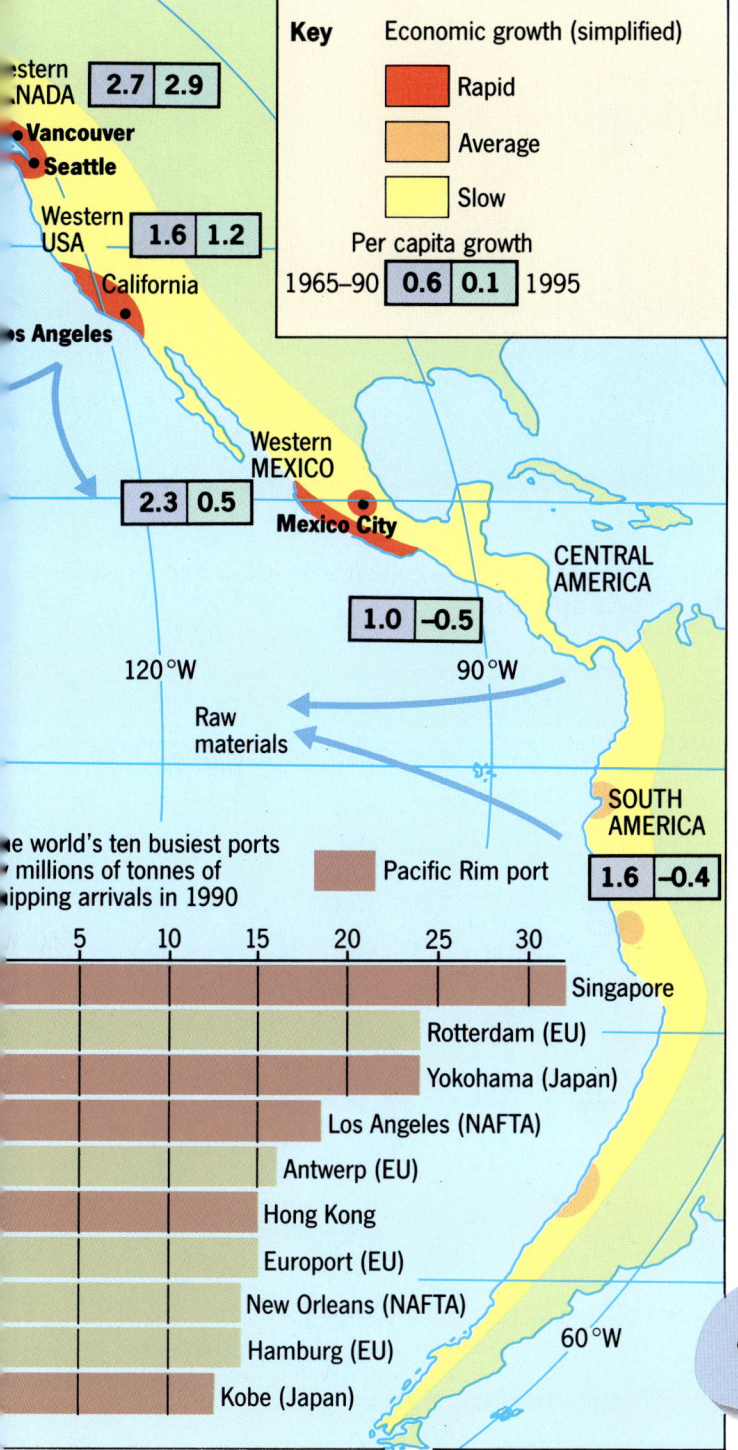

Key — Economic growth (simplified)

- Rapid
- Average
- Slow

Per capita growth
1965–90 | 0.6 | 0.1 | 1995

Western CANADA 2.7 | 2.9
Vancouver
Seattle
Western USA 1.6 | 1.2
California
Los Angeles
Western MEXICO 2.3 | 0.5
Mexico City
CENTRAL AMERICA 1.0 | –0.5
120°W   90°W
Raw materials
SOUTH AMERICA 1.6 | –0.4

The world's ten busiest ports
millions of tonnes of shipping arrivals in 1990

Pacific Rim port

5   10   15   20   25   30

- Singapore
- Rotterdam (EU)
- Yokohama (Japan)
- Los Angeles (NAFTA)
- Antwerp (EU)
- Hong Kong
- Europort (EU)
- New Orleans (NAFTA)
- Hamburg (EU)
- Kobe (Japan)

60°W

Activities

1 a) What is the Pacific Rim?
  b) Which two Pacific Rim countries used to have most wealth and trade?
  c) Which four Pacific Rim countries have developed their economies and trade the most since 1980?
  d) Name four large ports in the Pacific Rim. In which country is each port located?

2 a) i) What is the meaning of GATT?
     ii) What are the G7?
  b) Why were some countries:
     i) in favour of the GATT proposals
     ii) against the GATT proposals?

Summary   Recent trends have seen a growth in trade between the Pacific Rim countries. The GATT agreement should increase free trade and reduce protectionism.

What are hurricanes?

The tropics experience some of the fiercest and most destructive storms on Earth. The **hurricanes** that occur in that region claim an average 20 000 lives each year and cause immense damage to property, vegetation and shipping.

A hurricane (also called a cyclone, typhoon or willy-willy) is a particularly powerful **tropical storm**. It rotates around an area of intense low pressure and produces very high winds and torrential rain. Wind speeds commonly exceed 118 km/h (73 mph) and in the most powerful storms have been known to reach 300 km/h (186 mph) in gusts. Rainfall is almost continuous throughout the storm but is heaviest near the centre where 300 mm may fall in just 24 hours. (London can expect 610 mm in a year.) Hurricanes vary from 80 to 650 km in width and move generally westwards, often on an erratic and unpredictable course. At their centres are calm areas or 'eyes' where the sky is clear and winds are light.

As map **C** shows, most tropical storms originate over warm oceans close to the Equator. They are most common in late summer or autumn when sea temperatures are at their highest (at least 26°C). At these temperatures water evaporates rapidly and as the rising air cools it condenses and releases enormous amounts of heat energy which powers the storm. Once the hurricane reaches land, however, the source of energy is lost and the storm quickly declines in strength and eventually blows itself out. Diagram **B** shows the development and structure of a typical hurricane.

A A hurricane viewed from space: notice the swirling shape, thick cloud and the 'eye' of the storm

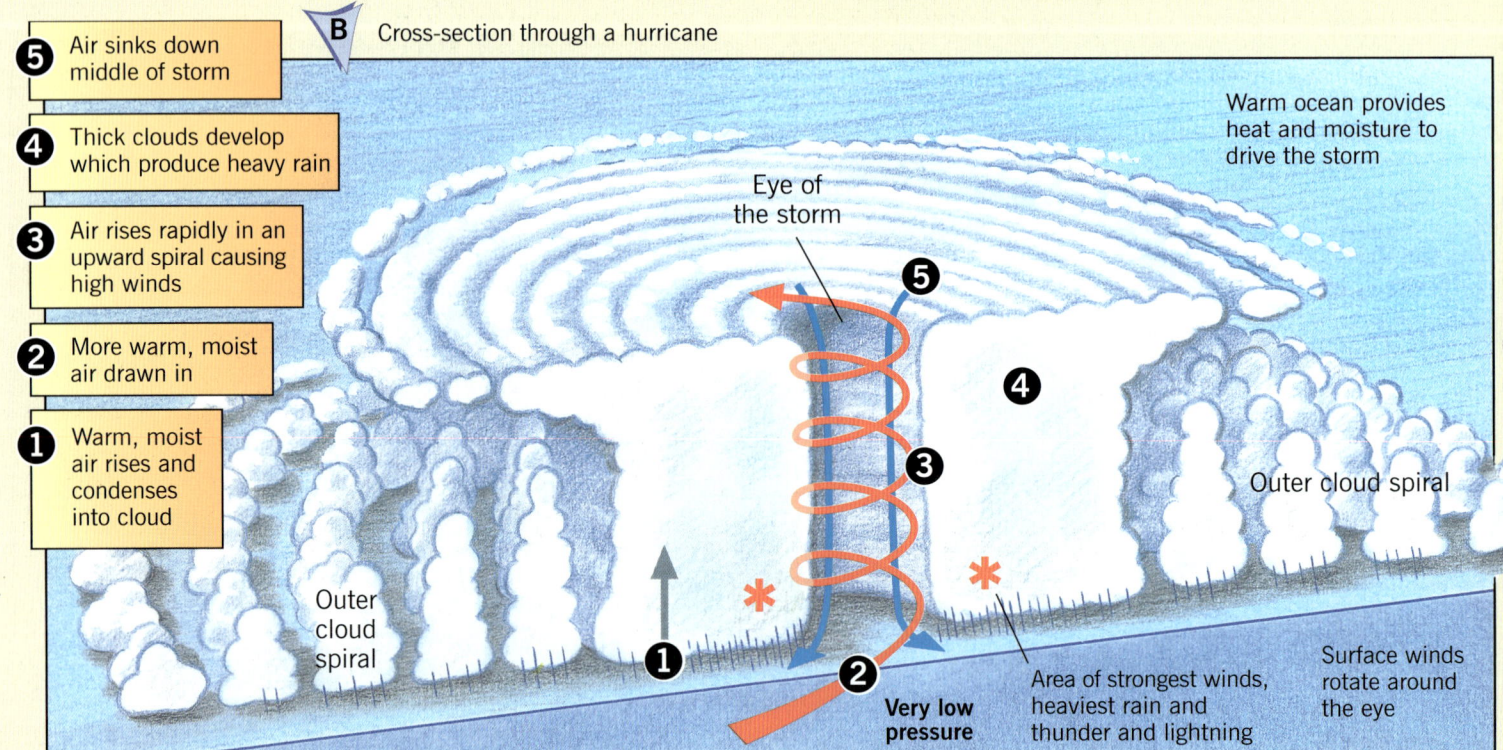

B Cross-section through a hurricane

5 Air sinks down middle of storm

4 Thick clouds develop which produce heavy rain

3 Air rises rapidly in an upward spiral causing high winds

2 More warm, moist air drawn in

1 Warm, moist air rises and condenses into cloud

Warm ocean provides heat and moisture to drive the storm

Eye of the storm

Outer cloud spiral

Outer cloud spiral

Very low pressure

Area of strongest winds, heaviest rain and thunder and lightning

Surface winds rotate around the eye

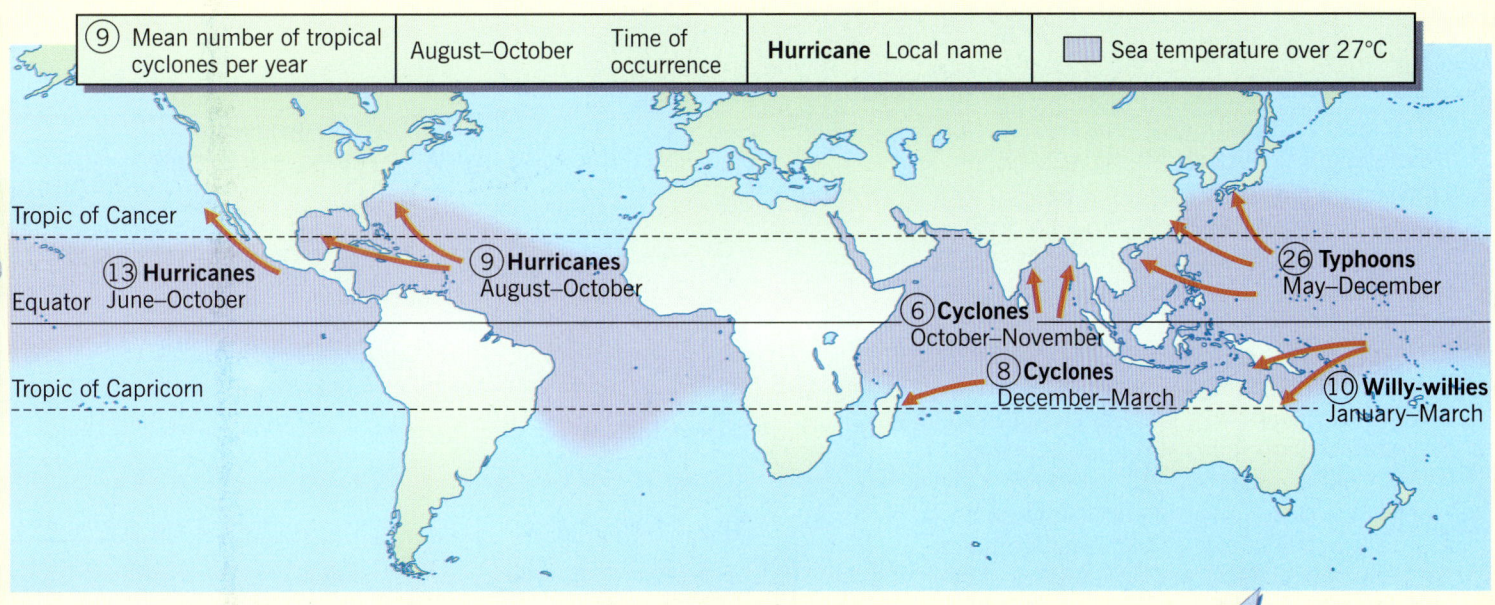

⑨ Mean number of tropical cyclones per year	August–October	Time of occurrence	**Hurricane** Local name	Sea temperature over 27°C

Tropic of Cancer

⑬ **Hurricanes** June–October

Equator

⑨ **Hurricanes** August–October

Tropic of Capricorn

⑥ **Cyclones** October–November

⑧ **Cyclones** December–March

㉖ **Typhoons** May–December

⑩ **Willy-willies** January–March

C

Hurricanes are a major natural hazard. Their effects can be catastrophic, causing widespread damage to property, disrupting communications, destroying crops and resulting in considerable loss of life. They have probably caused more deaths worldwide than any other form of natural hazard except perhaps droughts. Although the extremely strong winds and intense rainfall cause a huge amount of damage, by far the most dangerous feature of a hurricane is the **storm surge**. This occurs at the **eye of the storm** where very low pressure causes the sea-level to rise by up to 10 metres. The resulting high seas and tidal waves lead to serious flooding of low-lying coastal areas close to the hurricane track. The storm surge that swept up the Bay of Bengal in 1970 killed 300 000 people in north-east India and Bangladesh and made a further 2.5 million people homeless.

The extent of the damage and loss of life caused by tropical storms varies and is closely related to the stage of development of the affected area. Poorer countries suffer most because their buildings, warning systems, defences and emergency services may be inadequate. Wealthier countries, however, can afford to prepare for such disasters and so minimise the potential destruction and loss of life.

Activities

1 **a)** Draw a sketch of photo **A** and label the thick cloud, swirling shape and the eye of the storm.

b) Describe the main features of a hurricane. Include the following in your description:
- pressure • winds • rainfall • size
- movement • the 'eye' of the storm.

2 With the help of a simple diagram, describe how hurricanes develop.

3 **a)** From map **C**, describe and explain the distribution of tropical storms.

b) Why do these storms weaken when they move over land or cross cooler areas of ocean?

4 With help from diagram **D**:
a) Explain how a storm surge happens.
b) Suggest why its effects can be devastating.

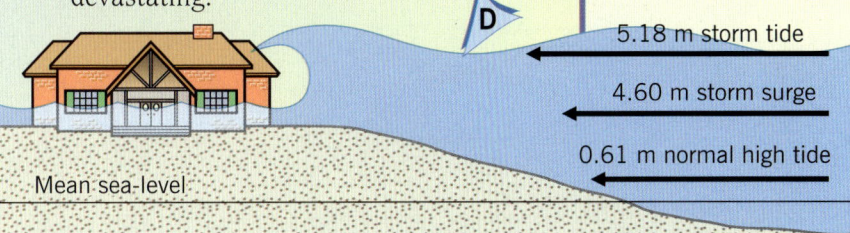

D

5.18 m storm tide

4.60 m storm surge

0.61 m normal high tide

Mean sea-level

Summary

Hurricanes are tremendously powerful tropical storms that can cause widespread destruction. They develop over warm tropical oceans but soon decline on reaching land where they lose their source of energy.

137

Hurricane Andrew: what happened?

In late August 1992, Hurricane Andrew hit Florida and quickly became 'the most destructive natural hazard in the history of the United States'. The storm began its life in the mid-Atlantic as a low pressure area heading westwards towards the West Indies. Satellites and aircraft plotted its progress as it approached the eastern seaboard of America until, on the afternoon of 23 August, it hit The Bahamas, killing four people and causing widespread damage. The US National Hurricane Centre in Florida issued warnings that this would be one of the worst storms of the century and predicted wind speeds of over 240 km/h along with torrential rain and a storm surge of 5 metres.

People in the area are well used to hurricanes and they quickly responded to the warnings by following the recommended and well-practised emergency procedures. Radios were left on, windows and doors boarded up and gas and electricity turned off. Food supplies were stockpiled, torch and radio batteries checked and any property like rubbish bins, cars or boats that were likely to be moved by the hurricane, were secured or carefully locked away. The State then issued a mandatory evacuation order, and up to a million people moved out of their homes near the coast and away to safer ground inland. Here they stayed with friends or in designated shelters until the storm had passed by.

A A satellite image of Andrew over Florida, 24 August 1992. The colours indicate cloud thickness on a scale from white (thickest) through yellow and grey to blue (clear sky – land areas are green).

B The track of Hurricane Andrew, 20–27 August 1992

0 200 400 km   N

⊙ Eye of hurricane

72 Wind speeds in km/h

LOUISIANA
62
Aug 27

New Orleans

Aug 26
194

FLORIDA

Highest storm surge ever recorded

Atlantic Ocean

Wind speed meter jams at top of scale

Andrew reaches hurricane strength

218
Aug 25

Gulf of Mexico

Miami

232
Aug 24

164
Aug 23

94
Aug 22

50 km wide zone of destruction

BAHAMAS

82
Aug 21

Tropic of Cancer

CUBA

Aircraft reports 320 km/h in eyewall

72
Aug 20

MEXICO

Caribbean Sea

WEST INDIES

Those who sought safety were not disappointed. Early in the morning of 24 August, Hurricane Andrew hit the coast of south-east Florida with winds gusting up to 280 km/h. The pounding lasted for about eight hours, during which time the area was devastated by wind, rain and flood. The storm surge, as expected, did considerable damage. It was near to the predicted height of 5 metres and flattened coastal developments to the south of Miami and particularly along the length of Biscayne Bay.

Andrew was not finished yet, however. After leaving Florida it tracked across the Gulf of Mexico, gathering strength over the warm sea. Like Florida before it, Louisiana was well prepared and had evacuated over 800 000 people. The hurricane eventually hit the coast near to New Orleans and caused extensive damage with winds this time peaking at 225 km/h. Andrew then continued toward Texas and Alabama but quickly lost strength as it moved inland.

C Few people venture out to brave the fury and torrential rain during a hurricane

Activities

1 Complete a timeline like the one in figure **D** to show the progress and effects of Hurricane Andrew.

E

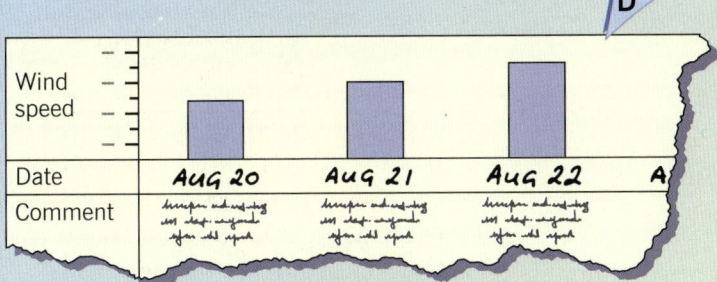

2 **a)** Sketch the main part of the hurricane shown in satellite image **A**. Colour and label the eye, the thickest cloud, thinner cloud and the coast of Florida.
 b) With the help of map **B**, describe the location of the storm's centre.

3 As it reached Florida, Hurricane Andrew was on the threshold of a category 5 storm, the highest level on the Saffir/Simpson hurricane scale. Look at figure **E** and list the main problems faced by residents:
 a) living some distance inland on higher ground
 b) living on the low-lying coast of Biscayne Bay
 c) planning late evacuation from their coastal homes.

Category 5

Winds greater than 250 km/h. Shrubs and trees blown down; considerable damage to roofs of buildings; all signs down. Very severe and extensive damage to windows and doors, with extensive shattering of glass. Complete failure of roofs on many residential and industrial buildings. Some complete building failures. Small buildings overturned or blown away. Complete destruction of mobile homes.

Storm surge greater than 5.5 metres. Major damage to lower floors on all structures less than 4.5 metres above sea-level within 500 metres of shore. Low-lying escape routes made impassable by rising water 3–5 hours before hurricane centre arrives. Massive evacuation of residential areas on low ground within 8–16 km of shore possibly required.

4 Draw a poster to give residents of Florida advice on what they should do in the event of a hurricane. Make your poster simple but clear. Include drawings to give it impact.

Summary Hurricane Andrew was one of the fiercest and most destructive storms to hit the USA in the twentieth century. The states of Florida and Louisiana were the worst affected. Much damage was caused by the storm surge which devastated coastal areas.

139

Hurricane Andrew: what were the effects and...

The full extent of the damage caused by Hurricane Andrew took some time to sink in. At first people were in shock and disoriented. Many people were living in temporary shelters far from their homes, and were short of food and clean water. Others who had been evacuated to places further inland were unable to return to their homes on the coast because roads, railways and airfields had been damaged.

The US government reacted quickly to the situation. President Bush declared south Florida a national disaster area and the state mobilised its well-planned and generously funded hurricane relief programme. Through this programme, first aid, food and shelter should have been available to everyone in need within a few hours of the disaster. Unfortunately, due to confusion and difficulties

of access, much of this help failed to arrive until several days after the storm had passed. Once it was under way, however, the relief effort ran smoothly and efficiently. About 8000 soldiers were brought in to oversee the programme, and military aircraft delivered food kitchens, tents, portable toilets, generators, water purifiers, and other essential items. Organisations like the Red Cross also arrived, and offers of help from other countries were received.

Gradually, as the immediate problems were sorted out, the full picture of the hurricane and the damage that it had caused became evident. As map **A** shows, these were both spectacular and substantial, and it quickly became clear that Florida had experienced a weather hazard from which it would take years to recover.

A

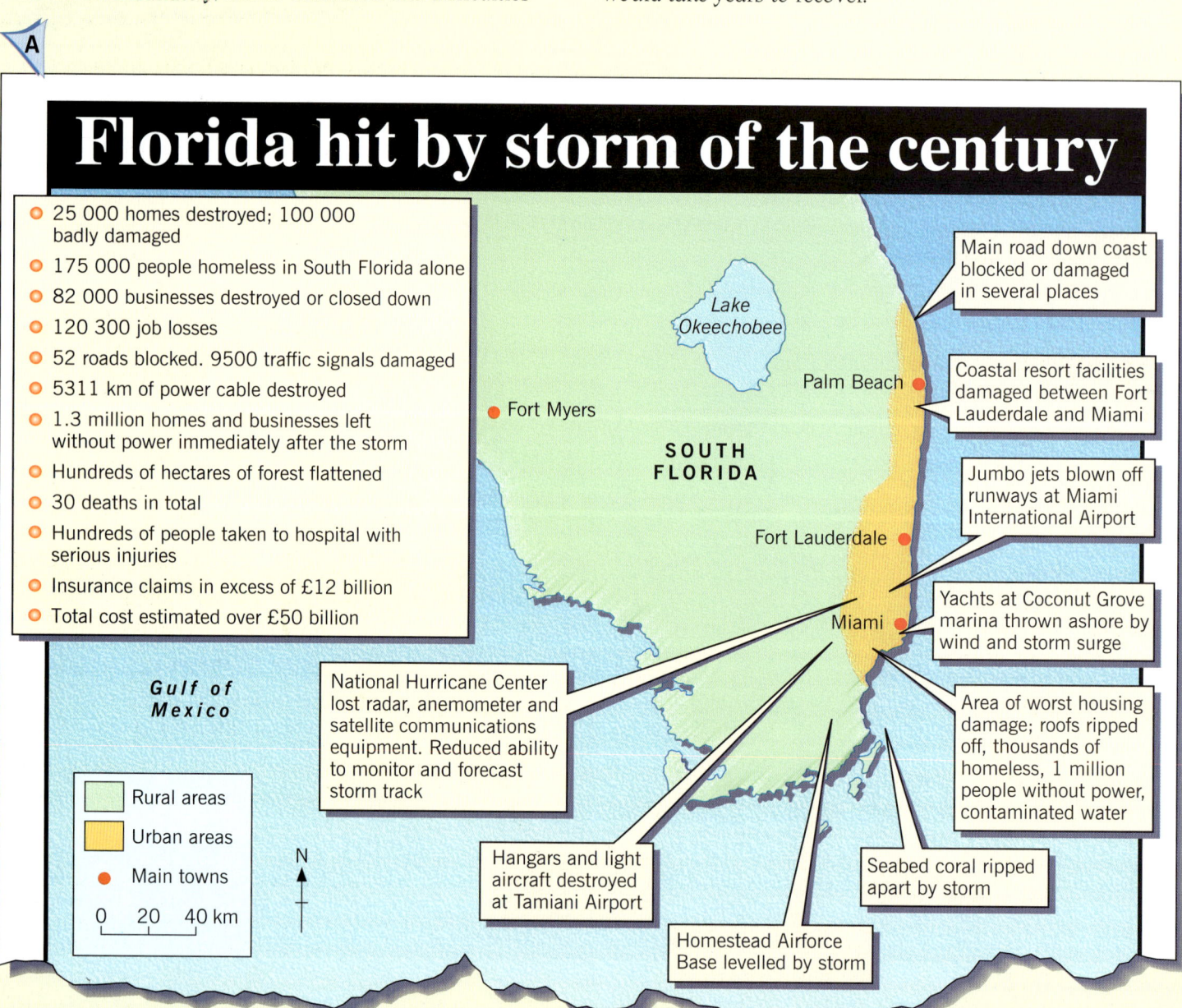

Florida hit by storm of the century

- 25 000 homes destroyed; 100 000 badly damaged
- 175 000 people homeless in South Florida alone
- 82 000 businesses destroyed or closed down
- 120 300 job losses
- 52 roads blocked. 9500 traffic signals damaged
- 5311 km of power cable destroyed
- 1.3 million homes and businesses left without power immediately after the storm
- Hundreds of hectares of forest flattened
- 30 deaths in total
- Hundreds of people taken to hospital with serious injuries
- Insurance claims in excess of £12 billion
- Total cost estimated over £50 billion

Main road down coast blocked or damaged in several places

Coastal resort facilities damaged between Fort Lauderdale and Miami

Jumbo jets blown off runways at Miami International Airport

Yachts at Coconut Grove marina thrown ashore by wind and storm surge

Area of worst housing damage; roofs ripped off, thousands of homeless, 1 million people without power, contaminated water

National Hurricane Center lost radar, anemometer and satellite communications equipment. Reduced ability to monitor and forecast storm track

Hangars and light aircraft destroyed at Tamiani Airport

Seabed coral ripped apart by storm

Homestead Airforce Base levelled by storm

Lake Okeechobee

Fort Myers

Palm Beach

SOUTH FLORIDA

Fort Lauderdale

Miami

Gulf of Mexico

Rural areas
Urban areas
Main towns
0 20 40 km

N

... what was done to reduce its impact?

Whilst the damage and loss of life caused by Hurricane Andrew was indeed very serious, there can be no doubt that its impact was reduced because it happened in one of the richer parts of the world. Here in America, for example, money and resources are available to:

- inform and advise people of the dangers and necessary precautions that should be taken
- prepare and implement emergency plans to be used before, during and after the storm
- provide research and information on storm development and its predicted track
- develop a supporting infrastructure and communications network that can provide warnings and information throughout the life of a storm
- give help after the storm, in the form of rebuilding programmes and financial support.

B

Hurricane Relief Programme Improvements 1992–97

- A review of relief procedures to ensure that the slow response to the disaster will not be repeated.
- A change in building regulations to put an emphasis on concrete rather than timber building.
- A stricter policing of construction work to ensure that it meets with new criteria.
- Alternative provision for essential emergency services such as the National Hurricane Center, should they be damaged by the storm.
- A new £15 million research aircraft introduced in 1997. It can fly through the hurricane and provide 50 times more information than previous flights.

This preparation, planning and research is ongoing, and is constantly being updated. Much was learnt from Hurricane Andrew, and many changes have already been made to further reduce the damage caused by such storms. Some of these are listed in figure **B**.

Although the improvements were welcomed, the strategies used in 1992 had largely been effective. After all, Andrew was one of the most powerful storms on record, yet it killed just 30 people. For poorer countries like Bangladesh (see pages 142–143), where a less powerful storm in 1991 caused the deaths of more than 130 000 people, the impact can be very much more serious.

C

Activities

1 With the help of map **A** and photo **C**, and using the following headings, describe the effects of Hurricane Andrew.
   - Property • Transport • People • Cost • Others

2 The following is a list of problems facing authorities. List them in order of urgency, putting the most important first. Give reasons for your choice of the four most urgent points.
   - Help rebuild homes
   - Search for missing people
   - Rescue stranded people
   - Supply safe drinking water
   - Open up all roads
   - Provide first aid
   - Supply food
   - Re-open businesses

3 Make a larger copy of diagram **D** and complete it to show the methods used in Florida to reduce the impact of hurricanes. Give examples where possible.

D

| Before the storm | During the storm | After the storm |

Summary

Hurricane Andrew was one of the most powerful and expensive storms in American history. Careful planning helped to reduce the damaging effects of this natural hazard.

What can happen when a cyclone hits Bangladesh?

Bangladesh is one of the poorest and most densely populated nations in the world (pages 122–135). Most of the country is an extensive, flat, low-lying river delta with rich soils and a hot, wet climate which supports millions of rice farmers. Unfortunately Bangladesh is in a major hurricane belt and every year thousands die as these violent storms (called **cyclones** in this part of the world) sweep up the Bay of Bengal flooding villages and destroying everything before them.

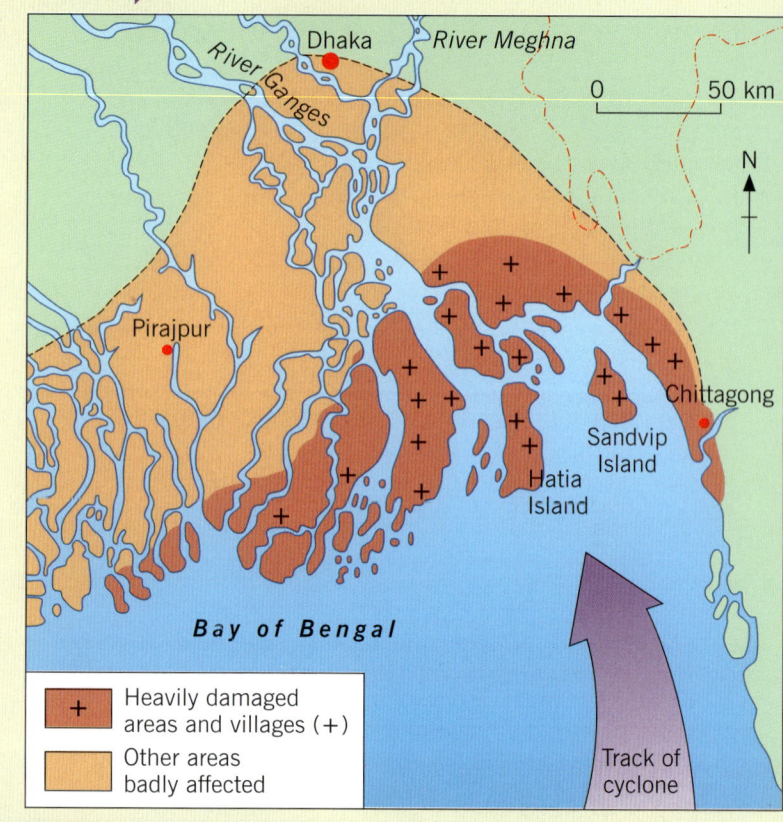

- The storm that ravaged the coast of Bangladesh in late April 1991 killed more than 130 000 people. Winds of 225 km/h and waves 7 metres high swept through eight of the coastal districts flattening houses and coastal defences. Nearly half a million head of cattle drowned and 63 000 hectares of crops were lost. Within hours entire villages were wiped out, food supplies washed away and livelihoods lost. Roads, bridges and electricity pylons were also destroyed. Chittagong, the main port of Bangladesh, was itself flooded, crippling communications with the outside world and severing links with other parts of the country.

- When the cyclone came it brought violent winds and serious flooding. The situation was worst in the coastal areas where for hundreds of miles the land is just a metre or two above sea-level. To escape the floods, people climbed trees and took refuge on the roofs of their homes. Most, however, were simply washed away and never seen again. Even as the flood subsided the problems remained. Food shortages were widespread and water supplies became contaminated with raw sewage and dead bodies. More than 4 million people faced starvation and disease during the weeks after the flood. The total death toll was never known.

- A potential cyclone was first detected from satellite pictures by Bangladesh's Space Research and Remote Sensing Organisation in Dhaka. They immediately informed the Meteorological Office and government that a storm was approaching.

- On 25 April the Meteorological Office passed on the information to the Red Crescent organisation in Dhaka which then radioed the information to the 21 000 field volunteers who make up the Cyclone Preparedness Programme. On the 28th, these volunteers warned people of the danger by megaphone or through the mosque loudspeaker systems, and advised them to evacuate the area. People were reluctant to leave their homes fearing that once they had gone away they would lose everything. The lack of any transport and shortage of safe places to go only added to their concerns.

- The main reason why more lives were not saved was that the government had failed to build the 3600 shelters that it had promised. Only 302 had been completed and most of these were not in the areas where the cyclone hit. If more had been built, more lives would have been saved.

- The coastal embankments that had been constructed were designed to protect villagers by slowing down the flood, so giving time for evacuation. Unfortunately these failed because they were not strong enough and had fallen into disrepair.

- Emergency supplies were stored in Chittagong but inadequate transport prevented them from being taken to the island communities that needed them. Boats had been destroyed by the storm surge and many of the crews had already been drowned in the flood. An attempt to drop supplies by air was not successful as most ended up in waterlogged fields which were inaccessible to villagers.

- After six days the government handed the relief operation over to the army. With their organisational abilities, manpower, helicopters, boats and trucks, the rescue programme speeded up and help eventually reached those most in need.

- Recommendations put forward after the disaster suggested that emergency services should be localised and each community made independent with its own cyclone shelter, its own food supplies and its own way of dealing with the disaster. Improvements in communications and transport should also be made so that warning messages could get through and evacuation made easier.

- Places like Bangladesh will never be safe from storms, and people living there will remain at risk whatever precautions are taken. It is simply not possible to provide full protection against the ferocity of a cyclone in low-lying coastal areas. What makes the Bangladesh situation worse, however, is the inability of the country to fund and provide adequate emergency services to reduce the effects of such storms both during and after the disaster.

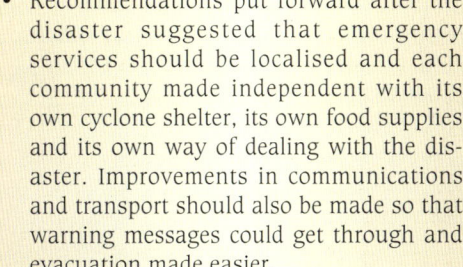

Activity

This activity is in the form of a mini-enquiry. Use the questions shown on the clipboard to help you structure your work. Use maps, diagrams, facts and figures where appropriate.

What were the effects and responses to the cyclone that hit Bangladesh?
- What happened?
  (Where, when, why?)
- What were the effects?
  (Damage, loss of life, after-effects, etc.)
- What was done to reduce its impact?
  (Before, during and after the storm)
- Why were the strategies taken to reduce the effects of the storm relatively ineffective?
  (Specific examples, general problems)
- What could be done in the future to limit the impact of cyclones in Bangladesh?
  (Local scale, foreign aid, etc.)

Summary

Cyclones are common in Bangladesh. Their effects are particularly serious because like most poor countries, the precautions taken to reduce their impact are rarely very effective.

Case study: Alaskan oil

What are the benefits and problems of Alaskan oil?

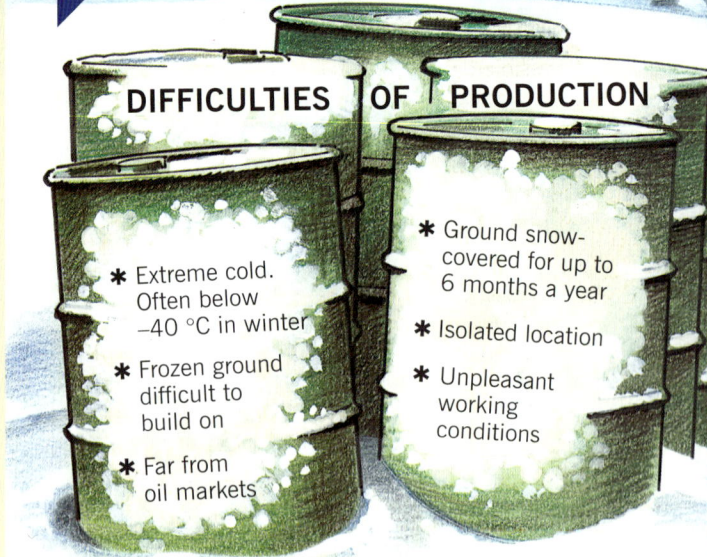

A

DIFFICULTIES OF PRODUCTION

* Extreme cold. Often below –40 °C in winter
* Frozen ground difficult to build on
* Far from oil markets
* Ground snow-covered for up to 6 months a year
* Isolated location
* Unpleasant working conditions

Short history of Alaskan oil

❄	1962	Oil discovered in Prudhoe Bay
❄	1968	Permission given to start construction
❄	1970	Conservationists delay pipeline
❄	1977	Oil flows along pipeline
❄	1986	300 minor oil spills recorded to date
❄	1989	Massive oil spill from grounded tanker
❄	1996	Permission sought for new exploration

The development of the oil industry in northern Alaska has brought many benefits but it has also caused problems. It is now more than 20 years since the first oil began to flow out of the ground near Prudhoe Bay. Since then Alaska has become rich, a serious oil spill has occurred, and environmentalists have continued to voice concerns about the damaging effects of the industry. Now, with reserves beginning to run out and the need for new fields to be explored and opened up, the arguments for and against development have become stronger.

The governor of Alaska, the State Congress and a majority of Alaskans are in favour of development. They point to the social and economic gains that the industry has already brought to the area as well as the importance of oil production to the nation as a whole. They rightly claim that Alaska owes much to oil. It has no state income tax or sales tax and has the highest average household income in all of America. Oil provides 85 per cent of the state's income and pays for virtually everything that Alaska needs. This

includes schools, hospitals, public buildings, water and sewerage schemes, new roads and improved communications with isolated communities. Even now that oil production is beginning to slow down, Alaska still produces a quarter of the nation's output and helps to provide over 700 000 jobs throughout the country.

Opponents to development have other views. Environmental groups and wildlife organisations are concerned about the effects of the oil industry in such an environmentally sensitive area. To protect the area from industrial development they want all of the Arctic National Wildlife

B

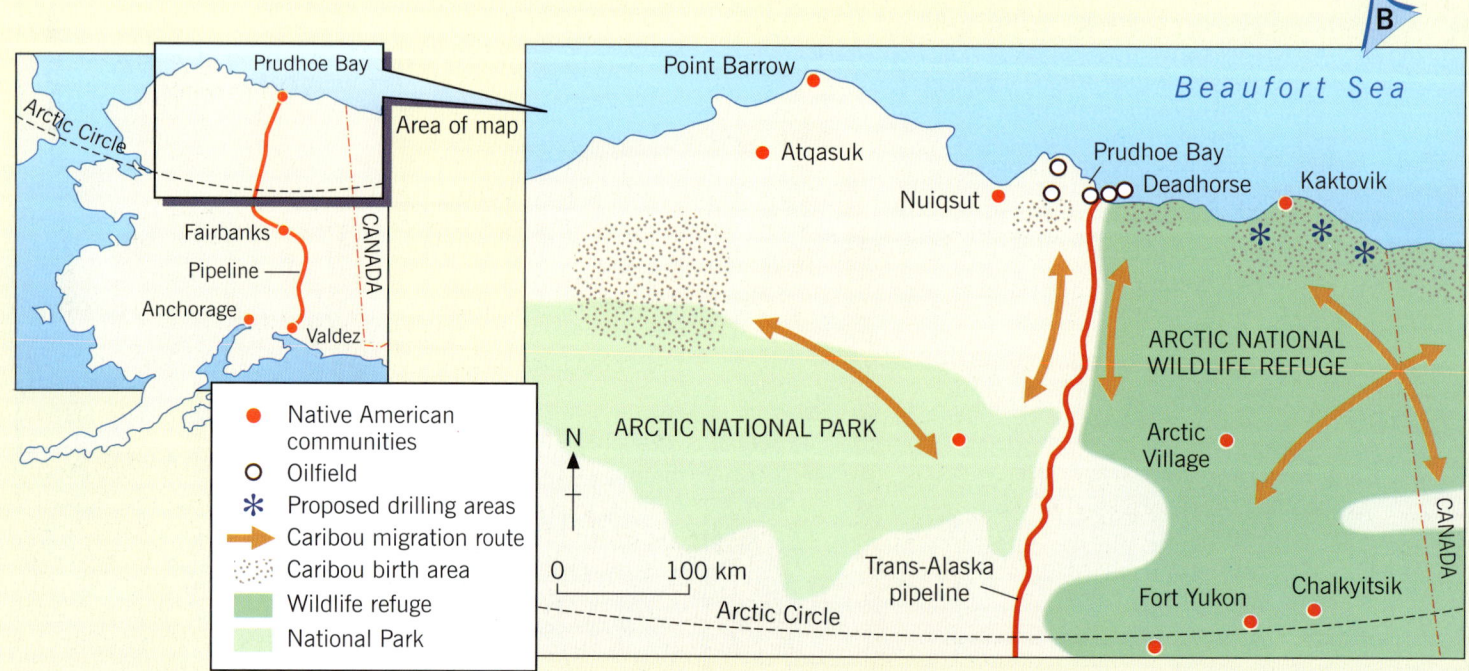

Prudhoe Bay
Area of map
Arctic Circle
Fairbanks
Pipeline
Anchorage
Valdez
CANADA

Point Barrow
Beaufort Sea
Atqasuk
Nuiqsut
Prudhoe Bay
Deadhorse
Kaktovik
ARCTIC NATIONAL WILDLIFE REFUGE
ARCTIC NATIONAL PARK
Arctic Village
CANADA
Trans-Alaska pipeline
Fort Yukon
Chalkyitsik
Arctic Circle

Legend:
- ● Native American communities
- ○ Oilfield
- ✳ Proposed drilling areas
- ➜ Caribou migration route
- Caribou birth area
- Wildlife refuge
- National Park

N

0   100 km

Prudhoe
Bay

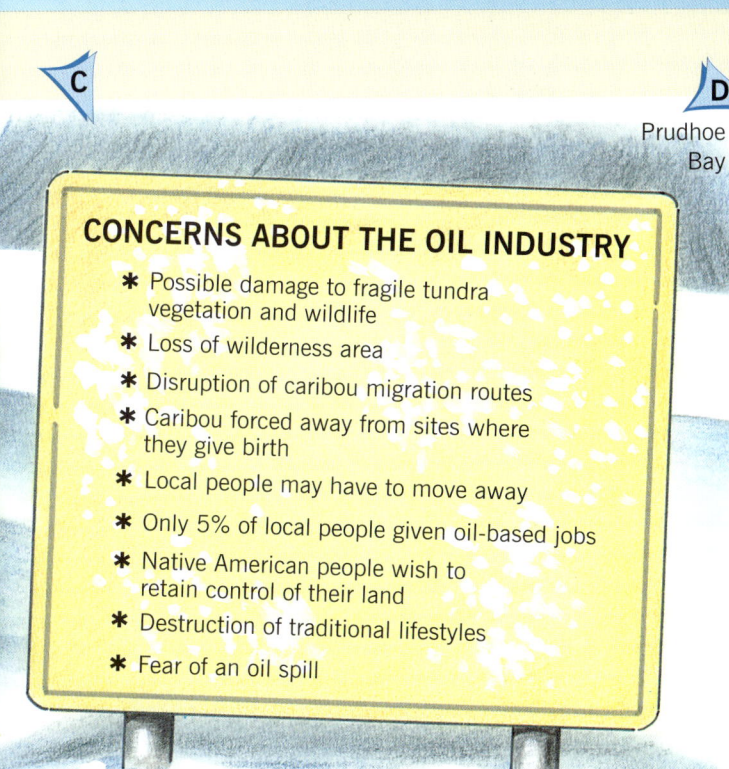

CONCERNS ABOUT THE OIL INDUSTRY

* Possible damage to fragile tundra vegetation and wildlife
* Loss of wilderness area
* Disruption of caribou migration routes
* Caribou forced away from sites where they give birth
* Local people may have to move away
* Only 5% of local people given oil-based jobs
* Native American people wish to retain control of their land
* Destruction of traditional lifestyles
* Fear of an oil spill

Refuge to be designated as a statutory wilderness. Local Native American groups including the Inupiat and Gwich'in are also actively opposed to the scheme, arguing that they don't want oil money but wish only to continue their unspoilt way of life. Even the US government through the Clinton administration has come out against drilling and has shown a reluctance to support further exploration. This is despite the obvious benefits that new oilfield discoveries would bring to the nation.

Activities

1 Draw a timeline to show the history of Alaskan oil.

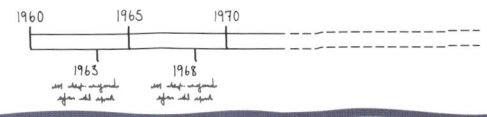

2 Describe the main features of Alaska's oil industry by completing fact file **E**.

3 Imagine that you work for the United States Department of the Interior and have been asked to write a report on the future of oil production in northern Alaska. Your report should be short, factual, and give both sides of the argument. It should provide reasoned recommendations as to whether further exploration and development should go ahead.

Fact file: Oil production in Alaska

1 Location
Maps and written description will be needed here to show Alaska and the oilfield area. An atlas and map **B** will help.

2 Main features
You could describe the features shown in photo **D** or draw a labelled sketch. Add any other relevant geographical information.

3 Benefits
Describe or list these under the headings 'Social' and 'Economic'. Remember to mention who has benefited.

4 Problems
Describe or list these under the headings: Environment, People, Transport, Climate. Try to be specific and give examples.

Summary Industrial activity in Alaska has brought social and economic gains. Many people are concerned about the damaging effects it may have on local communities and the environment.

What problems were there building the Alaskan pipeline?

When oil was first discovered at Prudhoe Bay, reserves were estimated to be in the region of 25 billion barrels. This made it the largest oilfield in America with a life expectancy of over 25 years. Unfortunately, the main demand for the oil came from thousands of miles away to the south, in America's great industrial cities. A major problem was how to transport the oil so far – a problem that was made even worse by the difficult physical and environmental conditions of the region.

The oil companies suggested three different routes.
1 Ship the oil directly by tanker from Prudhoe Bay. This was both difficult and dangerous as the Beaufort Sea is frozen most of the year.

2 Construct a Trans-Canadian pipeline to the east coast. This was an unpopular option because of its great length, danger to the environment and enormous cost.
3 Construct a pipeline south across Alaska to the ice-free port of Valdez on the Pacific coast. This was the most difficult route and attracted great opposition from conservation groups.

After much debate and a huge amount of technological research and expense, the third option was chosen and the 1285 km Trans-Alaska pipeline finally opened in June 1977.

A Trans-Alaska pipeline – the main problems

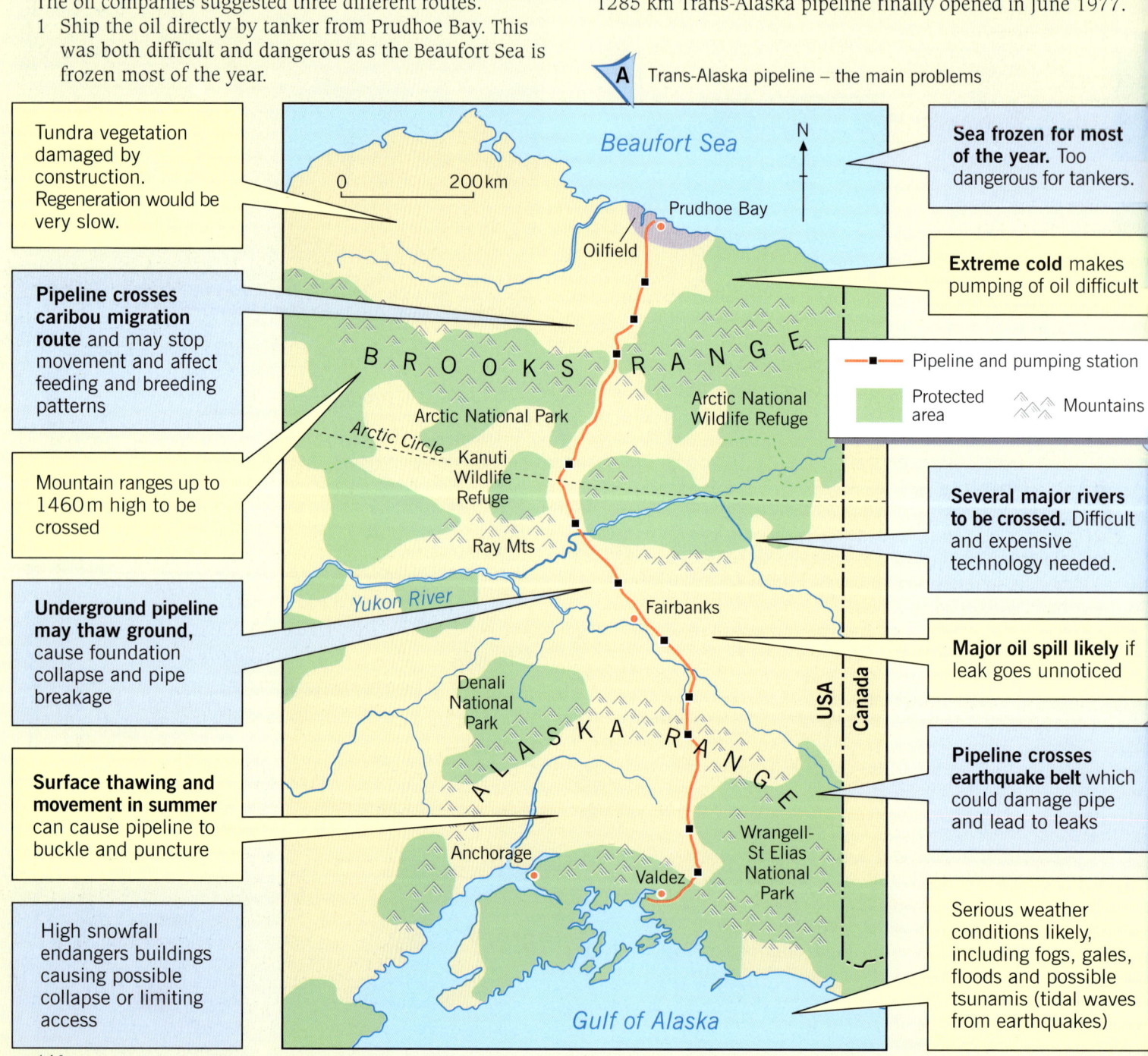

Tundra vegetation damaged by construction. Regeneration would be very slow.

Pipeline crosses caribou migration route and may stop movement and affect feeding and breeding patterns

Mountain ranges up to 1460 m high to be crossed

Underground pipeline may thaw ground, cause foundation collapse and pipe breakage

Surface thawing and movement in summer can cause pipeline to buckle and puncture

High snowfall endangers buildings causing possible collapse or limiting access

Sea frozen for most of the year. Too dangerous for tankers.

Extreme cold makes pumping of oil difficult

Several major rivers to be crossed. Difficult and expensive technology needed.

Major oil spill likely if leak goes unnoticed

Pipeline crosses earthquake belt which could damage pipe and lead to leaks

Serious weather conditions likely, including fogs, gales, floods and possible tsunamis (tidal waves from earthquakes)

B Trans-Alaska pipeline – attempted solutions

Permafrost causes many problems for builders in polar regions. Permafrost is permanently frozen ground and covers much of the pipeline route. It is difficult to build any structure on it because the warmth of the structure melts the permafrost and can cause movement and subsidence.

The active layer is up to 3 metres thick and causes further problems as it thaws in summer but freezes in winter.

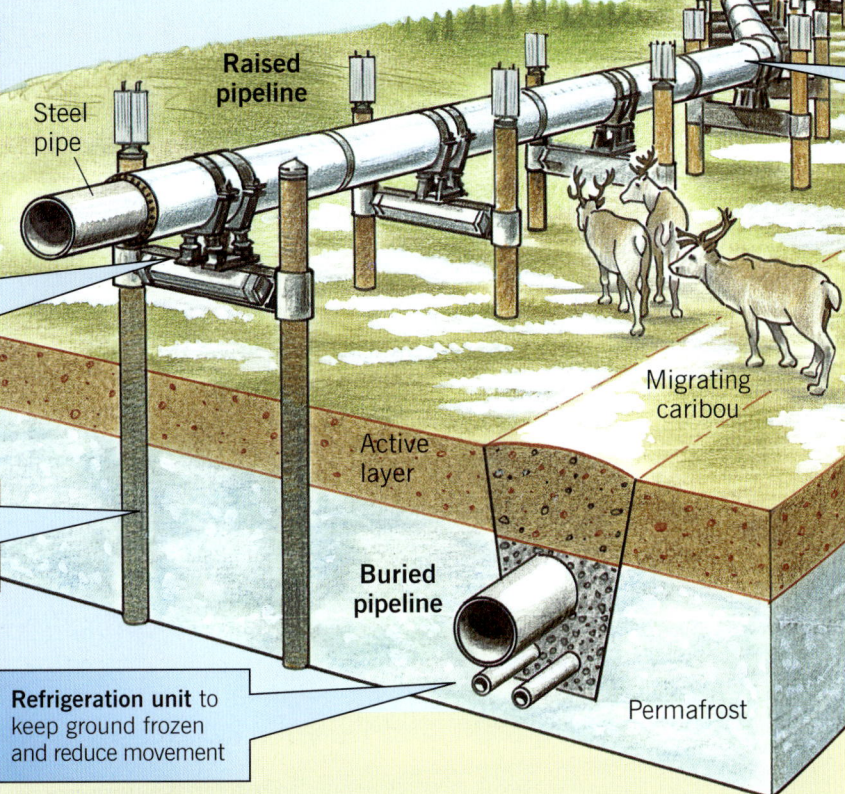

Pipeline built on stilts 3 metres above ground to reduce melting of permafrost and allow animal movement underneath

Raised pipeline

Steel pipe

Sliding shoes allow sideways movement in event of ground shaking from major earth movements

Support pylons sunk through active layer to give stability

Active layer

Buried pipeline

Refrigeration unit to keep ground frozen and reduce movement

Migrating caribou

Permafrost

Pipeline insulated and oil pumped at 80 °C

Trans-Alaska pipeline built from Prudhoe Bay to ice-free Valdez

Pumping stations can cut down oil flow in damaged sections

Suspension bridges built to carry pipeline across rivers

Activities

1 a) Using map **A** and cross-section **C** below, describe the route of the Trans-Alaska pipeline. Include any towns, mountain ranges and protected areas, and mention distances.

b) How might the route that you have described, cause problems for pipeline builders?

2 a) Make a larger copy of cross-section **C** below.

b) Write the following in the correct places and draw an arrow to each feature:
  • Brooks Range • Alaska Range • Yukon River
  • Beaufort Sea • Gulf of Alaska • 1460 metres.

3 a) Make a larger copy of table **D**.

b) Match each of the eight locations from the cross-section with a problem taken from map **A**. (Only write in the **bold** words.)

c) Write a solution from drawing **B** for each of the problems. (Again, use only the **bold** words.)

D

Location	Problem	Attempted solution
①		
②		

C

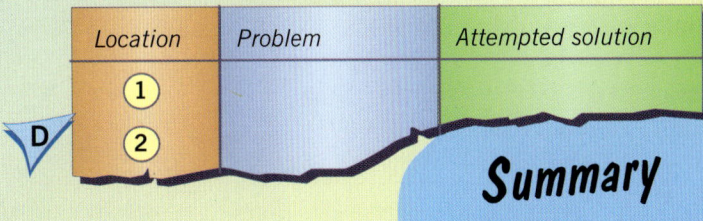

*   *   *   *   *

*

Prudhoe Bay

Valdez

① ② ③ ④ ⑤ ⑥ ⑦ ⑧

Summary

Difficult physical conditions have hindered oil production in Alaska. Builders of the pipeline had to overcome rugged countryside, extreme climatic conditions and complex environmental problems.

How has Alaskan oil damaged the environment?

24 March 1989 ... 12.28 a.m. ... *Exxon Valdez* ... 25 miles out of Valdez ... carrying 11 million gallons of oil ... off course ... run aground on reef ... badly holed ... oil pouring out ... need help immediately ...

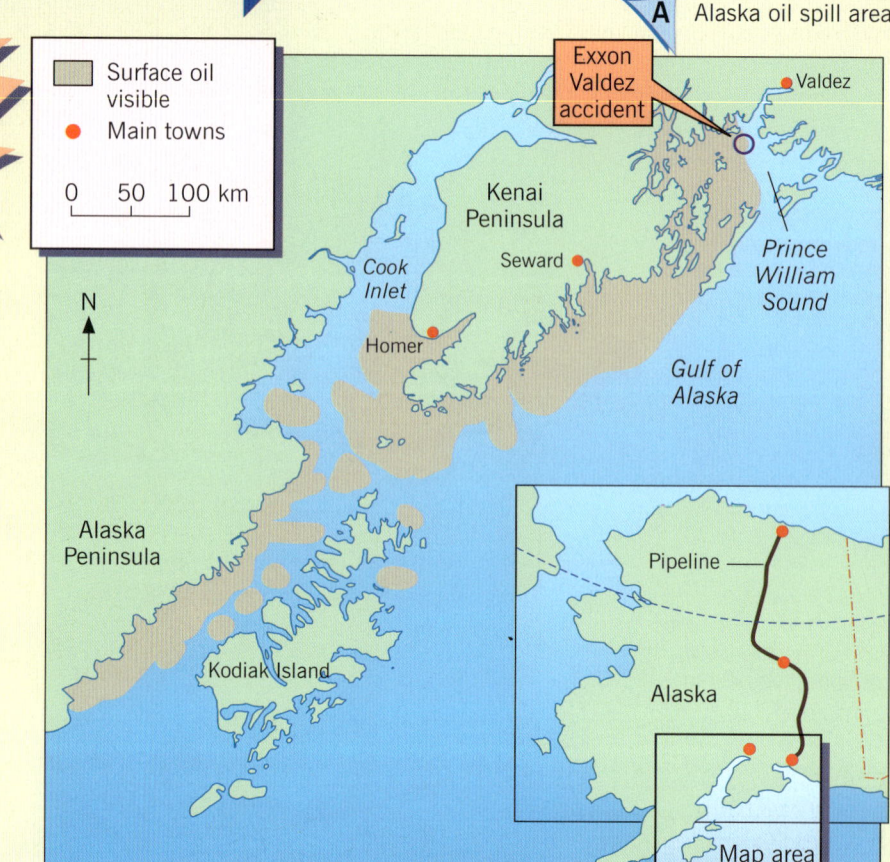

Alaska oil spill area

A

A short radio message on the coastguard's emergency wavelength and it was everyone's worst nightmare come true: a huge tanker pouring oil into the calm, crystal-clear waters of Prince William Sound. One of America's great wilderness environments perhaps damaged for ever by a single mistake. Coastguards could not understand why the ship was so far off course until they found out that the captain was drunk and an inexperienced third mate had been left in charge.

The effects of the spill were massive, deadly and long-lasting. An oil slick 10 cm thick quickly spread out from the stricken tanker, eventually reaching 1000 km to the south-west. An estimated 1700 km of coastline was oiled, and within days more than 10 million birds were reported dead and much of the local marine life poisoned and virtually wiped out (figure **C**).

The major problem was – and still is – how to clean up the oil and reduce the impact of the spill. Four main methods were used in Alaska.

1. Encircle the spill with booms and skim off the oil. This helped protect some areas and was successful on small patches of oil.
2. Disperse with chemicals. This was partially successful although the fumes are poisonous and kill wildlife.
3. Burning off the oil. This cleared some patches but also produced poisonous fumes and became dangerous in high winds.
4. Hand cleaning. A large team of workers scrubbed the rocks by hand and used high-pressure hot water to wash down the shoreline. This was a slow process and research now suggests that it may have washed the oil deeper into the beaches and caused more permanent damage.

B

The process of cleaning up has gone on for years, but a 1997 report showed that large areas of coastline remain contaminated. Some wildlife including harbor seals and several species of duck are still not showing any signs of recovery.

C Effects of oil spill

| Destruction of fragile ecosystem | At least 13 whales killed. Reduction in number of births since disaster |

| 10 million shore birds and water fowl dead | 1700 km of coast covered in oil |

| Commercial salmon hatcheries polluted | Loss of business for tourist industry |

| Land-based animals such as caribou poisoned by eating seaweed | Over 5000 sea otters killed. Recovery by 1997 reported as very low |

| | Serious loss of coastline vegetation and seaweeds |

| | Local fishing industry ruined |

The cost of the clean-up has been considerable and not totally successful. In the first year after the disaster, Exxon, the company found to be at fault, spent £843 million and employed 11 000 people to clear oil from the beaches. Exxon also agreed to pay £600 million over the next ten years to complete the clean-up and restore the environment as far as possible to its original state. Sadly, this has not yet happened. Oil remains on the coastline, and wildlife and its habitat have still not fully recovered. Many doubt if they ever will.

The failure to prevent a disaster or even to significantly reduce its impact has worried many people. Most worrying, perhaps, is the fact that this happened despite the most up-to-date technology, the latest advanced safety systems and the most expensive clean-up scheme ever undertaken.

The incident has made people think carefully about the impact of economic activity on the environment. There is no doubt that the oil industry has brought many social and economic benefits to Alaska and the United States as a whole. It has also, however, caused serious and irreparable damage to a fragile environment. People have to choose which is more important – to use these resources or to protect and conserve the environment.

Activities

1 Write a newsflash to be read out on television giving news about the *Exxon Valdez* disaster. The newsflash will be broadcast on the day of the incident. Write between 50 and 80 words.

2 Draw a star diagram to show the methods used to disperse the oil.

3 Produce two posters, one to show the benefits of the oil industry in Alaska and the other to show the problems and possible damage that it may cause.
   • Make the posters colourful and attractive.
   • Give facts and figures where possible.
   • Include headlines, maps and sketches for impact.

4 Do you think oil production should continue in places like Alaska? Give reasons for your answer.

 **Summary** Industrial activity may bring benefits but can also cause problems. The *Exxon Valdez* oil spill was the worst in the history of the United States, and caused extensive long-term damage to the environment.

Case study: Ecosystems

What are ecosystems?

A A woodland in northern England

Chaffinch
Beech
Sycamore
Squirrel
Owl
Hazel
Insects
Oak
Fox
Rabbits
Brambles
Deer
Voles and mice
Weasel
Wild flowers
Leaf litter

Look at diagram **A** which shows part of Wylam Wood, a typical area of deciduous woodland in northern England. Although it looks a very ordinary and rather tranquil scene, the woods are actually very complex and busy with over 1000 different species of plants and animals all living together in a carefully connected web of life. These plants and animals are part of a **community** and depend on each other for food and shelter. They also have close links with non-living elements of the environment such as the local relief, climate and soil. The relationship and interaction between plants and animals and the physical environment is called an **ecosystem**.

Diagram **B** shows the links between various elements of a simple ecosystem. Notice how the components are closely related and how each affects the other. These interactions are almost always at work although some are difficult to see either because they happen in the dark or because they are invisible to the human eye. An example of an invisible and important interaction is **photosynthesis**. In this process, plants take in carbon dioxide from the air through their leaves. In sunlight they then make sugars from carbon dioxide and water. These sugars are used by the plant to help it grow and are crucial to the **energy flows** within an ecosystem. Energy flows are explained in more detail on page 152.

B Links in a simple ecosystem

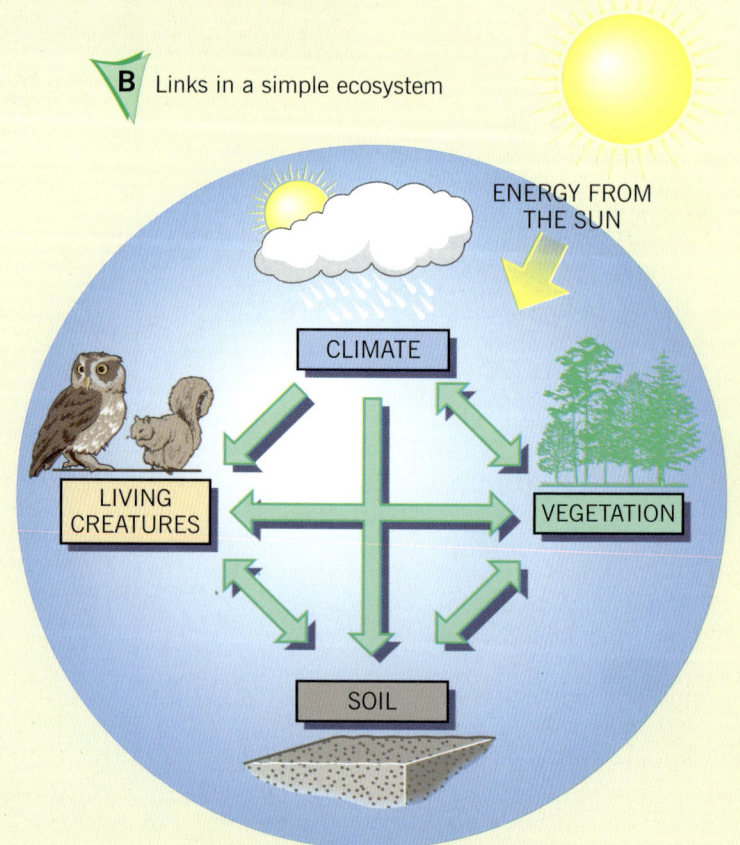

ENERGY FROM THE SUN

CLIMATE

LIVING CREATURES

VEGETATION

SOIL

Ecosystems can be any size, from the vast rainforests of the Amazon to a small woodland area or a tiny pond perhaps at the bottom of a garden. There are also many different types of ecosystem. They vary from place to place around the world as well as between and within areas such as woodland, moorland, streams, farms and even cities. These variations are due largely to the different physical conditions that exist in any particular location and they can be studied using a systems approach.

The systems diagram **C** summarises both the natural and human influences on a woodland ecosystem like the one in diagram **A**. In Britain, the influence of people is particularly important as there are few areas that have not been altered or affected by farmers, developers or industrial growth.

C

A simplified systems diagram for a woodland ecosystem

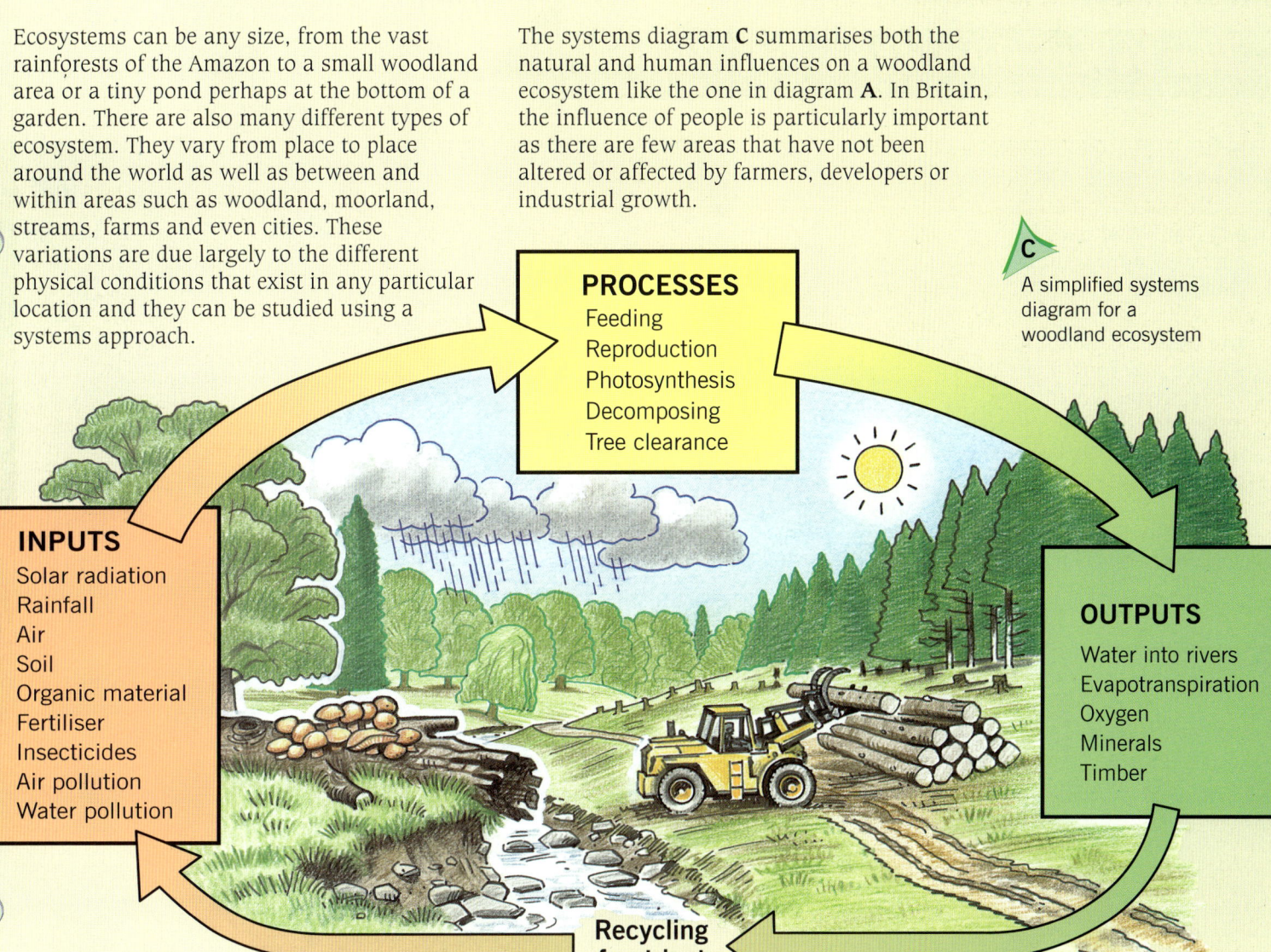

PROCESSES
Feeding
Reproduction
Photosynthesis
Decomposing
Tree clearance

INPUTS
Solar radiation
Rainfall
Air
Soil
Organic material
Fertiliser
Insecticides
Air pollution
Water pollution

OUTPUTS
Water into rivers
Evapotranspiration
Oxygen
Minerals
Timber

Recycling of nutrients

Activities

1 Explain the following terms and give two examples for each one.
   • Ecosystems
   • Living environment
   • Non-living environment.

2 Look out of the window and list:
   a) the natural features and
   b) the human features that are affecting the local environment.

3 Using diagram **B**, suggest what might be the effects on a woodland ecosystem if:
   a) half the trees were cut down
   b) chemicals were used to kill insects
   c) global warming caused climatic change.

4 a) Which of the influences shown in diagram **C** are human?
   b) Give three other ways in which people may affect ecosystems.

Summary

An ecosystem is a community of plants and animals which interact with each other and with the environment in order to survive. Ecosystems may be studied and compared using a systems approach of inputs, processes and outputs.

What are the features of a woodland ecosystem?

In the past much of Britain was covered in forest. The climate was colder and drier than it is today and coniferous trees such as Scots pine were most common. As the climate became gradually warmer and wetter so the type of vegetation and wildlife gradually changed to suit the new conditions. Wylam Wood is typical of the new forest cover where deciduous broadleaved trees such as oak, beech and elm are common.

Diagram **A** shows the main features of this type of ecosystem.

Rain gives water for growth

Sun provides warmth for growth and light for photosynthesis

Leaves trap energy from the sun through photosynthesis and release oxygen to the air

Tawny owls prey on smaller birds and animals such as field mice

An oak tree may contain 270 species of insect

Carbon dioxide in air combines with water and mineral nutrients to make sugars and starches

Birds feed mainly on insects and seeds

A

Animals add nutrients to the soil through their droppings

Rabbits, field mice, hedgehogs and squirrels eat nuts and berries

Weasels eat mice, voles, young rabbits and birds

Grasses and wild flowers grow in the damp shade under the tree

Soil contains minerals (rock particles), nutrients (dead organic matter) and water

Fungi and bacteria feed on dead organic matter and decompose it

Roots hold the soil together and prevent soil erosion

Worms and insects eat dead plants and break up the soil

Weathered rock releases minerals into the soil

Energy flows

Within the woodland area, trees, plants, animals and elements of the physical environment such as the weather and soils are all linked by **flows of energy**. The main source of energy is sunlight. The sun's energy is taken in by the green leaves of plants through the process of **photosynthesis**. Animals then eat the plants. These animals in turn may be eaten by other animals. This process of energy transfer through the ecosystem is called the **food chain**.

B

A woodland ecosystem

Sun

Air

Rain

Soil
Water
Rock

TOP CARNIVORES

Death

Eaten by

CARNIVORES (meat eaters)

Death

Eaten by

HERBIVORES (plant eaters)

Death

Eaten by

PRODUCERS

Death

DECOMPOSERS

Nutrient recycling

All animals and plants require nutrients. These come from the weathering of rocks and are taken up by the roots of plants. They are then transferred to animals through the food chain. Eventually, when the plants or animals die, they rot away and decompose due to the action of fungi and bacteria. In this way the nutrients return to the soil and may be used again. Without this recycling process, the ecosystem would quickly run out of mineral nutrients.

Human influences

Ecosystems are made up of several components which depend upon and affect each other. The interdependence means that changes in inputs or outputs are likely to have a knock-on effect through the system. The people of Wylam are concerned that developers might want to cut down trees to build a housing estate. This would obviously have a visual impact but would also destroy the habitat of numerous plants and animals and affect other elements of the ecosytem. Air and water pollution, the use of fertilisers, litter and even the widening of footpaths through the woods, can similarly cause severe and irreversible damage to the delicately balanced woodland ecosystem.

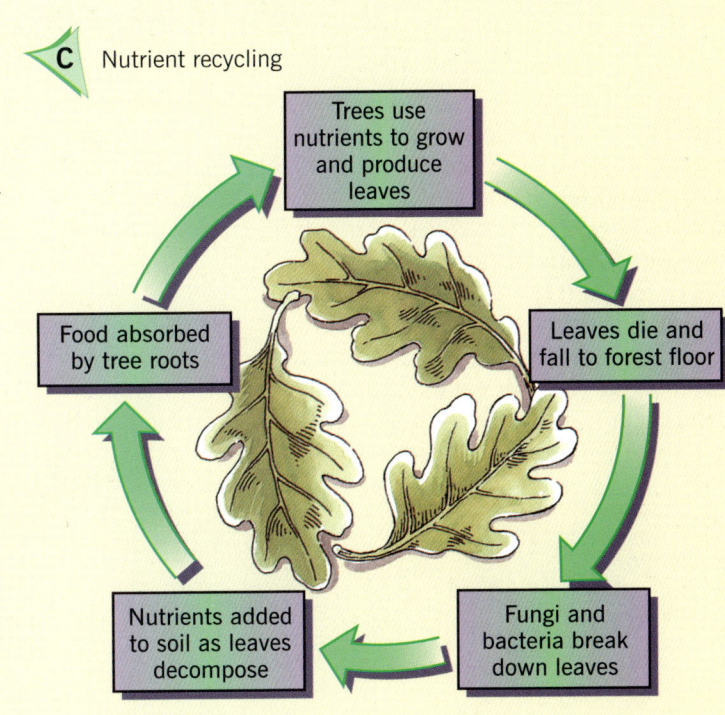

C Nutrient recycling

Trees use nutrients to grow and produce leaves → Leaves die and fall to forest floor → Fungi and bacteria break down leaves → Nutrients added to soil as leaves decompose → Food absorbed by tree roots

Activities

1 Explain the following terms.
   - Energy flows • Photosynthesis
   - Food chain • Nutrient recycling
   - Decomposition

2 Make a larger copy of diagram **D** and add two examples to each box from the following list.
   - fungi • weasel • rain • oak tree • sun
   - rabbit • insect • flower • tawny owl
   - bacteria

D

| Non-living environment e.g. | → | Producers e.g. | → | Herbivores e.g. | → | Carnivores e.g. | → | Decomposers e.g. |

SAVE OUR WOODS

E

3 Look at diagram **C** which shows how nutrients are recycled through leaf growth and decomposition. Draw a similar diagram to include animal life as well as plants, in the recycling process.

4 **a)** Design a poster to show the effects that tree felling would have on a woodland ecosystem. Give examples from both the living and non-living environment. Figure **E** could be your poster centrepiece.
   b) Describe two other ways that people may affect the woodland ecosystem.

Summary

Woodland environments are common in many areas of Britain and illustrate the features of complex ecosystems. Ecosystems depend on energy flows and nutrient recycling. They may be altered and damaged by human influences.

13 Map projections and geographical information systems (GIS)

► Which map projection is best? ◄

Does your geography room have a globe? A globe shows the actual shape of the Earth. You will notice that it is circular and has three dimensions. These two features, however, make it impossible to draw the Earth accurately onto a flat piece of paper (see Activity 1). Parts of the map will be either the wrong **shape** or the wrong **size**.

Map projections result from the various attempts made to try to 'project' the three-dimensional globe onto a two-dimensional sheet of paper. Each map projection therefore has to be a compromise. Which is the most suitable type of

projection depends upon what the **cartographer** (a person who draws maps) is trying to show.

Correct shape

In diagram **A**, which is a Mercator projection, the continents have been given their correct shape but their size (area) is wrong. This is because, while on a globe the poles appear as a point, on this projection they have been 'stretched' and so become as wide as the Equator. The further a place is from the Equator, the greater is the exaggeration of its size. The Mercator projection is still used by navigators as any straight line on the map has a constant bearing (direction).

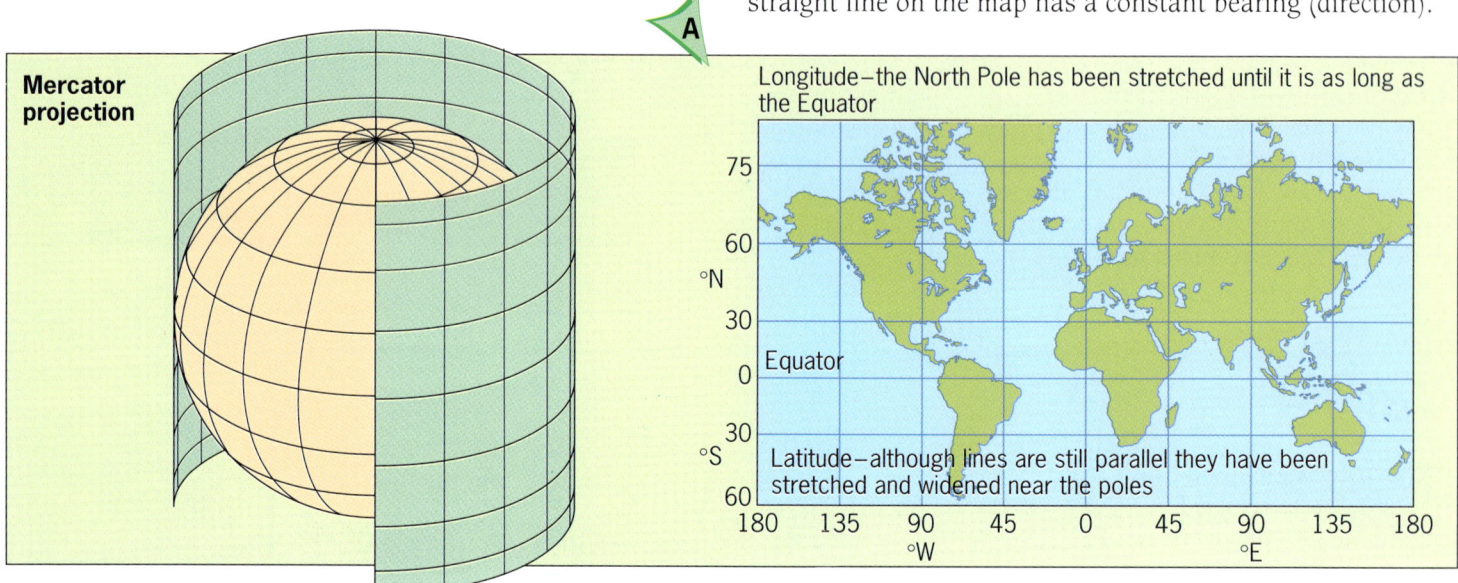

A

Mercator projection

Longitude–the North Pole has been stretched until it is as long as the Equator

Equator

Latitude–although lines are still parallel they have been stretched and widened near the poles

Correct area (size)

In diagrams **B** and **C**, the Mollweide and Peters projections, the continents have been given their correct size (area) but this time their shape is incorrect (distorted). The Peters projection is becoming increasingly favoured for showing

developing countries in relation to developed countries. In order to get the size correct, the continents have had to be drawn narrower and longer. Equal area maps are used to show distributions, e.g. world population.

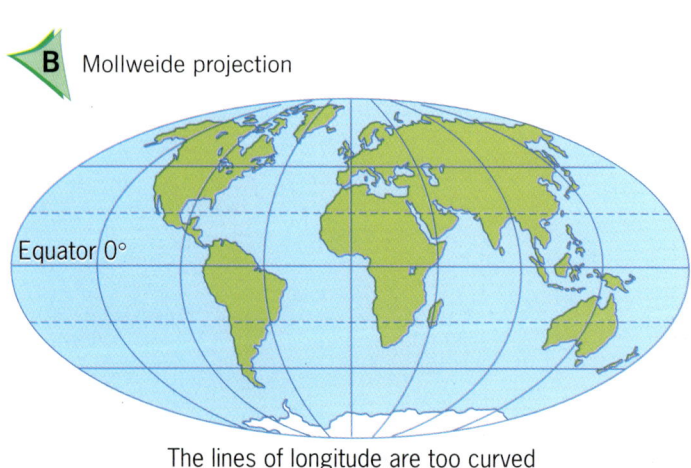

B Mollweide projection

Equator 0°

The lines of longitude are too curved

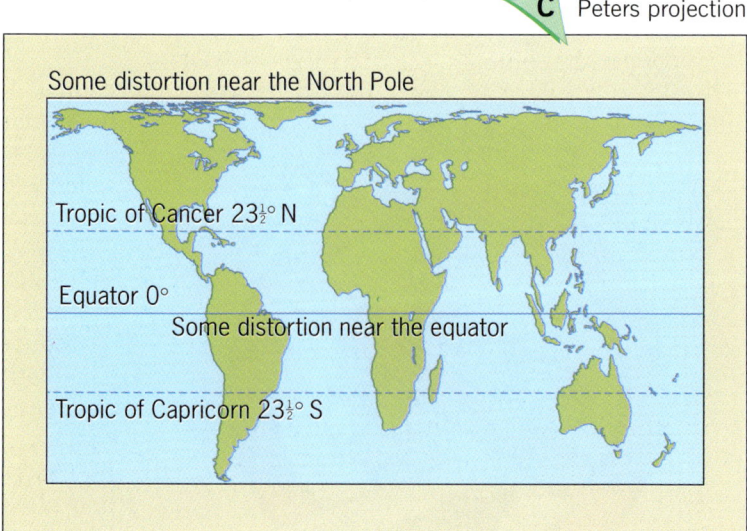

C Peters projection

Some distortion near the North Pole

Tropic of Cancer 23½° N

Equator 0°

Some distortion near the equator

Tropic of Capricorn 23½° S

Correct distance

In diagram **D**, a zenithal projection, the scale is correct along any line drawn from the centre of the projection, but both the shapes and sizes of places are incorrect. (Zenith means a point directly overhead, e.g. the position of the midday sun on the Equator, page 8.) A map centred on the North Pole (or London as in diagram **E**) is effective for the northern hemisphere but greatly distorts places to the south of the Equator. This type of projection is useful for plotting air-routes as it shows the shortest distance, known as a great circle route, and the correct direction (bearing) between two places. One great circle route, between Europe and the Pacific countries, passes over the Arctic. A map showing the Pacific Rim (pages 134–135) is a zenithal projection centred on the Pacific Ocean.

Compromise projections

Several projections used in an atlas try to compromise so that while neither the shape, the size nor the distance is correct, their distortion and exaggeration are minimised.

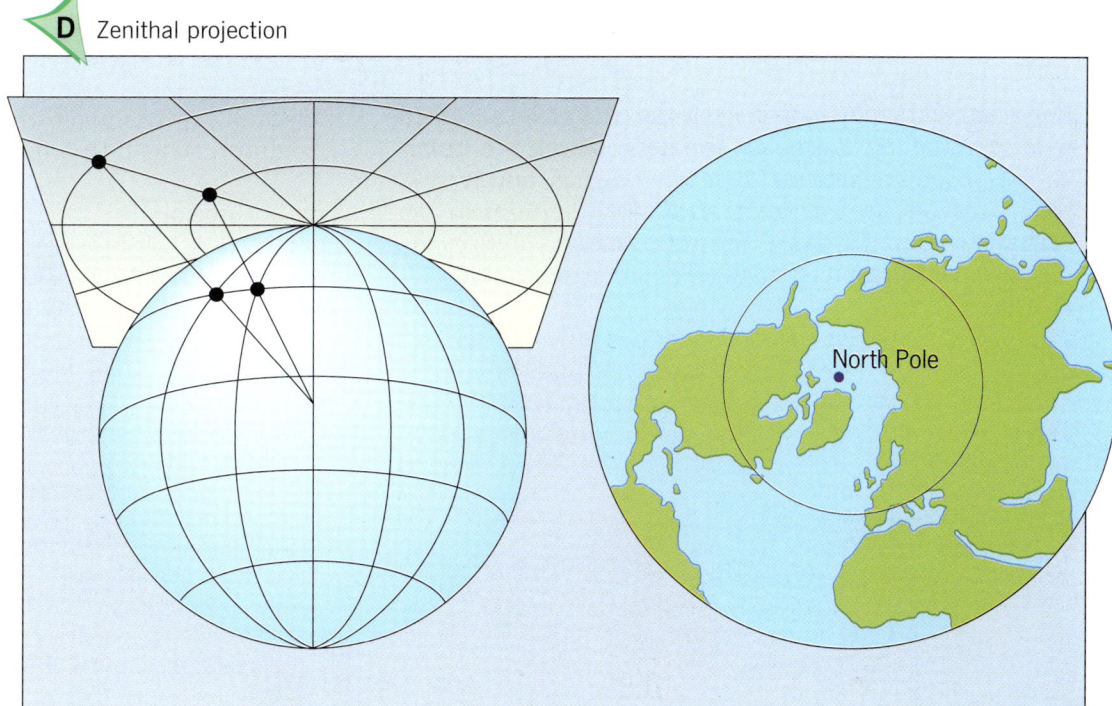

D Zenithal projection

North Pole

E

Wellington
Los Angeles
Mexico City
Miami
Beijing
Sydney
North Pole
New York
Dehli
Moscow
Singapore
London
Caracas
Cairo
Lagos
Nairobi
Buenos Aires
Rio de Janeiro
Cape Town

Activities

1. In an atlas the ball-shaped globe has to be projected onto a flat surface. Is this possible?
   a) Peel an orange in one piece and try to lay the peel flat onto a piece of paper.
   b) Describe what happens to the peel, and say how many shapes you produced.

2. Match the types of projection shown here with the correct:
   i) description and
   ii) use.

Peters	shows the correct shape but size is greatly distorted	navigation
Zenithal	shows the correct distances but size and shape are incorrect	air-routes
Mercator	shows the correct size but shape is greatly distorted	population distribution

3. Make a list of the various types of map projection used in your atlas. Try to divide them into those that have the correct shape, correct size, correct distances, or are a compromise between the three.

Summary

No atlas map can be totally accurate. All will have some good qualities such as correct shape, size or distance, but all will have limitations. The choice of projection depends upon the purpose of a particular map.

▷ *What are geographical information systems (1)?* ◁

Geographical information systems (GIS) are concerned with the handling of geographical data, collected from a variety of sources, and its storage in a digital form on computers. GIS need not be limited to IT (information technology) but, due to the amount of data involved, it is ideally suited to computers. One definition states that GIS provides:

> A powerful set of tools for collecting, storing, retrieving at will, transforming and displaying spatial data from the real world for a particular set of purposes. (P. A. Burrough, 1986).

As with other systems, GIS has inputs, processes, stores and outputs (diagram **A**).

A

Inputs	Stores	Processes	Outputs
Data from a variety of sources. • Satellite images, aerial photos, Landsat images • Different types of map – OS maps, maps of soils, relief, settlement • Digital data and graphs	a) Data stored in digital form b) Vast quantities of data	a) Retrieval, transformation and analysis of data b) Data in digital form can be easily updated (unlike atlases or textbooks) c) Can select and enlarge material for display d) Display colours can be changed at the press of a button	a) Several maps or sources of data can be displayed on the screen at the same time b) A final composite map is achieved by superimposing several maps on each other (overlays) c) Maps, graphs, tables

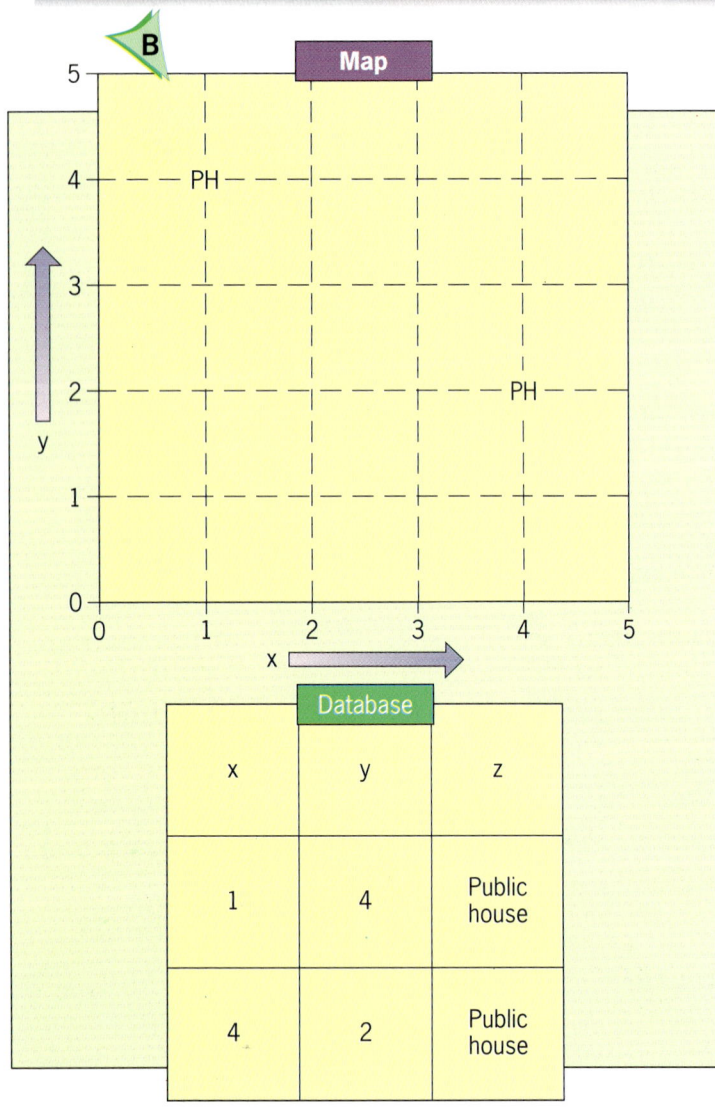

B

Principal role of GIS

The main role of GIS is to process raw geographical data in order to produce further information that can be used for informed decision-making. This is achieved through the development of new and exciting ways of manipulating and displaying spatial data (maps), and by performing simple and complex spatial analysis on the geographical data quickly and efficiently.

A map is the traditional way of showing spatial data. A map records and displays geographical data by using (x, y) co-ordinates together with a (z) value that records the features found at each (x, y) location (diagram **B**). Maps are usually drawn on two-dimensional flat sheets of paper (page 154). A map, once drawn in an atlas, is difficult to update.

Advances in computer technology have enabled huge amounts of data to be stored in a **database**. A database within a GIS acts as a storage facility for geographical information. For example, diagram **B** shows a small database recording information for public houses. The computer can access this database, and display the spatial data using the (x, y) co-ordinates recorded and the associated (z) feature. On a standard two-dimensional map, each (x, y) co-ordinate can only store and display, at the most, two (z) features (e.g. height of land and either soils, or settlement, or vegetation, etc.). With improvements in technology, a computerised GIS can store hundreds of (z) features for each (x, y) location. These can then be selected depending upon what particular features the map is to display. It is also possible to display maps in three dimensions using a computer, with each (x, y) location recording a particular (z) height feature. Data can then be displayed using a range of graphics.

Map features

Data can be displayed on a map in one of three ways (diagram **C**).

Point	Line	Polygon
A point feature is displayed at one particular (*x,y*) location on the map.	A line consists of a series of (*x,y*) co-ordinates that join together, with each having the same (*z*) feature (e.g a railway line).	A polygon consists of a series of (*x,y*) co-ordinates that join together to complete a boundary. Everything inside this boundary is assigned the same (*z*) feature (e.g. a wood).

Maps

Point

x	y	z
1	3	PH

Line

x	y	z
0	1	Railway
1	1	Railway
2	2	Railway
2	3	Railway
3	3	Railway

Start and finish points must be equal

Polygon

x	y	z
1	1	Wood
1	2	Wood
2	3	Wood
2	2	Wood
3	2	Wood
3	1	Wood
1	1	Wood

Database

GIS can then display the complex spatial data, using the (*x, y, z*) values, and analyse it. Two of the most common techniques used for performing spatial analysis are **buffering** and **overlaying**. These techniques are described in the following section which seeks to select the ideal site for a rubbish dump.

Locating a rubbish dump

The local council have asked you to locate a suitable site for a new rubbish dump. The rubbish dump has to be located within the council boundary. In locating the new site, the council have specified the following requirements:

1. The site should be located at least 500 metres away from all urban areas.
2. The soil must be of poor quality.
3. The land should be sufficiently flat to allow easy vehicle access (slope of under 2°).

To identify the possible sites that satisfy the above criteria, you should first locate the extent of the council's boundary. You will then need the three maps which contain the relevant information. These maps, which should all be at same scale, will be:

- a settlement map highlighting the urban areas
- a soil map
- a slope angle map.

Each of the above criteria should then be examined in turn (pages 158–159).

Each of the above criteria should then be examined in turn (pages 158–159).

Activity

a) What are geographical information systems (GIS)?

b) What are the main inputs, stores, processes and outputs of a GIS?

c) What is the difference between a map and a database?

d) Why is a GIS of more value than an atlas?

Summary

A geographical information system (GIS) collects, stores, retrieves, analyses and displays geographical data. A wide range of maps, together with satellite images and aerial photographs, can be used to reveal spatial patterns and relationships.

▶ What are geographical information systems (2)? ◀

1 Locate all the places that lie at least 500 metres from an urban area This involves a process called **buffering**. A boundary must be drawn around the limits of all the urban areas on the map. A minimum of 10 houses is needed to constitute an urban area. This produces a number of polygons (diagram **A**). Each polygon should then be studied in turn. From each point on the polygon boundary a second point has to be located 500 metres away, and at an exact angle of 90°. When this has been done you should be able to draw an exact replica shape of the original polygon

but at a distance of 500 metres from its boundary. The area between the urban area and the new polygon is referred to as the **buffered zone**.

Any point located **inside** the buffered zone, or inside the urban boundary, is considered unsuitable according to the council's criteria. Any point outside the buffered zones should be highlighted as a possible site. The map should then be traced onto a transparency, highlighting all those areas that lie **outside** the buffered zones.

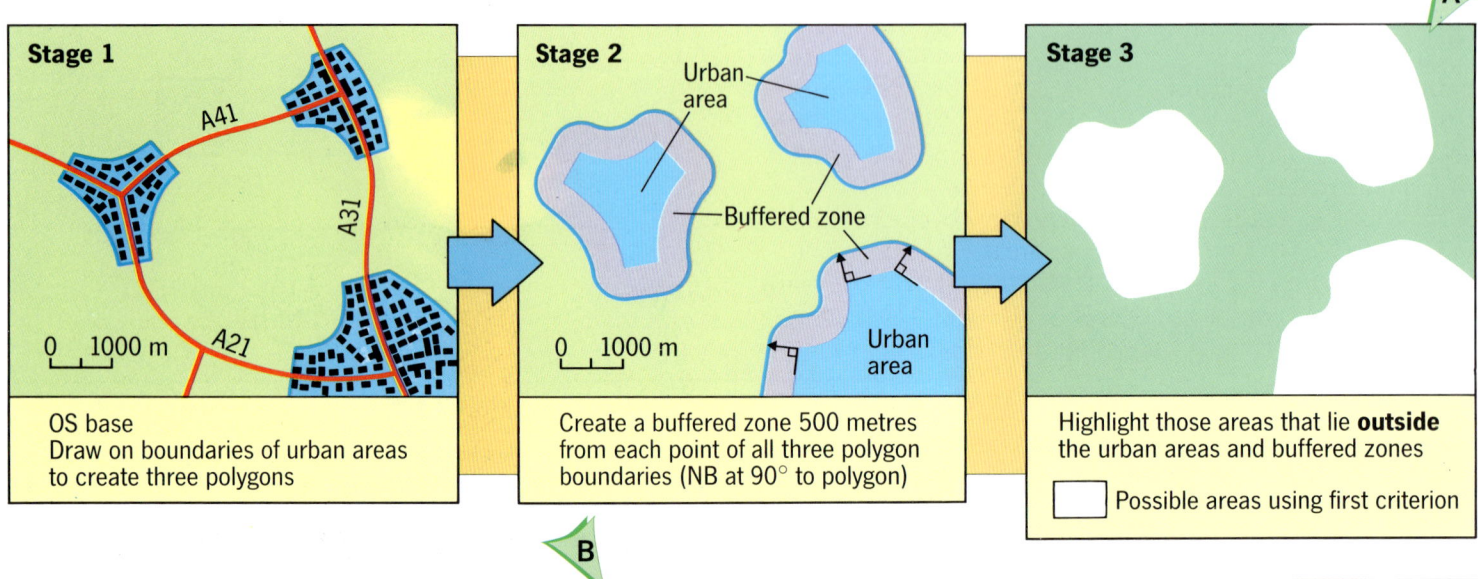

A

Stage 1
A41
A31
A21
0 — 1000 m
OS base
Draw on boundaries of urban areas to create three polygons

Stage 2
Urban area
Buffered zone
Urban area
0 — 1000 m
Create a buffered zone 500 metres from each point of all three polygon boundaries (NB at 90° to polygon)

Stage 3
Highlight those areas that lie **outside** the urban areas and buffered zones
☐ Possible areas using first criterion

B

2 Locate all places with poor soils
The soil map, needed to locate areas of poor soil, should have the same scale as the one previously used for highlighting the urban areas in stage 1. A line can be drawn on the map to show the boundary between good-quality and poor-quality soil (diagram **B**). This map should be traced onto a transparency in the same manner as in diagram **A**, with the poor soils highlighted.

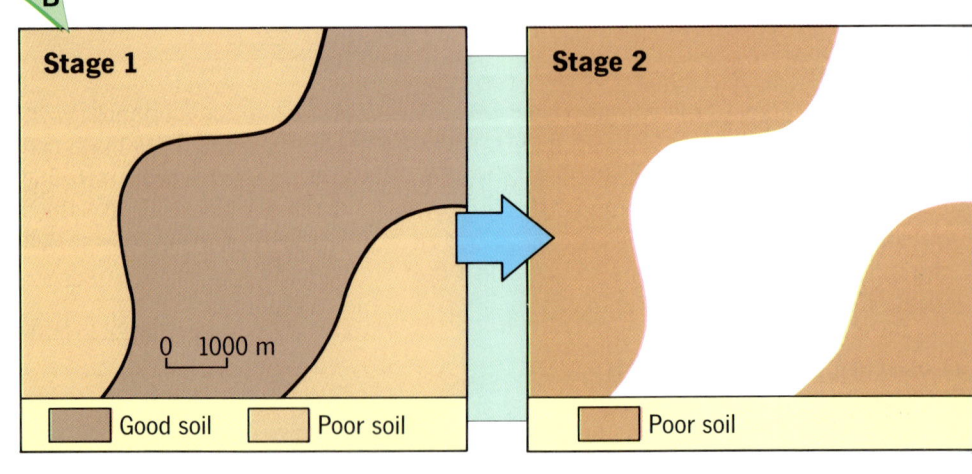

Stage 1
0 1000 m
☐ Good soil ☐ Poor soil

Stage 2
☐ Poor soil

3 Locate all areas of flat land A slope angle map is needed to locate all those areas within the council's boundary that have, as specified by the council, a slope angle of under 2°. The map should be at the same scale as the previous maps. On it, a line can be drawn to indicate the boundary between land that has a slope greater and less than 2° (diagram **C**). The areas under 2°, indicating flat ground, can be highlighted and traced onto a third transparency.

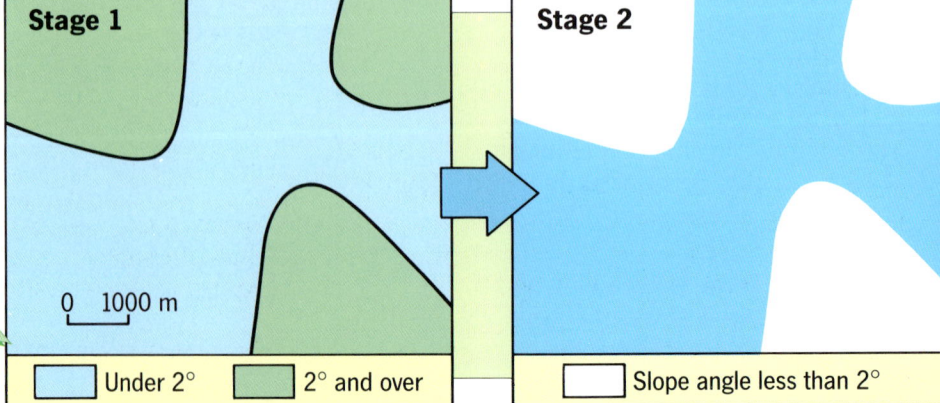

C

Stage 1
0 1000 m
☐ Under 2° ☐ 2° and over

Stage 2
☐ Slope angle less than 2°

Overlaying the transparencies

To find the areas that satisfy the council's three specified criteria, the transparencies should be placed one on top of each other. This process, called **overlaying**, is a fundamental operation of a GIS (diagram **D**). It can only be performed, however, using maps that have the same scale and a common origin. The areas, in our example, that contain all three types of highlighting can then be isolated and traced onto a base map. This composite map can then be forwarded to the council as it fits their criteria and shows all the possible sites in which to locate the rubbish dump. It is possible to use many more overlays than just the three described in this example (e.g. access roads, visibility of the dump from urban areas, direction of prevailing winds should the dump smell, soil permeability, etc.).

Computer enhancements to highlight the best sites

With improvements in computer hardware and software, this process can be undertaken much more efficiently and quickly than the manual method described, yet still using the same techniques. The computer performs the same operation by studying each criterion in turn. Those areas that satisfy one particular criterion are assigned the value 1, while those that fail to satisfy the criterion are given the value 0. Those areas of land within the council's boundary that obtain the value 3 are given the highest priority as they fit all three criteria, i.e. they are away from urban areas and are on poor soil and flat land. Areas that satisfy two of the three criteria are assigned the value 2 and are considered medium priority. Those areas with a value of 1 or 0 will be rejected.

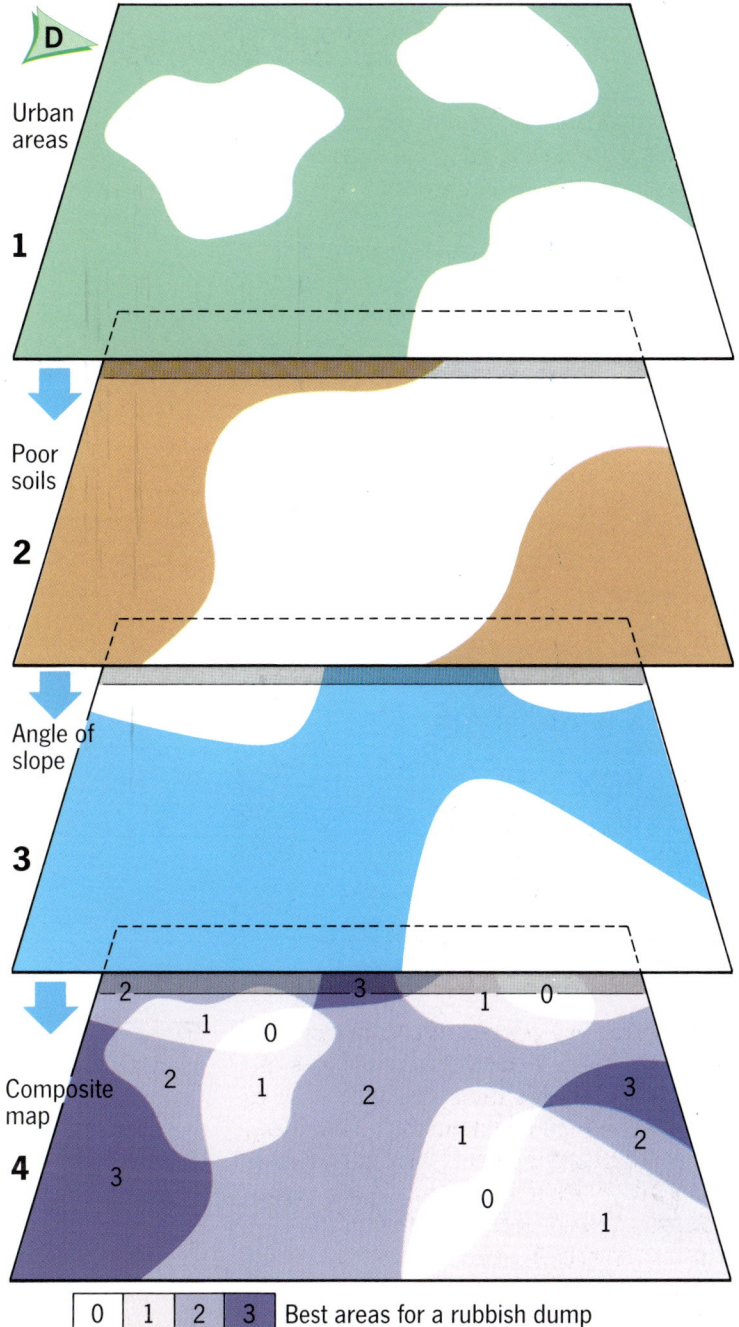

D

1 Urban areas

2 Poor soils

3 Angle of slope

4 Composite map

| 0 | 1 | 2 | 3 | Best areas for a rubbish dump |

GIS and the future

GIS has arisen from the joining of information technology and the demand for the storage and manipulation of data. Its strengths lie particularly in the ability to use it to 'model' geographical reality and to consider the impact of proposed or possible changes in spatial patterns in the natural or human environment. It is a technology where the role and value of geographers is beginning to be felt.

Source: Geographic Information Systems, *Geofile, April 1993*

Activity

a) Attempt to locate a new rubbish dump within your own local council's boundary. (You may prefer, as an alternative to the rubbish dump, to try to locate the best possible site for some other feature, such as a hypermarket, a caravan park or a wind farm.)
You will need to find a range of maps, some of which may use the same criteria as used on these two pages; some may use criteria that you can think of for yourselves.

Complete the location exercise either manually or with the use of a computer.

b) How effective do you think a geographical information system is when trying to produce a composite map to show the best possible sites for a new rubbish dump (or hypermarket, caravan park or wind farm)?

c) What other uses can be made of geographical information systems?

Summary

Composite maps for specific purposes can be constructed by overlaying various distributions of thematic data that can be combined to show interrelationships. This can be done either manually or with the help of a computer (information technology).

Index